COMMON CORE BASICS

Building Essential Test Readiness Skills

SOCIAL STUDIES

Mc Graw Hill Education

Bothell, WA • Chicago, IL • Columbus, OH • New York, NY

Contents

To the Student

Common Core Basics: Building Essential Test Readiness Skills, Social Studies will help you learn or strengthen the skills you need when you take any Common Core State Standards–aligned social studies test. To answer some questions, you will need to read passages, graphs, charts, and maps. Questions will focus on the content areas of US history, civics, political systems, economics, and geography.

Before beginning the lessons in this book, take the **Pretest**. This test will help you identify which skill areas you need to concentrate on most. Use the chart at the end of the Pretest to pinpoint the types of questions you have answered incorrectly and to determine which skills you need to work on. You may decide to concentrate on specific areas of study or to work through the entire book. It is highly recommended that you do work through the whole book to build a strong foundation in the core areas in which you will be tested.

Common Core Basics: Building Essential Test Readiness Skills, Social Studies is divided into eight chapters:

- **Chapter 1: US Government and Civics** describes government at the local, state, and national levels and the responsibilities of citizenship.

- **Chapter 2: US History: Revolutionary War through the Depression** explores events from time of the early settlers through the 1930s.

- **Chapter 3: US History: World War II through Modern Times** continues the story from the 1940s through the current day.

- **Chapter 4: World History and Political Systems** discusses various government systems and international organizations. It gives an overview of relations among the nations of the world.

- **Chapter 5: Economic Foundations** explains economic concepts and discusses the roles of individuals, businesses, and governments in economics.

- **Chapter 6: Economic Events in History** explores major economic events of the past and relates them to today's economy.

- **Chapter 7: Economics in the Twenty-First Century** reviews modern economics from national and global perspectives.

- **Chapter 8: Geography and People** explores how geographic features and humans interact on Earth.

In addition, *Common Core Basics: Building Essential Test Readiness Skills, Social Studies* has a number of features designed to familiarize you with standardized tests and to prepare you for test taking.

- The **Chapter Opener** provides an overview of the chapter content and a goal-setting activity.

- **Lesson Objectives** state what you will be able to accomplish after completing the lesson.

- **Vocabulary** critical for understanding lesson content is listed at the start of every lesson. All boldfaced words in the text can be found in the Glossary.

- The **Key Concept** summarizes the content that is the focus of the lesson.

- In the lessons, the **Core Skill** and **Reading Skill** are emphasized with direct instruction and practice in the context of the lesson. The Core Skills align to the Common Core State Standards.

- In the lessons, the special features **21st Century Skills**, **Technology Connections**, **Workplace Connections**, and **Research It** will help you activate high-level thinking skills by using real-world application of these skills.

- **Think about Social Studies** questions check your understanding of the content throughout the lesson as you read.

- **Write to Learn** is a quick activity that provides you with a purpose for practicing your writing skills.

- End-of-lesson **Vocabulary Review** checks your understanding of important lesson vocabulary, while the **Skill Review** checks your understanding of the content and skills presented in the lesson.

- **Skill Practice** and **Writing Practice** exercises appear at the end of every lesson to help you apply your learning of content and skill fundamentals.

- The end-of-chapter **Review** and **Essay Writing Practice** test your understanding of the chapter content and provide an opportunity to strengthen your writing skills.

- **Check Your Understanding** charts allow you to check your knowledge of the skill you have practiced.

- The **Answer Key** explains the answers for the questions in the book.

- The **Glossary** and **Index** contain lists of key terms found throughout the book and make it easy to review important skills and concepts.

After you have worked through the book, take the **Posttest** to see how well you have learned the skills presented in this book.

Good luck with your studies! Keep in mind that knowing how to read and analyze various types of social studies materials is a skill worth learning.

Social Studies

The Pretest is a guide to using this book. It will allow you to preview the skills and concepts you will be working on in the lessons. The Pretest is intended to be a check of your current level of knowledge and understanding of social studies. It will serve as a starting point as you work through these lessons and develop your skills.

The Pretest consists of 25 multiple-choice questions. To answer these questions, you will need to read passages, maps, tables and charts, and photographs.

Directions: Read each question carefully. Then choose the <u>one best answer</u> to the question.

When you have completed the Pretest, check your work with the answers and explanations on pages 12 and 13. Then use the Evaluation Chart on page 14 to determine which areas you need to pay special attention to as you work your way through this book.

Social Studies

Directions: Question 1 refers to the following passage from the Declaration of Independence.

> "We . . . declare, that these united colonies are, and of right ought to be free and independent states; that they are absolved from all allegiance [loyalty or commitment] to the British Crown, and that all political connection between them and the state of Great Britain, is and ought to be totally dissolved; and that as free and independent states, they have full power to levy war, conclude peace, contract alliances, establish commerce, and to do all other acts and things which independent states may of right do."

1. In the passage, the colonists declare that they have "full power to levy war, conclude peace, contract alliances, establish commerce, and to do all other acts and things which independent states may of right do." In essence, what are the colonists declaring that they are doing?

   A. establishing a government that is self-sufficient and separate from Great Britain
   B. strengthening the connection between the colonies and Great Britain
   C. declaring allegiance to one another
   D. severing economic ties with Great Britain

Directions: Questions 2 and 3 refer to the following passage.

> The Articles of Confederation were passed by the Continental Congress in 1781 as the constitutional framework for the new United States. The articles gave a great deal of power to the states and relatively little power to the central, or federal, government. Later developments proved that the new federal government was too weak to secure the country's frontiers, create a strong military defense, protect trade, and handle unrest during the troubled 1780s.
>
> The leaders of the revolution called for a Constitutional Convention in 1787. The new constitution established a strong federal government.

2. Why were the Articles of Confederation replaced?

   A. They gave too much power to the president.
   B. They created a powerful federal government.
   C. They gave too much power to the states.
   D. They created a weak and ineffective federal government.

3. You can infer from this passage that the leaders of the revolution supported a more centralized system. Why was that so?

   A. to ensure the nation's survival
   B. to have political power for themselves
   C. to make the United States a world power
   D. to protect their own wealth and investments

Social Studies

Directions: Questions 4 and 5 refer to the following chart.

Federal Government Expenditures	
Defense	20.0%
Medicare	13.1%
Health	10.7%
Social Security	21.4%
Income security*	18.0%
Veterans' benefits	3.1%
Education, training, employment, and social services	3.7%
Transportation	2.7%
Interest on public debt	5.7%
Administration of justice	1.5%
Natural resources and environment	1.3%
International affairs	1.3%

Source: Statistical Abstract of the US, 2010

*Includes housing assistance, food and nutrition assistance, unemployment compensation, and federal employees' retirement

4. According to the chart, which responsibility of the federal government is the most costly?

   A. national defense
   B. Social Security
   C. Medicare
   D. education and employment

5. Which statement is most likely to be true?
   A. Americans are living longer, so Social Security costs will increase.
   B. Paying off the national debt is the country's top priority.
   C. Federal spending on education has steadily decreased.
   D. The United States is a leader in providing international aid.

6. The US political system is described as pluralist. A pluralistic system gets its strength from the large number of interest groups that participate in politics. These groups must share power and make compromises to get things done.

   Which of the following would be characteristic of decision making in such a system?

   A. Political decisions are usually made quickly.
   B. One group tends to dominate the system.
   C. No single group wins all the time.
   D. Political parties play a small role.

Social Studies

Directions: Questions 7 and 8 refer to the following passage.

> Today almost all US citizens age 18 and over have the legal right to vote. However, this was not always the case. Originally the Constitution let the states determine qualifications for voting. The right to vote was at first limited to white male property owners.
>
> Property qualifications were gradually eliminated. By 1830 most white males over the age of 21 could vote. African American men gained the right to vote when the Fifteenth Amendment was passed in 1870. Women gained the right to vote with the passage of the Nineteenth Amendment in 1919.
>
> Some states still tried to deny African Americans the right to vote. Poll taxes, literacy tests, and scare tactics were sometimes used to stop African Americans from voting.
>
> The poll tax on voting in federal elections was finally eliminated in 1962 by the Twenty-Fourth Amendment. The Voting Rights Act of 1965 guaranteed the right to vote to all citizens, regardless of race or sex.

7. Legislation passed in 1962 and in 1965 guaranteed all citizens the right to vote. Which event likely led to the passage of this legislation?

   A. the American Revolution
   B. the Civil War
   C. World War I
   D. the civil rights movement

8. Which conclusion could be supported by the information in the passage?

   A. Equal voting rights for all Americans were mandated by the Constitution when it was written.
   B. White men and women were the only people who had the right to vote when the country was founded.
   C. Minorities and women have had to struggle to get the right to vote.
   D. It was illegal for white women to own property in the early 1800s.

9. Colonization is the act of one country directly controlling another. In the 1800s and 1900s, many European nations established colonies in India, China, Africa, and South America.

At this same time, the Industrial Revolution was taking place in Europe. Why was the Industrial Revolution an important factor in the establishment of European colonies?

   A. Europeans wanted to learn about other cultures.
   B. European countries wanted an equal share the world's wealth.
   C. Europeans feared the spread of communism.
   D. European industries were more advanced and more productive.

Social Studies

Directions: Questions 10 and 11 refer to the following chart.

WORLD'S MOST POPULOUS COUNTRIES: 2012 AND 2050

2012			Projection for 2050		
Rank	Country	Population (millions)	Rank	Country	Population (millions)
1	China	1,350	1	India	1,691
2	India	1,260	2	China	1,311
3	United States	314	3	United States	423
4	Indonesia	241	4	Nigeria	402
5	Brazil	194	5	Pakistan	314
6	Pakistan	180	6	Indonesia	309
7	Nigeria	170	7	Bangladesh	226
8	Bangladesh	153	8	Brazil	213
9	Russia	143	9	Democratic Republic of the Congo	194
10	Japan	128	10	Ethiopia	166

Source: 2012 World Population Data Sheet of the Population Reference Bureau, Inc.

10. Which statement best describes how the data changes from 2012 to 2050?
    A. All countries will increase in population.
    B. The first five most populous countries will be the same.
    C. The majority of the most populous countries will continue to be the most populous countries.
    D. Countries that will be the most populous in 2050 were not the most populous in 2012.

11. Which reason best explains why Russia and Japan might drop from the list by 2050?
    A. lower birthrates in Russia and Japan and higher birthrates in other countries
    B. higher birthrates in Russia and Japan and lower birthrates in other countries
    C. lower birthrates in Russia and Japan and lower birthrates in other countries
    D. higher death rates in Russia and Japan because of disease

Social Studies

Directions: Questions 12 and 13 refer to the following passage.

> James Watt invented the steam engine, which was first put to use in 1776. During the 1800s, steam-driven machines started doing work that had previously been done by human hands.

12. Which statement describes the significance of the invention of the steam engine?

  A. It was not as important as other inventions.

  B. Its effects lasted only a short period of time.

  C. Its development was brought about by the Industrial Revolution.

  D. It was a technological advancement that helped spur the Industrial Revolution.

13. What would most likely have been the reaction of factory workers to the steam engine?

  A. relief that their jobs would become easier

  B. fear they would lose their jobs

  C. confusion about what the steam engine could do

  D. excitement about the steam engine's potential

14. During the 1970s and 1980s, there were several federal court decisions concerning the powers of the president and Congress. During the Watergate affair, the courts ruled that the president could not claim executive privilege as a reason to keep certain information from Congress. In 1983, the Supreme Court halted the use of the so-called "legislative veto," which had been used by Congress to control and limit many actions of the executive branch.

What do the events described in the passage show about the separation of powers provided for under the Constitution?

  A. It is open to interpretation and change.

  B. It is too rigid.

  C. It encourages a dictatorial government.

  D. It is not an effective way to organize the government.

Social Studies

Directions: Questions 15 and 16 refer to the following map..

RAILROADS IN THE EASTERN UNITED STATES, 1860

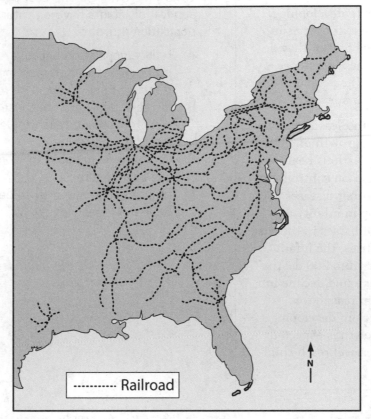

---------- Railroad

15. What does the map show?
   A. geographical features in the East
   B. state boundaries in the East in 1860
   C. transportation in the East in 1860
   D. communication in the East in 1860

16. What can you infer from this map?
   A. The Northeast had more commerce and industry than the Southeast.
   B. River travel was more common in the Northeast than in the Southeast.
   C. Communication between cities in the Northeast was not well developed in 1860.
   D. Few highways had been built in the Southeast.

Social Studies

Directions: Questions 17 and 18 refer to the following passage.

The term *Third World* refers to developing nations. These are the poorest countries in the world. Unlike the United States, they do not have large industries. These countries remain largely agricultural. The people depend on farmland for their survival.

In recent years, public health measures have greatly influenced the rapid growth of Third World populations. United Nations health efforts have had a big impact on controlling malaria, yellow fever, and other diseases. One result has been a great drop in infant mortality (the death rate of babies in the first year of life). In some countries, the infant mortality rate has dropped from 200 deaths per 1,000 births to 50. This rapid decline in infant mortality is the main reason for increased population growth in developing countries. Even further growth is expected because more young women will reach child-bearing age.

18. What effect will the increased survival of infants have on future population growth?

   A. reduce population because governments will provide more effective family planning

   B. increase population because more girls will grow up and reach the age where they can bear children

   C. decrease the number of women who can bear children

   D. reduce population growth because of food shortages

17. What has been a major cause of the reduction in infant mortality?

   A. more young women reaching child-bearing age

   B. public health measures that help control diseases

   C. increased population growth

   D. better food and housing conditions

19. In the 1880s and 1890s, many American small farmers were driven off the land or forced to become tenants by changing economic conditions. They formed protest organizations and demanded government reforms. They thought reforms would save the small farmers and their way of life, but their efforts were unsuccessful. The small farmers continued to decrease in number as agriculture became more mechanized and larger farms took over the small ones.

Which group did small farmers belong to in the late nineteenth century?

   A. the upwardly mobile social class

   B. the rich elite class

   C. the powerful middle class

   D. the social class in decline

Social Studies

Directions: Questions 20 and 21 refer to the following passage and photograph.

Many Americans are shocked about the large number of deaths caused by guns and want strict gun control. Other Americans are equally determined to have the right to own guns. They point to the Second Amendment for constitutional support. It clearly states that "the right of the people to keep and bear arms shall not be infringed."

20. Which statement most likely sums up the photographer's view of gun rights?
   A. There should be no restrictions on the right to own and carry guns.
   B. The courts should decide who can own guns, not Congress.
   C. Some restrictions on gun ownership is logical in today's world.
   D. The gun lobby is a powerful political interest group.

21. Which statement could be considered a synthesis of the information in the photograph and the passage?
   A. People should not fire guns at night.
   B. The Constitution clearly allows for handguns.
   C. Strict gun control is needed to save lives.
   D. The meaning of the Second Amendment is open to interpretation.

Social Studies

Directions: Questions 22 and 23 refer to the following map.

ANCIENT MIDDLE EAST

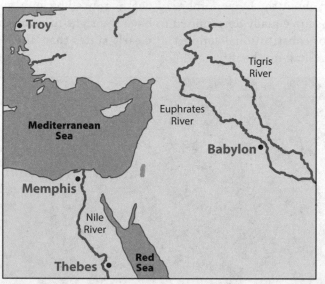

22. Maps can be used to present many kinds of information, such as the political borders of countries, regional rainfall averages, and population density.

Which kind of map is shown here?

A. climate map
B. historical map
C. road map
D. topographic map

23. What do all the cities shown on the map have in common?

A. They are located near bodies of water.
B. They are within a few miles of one another.
C. They are located along the Tigris River.
D. They are important trading ports.

Social Studies

24. On the basis of this table, which statement can you make about unemployment?

SAMPLE WORLDWIDE UNEMPLOYMENT RATES

Country	2009	2011
Chili	9.6%	6.6%
Egypt	9.4%	12.2%
France	9.1%	9.3%
India	10.7%	9.8%
Iraq	15.2%	15.0%
Nigeria	13.0%	21.2%
South Korea	3.7%	3.4%
United States	9.3%	9.0%

A. Throughout the world, unemployment rates decreased between 2009 and 2011.

B. In all African countries, unemployment rates are increasing at a rapid pace.

C. The population of India is so large that it will be impossible to achieve full employment there.

D. Unemployment rates vary widely from country to country, from year to year.

25. A budget is a plan for spending your income. It involves figuring out how much money you have and how you will use it. The first step is to figure out your fixed costs. These are expenses you must pay each month. Examples include rent, food, utilities, and car payments. The difference between what you must spend and your total income is called discretionary income. This is income you can spend as you choose.

The Garcia family is making a budget. Which of these would be considered part of their discretionary income?

A. entertainment
B. rent
C. car payment
D. electricity bill

Answer Key

1. **A.** The colonists were establishing a new government independent of Great Britain. The powers listed are all powers that would belong to an independent government.

2. **D.** The passage says the federal government had "little power" and was "too weak."

3. **A.** The last sentence in paragraph 1 lists the problems facing the new nation. These problems suggest that survival of the nation was a concern.

4. **B.** The highest percentage of government expenses is Social Security. Therefore, this is the most expensive service provided by the government.

5. **A.** You know people are living longer, so you can infer that more people will receive Social Security payments for longer times. There is no information to suggest that the other options are true.

6. **C.** The last sentence says, "These groups must share power and make compromises to get things done." This sentence suggests that all groups get some of what they want but no single group dominates.

7. **D.** The amendments were passed in the 1960s. This was the time that the civil rights movement was active.

8. **C.** Women and minorities had to fight for the right to vote. The 15th, 19th, and 24th Amendments guaranteed their rights.

9. **D.** Europe was able to dominate other countries because its factories were producing more and more goods. Therefore, Europe was richer and more advanced than other parts of the world. It had the money and equipment necessary to colonize other nations.

10. **C.** The chart shows that eight of ten of the most populous countries in 2012 are expected to be on the list of the most populous countries in 2050.

11. **A.** Only a lower birthrate in Russia and Japan and a higher birthrate in other countries could explain why Russia and Japan would move further down the list.

12. **D.** The steam engine was the key to the Industrial Revolution. It changed the way things were made and transported.

13. **B.** Generally inventions that have replaced workers have not been popular among workers themselves because workers quickly realize that machines can work better and faster than they can.

14. **A.** The paragraph describes how the courts re-interpret the constitutional balance of power. This means that the way we understand the Constitution changes with time.

15. **C.** The title of the map indicates that the map gives information about railroads, which are a form of transportation.

16. **A.** The map shows more railroads in the Northeast than in the Southeast. Railroads moved raw matrials and manufactured goods. They enabled the Northeast to develop economically much faster than the Southeast.

17. **B.** Public health measures in the Third World are controlling many of the diseases that have caused infant deaths. More babies are surviving, which results in an increased population.

18. **B.** Because more infants are surviving, more children are growing up. This means more young women will reach the age where they will be able to have children.

19. **D.** The passage says small farmers were losing their land and their way of life. Therefore, this class of people was getting smaller in number.

20. **C.** The photograph shows children demonstrating for gun restrictions. The message is that limiting guns is logical. Nothing in the photo relates to the courts or to the gun lobby.

Answer Key

21. **D.** The passage states that people have different ideas about the Second Amendment. The children in the photo are trying to convince others to agree with their point of view.

22. **B.** The title of the map, "Ancient Middle East," indicates that this is a historical map. It shows some cities, like Troy, that no longer exist.

23. **A.** Every city shown on the map is located near a body of water, either a river or a sea.

24. **D.** The unemployment rates shown on the table vary greatly. Although most countries had lower rates in 2011 than in 2009, no worldwide trend is shown. No general statement about Africa or India can be made from so little data.

25. **A.** Entertainment is a want, not a need, so it is part of discretionary income. All the other choices are part of the Garcia family's fixed costs that must be paid every month.

Evaluation Chart

Check Your Understanding

On the following chart, circle the number of any question you answered incorrectly. Under each lesson title, you will see the pages you can review to study the content covered in the question. Pay particular attention to reviewing those lessons in which you missed half or more of the questions.

Chapters	Item Number	Study Pages
US Government and Civics	6, 14	18–65
US History: Revolutionary War through the Depression	1, 2, 3, 15, 16, 19	74–101
US History: World War II through Modern Times	7, 8, 20, 21	110–143
World History and Political Systems	17, 18	152–175
Economic Foundations	4, 5, 25	184–235
Economic Events in History	9, 12, 13	244–261
Economics in the Twenty-First Century	24	270–277
Geography and People	10, 11, 22, 23	286–319

UNIT 1

US History and Civics

US Government and Civics

Think about a time you worked with a group of people to get something done. Maybe you worked on a project at school, for your job, or with your family members. Did everyone work together and share ideas, or did one person make all the decisions and tell everyone else what to do? Usually people think it is unfair for one person to take control of a group. In a similar way, the US government divides its responsibilities and powers so one branch or one group does not have too much power.

In this chapter, you will learn how the US government is structured. As you read, think about how you can participate in our democracy. What can you do to change laws or policies at the local, state, or national level?

In this chapter you will study these topics:

Lesson 1.1: Types of Modern and Historical Governments
Throughout history, people have formed governments. Three types of government are common today: democracy, monarchy, and dictatorship. None of these types are new. For example, more than two thousand years ago, some of the Greek city-states had democratic governments, but this was not the same type of democracy that we have in the United States today.

Lesson 1.2: The US Constitution
The Constitution outlines the responsibilities and structure of the government. It also describes the rights of citizens. The Constitution can be changed, but changes have been made only a few times in more than two hundred years.

Lesson 1.3: The Executive, Legislative, and Judicial Branches of Government
The US Constitution establishes three branches of government. The executive branch, led by the president, is in charge of the daily activities of government. The legislative branch, which includes the House of Representatives and the Senate, passes laws. The judicial branch, made up of the Supreme Court and other courts, interprets the laws.

Lesson 1.4: State and Local Government
The Constitution names the powers given to the federal government. Other responsibilities belong to state or local governments. Some powers, such as taxation, belong to all levels of government.

Lesson 1.5: Political Parties and Interest Groups
Though political parties are not described in the Constitution, they have dominated politics since the 1800s. Interest groups try to influence political decisions, working to promote their ideas at all levels of government.

Lesson 1.6: Civil Liberties and Civil Rights
The Bill of Rights protects the rights of individuals. Originally some of these rights applied only to white males, but today they apply to all citizens, regardless of race or gender.

Lesson 1.7: The US Role in Global Society

At a time when nations are more interconnected, the United States has a greater role in the global society because it is the world's only superpower. This role includes expanding businesses, spreading American culture, and providing aid to foreign countries.

Lesson 1.8: Contemporary Public Policy

Public policy is made at all levels of government—local, state, and national. Public policies address concerns such as health, the environment, and the economy. Voting is one way citizens can participate in making public policy.

Goal Setting

Why is it important to study government?

- to understand how democracy is different from other forms of government
- to understand why there are separate branches of government
- to understand what rights citizens have
- to understand how laws can change society

Think about the reasons people study government.

- to understand how to amend a law or get a new law passed
- to understand their rights and protections under the law
- to find out how to run for public office
- to understand how political parties work
- to understand the role of lobbyists
- to influence public policy

What do you hope to learn from the lessons in this chapter? As you read through this chapter, fill in the graphic organizer below with words and concepts related to government.

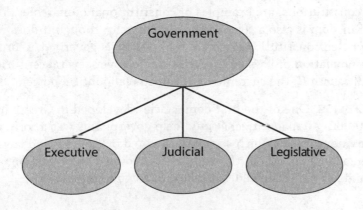

Types of Modern and Historical Governments

Lesson Objectives

You will be able to

- Identify and compare types of modern and historical governments

- Explain how types of government are related

- Explain how governments develop

Skills

- **Reading Skill:** Analyze Ideas

- **Core Skill:** Make Inferences

Vocabulary

absolute
amendments
analyze
confederacy
democracy
dictatorship
government
monarchy
peers

KEY CONCEPT: Within a state, a country, or a region, the government is made up of a group of people responsible for the direction and supervision of public affairs.

Have you ever been part of a sports team or planned a family reunion? The people who lead such groups or events decide how things should be done and who will do what. These people have something in common with different types of governments. Local and national governments accomplish many of the same tasks, but they operate on a larger scale.

Identify Types of Government

Throughout history, people have developed different forms of **government**, or ruling authority. Three types of government are common today. A **monarchy** is a government in which a king or queen serves as head of state. A **democracy** is a government in which the people decide what kind of society they will have and what laws and services they want. A **dictatorship** is a government in which one person decides how the government functions and what the laws are. Each of these basic forms of government has variations.

Monarchies Monarchies were one of the earliest forms of government. As people began to live in groups, the strongest leaders took charge. Kings and queens passed on their leadership roles to their sons or daughters. Early monarchs had absolute power—they made all decisions. But by the year 1215, the power of monarchs began to weaken. In England, the barons (men who had been given land by the king in return for their loyalty) were angered by King John's cruel conduct and high taxes. They forced the king to sign the **Magna Carta**, a document limiting his power.

Gradually the power of monarchs became more limited. In 1789, for example, the French Revolution brought an end to King Louis XVI's absolute power. **Constitutional monarchies** replaced the earlier monarchies.

Today there are only a few monarchies. Japan and Norway, which have written constitutions, are examples of constitutional monarchies. The United Kingdom is also a constitutional monarchy, though it does not have a written constitution. Instead, the country is governed according to an accumulation of laws and treaties created over several centuries. Queen Elizabeth II, the current ruler, has no real political power.

Democracies One of the first democracies developed in Greece in about 500 BC. All male citizens could help govern. This was a form of **direct democracy**, in which each citizen voted on policies and laws. However, a large portion of the population had no rights. Women, slaves, and non-Greeks could not take part in government.

ANALYZE IDEAS

When you **analyze** ideas, you carefully examine all the information in order to understand it. Be an active reader. Ask yourself questions as you read. Jot notes in the margin when you don't understand an idea. When you have finished reading, review the important ideas and think about how these ideas fit together.

Read the following paragraph. As you read, write questions beside the text. After reading, go back and answer your questions. If some of your questions are not answered in the text, you may have to look for information in other sources.

> The government of the United States is a democracy. To be more accurate, the United States is both a **representative democracy** and a **constitutional democracy**. In a representative democracy, the people vote for leaders who represent them and speak for them in the government. Senators, representatives, and the president are all elected by the people. These leaders are expected to do what the majority of the people want. In a constitutional democracy, the powers of the government are described in a document called a constitution.

You might have written *What's the difference?* beside the two boldfaced terms. Next to the sentence that begins "These leaders . . ." you might have written *What if they don't do what the people want?* This last question is not answered in the text. But if you read on through this chapter, you will find the answer to your question.

Reading Skill
Analyze Ideas

When you analyze something, you read carefully to understand the ideas in the text. When you analyze monarchies and democracies, you try to understand the differences between these two forms of government.

As you read "Types of Government," make a list of key differences between a monarchy and a democracy. Then write a short paragraph explaining why democracies have become more common, while the number of monarchies has decreased.

Democracy did not become a common form of government for hundreds of years. But in the 1700s, people in Europe began to push for greater freedom. Many of their efforts resulted in constitutional monarchies. This set the stage for the first modern democracies.

The colonists who came to America knew about the changes in government that were occurring in Europe. When Americans won their freedom, these new ideas about government led to our representative democracy.

Other countries, however, took different approaches. Canada, for example, developed a **parliamentary democracy**. Canadians vote for representatives who become members of their **parliament**, or legislature. The leader of the political party with the most seats in parliament becomes the prime minister. This means the nation's chief executive answers to representatives rather than directly to the people.

Dictatorships   A dictatorship is a government ruled by one person or by a small group that has absolute power. The dictator determines the laws and holds power over everyone in the country. Dictators often come to power by force or by misleading the people. Adolf Hitler of Germany and Idi Amin of Uganda were dictators.

REAL WORLD CONNECTION

Apply Knowledge

As part of the legislative process in the United States, the president may veto, or turn down, laws passed by Congress. However, Congress may override a presidential veto if two-thirds of its members vote in favor of the law.

In a notebook, write several sentences analyzing why it is important for both the president and the Congress to have a say in the final passage of laws.

The Virginia Declaration of Rights and the Declaration of Independence are primary documents. Both are original papers written by early leaders of the new American colonies. By studying them, we can learn what the colonists were thinking about government.

In a notebook, write answers to these questions:

Why do you think these documents are so similar?

What does their similarity tell you about the individuals who wrote the two documents?

READING PRIMARY DOCUMENTS

Primary documents are original papers. They include letters, autobiographies, speeches, and official records.

The Declaration of Independence is one of the most important documents ever written. The Declaration of Independence states that the American colonists had the right to rebel against rule by England and to establish a new nation. It was drafted by Thomas Jefferson in 1776 while he was representing Virginia at the Second Continental Congress.

Jefferson drew on earlier documents to create his powerful statement of the values and beliefs of the colonists. One of these documents was the Virginia Declaration of Rights, which was written by George Mason and adopted in June 1776. This statement of the rights of the people of Virginia also set out the plan for the government of Virginia.

Directions: Read the passages below from the Virginia Declaration of Rights and the Declaration of Independence. In a notebook, list the similarities regarding the freedom of all humans and the right of people to govern themselves.

These are the first two sections of the Virginia Declaration of Rights.

Section 1. That all men are by nature equally free and independent and have certain inherent rights, of which, when they enter into a state of society, they cannot, by any compact, deprive or divest their posterity; namely, the enjoyment of life and liberty, with the means of acquiring and possessing property, and pursuing and obtaining happiness and safety.

Section 2. That all power is vested in, and consequently derived from, the people; that magistrates are their trustees and servants and at all times amenable to them.

The passage below is the beginning of the second paragraph of the Declaration of Independence.

We hold these truths to be self-evident, that all men are created equal, that they are endowed by their Creator with certain unalienable Rights, that among these are Life, Liberty and the pursuit of Happiness.—That to secure these rights, Governments are instituted among Men, deriving their just powers from the consent of the governed,—That whenever any Form of Government becomes destructive of these ends, it is the Right of the People to alter or to abolish it, and to institute new Government, laying its foundation on such principles and organizing its powers in such form, as to them shall seem most likely to effect their Safety and Happiness.

THE MAGNA CARTA AND THE US CONSTITUTION

Magna Carta   Bill of Rights

TECHNOLOGY
CONNECTION

Internet Research

Research the Virginia Declaration of Rights, the Declaration of Independence, and the US Constitution on the Internet.

In an essay, explain how the Virginia Declaration of Rights influenced the other two documents. Cite details showing similar ideas and wording in the three documents.

The Magna Carta and the US Constitution are important primary documents. They are studied by people learning about government.

The Magna Carta was written in 1215 by nobles wanting to protect their rights from a king who had absolute power. It formed the basis for Great Britain's development as a constitutional monarchy.

Following is a paraphrase of part of the Magna Carta.

Item 20: A freeman shall not be punished for a minor crime except to the degree of the crime. For a serious offense, he shall be punished according to the seriousness of that crime.

Item 39: No freeman shall be imprisoned or have his rights taken away except by the lawful judgment of his **peers**, or equals, and by the law of the land.

Item 40: No one shall be denied or delayed the right to justice.

The US Constitution, written in 1787, is the document that establishes US laws. Some of its authors, including Thomas Jefferson and James Madison, believed the document did not do enough to protect the rights of individuals. In 1789, Madison presented Congress with a list of suggested Constitutional **amendments**, or changes. The ten amendments added to the Constitution in 1791 became known as the Bill of Rights. The following text is taken from three of the amendments.

Amendment 5: "No person shall be . . . deprived of life, liberty, or property without due process of law."

Amendment 6: "In all criminal prosecutions, the accused shall enjoy the right to a speedy and public trial, by an impartial jury of the state and district wherein the crime shall have been committed."

Amendment 8: "Excessive bail shall not be required, nor excessive fines imposed, nor cruel and unusual punishments inflicted."

The US Constitution was written more than 550 years after the Magna Carta. However, over that long period of time, many of the same ideas about government remained important to people.

Reading Skill
Analyze Ideas

You have just read parts of the Magna Carta and the three of the first amendments to the US Constitution. Analyze the important ideas in these passages.

In a notebook, write one paragraph explaining why the ideas in the Magna Carta were important to the writers of the Constitution.

(l)KAREN BLEIER/AFP/Getty Images, (r)Comstock Images/Getty Images

When you make an **inference**, you figure out an idea that was not stated directly.

Begin by thinking about what you know. Consider facts, examples, and other details. Think about your own experiences. All of this information provides clues that give you a new understanding. Then add up these clues in your head and make an inference.

As you read the information regarding the Iroquois constitution, think about the facts that are presented. Consider what you already know about government.

Then answer these questions in a notebook:

What can you infer that the authors of the US Constitution knew regarding the Great Binding Law?

Do you believe the writers of the Constitution shared the same values as the Iroquois?

Do you think all people value these ideas?

Directions: Read this passage about the constitution of the Iroquois. As you read, think about how the Iroquois organized their government. In a notebook, explain one way that the Great Binding Law is similar to both the Magna Carta and the US Constitution.

The Iroquois are a group of closely connected Native American tribes. Sometime between the years 1300 and 1450, the Iroquois created a document known as the Great Binding Law. This law, which was like a constitution, bound the five nations, or tribes, of the Iroquois into one **confederacy**. A confederacy is a union, or a group of people who join together for a common purpose. The individuals who wrote the US Constitution were familiar with the Great Binding Law. Some of the ideas in that law influenced them when they began writing the Constitution.

The Great Binding Law included these ideas:

- All members of the Iroquois—men and women alike—could participate in government.

- The welfare of the individual, and of the people as a whole, was most important. The role of the leaders was to look after the people. The people were not there to serve the leaders.

- There were five Iroquois nations. The nations shared a single territory. The nations cooperated and were represented by leaders in the same government. They joined together in war.

- The Iroquois had a Grand Council that met in the central nation of the confederacy.

- The Grand Council was made up of two separate groups. Each group discussed an issue and came to a decision. Then the members reached a final agreement.

Directions: Read the following passage. It includes a quotation from a letter that George Washington wrote to a man who wanted him to be a king. In a notebook, write an inference you can make about how George Washington saw his role as a leader.

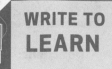

WRITE TO LEARN

Write a journal entry from the point of view of one of the authors of the US Constitution. Explain whether you think the United States should have a representative democracy or a constitutional monarchy. Give reasons that support your choice.

During the American Revolutionary War, George Washington was Commander in Chief of the Army. As a war hero and statesman, he was held in high esteem in America.

Some people believed that Washington should become king of the United States. Washington, however, refused to be a king. He wrote to one man who proposed the idea, "I am much at a loss to conceive what part of my conduct could have given encouragement to an address which to me seems big with the greatest mischiefs that can befall my Country." He went on to tell the man, "If you have any regard for your Country . . . or respect for me, to banish these thoughts from your Mind."

After the war, Washington was president of the Constitutional Convention, which produced the US Constitution in 1787. After the Constitution was ratified, or approved, he was elected the first president of the new country.

THINK ABOUT SOCIAL STUDIES

Directions: In a notebook, list three of the documents that helped determine the type of government established in the United States. Describe one important idea that came from each of these documents.

_____

_____

_____

_____

_____

Vocabulary Review

Directions: Use words from the list to complete the following sentences.

absolute	amendments	confederacy	democracy
dictatorship	government	monarchy	peers

1. When the suspect appears in court, her case will be judged by a group of her _____.

2. The power of president of the United States is not _____. It is limited by the Constitution.

3. A _____ is a government in which the people hold the power.

4. A harsh _____ was set up to govern a country after the army generals threw the president out of power.

5. Today the Constitution of the United States has 27 _____.

6. The American colonies joined together in a _____ to fight against the British.

7. In a _____, a king or queen is the head of state.

8. A monarchy, a democracy, and a dictatorship are all types of _____.

Skill Review

Directions: Choose the one best answer to each question.

1. A direct democracy would work best in which of these situations?

   A. A nation wants to vote for leaders who represent them in the government.
   B. In a small nation, each citizen wants to vote on policies and laws.
   C. A nation wants to describe the powers of its government in a constitution.
   D. A nation has been taken over by a leader who will exert nearly absolute power.

2. How is a constitutional monarchy different from an absolute monarchy?

   A. Only an absolute monarchy is headed by a king or queen.
   B. In a constitutional monarchy, the king or queen can change the laws. In an absolute monarchy, the ruler does not have that power.
   C. In a constitutional monarchy, the ruler's power is mainly ceremonial, and a prime minister governs the country. In an absolute monarchy, the ruler's power is unlimited.
   D. Only an absolute monarchy protects the rights of citizens.

3. What do the Magna Carta, the Great Binding Law, and the US Constitution have in common?

   A. Each established a dictatorship.
   B. Each created a democracy.
   C. Each eliminated a monarch.
   D. Each protected the rights of the people.

Skill Practice

Directions: Read the two passages. Then answer the questions that follow.

The English Bill of Rights

The 1600s were a time of conflict between the British king, the English people, and Parliament (the British legislature). The conflict ended in 1689 when new monarchs, William III and Mary, accepted the English Bill of Rights. This document helped create a constitutional monarchy. The English Bill of Rights stated that the monarch served at the will of Parliament. The Bill of Rights strengthened the rights of common people. For example, people could no longer be taxed simply because the king wanted money. Laws could not be changed without Parliament's approval. Members of Parliament were to be freely elected. The Bill of Rights guaranteed a just and fair government that answered to the people.

The US Bill of Rights

To protect the rights of Americans, the US Congress approved the Bill of Rights in 1789. Among the rights protected are the following:

Amendment 1: People have the right to practice any religion they choose.

Amendment 4: People and their homes cannot be searched without probable cause.

Amendment 8: Persons arrested cannot be punished in cruel or unusual ways.

Amendment 9: The rights of the people are not limited to the rights listed in the Constitution.

---

1. Why do you think the authors of the US Bill of Rights thought it was necessary to include these rights in the Constitution?

   _____

   _____

2. In what way did the English Bill of Rights influence the US Bill of Rights?

   _____

   _____

3. Why do you think the authors of the US Bill of Rights included Amendment 9?

   _____

   _____

   _____

Writing Practice

Directions: Write a paragraph explaining how monarchies influenced the development of the US government.

The US Constitution

Lesson Objectives

You will be able to

- Identify the factors that led to the Constitutional Convention

- Describe some of the compromises in the Constitution

- Summarize the process of amending the Constitution

Skills

- **Core Skill:** Read a Bar Graph

- **Reading Skill:** Paraphrase Information

Vocabulary

category
checks and balances
guarantee
paraphrase
separation of powers

KEY CONCEPT: Changes and compromises were needed to create and pass the US Constitution.

Computers have operating systems that tell them how to work. Programmers update the operating systems as they make improvements and see features that need to be changed.

In a similar way, governments rely on operating systems. The United States tried one system that had several bugs in it. Then legislators made changes to the documents that defined the government. In this way, the system became more effective.

The US Constitution

After the Revolution, the new nation was deeply in debt. In 1786, farmers in Massachusetts took part in Shays's Rebellion. They seized courtrooms to prevent mortgage foreclosures. After seven months of fighting, the militia put down the rebellion with little bloodshed. The conflict, however, showed the need for a strong central government. Some aspects of the economic crisis, especially problems of interstate commerce, had to be dealt with. It was clear that the Articles of Confederation—the agreement made by the original thirteen states to establish the United States as a nation—needed to be changed.

A Constitutional Convention was called. It began meeting in Philadelphia in May 1787. Its purpose was to amend the Articles of Confederation.

To prevent the leaders of the central government from becoming too powerful, the new government would be based on the principle of **separation of powers**; that is, the government would be divided into three branches. The legislative branch was to enact laws. The executive branch, headed by the president, was to administer the government. The federal **judicial** (court) system was created to settle disputes and legal matters. This system of **checks and balances** was designed to prevent any single branch of government from having too much power.

Another important issue was the fair distribution of power between large and small states. To resolve the issue, two separate bodies were created in the legislative branch. Each state received equal representation in the **Senate**. Representation in the **House of Representatives** was determined by the size of the state's population. In this way, the House protected the rights of large states, and the Senate protected the rights of small states.

The Constitution addressed other areas of government as well. Sections discussed choosing the president, structuring the federal court system, and amending the Constitution. The finished Constitution was sent to conventions in each of the thirteen states. It needed to be ratified by nine states before the Constitution became the law. Eleven states had ratified the Constitution by March 1789.

PARAPHRASE INFORMATION

When you read, you may come across a long, complicated sentence or paragraph. To make sure you have understood what you just read, go back and read it again, slowly. Then **paraphrase** the passage, or use your own words to tell what you just read.

To paraphrase a passage, look for key words and ideas. Imagine that you are explaining the text to someone else. How could you explain the text in your own words?

Read the following paragraph. Then read the two paraphrases below and choose the best one.

> The US Constitution has three major sections. The first section is the preamble, or introduction. It outlines the document's purpose. The second section is the main text. It has seven parts, called Articles, which are numbered with roman numerals. Each article explains how the government will work or how the Constitution will be ratified (approved). The last section lists the amendments to the document. The first ten amendments were proposed in 1789. The most recent amendment passed in 1992.

1 The three sections of the US Constitution are the preamble, the articles, and the amendments. The articles explain how the government works.

2 The US Constitution has three sections. The third section is the amendments. The first ten amendments were added at the same time.

The first paraphrase summarizes the important information in the paragraph. The second paraphrase leaves out key information and focuses on one detail. The first paraphrase is better.

THINK ABOUT SOCIAL STUDIES

Directions: Write a short response to this question.

1. How did the new US Constitution balance the power between small states like Rhode Island and large states like Pennsylvania?

_____

_____

Research It
Compare Government Documents

Go to the National Archives website (www.archives.gov), and enter the search term "Rotunda for the Charters of Freedom." Choose "Charters of Freedom." Read the bullet points that describe the Declaration of Independence, the Constitution, and the amendments to the Constitution. Then click the links to look at the original documents.

Next, visit the THOMAS Library at the Library of Congress (http://thomas.loc.gov/home/bills_res.html) and choose Browse Bills & Resolutions. Then select Popular and Short Titles. Choose a bill that is interesting to you. Open the bill. Click the number of the bill (such as S.674 or H.R.1274). Finally, select Text of Legislation to read the bill.

In a notebooks, compare and contrast the historic documents with the modern documents. How are the historical documents similar to modern government documents? How are they different?

Bar graphs have two axes: the vertical axis along the side and the horizontal axis across the bottom. Each axis is labeled. To understand a graph, it is important to read the title and labels.

Bar graphs make it easy to compare amounts. The longer the bar, the greater the amount being measured.

Look at the graph and answer these questions:

- In which time period were the fewest amendments passed?

- During which century were the most amendments passed?

Key Principles of the Constitution

The framers of the Constitution relied on eleven key ideas when writing the Constitution. These ideas are explained in the chart below.

Principle	What It Means
Popular Sovereignty	The government gets its power and authority from the people.
Federalism	Power is shared between state and national government.
Separation of Powers	Responsibilities are shared among three branches of government, each with its own powers.
Checks and Balances	Each of the branches of government has some control over the other.
Judicial Review	The judicial branch (the courts) can declare a law passed in Congress or an action taken by the president to be unconstitutional.
Limited Government	The national government can do only what the Constitution specifically states it can do.
Natural Rights Philosophy	Government has authority only because the people give it authority to protect their natural rights.
Constitutionalism	A constitution limits a government's power.
Majority Rule and Minority Rights	The majority rules, but it must respect and protect the rights of individuals.
Rule of Law	Laws are clear and fair, and no one is above the law—not even the government.
Individual Rights	All people naturally have certain individual rights, such as life, liberty, and property.

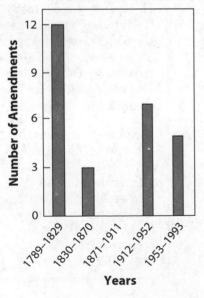

AMENDMENTS TO THE CONSTITUTION

Amendments to the Constitution

At the first session of Congress in 1789, popular pressure forced the Constitution's supporters to add ten amendments aimed at protecting individual rights. This Bill of Rights gives citizens the following freedoms:

- freedom of speech and the press
- the right to assemble and petition the government
- the right to keep and bear arms
- protection against unreasonable search and seizure
- the right to trial by jury
- the right to due process and protection against self-incrimination
- the right to a public trial
- the right to have an attorney
- protection against excessive bail or cruel or unusual punishment
- separation of church and state

Congress submitted this **guarantee**, or assurance, of rights to the states. All ten amendments were approved by 1791.

Since the Bill of Rights, seventeen more amendments have been added. Each amendment has been passed to solve a problem. Only one amendment has been **repealed**, or withdrawn. The Eighteenth Amendment (1919) prohibited the drinking and sale of alcohol. It was repealed by the Twenty-First Amendment (1933).

The procedure for changing the Constitution is complicated. Amendments must be proposed by a two-thirds majority vote of both houses of Congress or by two-thirds of the state legislatures. Amendments must be approved by three-fourths of the states. Because of this complex procedure, many proposed amendments have never been ratified. For instance, the Equal Rights Amendment passed Congress in 1972. However, it was not adopted because it fell short of the 38 states required for ratification.

The seventeen amendments passed after the Bill of Rights fall in three broad **categories**, or groups. One category is amendments that extend voting rights and the power of voters. Among the more important examples of this group are the Fifteenth (1870), guaranteeing African American males the right to vote; the Nineteenth (1920), giving women the right to vote; and the Twenty-Sixth (1971), lowering the voting age to 18. A second category is amendments that change the powers of state and national government. For example, the Thirteenth (1865) abolished slavery, the Fourteenth (1868) granted citizenship to the former slaves, and the Sixteenth (1913) established the federal income tax. The final group involves changes in the function or structure of government. One example of this category is the Twenty-Second (1951), which limits a president to ten years in office.

Even with its amendments, the Constitution is short, probably shorter than the bylaws of many organizations. It has vague guidelines concerning the powers and functions of the different levels of government. However, this flexibility has allowed the Constitution to survive as a symbol of national unity. The meaning of its various paragraphs has constantly evolved as the country has grown and changed.

21st Century Skill
Critical Thinking and Problem Solving

In 1789, Congress proposed 10 amendments to the Constitution. This was done as a solution to a problem.

In your notebook, state the problem that Congress wanted to solve. Then tell whether you think the solution was effective. Explain your answer.

Reading Skill
Paraphrase Information

When paraphrasing a passage, look for key words and ideas.

As you read the second paragraph on this page, ask yourself, *What is the main point of this paragraph? How could I state that more simply?*

In a notebook, paraphrase the second paragraph.

THINK ABOUT SOCIAL STUDIES

Directions: Write a short response to the following questions.

1. How is an amendment added to the Constitution?

   _____

   _____

2. List three categories of amendments.

   _____

   _____

   _____

WRITE TO LEARN

After completing this lesson, think about a time you were in a group that divided responsibilities among all members. Then write a few sentences describing the situation and explaining why sharing responsibility was a good idea.

Vocabulary Review

Directions: Use these words to complete the following sentences.

categories   checks and balances   guarantees   separation of powers

1. The Bill of Rights _____ certain rights and liberties to US citizens.

2. The _____ means that no one branch of government has all the authority.

3. The president's vetoing a bill passed by Congress is an example of _____.

4. Voting rights, powers of state and national governments, and functions of government are

_____ of amendments made to change the Constitution.

Skill Review

Directions: Use the graph on page 28 to answer this question.

1. Which statement about the 40 years after the Constitution was passed is best supported by the graph?

   A. More amendments were adopted in that time period than in any other time period.
   B. No amendments were adopted during that time period.
   C. Fewer amendments were adopted in that time period than in any other time period.
   D. The early 1800s represent a time of great changes.

Directions: Write a paraphrase of the following paragraph.

Until 1933, presidents were inaugurated in March following the November election of the previous year. In 1932, Franklin Delano Roosevelt was elected president. The outgoing president, Herbert Hoover, was blamed for the economic troubles of the Great Depression. About 25 percent of the nation's people were out of work, and the situation did not improve during the four months following the election. The new president had no authority to resolve the financial crisis. To avoid the problems that occurred with a powerless president, the Twentieth Amendment to the Constitution moved Inauguration Day to January 20. Congressional sessions were to begin on January 3 so that Congress could have drafts of new laws ready for the incoming president.

_____

_____

_____

_____

Skill Practice

Directions: Choose the one best answer to each question. Questions 1 and 2 refer to the passage.

> In 1987, the Supreme Court heard the case of *Bethel School District #43 v. Fraser*. A student at Bethel High School made an obscene speech to an assembly of students and was suspended. The student, Fraser, argued that his right to freedom of speech was violated. However, the Supreme Court ruled that students do not have a First Amendment right to make obscene speeches in school. This case is an example of the Supreme Court's limiting the meaning of an amendment. The decision shows that there are conditions to freedom of speech.

1. What is the main idea of this passage?

   A. The Bill of Rights should have clearly defined individual rights and freedoms.
   B. Freedom of speech has always been upheld by the government.
   C. Freedom of assembly was not clearly defined in the Bill of Rights.
   D. Some Supreme Court decisions limit freedoms in order to prevent these freedoms from being abused.

2. The Supreme Court's decision in *Bethel v. Fraser* was based on its interpretation of which freedom?

   A. assembly
   B. speech
   C. political beliefs
   D. religion

3. The Fifth Amendment states "nor shall any person be subject for the same offense to be twice put in jeopardy of life or limb; nor shall be compelled in any criminal case to be a witness against himself, nor be deprived of life, liberty, or property, without due process of law; nor shall private property be taken for public use without just compensation."

   When people are arrested, they must be read their Miranda Rights. The Miranda Rights tell suspects that they have the right to remain silent and warns them that anything they say can be used against them in a court of law.

   Which clause in the Fifth Amemdment is the basis for the Miranda Rights?

   A. "nor shall any person be subject for the same offense to be twice put in jeopardy of life or limb"
   B. "nor shall be compelled in any criminal case to be a witness against himself"
   C. "nor be deprived of life, liberty, or property, without due process of law"
   D. "nor shall private property be taken for public use without just compensation"

Writing Practice

Directions: The Bill of Rights protects freedoms that many people take for granted. Choose one of the first ten amendments and write an essay describing how you have used the freedoms it guarantees. For example, you might write about freedom of speech or freedom of religion.

The Executive, Legislative, and Judicial Branches of Government

KEY CONCEPT: Each of the three branches of government has unique roles and responsibilities.

If you have ever worked on a group project, you know that each member has a role to play. Running for an office at school or in an organization requires teamwork. Someone may provide artwork for a campaign poster, while another person creates a memorable slogan. A third team member may write a campaign speech.

In the same way, the three branches of the federal government work together toward the goal of good government. Each branch has its own work to do.

The Federal Government

To prevent an **imbalance** (lack of equality) of power, the Constitution divided the power and functions of government among three branches: executive, legislative, and judicial. The Constitution also instituted a system of checks and balances. This would keep one branch of government from controlling any other branch.

This graphic shows the branches of US government.

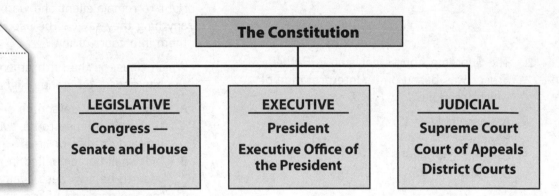

The Constitution

LEGISLATIVE	EXECUTIVE	JUDICIAL
Congress — **Senate and House**	President Executive Office of the President	Supreme Court Court of Appeals District Courts

The Executive Branch

The **executive branch** oversees the day-to-day activities of the government. The president, who is the head of this branch, must be at least 35 years old and a natural-born citizen of the United States. The presidential term is four years. The Twenty-Second Amendment (1951) limits a person to ten years in office. If the president dies or resigns while in office, the vice president becomes president.

The executive branch includes all federal agencies, such as the Environmental Protection Agency (EPA). With Senate approval, the president appoints cabinet officers, who are called secretaries. These secretaries head the major government agencies. The president also appoints the major executive positions.

COMPARE AND CONTRAST

Writers **compare** people, things, and ideas when they examine similarities, or likenesses. They **contrast** people, things, or ideas when they look at differences. For example, a writer might compare and contrast the three branches of government.

To show how the branches are alike and different, a writer might compare and contrast

- members and their terms of office

- functions and responsibilities

- powers and limitations

In comparing items, writers use terms such as *similar*, *both*, or *alike*. When contrasting items, terms such as *different*, *but*, *in contrast*, and *instead of* are often used.

Read the following paragraph and underline the words that signal comparisons and contrasts.

> In 1790 the Supreme Court had a Chief Justice and five associate justices, all of whom were men. Since the first female justice was appointed in 1981, the Court has had a different makeup. Presidents George Washington and Franklin D. Roosevelt are alike in one respect. They appointed more Supreme Court justices than any of the other presidents.

The signal words in the passage include *all*, *different*, and *alike*. The comparison in the passage is between Presidents Washington and Roosevelt: both appointed a large number of Supreme Court justices. The contrast is relates to the makeup of the Supreme Court (all men in 1790 versus a court with at least one female justice since 1981).

Core Skill
Identify Comparisons and Contrasts

Sometimes writers organize information into tables. A table lists information in columns and rows. Tables make it easy to compare and contrast.

Look at the table below. Read the title of the table and study the headings of the columns.

Candidates for president spend a great deal of money running for office. Their campaigns pay for travel, advertising, and advisors.

Presidential Campaign Spending	
Year	Amount (in Millions)
1952	$16
1972	$90
1996	$120
2004	$820

Write one sentence comparing or contrasting the money spent on two of the campaigns listed in the table. Then state your opinion about what you think will happen to campaign spending in the future.

The executive branch enforces acts of Congress, court decisions, and treaties. The president can also issue **proclamations** (formal public statements) and executive orders. These powers have been **delegated**, or assigned, to the president by law or by court decision.

All bills passed by Congress must be sent to the president. If the president signs the bill, it becomes law. However, the president can refuse to sign the bill and return it to Congress. This action is called a **veto**. Congress may override the president's veto by a two-thirds vote of both houses of Congress. However, if the president does not return the bill within ten days, the bill automatically becomes a law, unless Congress adjourns during that period. A pocket veto occurs if Congress adjourns during that 10-day period and the president does not sign the bill. Congress cannot override this kind of veto. The president's veto power shows how the executive branch checks the legislative branch. However, the legislative branch also has a check over the executive branch.

THINK ABOUT SOCIAL STUDIES

Directions: Write a short response to these questions.

1. What qualifications must a person have to become president?

   _____

2. What kinds of veto power does the president have?

   _____

   _____

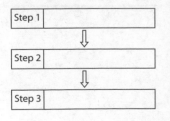
The Legislative Branch

The **legislative branch** of the federal government is called the Congress. It is responsible for writing the laws of the country. Congress is made up of two houses: the Senate and the House of Representatives. The Senate is made up of two senators from each of the 50 states, making 100 members. The House of Representatives has 435 members, a number that Congress has limited since 1910. The number of representatives from a state is determined by the population of the state.

A senator is elected for six years, must be at least 30 years old, and must have been a US citizen for nine years. A representative in the House is elected for two years, must be at least 25 years of age, and must have been a US citizen for seven years.

Powers Congress is responsible for taxing people. Taxes are used to provide services to people, to defend the country, and to pay the government's debts. Congress has the power to coin money, to declare war, and to override a presidential veto with a two-thirds vote of both houses. Congress proposes amendments to the Constitution, has the power of impeachment, and organizes the federal court system.

Congress operates as a check on the executive branch. It defines the **functions**, or roles, of the departments in the executive branch and controls the money set aside for those departments. Congress has the power to investigate many areas inside and outside of the government, including the executive branch. A congressional committee, like the court system, has the power to **subpoena** witnesses, or issue a formal command that requires a person to testify. Congress can exert a great deal of influence when it assumes a "watchdog" role over the executive branch.

Organization The vice president presides over the Senate but has little real power to direct the workings of the Senate. The vice president can cast a vote only to break a tie. The party that has the majority of delegates in the Senate elects a Senate Majority Leader, who leads the legislative activity in the Senate. The Speaker of the House is elected by the majority party in the House of Representatives. The Speaker presides over the meetings of the House and is responsible for organizing its activities.

Both houses of Congress are organized into committees to carry out the tasks of researching, holding hearings, and writing legislation. All legislation must go through a committee before it can be considered for a vote. Two important committees are the House Ways and Means Committee, which considers **revenue** (tax) bills, and the Senate Committee on Foreign Relations, which reviews all treaties.

The Judicial Branch

The **judicial branch** of the federal government interprets laws. It is the federal court system's responsibility to hear cases involving federal law.

The Supreme Court in Washington, DC, heads the federal courts. It consists of a chief justice and eight associate justices. The president appoints these justices with the Senate's approval. The justices serve for life, but they can be impeached for misconduct. The major functions of the Supreme Court are to hear appeals of lower federal-court decisions and to hear cases from state courts about whether a law is constitutional.

Prior to the second half of the twentieth century, all the justices were white men. In 1967 President Lyndon B. Johnson appointed his friend, Thurgood Marshall, to the court. Marshall became the first African American justice. President Ronald Reagan appointed Sandra Day O'Connor, the first woman on the Court, in 1981. She retired after serving nearly 25 years. Ruth Bader Ginsburg joined her as the second female associate justice in 1993. In 2009, Sonia Sotomayor became the first Hispanic American to serve on the Court.

Below the Supreme Court are the federal circuit courts of appeals. They hear appeals and review decisions of the federal district court and federal administrative bodies. At the lowest level are the federal district trial courts. The president appoints all federal judges.

The single most important power of the Supreme Court is its power of **judicial review**. This means that the Supreme Court rules on the constitutionality of laws passed by the legislative branch or on actions taken by the executive branch. The power of judicial review was first used by the Supreme Court in 1803 in *Marbury v. Madison*. In that case, the court refused to enforce a law that it believed was unconstitutional. The judicial branch has become an equal partner in the three-way separation of powers in the federal government.

Reading Skill
Compare and Contrast

There are two ways to organize an essay of comparison and contrast: block or point-by-point.

Sometimes writers cover each idea in a block. For example, one paragraph might focus on the Senate and the next paragraph on the House of Representatives.

At other times writers do a point-by-point comparison. In this case, one paragraph might contrast the length of terms for senators and representatives. The next paragraph might compare the responsibilities of each house of Congress.

Reread the first paragraph in the section titled "Organization." Use colored markers to indicate which sentences relate to the Senate and which relate to the House of Representatives. Then write one sentence describing the method used to organize the paragraph.

WRITE TO LEARN

In a notebook, write one paragraph comparing and contrasting the three branches of government. Use one of the methods described above to organize your essay.

Vocabulary Review

Directions: Use these words to complete the following sentences.

delegated   functions   imbalance   judicial review   veto

1. The federal government's system of checks and balances prevents a/an _____ of power among the three branches.

2. Congress checks the power of the executive branch because it defines the _____ of government departments.

3. _____ is one of the primary tasks of the Supreme Court.

4. The president can _____ a bill that Congress has approved.

5. The power to issue executive orders and proclamations has been _____ to the president.

Skill Review

Directions: Read the passage below. Choose the best answer to the questions.

> Members of the Supreme Court look carefully at each case. In 1969 in the case of *Tinker v. Des Moines Independent Community School District*, the justices voted seven to two in favor of students who wore black armbands to school to protest the Vietnam War. The students believed that this act was part of their First Amendment right to free speech. It did not pose a threat to the school or to the students. Most of the justices agreed.
>
> In contrast, the 1988 case of *Hazelwood School District v. Kuhlmeier* resulted in a different decision, though the issue was similar. The justices did not uphold what some high school students believed to be free speech. The principal had censored several pages of the school newspaper. The Court upheld his right to do so, stating that publications produced in the name of the school had to be consistent with the school's educational mission.

1. What do the two cases show about the Supreme Court?

   A. The Court does not understand adolescents.
   B. The Court is not sympathetic to teenagers.
   C. The Court always upholds First Amendment rights.
   D. The Court judges each case individually.

2. How does the writer show contrast between the two cases?

   A. The writer describes how each case came to the Supreme Court.
   B. The writer shows that the two cases had different outcomes.
   C. The writer writes about two events that happened in a similar setting.
   D. The writer describes two cases that were judged on the First Amendment.

Skill Practice

Directions: Choose the <u>one best answer</u> to each question.

> "The President of the US is to have power to return a bill, which shall have passed the two branches of the legislature for reconsideration; but the bill so returned is not to become a law unless upon reconsideration, it be approved by two-thirds of both houses."
>
> —Excerpted from *The Federalist Papers*, by Alexander Hamilton

1. To which of the following processes was Hamilton referring?

   A. pocket veto
   B. power of impeachment
   C. executive order
   D. presidential veto and congressional override

2. Who must approve a returned bill before it can become a law?

   A. the president
   B. two-thirds of the Senate
   C. two-thirds of each house
   D. all of the House of Representatives

Directions: <u>Questions 3 and 4</u> refer to the following passage.

The Supreme Court Reverses Itself

People make the laws and interpret them according to their beliefs. What the Constitution "really means" is subject to judicial review. Although the Constitution has changed little over the years, the values of society have changed. This has led to new rulings on earlier decisions. Consider these two cases concerning racial segregation:

(1) In 1896, in a period marked by extreme expressions of racial discrimination, the Supreme Court ruled in *Plessy v. Ferguson* that segregation in public facilities, including public schools, was constitutional so long as the facilities were "separate but equal."

(2) In 1954, the Supreme Court ruled, in the case of *Brown v. the Board of Education* that "separate but equal" schools were unconstitutional and they violated laws granting equal protection.

3. Which best describes the decisions of the Supreme Court?

   A. influenced by current developments
   B. based on the written Constitution
   C. not subject to major revisions
   D. based on the opinions of the individual justices

4. The passage suggests that the *Plessy v. Ferguson* decision was very heavily influenced by what?

   A. politicians
   B. the civil rights movement
   C. racial discrimination
   D. black power movement

Writing Practice

Directions: Write an essay comparing and contrasting the role of the executive branch with the role of the legislative branch.

State and Local Government

Lesson Objectives

You will be able to
- Explain the ways in which national and state governments are alike and different
- Identify the different levels and forms of local government
- Distinguish between the various forms of city government

Skills

- **Core Skill:** Judge the Relevance of Information
- **Reading Skill:** Identify Facts and Details

Vocabulary

contradict
direct initiative
recall
referendum
relevant information
reserved

KEY CONCEPT: State and local governments have powers and duties not granted to the federal government.

At work, each employee has specific duties. One person may run the cash register, while another stocks shelves. Sometimes duties overlap, so people are cross-trained to work in more than one department.

In the same way, national, state, or local governments have different duties, and sometimes their responsibilities overlap.

Who Has Power?

Under the federal system, the central government and the states share political power. The federal government has the power to tax, make war, and regulate interstate and foreign commerce. In addition, it has the right to "make all laws which shall be necessary and proper" for carrying out the powers granted to it under the Constitution. Any powers not specifically granted to the federal government are **reserved**, or set aside, for the states.

The Constitution established a general framework; however, the actual relations between local governments and the federal government have grown and changed over time. The general trend has been toward the federal government increasing its power. The rise of a national economy, several major wars, the trauma of the Great Depression, complicated international relations, and serious urban problems have all helped create a strong federal government.

State Governments

State governments are organized much like the federal government. Each state has a written constitution and a **governor**, the chief executive officer. All states have a **bicameral** (two-house) legislature, except Nebraska, which has a unicameral (one-house) legislature. All states also have court systems. However, there are wide variations in how state governments operate. One common trend is toward increased power in the executive branch, headed by the governor.

IDENTIFY FACTS AND DETAILS

Writers support their main ideas with details. Details expand on the main idea or make it clearer. Details that can be proven are facts. Facts are recorded in reference books, such as encyclopedias.

For example, a writer who is discussing a war might include such facts as the dates of the war, the countries involved, and the number of casualties suffered. The causes and outcomes of the war might also be discussed. These details are not facts, because they cannot be proven.

To find details, look answers the questions *Who? What? Where? When? How? Why?*

Read the following paragraph. Then underline the details and note which question each detail answers.

> (1) The issue of the rights of state and federal government has long been a source of argument. (2) In 1830 at a celebration in Washington, DC, President Andrew Jackson and Vice President John C. Calhoun gave contradictory toasts about loyalty to the nation regarding the issue of slavery. (3) Jackson gave the first toast: "Our Union—it must be preserved." (4) Calhoun, a Southerner who believed in states' rights above national unity, followed by saying, "The Union—next to our liberty, most dear." (5) Eventually, Calhoun resigned as vice president and several states seceded from the Union because of this issue.

Sentence 2: *When?* 1830; *Where?* Washington, DC; *Who?* Jackson and Calhoun; *What?* gave contradictory toasts
Sentence 3: *Who?* Jackson; *What?* gave the first toast
Sentence 4: *Who?* Calhoun; *What?* gave the next toast
Sentence 5: *Who?* Calhoun; *What?* resigned from office

THINK ABOUT SOCIAL STUDIES

Directions: Choose the term that best completes each sentence.

1. Conditions such as major wars, complicated international affairs, and serious problems in major cities have led to a stronger (state, federal) government.

2. Nebraska is the only state that has a unicameral, or (one-house, two-house), legislature.

3. The powers that the Constitution does not give to the federal government are given to the (individual, states).

It is important to be able to determine **relevant information**. When something is relevant, it is connected to what you want to know.

For example, read this paragraph about Barack Obama.

Barack Obama is the 44th president of the United States. He was born in Honolulu, Hawaii. Eventually he moved to Chicago, and later he represented the state of Illinois in the US Senate. During his time in office, he worked to bring the United States out of recession. He also focused efforts on changing the health care system. Obama adopted a dog named Bo during his first months in office.

Imagine you are writing an essay about President Obama's goals and achievments during his term as president. In a notebook, identify facts from the paragraph that would be relevent to your essay. Then explain why the other details in the paragraph are not relevent to your topic.

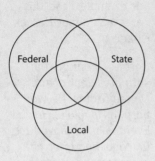

DUTIES AND POWERS OF THE GOVERNOR	
Role	**Responsibilities**
Chief Executive	Sees that state laws are carried out; prepares budget; appoints officials
Chief Legislator	Proposes, approves, or vetoes legislation
Judicial Leader	Grants paroles, pardons, and reprieves
Commander in Chief	Is commander of the National Guard (the state militia)
Party Leader	Heads the political party in the state
Ceremonial Leader	Represents the state; greets key visitors

Some functions of government overlap. Both the national and state governments have the power to tax, for example. Both make and enforce laws and establish courts. However, the Constitution denies some powers to the states. A state cannot coin its own money or enter into a treaty with a foreign country. States cannot tax their exports or imports. State laws cannot **contradict**, or conflict with, the Constitution.

States provide a wide range of public services. They maintain highways and regulate **intrastate** commerce, which is marketing within the state. States also provide for both education and public welfare.

Creating laws that determine the formation and powers of local governments is one of the most important powers of the state. Counties, towns, and cities are the legal units of the states. Many states have strong **home rule laws**. These laws give the local governments a great deal of freedom to set up their own systems of government.

Many states also provide for direct initiative and referendum voting. A **direct initiative** allows citizens to draft proposed laws. If citizens can acquire the required number of signatures on a petition, the state's voters decide whether the law is enacted. A **referendum** allows voters to **repeal**, or overturn, legislation that has already been passed by voting on that law in general elections. Several states also provide for **recall**, a special election that permits citizens to vote an official out of office before the official's term is over.

Local Governments

Local governments include municipalities (cities, towns, villages), counties, and special districts. The governing bodies in towns, villages, and boroughs provide some of the services that cities do but on a smaller scale. Special districts serve schools, public transportation, and housing. Special districts may also maintain parks, bridges, libraries, and airports.

Town meetings were the earliest form of government meetings in the New England settlements of the 1600s. They remain important in regions where towns have the powers usually reserved for counties. At town meetings, voters set aside money to run the town, pass town laws, and determine the salaries of elected officials. Elections at town meetings are **nonpartisan**, or not related to political parties. The candidate's political party is not named on the ballot. Anyone in the town can attend town meetings.

In a similar way, township government is popular in some northeastern and north-central areas of United States. A township is commonly 36 square miles. Generally townships distribute public assistance and maintain roads. In some states, school administration is part of the township's responsibility.

County governments enforce state laws and perform any additional duties the state may assign. In county governments, power is usually vested in an elected board of supervisors or commissioners. County governments collect taxes, maintain roads, and manage county property such as jails, hospitals, parks, and forest preserves. County governments also protect the public health by passing public health ordinances. Counties record documents such as deeds, mortgages, and marriage licenses. Some counties provide water and sewage services, operate airports, and maintain recreational facilities.

Counties are divided into smaller units of local government. These can include cities, towns, villages, and boroughs. Cities provide services that include police and fire protection, schools, public utilities, libraries, street and sidewalk repairs, and garbage collection.

A city is governed under a charter that is granted by the state legislature. There are three forms of city government. The first is strong mayor/weak city council (the mayor has wide authority to run the local government and to veto council actions). The second form is weak mayor/strong city council (the mayor usually has little actual power). The third is city manager/city council (an elected council appoints a city manager and retains the power to make all policy).

Research It
Extend Your Knowledge

Local governments have websites where citizens can learn more about their area and its leaders. Search online to locate your local government's website. Then use that website and other online resources to find answers to the following questions. Write your answers in a notebook.

- What form of government (board of supervisors, city council with strong mayor, etc.) governs your area?

- When does your local government host meetings that are open to local citizens?

- As a citizen, what role might you play in local government?

- How could you officially become a part of local government in your area?

THINK ABOUT SOCIAL STUDIES

Directions: Write a short response to the following questions.

1. What powers are denied to the states? _____
   _____

2. List three examples of local governments. _____
   _____

3. What are the three forms of city government?_____
   _____

Vocabulary Review

Directions: Use these words to complete the sentences below.

contradict   direct initiative   recall   referendum   reserved

1. The group was trying to collect enough signatures to get a _____ on factory farms on the November ballot.

2. After the governor confessed to an affair, a move was made to _____ him.

3. Powers that are not explicitly given to the federal government are _____ for the states.

4. There was a _____ on the new state sales tax law.

5. States are not allowed to pass laws that _____ the Constitution.

Skill Review

Directions: Read the passage below. Then answer the questions that follow.

(1) The move for unicameral legislatures began shortly after the Revolutionary War. (2) The one-house system is similar to the way that most cities and counties are governed. (3) Until 1937, however, all states had two-house legislatures. (4) That year, Nebraska adopted a unicameral system, in part to save money during the Great Depression. (5) In its first year, the new system cut personnel by nearly 70 percent. (6) It passed more bills in fewer days at a lower cost. (7) Although several states have considered a unicameral legislature, Nebraska remains unique.

1. When did Nebraska adopt a unicameral legislature?

     A. in 1937
     B. after becoming a state
     C. during the 1960s
     D. Nebraska has a bicameral legislature.

2. Which statement best summarizes the relevant information in the passage?

     A. Most states have unicameral legislatures.
     B. A unicameral legislature can save money and be more efficient.
     C. States that have a unicameral legislature spend more money.
     D. The Great Depression greatly affected politics in the West.

3. Which sentence answers the question *Where?*

     A. Sentence 1
     B. Sentence 2
     C. Sentence 4
     D. Sentence 6

4. Which sentence contains the relevant information about how many states have bicarmel legislatures?

     A. Sentence 2
     B. Sentence 3
     C. Sentence 6
     D. Sentence 7

Skill Practice

Directions: Choose the <u>one best answer</u> to each question. <u>Questions 1 and 2</u> refer to the chart and information on page 40.

1. Which role gives the governor the power to activate the National Guard in an emergency?

   A. chief legislator
   B. judicial leader
   C. commander in chief
   D. party leader

2. Which statement best summarizes the similarities between the federal government and state governments?

   A. Both have a written constitution, a chief executive, and a court system.
   B. Both have a unicameral legislature.
   C. Both are led by the same political party.
   D. Both make treaties with foreign countries.

3. A state legislator with one year left in her term goes against overwhelming public opinion in her district and votes for a state income tax. Voters who wish to remove the legislator before the next general election could set in motion the process for which action?

   A. petition
   B. referendum
   C. impeachment
   D. recall

4. A group of citizens became angered by a law that the state legislature passed. They circulated a petition to have the law put to a vote by the people of the state. This is an example of what?

   A. direct initiative
   B. recall
   C. referendum
   D. home rule

5. The mayor of a city tries to start a project to build a new sports stadium, and the city council overrules him. Which form of local government does the city probably have?

   A. city manager/city council
   B. strong city council/weak mayor
   C. strong mayor/weak city council
   D. bicameral

6. Why do some states give voters the power to recall officials from office?

   A. Governors want voters to be able to remove officials they don't like.
   B. States are required to give voters this power under the Constitution.
   C. Voters only rarely use their power to recall officials.
   D. It is important for voters to have some control over officials who abuse their power or break the law.

Writing Practice

Directions: Research the local government structure in your city or town. Write two paragraphs describing the structure of your local government and its effectiveness.

Chapter 1 US Government and Civics   **43**

Political Parties and Interest Groups

KEY CONCEPT: Political parties and interest groups play important roles in government at all levels.

When you watch a sports event, generally you are rooting for one of the teams. You have a point of view, and it influences the way you evaluate the referee, the other team, and even the band and the cheerleaders.

Political parties and interest groups also have points of view in favor of ideas and policies or against them. Politicians generally identify themselves with one party. Interest groups can advocate, or promote, one particular issue, or they can support an industry or a specific group of people.

Ideas and Influence in Politics

When representatives take office, many people try to **influence**, or have an effect on, their decisions. Individuals, groups, and organizations try to get support for their interests.

Political Parties The US Constitution did not provide for political parties. However, leaders of the young nation soon found themselves grouping together to gain support for their ideas.

Some nations have a one-party system. Dictatorships, where differing opinions are not allowed, often have one-party systems. Countries such as Cuba, China, and North Korea have one-party systems. Some other countries, such as Germany, have multiple parties. These parties may work together in **coalitions** (teams made up of several parties that join together for a common purpose).

In the United States, however, two major parties have dominated the political system since the 1800s. The Democratic Party officially began in 1848. It is the oldest continuously active political organization in the world. The Republican Party began in the 1850s as a **third party**—that is, a party other than one of the two major parties.

Each party has an animal as its symbol. Thomas Nast, a famous cartoonist of the late 1800s, was first to use the donkey to represent the Democratic Party and the elephant represent the Republican Party. Today the donkey and elephant are well-known symbols.

Political parties select presidential candidates at national conventions. Since the 1850s, there have been 18 Republican presidents and 14 Democratic presidents.

Presidential elections are held every four years. In the summer before the November election, each party meets for a convention. The candidates for president and vice president are officially introduced. Before these meetings, key party members develop a statement of issues that the party supports. This document is called a **platform**. Each individual issue, such as health care reform, is called a **plank**.

SYNTHESIZE IDEAS FROM MULTIPLE SOURCES

When doing research, always read more than one reference source. By using multiple sources, you are more likely read a variety of points of view. Then you can **synthesize**, or combine, information in order to draw conclusions based on your various sources.

To synthesize information, look for ideas that are similar and ideas that are different. Then combine what you have learned to draw a conclusion, or come up with a new idea.

Synthesize the information below to answer this question: Why is the two-party system important in the United States today?

SPEAKER A

I think people are less loyal to the major political parties today, since voters tend to vote for the person rather than the party. This trend worries me. We need stability in our political system more than ever. The two-party system has worked well for us for more than 150 years.

SPEAKER B

You're right about the trend, but I think it's great. The big parties must work to earn the independent vote. This way, they have to find out what people really want.

The two-party system provides a more stable government. It forces both parties to support issues that will attract independent voters.

Bolinger, Bruce/CartoonStock.com

"You can try but it's pretty small in here...the water's going cold and the good soap is gone."

Core Skill
Recognize the Cartoonist's Point of View

People create political cartoons to express their opinions and to persuade others to agree with them. Cartoonists often make use of **irony**. That is, they use words to express the opposite of what the words say literally.

When looking at an political cartoon, pay attention to these features:

• the title or caption

• the characters

• the labels or dialogue

Look at the cartoon below.

• What is the topic?

• What are the characters saying or doing?

• What opinion is the author expressing?

Many people vote for the same political party at each election. Others consider themselves **independents**. They switch parties depending on the issues or candidates. Sometimes they support third parties, such as the Libertarian or Populist parties. Third parties tend to have narrower interests compared to the broader platforms of the two major parties.

Interest Groups An **interest group** is a group that tries to influence political decisions. They may represent the interest of the public (clean water), the economy (the pharmaceutical industry), institutions (colleges), or groups (the American Cancer Society). Interest groups may act on the local, state, and national levels. Some interest groups, such as the World Wildlife Fund, are global in their efforts.

Many groups have **lobbyists**, people who work to influence legislation. When issues of interest to the lobby are scheduled for debate in Congress, lobbyists try to persuade members of Congress to vote in a way that will benefit their group. They may also try to get government funding for their causes or organize protests against measures they do not support.

Following World War II, political action committees (PACs) formed to help raise money for candidates running for office. The first PAC was formed to support union interests. Soon a PAC supporting business interests was formed. Today some PACs, such as the National Organization for Women, support an idea. Other PACs are formed by members of Congress to support their ideas and to help them get re-elected. People connected to these PACs may campaign for their candidate.

THINK ABOUT SOCIAL STUDIES

Directions: Write P for *political party* or I for *interest group* to identify the groups listed below.

_____ **1.** antismoking lobby

_____ **2.** Republicans

_____ **3.** Populists

_____ **4.** Save the Whales

Vocabulary Review

Directions: Use these words to complete the following sentences.

influence   interest group   platform

1. A statement of beliefs is called a(n) _____.

2. Lobbyists try to _____ the decisions of elected officials.

3. Members of a(n) _____ try to influence government.

Directions: Read the passage and study the photograph. Then answer the question.

> Third parties are important because they bring attention to social, economic, or political issues that neither the Democratic Party nor the Republican Party addresses. They provide an addition option for voters dissatisfied with the platforms of the two major parties. Third parties get citizens more interested in political affairs and increase voter turnout.

1. Which statement best sums up the author's view of third parties?

   A. He thinks third parties need to make significant changes.
   B. He favors them because they activate voters.
   C. He thinks they are overshadowed by the major parties.
   D. He supports making them one of the major parties.

Skill Practice

Directions: Choose the one best answer to each question.

> The low voter turnout in this country is due to the relatively small number of voters who control elections. Most close congressional races are decided by fewer than 7,000 votes. Primary elections and state and local races are often decided by much smaller margins.
>
> Senior citizens have protested every hint of cuts in Social Security. Elected officials know this, and Social Security is untouched because a high percentage of senior citizens vote.
>
> On the other hand, surveys show that only 25 to 35 percent of eligible low-income people vote. When so few low-income people vote, their interests are ignored.

1. What does the writer believe is a result of voter turnout patterns?

   A. The elderly do not have much influence.
   B. The poor have too much influence on elections.
   C. Poor people do not have much influence on elections.
   D. Elections are meaningless and a waste of time.

2. If lower-income people voted in larger numbers, what could you conclude?

   A. Social welfare programs would probably be expanded.
   B. Social welfare programs would probably be decreased.
   C. Social Security payments would be decreased.
   D. Social Security payments would be increased.

Writing Practice

Directions: Search for a recent political ad online, in a newspaper, or on television. Find out what group paid for the ad. Then write a paragraph that explains why you think the sponsoring group would have created the ad and how the group would benefit from it.

Civil Liberties and Civil Rights

KEY CONCEPT: Through Constitutional amendments, civil rights in the United States have been extended to more people.

Think about a belief you have that has changed over time. Perhaps you had an experience that changed your point of view. Perhaps you learned something new that influenced how you felt. Events can change people's perspectives on important issues. For example, the civil rights movement changed some people's interpretations of the civil rights and civil liberties that are guaranteed in the Constitution.

Lesson Objectives

You will be able to

• Identify the general provisions of the Bill of Rights

• Explain how civil rights expanded been to include more people

• Understand how African Americans and women gained the right to vote

Skills

• **Core Skill:** Identify Cause-and-Effect Relationships

• **Reading Skill:** Identify Point of View

Vocabulary

civil liberty
civil right
disenfranchise
provision
seize
suffrage

The Expansion of Civil Liberties

Civil liberties are the freedoms that protect individuals from the government. Being able to act and think without interference from the government is a right we often take for granted. The civil liberties we enjoy are guaranteed in the Constitution. In 1789 several states agreed to a new federal Constitution on the condition that a Bill of Rights be added. Two years later, the first ten amendments became part of the highest law of the nation. States often added a Bill of Rights to their own constitutions.

The Bill of Rights exists to protect citizens against abuses by the federal government. The first amendment guarantees four freedoms: freedom of religion, freedom of speech, freedom of the press, and freedom to **assemble**, or gather, peacefully.

The first part of the amendment states that there will be "… no law respecting an establishment of religion." This is known as the establishment **clause**. A clause is a section in a legal document. This clause means that the United States does not have an official religion. The next clause is known as the free exercise clause. It says that the government cannot make laws that keep people from worshiping as they choose.

Freedom of speech refers not only to the spoken word but also to symbolic acts such as burning a flag or wearing a T-shirt with a slogan on it. The writers of the Constitution wanted to assure that people could criticize the government without fear of being imprisoned.

The third clause, freedom of the press, refers to the written word. The newspapers—and also the electronic media—are free to publish criticism of the government and government officials. The press has two major responsibilities: to inform the public and to act as a check against the government and elected officials. The press is free to write what it wants in order to fulfill these tasks.

The last part of this amendment makes sure that people can gather peacefully to discuss political ideas. In addition, people can **petition**, or formally question, when they feel their rights have been violated by political institutions or elected officials.

IDENTIFY POINT OF VIEW

When you read an article, it is important to notice the writer's point of view. Does the writer explain only side of an issue? Does the writer exaggerate details to support a point? Does the writer make statements that cannot be proven?

Read the following paragraph and identify the writer's point of view. What words give you clues?

> (1) This nation must reform the way presidential campaigns are conducted. (2) During the 2012 run for the presidency, both sides ran shamelessly negative campaigns. (3) Candidates and their supporters spread rumors, exaggerations, and even blatant lies about their opponents. (4) Presidential candidate Governor Mitt Romney, for example, falsely accused President Obama of being the only president ever to cut Medicare. (5) At the same time, the Democrats were openly claiming that "Republicans voted to end Medicare." (6) Who can the voters believe? (7) We have to make it illegal for politicians, their campaigners, PACs, and—yes—even the media to mislead US citizens in this way. (8) There is a clear line between free speech and libel, and American political campaigns have crossed that line.

Point of view: The writer is opposed to candidates and their supporters misleading the voters.

Clue words: *must reform, shamelessly negative, even blatant lies, falsely accused, openly claiming, yes—even, clear line . . . crossed that line, libel.*

REAL WORLD
CONNECTION

Apply Your Experience
As Americans, it is easy to take our civil liberties for granted. The world news, however, provides numerous examples of people whose civil liberties are being denied.

Think about the rights you enjoy every day, such as freedom of speech and freedom of the press. How do they affect your daily life? In what way do you rely on them? What might your life be like if these freedoms were taken away?

Identify one freedom that you especially value. Write a short essay examining its importance in your life. Name the freedom in your introduction and conclusion. In the body of your essay, support your main idea with details.

The remaining amendments in the Bill of Rights cover a variety of topics, such as being protected against unreasonable searches and seizures. This means that government officials need a search warrant to enter a home.

In the same way, we cannot be **seized**, or arrested, without a warrant. **Double jeopardy** (being tried twice for the same crime) is illegal. Citizens cannot be subjected to cruel and unusual punishment. Trials are to take place quickly, and they must be public.

Some of these **provisions**, or legal statements, can be interpreted in a variety of ways. What does the right to bear arms mean? What are cruel and unusual punishments? People have gone to court to define these ideas.

The last amendment in the Bill of Rights refers to powers not specifically given to the federal government and not specifically forbidden to the states. The states have these powers.

Writers frequently use a
cause-and-effect pattern
to organize social
studies passages. They
show how one event
causes another event to
happen.

For example, some
states would not
accept the Constitution
unless a Bill of Rights
was added. The effect
was the addition of
ten amendments that
protect the rights of
citizens.

The Bill of Rights is
open to interpretation.
Certain groups have
used portions of the Bill
of Rights to deny rights
to other groups.

CAUSE	EFFECT
States insist on a Bill of Rights in the Constitution.	Bill of Rights, protecting citizens from abuses by government, is added.
The Bill of Rights can be interpreted in various ways.	Some people have been denied their rights.

How do you identify
a cause-and-effect
relationship? Look for
key words and phrases
such as *because, since,
therefore, consequently,*
and *if … then.*

Make a chart listing
causes and effects
related to one freedom
guaranteed by the Bill
of Rights. For example,
you might choose gun
ownership. State the
effects that gun-related
laws have had or may
have in the future.

Gains and Losses in African American Suffrage

When the Framers wrote the Constitution, they had in mind the rights of men like themselves. This was also true of those who wrote the state constitutions. At first, only white men who owned property could vote. Gradually other groups gained **suffrage**, or the right to vote.

In 1865, the Thirteenth Amendment ended slavery, but it did not extend suffrage to African Americans. The Fourteenth Amendment stated that everyone born or **naturalized** (made a citizen) in the United States was a citizen and had all the rights of a citizen. The Fifteenth Amendment stated that the right to vote could not be denied on the basis of "race, color, or previous condition of servitude."

The states that had seceded from the Union at the beginning of the Civil War needed to be reinstated. Conditions of their rejoining included accepting these amendments and rewriting their constitutions to incoporate them. State constitutional conventions took place in 1868.

Despite the new constitutions, efforts were made to **disenfranchise** African American males in the South, that is, to take away their right to vote. The poll tax—a tax on voters—was one attempt. Poor people, both African American and white, often did not have the money to vote. The Twenty-Fourth Amendment (1964) made poll taxes illegal.

Another device used to disenfranchise African Americans was a literacy test. When people came to vote, they were given a section of the Constitution to read and explain. African Americans were given very difficult passages, while whites were given simple passages.

CAUSES AND EFFECTS OF LEGISLATION AFTER THE CIVIL WAR	
Cause	**Effect**
Fourteenth and Fifteenth Amendments were passed.	Formerly enslaved persons were given the right to vote.
Formerly enslaved persons were given the right to vote.	Southern states begin to disfranchise these voters.
Poll taxes and literacy tests were set up.	Poor and uneducated people could not vote.

Women Gain the Right to Vote

In 1848, a group met in Seneca Falls, New York, at the invitation of Elizabeth Cady Stanton, a young mother, and Lucretia Mott, a Quaker. Stanton wrote a Declaration of Sentiments, modeled on the Declaration of Independence. The Seneca Falls convention called for an extension of women's rights, among them the right to vote. This was a radical notion at the time. In many states, women could not own property, divorce their husbands, or have sole custody of their children.

In the last half of the 1800s, some states, generally in the West, gave women limited voting rights. In 1869, Wyoming became the first state to grant this right. In 1916, Jeannette Rankin of Montana became the first woman elected to the House of Representatives. Ten states west of the Mississippi River had granted women full suffrage by 1912.

The movement split into two groups. African American women—who realized that many white women, especially in the South, were opposed to black women voting—formed their own groups.

Then another generation took up the cause. Their demands intensified after World War I, in which women had aided the war effort and worked as nurses.

Women were the first to use the nonviolent tactics that later would be popular in the civil rights movement. In 1917, more than 200 women were arrested for civil disobedience. Some were force fed when they went on hunger strikes in prison. Women picketed the White House and lobbied members of Congress. Thousands marched in parades demanding full voting rights. Some lost their jobs, health, homes, or families.

President Wilson finally supported the suffragists in 1918 and encouraged Congress to pass the amendment that had first been proposed to the Senate in 1878. The Nineteenth Amendment was ratified in 1920. It was the largest single extension of voting rights in the nation's history.

THINK ABOUT SOCIAL STUDIES

Directions: Write a short response to these questions.

1. Why was women's suffrage the largest single extension of voting rights in the nation's history?

2. What geographical region most likely resisted giving women voting rights before ratification of the Nineteenth Amendment? Why do you think that?

Civil Rights for African Americans

African Americans remained largely disenfranchised in many states. They continued to experience discrimination, or unfair treatment, as a result of prejudice. The effects of poll taxes and literacy tests meant that the rights of full citizenship and equality, or **civil rights**, were effectively denied to them. Further Supreme Court rulings and Constitutional amendments were needed before African Americans had full rights.

In 1954, the Supreme Court reversed a decision it had made in 1896. That decision had declared that "separate but equal" facilities, including schools, restrooms, and restaurants, were legal. In the 1954 decision *Brown v. Board of Education of Topeka, Kansas*, the Court recognized that racial segregation in public schools violated the Fourteenth Amendment.

The poll tax was abolished in 1964 with the passage of the Twenty-Fourth Amendment. That same year, the Civil Rights Act made discrimination in employment, education, and voter registration illegal. The Voting Rights Act of 1965 made literacy tests illegal.

The effect of these new laws was dramatic. In 1940, only 5 percent of African Americans in the South were registered to vote. This figure rose to 66 percent in 1969. The voting laws also changed who was elected. In the mid-1960s, about 70 elected officials in the South were African Americans. By the beginning of the twenty-first century, the number had grown to about 5,000. African American members of Congress increased during that same time from 6 to about 40.

Reading Skill
Identify Point of View

Many factors influence a writer's point of view, including the writer's age, gender, family background, political beliefs, and experiences.

To identify the writer's point of view, watch for statements beginning with phrases such as *I feel*, *I believe*, and *I think*. They often provide a direct statement of the writer's point of view.

To practice identifying point of view, write two sentences from the point of view of people in the early 1900s. In the first sentence, state why you oppose women's suffrage. In the second sentence, state why you favor it.

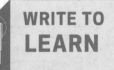

WRITE TO LEARN

In a notebook, make a cause-and-effect chart like the one on page 50. As you read about women's suffrage on this page, fill in your chart.

Civic Responsibilities

As citizens, Americans have not only rights, they also have responsibilties. These include obeying the law, paying taxes, and acting as a juror. Failure to perform these duties can lead to fines or imprisonment. Citizens also have voluntary responsibilities, such as voting.

Vocabulary Review

Directions: Use these words to complete the following sentences.

civil liberty   civil rights   disenfranshised   provision   seized   suffrage

1. The Nineteenth Amendment guaranteed the _____ of women.

2. A _____ is a legal statement.

3. Freedom of the press is a _____ guaranteed in the Bill of Rights.

4. The Fourth Amendment protects Americans from being illegally _____ by the police.

5. Many African Americans were _____, or denied the right to vote.

6. _____ are the rights of all people to equal protection and treatment under the law.

Skill Review

Directions: Read the passage below. Choose the best answer to the question.

(1) The best political system ever developed is the two-party system found in the United States. (2) Since the Civil War, no third party has been able to threaten the political power of either the Democratic Party or the Republican Party. (3) Every president in the last 100 years has been a member of one of these two parties. (4) No third party has been able to gain control of either house of Congress. (5) The country has been spared the chaos that results when there are more than two parties. (6) And Americans have not had to endure the tyranny of one-party rule.

1. Which sentences contain clues about the writer's point of view of the two-party system?
   A. sentences (1), (2), and (3)
   B. sentences (2), (3), and (4)
   C. sentences (3), (4), and (5)
   D. sentences (1), (5), and (6)

Skill Review (continued)

Directions: Study the chart below. Then choose the best answer to the question.

NATIONAL VOTER TURNOUT, SELECT YEARS, 1960–2008	
Year	**Percentage of Registered Voters Participating**
1960	63.1
1972	55.2
1980	52.6
1996	49.1
2000	51.3
2008	56.8

2. What is one effect of the trend shown in the chart?

   A. Fewer qualified people run for office.
   B. Young people vote more consistently than other age groups.
   C. Women choose not to go to the polls.
   D. A president is elected with less than half of registered voters voting.

Skill Practice

Directions: Choose the one best answer to each question.

> After the Civil War, the Radical Republicans were the strongest supporters of civil rights for African Americans. One of their most significant successes was the passage of three constitutional amendments guaranteeing basic civil rights. They also established the Freedmen's Bureau, an agency that helped former enslaved persons. The bureau provided food and clothing and helped African Americans find work. It also set up many schools.

1. Which civil liberties did the Radical Republicans support?

   A. poll taxes
   B. separate but equal facilities
   C. voting rights for former slaves
   D. limited civil rights for African Americans

2. What did the Freedmen's Bureau do?

   A. taught reading and writing
   B. trained new servants
   C. moved former slaves to the North
   D. worked for constitutional amendments

Writing Practice

Directions: Voting rights has been a major issue for many groups of people. Write an essay explaining why the right to vote is important to minority groups.

The US Role in the Global Society

KEY CONCEPT: The world is becoming more interconnected. In this new global society, the United States bears heavy responsibilities but also looks forward to important opportunities.

The Internet allows events from all over the world to be tracked and ideas to be exchanged. Satellites enable news and cell-phone conversations to be broadcast over vast distances. Trade between countries is easier than ever before due to improved storage and transportation methods and new trade agreements. This global exchange of news, goods, ideas, and services has tightened the connections between the United States and other countries. The United States is a leader in this international community.

Opportunities and Challenges in a Global Society

In today's world, people communicate instantly across vast distances. Travel is easier and faster than ever before. This seemingly smaller world is known as the **global society**. It presents many opportunities, perhaps most obviously in the economic **realm**, or area. Businesses can expand across the globe, and individuals can **transact**, or carry out, private business from one country to another via the Internet. Opportunities also abound in education, politics, and government. Today's technology makes it easier than ever before to engage in meaningful **dialogue**, or discussion. Technology also provides a way to reach those who previously had no access to information or education.

Internet technology allows people around the globe to communicate quickly and easily. This has a deep impact on society. For example, social media, especially Facebook and Twitter, played a significant role in the 2011 uprisings referred to as the Arab Spring.

Today's global society also presents important challenges. Because world markets are all interconnected, an economic slowdown in one country affects all countries. Terrorism and the spread of nuclear arms are two serious problems in the world today. Health threats (such as AIDS) and environmental issues (such as climate change) are also global in scope. Censorship and human rights violations in one part of the world threaten freedom everywhere.

The US Role

The United States is a superpower. It has a responsibility to meet the challenges and explore the opportunities of the global society.

The State Department, which is part of the executive branch of the federal government, is responsible for US relations with other countries. The department helps ensure the safety and well-being of US citizens living or traveling in foreign countries. It also has responsibilities for foreign aid and international trade agreements.

MAKE PREDICTIONS

A **prediction** is an attempt to answer the question "What will happen next?" Predicting helps get you involved in what you are reading. When predicting, readers use clues in the text, along with their prior knowledge and experience, to make reasonable guesses (that is, guesses that make sense) about what will occur next.

Here are some key points to keep in mind when predicting:

- Look at the title of the passage.

- Make predictions before you reading. Then continue to make predictions while reading.

- Use prior knowledge. Ask yourself these questions: *Have I read something like this before? Have I experienced something like this myself? What happened next in those cases?*

- **Adjust**, or change, your predictions as you read. Predictions should make sense, but they don't have to be correct.

Read this passage. What do you think the president might do next?

> The US president sat in a closed meeting with the prime minister of Israel. The president had flown to Israel the day before for high-level talks about international security issues. The US secretary of state had accompanied the president and was waiting to join the meeting. As the president and the prime minister talked, an aid knocked on the door and rushed in to report new fighting between Israeli and Arab troops.

One prediction you might have made is that the president would discuss the issue with the secretary of state. This is a logical prediction. The president and the secretary of state are together in Israel. They would work together in facing this crisis.

Research It
Compare Viewpoints

In a global society, it is important to recognize that people in different countries may have different opinions about the same events.

Think about an recent event that you have read about in US news reports. Then go to these websites to read more about the event.

- Spiegel Online (Germany)—http://www.spiegel.de/international/

- Al Jazeera (Qatar)—http://www.aljazeera.com/

In your notebook, write a brief paragraph telling how the viewpoints expressed in the *Spiegel* and *Al Jazeera* reports differ from those in US news reports.

THINK ABOUT **SOCIAL STUDIES**

Directions: Write a short response to these questions.

1. List three areas of opportunity in today's global society.

   _____

2. Name three challenges of today's global society.

   _____

3. What part of the federal government shapes the US role in the global society?

   _____

Photographs can show cause-and-effect relationships in a visual way. At times, however, the photograph shows only the cause or only the effect of a particular event. The caption often describes the missing information. In other cases, the photographer leaves it to viewers to figure out the cause or the effect.

The photograph on this page shows a US Navy crewman delivering food supplies following the horrible destruction caused in 2004 by a massive tsunami that struck Indonesia. In this case, the tsunami was the cause. The relief effort is the effect.

Find a photograph in a newspaper or newsmagazine. Write one sentence identifying the cause and/or the effect that the photograph illustrates.

Foreign Aid **Foreign aid** is the help that one country offers to other countries. This aid can take many forms, including money, food, arms, and skilled personnel. US foreign aid promotes US interests abroad in the areas of both foreign policy and economics. It also helps people around the world and promotes democracy.

The major federal agency involved in managing US aid programs is known as the United States Agency for International Development (USAID). Aid programs are operating in Sub-Saharan Africa, Asia, Latin America and the Caribbean, Europe and Eurasia, and the Middle East. The agency offers aid in such areas as agriculture, government, environment, and education.

Trade Agreements **Trade agreements** are legal agreements or contracts relating to trade between two countries. US trade agreements are generally seen as beneficial to the US economy, although some people believe that US jobs can be lost as a result of these contracts.

In March 2013, the United States had free trade agreements (FTA) with 20 countries. The largest of these agreements was created in 1994, when the North American Free Trade Agreement (NAFTA) became effective. NAFTA permits trade with virtually no taxes or other restrictions between Canada, Mexico, and the United States. In 2012, the United States and other Pacific nations, including Australia, Chile, Malaysia, and Canada, began negotiations on a new FTA, the Trans-Pacific Partnership (TPP).

The World Trade Organization (WTO) is an international organization of 154 countries that provides a place for countries to negotiate trade-related issues, settle trade-related problems between nations, and keep trade flowing freely. The United States is a member of this group.

The Spread of US Culture

An interesting effect of the global society has been the spread of US culture to other countries. Blue jeans, McDonald's, Coca-Cola, American movie stars and musicians—these common features of daily life in the United States can be found across the globe. More and more, English is used for teaching at universities as diverse as Spain and South Korea. US universities are also setting up campuses around the world.

US Businesses Expand Globally

Just as US culture has spread across the world, so have US businesses. China, in particular, has seen the rise of many US businesses, whose workforces and profits have grown dramatically in recent years. Manufacturers such as Caterpillar find that the building boom in China has increased the need for Caterpillar products. Companies such as Starbucks, McDonald's, General Motors, and Motorola have found huge Chinese markets as well. Even small unknown companies have found that opening a Chinese branch is worthwhile.

There are two main reasons that US companies are interested in China. First, China's membership in the World Trade Organization has contributed to a growth in foreign investment. Second, improved financial opportunities in China have led to the growth of a Chinese middle class that can afford to buy foreign products.

While US business in China has exploded in recent years, US companies earn their highest profits in Japan. One US company, Aflac, has made as much as 70 percent of its profits in Japan. Other US businesses that have thrived are Coca-Cola, Apple, and McDonald's. Many other corporations operate around the globe. Walmart, for example, has retail stores in 27 countries outside the United States.

Fair Trade

The **fair trade** movement has arisen in recent years. Fair trade is trade that meets certain standards: workers are paid a living wage, and their working conditions are safe. Leaders of this movement insist that workers are not helped enough by free trade agreements. This is especially true in developing countries, where farm workers, for example, earn extremely low wages. The fair trade movement seeks to obtain a better price for goods so that workers can be paid better wages.

To accomplish its goals, the fair trade movement has devised a labeling system. Products—such as coffee, bananas, and handicrafts—that bear the fair-trade label have met health, safety, labor, and human rights standards.

US Nonprofit and Humanitarian Organizations

Beyond the government agencies that work to aid developing countries and countries that have suffered from natural disasters and war, the United States also has many private groups that seek to help in the same way. These groups are called **nonprofit organizations**, or nonprofits. **Nonprofit** means "not for the purposes of making money." Nonprofit organizations pour all money they earn into realizing the goals of their organization.

CARE is one well-known US-based humanitarian group. It seeks to eliminate poverty and to better the circumstances of women around the world. Doctors without Borders is a humanitarian organization created in France, but it has a branch in the United States. It sends volunteer doctors to help the victims of natural disasters, war, and famine. There are thousands of other US organizations that work to improve the lives of fellow humans around the world.

Reading Skill
Make Predictions

Before making a prediction, gather as many facts as possible. Knowing key facts can make your predictions more accurate.

Suppose a drought hit the United States and US crops suffered, causing a food shortage.

Review what you have learned in this lesson. In a notebook, write a paragraph predicting who would come to the aid of the United States and why. Give reasons for your predictions.

WRITE TO LEARN

A newspaper article often explains a particular event and then describes ways that event affected various people, policies, or other events. This is an example of cause-and-effect writing.

Write a short newspaper article that explains the possible effects of a UN-sponsored program that allows a remote African village to acquire the necessary technology to connect to the Internet.

Vocabulary Review

Directions: Use these words to complete the following sentences.

dialogue   **fair trade**   **foreign aid**   **global society**   **nonprofit organization**   **transact**

1. Because the price of coffee changes from month to month, a _____ agreement is needed to ensure that coffee-bean harvesters receive a decent wage.

2. After a _____ pays its expenses, it uses its funds to advance the goals of its organization.

3. _____ encourages the peaceful settlement of disputes or disagreements.

4. Most US _____ is channeled through the USAID.

5. Because of the _____, a recession in the United States threatens economies around the world.

6. The Internet helps people and companies _____ business around the globe quickly and easily.

Skill Review

Directions: Study the cartoon below. Then write a paragraph identifying the subject of the cartoon, the artist's message, and the cause and effect that the cartoon addresses.

1.

"I have to break into houses to fund my addiction to organic and fair trade produce."

_____

_____

_____

_____

Skill Review (continued)

Directions: Read the passage below. Then, in a notebook, write a paragraph in which you make a prediction about US business profits in China in the years 2009 and beyond. Explain how the information in the passage led you to make this prediction.

2. BEIJING – The American Chamber of Commerce in China (AmCham-China) announced results of its 2009 Business Climate Survey Tuesday. . . . About 74 percent of the respondents, most of which are American companies in China, reported a profitable 2008, almost consistent with the situation in 2007, according to the survey of more than 400 member companies of the Chamber.

Skill Practice

Directions: Choose the one best answer to each question.

1. Which factor has played the greatest role in creating a global society?

   A. communication technologies
   B. medical technologies
   C. international alliances
   D. global treaties

2. Why has the fair trade movement grown in recent years?

   A. It improves the quality of the food supply.
   B. It offers a variety of goods to all people.
   C. The global society has increased awareness of how goods are made.
   D. It ends US dependence on overseas goods.

3. Which statement about the global expansion of US businesses can be supported by the information in the lesson?

   A. They have not benefited from overseas growth.
   B. They are exploiting workers in other countries.
   C. They are against free trade agreements.
   D. They grow and prosper when they open overseas branches.

4. Which issue would require the involvement of the World Trade Organization?

   A. California strawberry growers want the US government to set minimum prices for strawberries.
   B. The United States claims that Mexico is shipping uninspected beef to the United States.
   C. A developing country wishes to expel the Red Cross.
   D. Texas wants to stop produce being shipped into the state from Colorado.

Writing Practice

Directions: What effects do you think the expansion of US business and culture will have on people in China? In a notebook, write one paragraph stating your predictions and explaining why you believe they will occur.

Contemporary Public Policy

Lesson Objectives

You will be able to

- Define contemporary public policy

- Identify examples of public policy

- Describe how public policy is made

Skills

- **Reading Skill:** Draw Conclusions

- **Core Skill:** Evaluate Reasoning

Vocabulary

accountable
bias
contemporary
domestic
implement
issues
log
public policy

KEY CONCEPT: Public policy refers to the actions taken by government to address public issues.

Do you think the speed limit on a certain road should be changed? Do you wish that you paid less taxes? Do you think the government should do more to help people? Most people have opinions on these issues. If you do, then you have opinions about contemporary public policy.

Contemporary Public Policy

To understand contemporary public policy, you need to understand the three words *contemporary public policy*.

First, a **policy** is a plan or a course of action. You probably have several policies yourself. You may have a policy of eating a healthy breakfast every morning or a policy of never missing your favorite team's game. These are personal policies. There are also plans for action addressing issues that affect the public.

Second, **public** means "affecting all the people." For example, a public park is open to everyone. **Public policy** refers to actions that affect everybody. Who has the power to affect everybody? Neither individuals nor businesses have this power, but the government does. Therefore, public policy refers to the laws and actions of the government.

Third, **contemporary** means "current" or "existing now." Contemporary public policy is the policy of today—not policies of the past or the future.

Contemporary public policy really means "current government actions." Read on to investigate the impact that contemporary public policy has on your life.

Types of Public Policy

There is not just one contemporary public policy in the United States today. There are actually hundreds, or even thousands, of public policies. This is because the government is very large and it addresses many **issues**, or concerns. We can organize contemporary public policies according to types of policies.

One way to organize public policy is by the level of government—local, state, or national—that is making the policies. Local public policies are made by local governments, such as cities or counties. For example, city governments have policies describing the health codes that must be maintained in restaurants within the city. State governments have polices too. Most states have policies related to income taxes and sales taxes. Policies made by the national, or federal, government affect everyone in the United States. For example, federal policy allows citizens who are 18 years of age and older to vote in elections.

A second way of organizing public policy is by topic, such as health policies, environmental policies, and economic policies. A local government that chooses to **implement**, or put into practice, restaurant inspections is implementing a health policy. A state government fining a company for polluting would be implementing an environmental policy. The federal government deciding to lower income taxes would be implementing an economic policy.

Public policies also include agricultural policies, drug policies, and energy policies. There are recycling policies and hiring policies. There are land-use policies and transportation policies. The list goes on and on.

All the policies that deal with people in the United States are domestic policies of the US government. In this context, **domestic** means "within the country." Because the federal government deals with other countries, it also has foreign policy.

THINK ABOUT SOCIAL STUDIES

Directions: Consider each public policy described below. Use the labels in the box to identify the type of public policy. You will use two labels for each public policy.

local	business
state	economic
national	foreign
	public safety

1. _____ The US government requires that individuals pay income taxes.

2. _____ Texas requires cars and trucks to pass safety inspections.

3. _____ The city of Springfield makes it illegal to operate businesses out of homes.

4. _____ The United States sends soldiers to Afghanistan.

5. _____ The US Congress extends the length of time people can receive unemployment benefits.

REAL WORLD CONNECTION

How Public Policy Affects You

One way to determine how public policy affects you is to keep a public policy diary, or log. A **log** is a record of events.

In a notebook, make a chart like this one.

Label the columns "Public Policy," "Type of Policy," and "Effect on Me."

Spend one week noting any time public policy affects you. For example, if you ride a city bus, fill in your log this way:

Public Policy
    provide city buses

Type of Policy
    local transportation

Effect on Me
    can ride bus to work

After your week of entries, write one paragraph explaining how your life is affected by public policy.

Then, with other students in your class, make a list of all the public policies named by your class. This will help you see how much your lives are affected by public policy.

When you draw a conclusion, you use more than one piece of information to figure out a new idea.

Use the Internet to learn about the ideas that one of your elected officials has regarding a public policy issue. In a search engine, write the name of a senator or representative, and then write a phrase describing the policy. For example, you may write "Maria Mendez health care."

In a notebook, write one conclusion you can draw about this official's views. Give evidence for your conclusion.

Who Makes Contemporary Public Policy?

In the United States, the government is **accountable**, or responsible, to the people. Elected officials make public policy, but the people choose these officials. Your choice of who to vote for has a direct effect on public policy. Millions of people have the right to vote. Each voter helps shape public policy. Every vote counts.

Within the United States, public policies are the work of all three branches of government (legislative, executive, and judicial). All three levels of government (national, state, and local) make public policies.

Take, for example, one of the greatest changes of public policy in US history: the changes brought by the civil rights movement. The legislative branch (Congress) passed laws such as the Civil Rights Act of 1964. The executive branch (headed by the president) enforced these laws and passed regulations requiring desegregation. The judicial branch (the Supreme Court), in the case of *Brown v. Board of Education*, declared schools segregated by race to be unconstitutional.

All these governmental decisions were influenced by the men, women, and children who marched and protested for civil rights. These people helped shaped public policy.

Public policy issues affect all parts of our lives. Examples include taxes (economic issues), recycling (environmental issues), funding (scientific research), workplace safety (health issues), and public transportation access for disabled people (transportation issues). How can individual citizens in the United States help shape public policy?

Besides voting, you can help shape public policy in many other ways. You can write letters to the editors of newspapers or post comments online to try to convince others of your position. You can join a political party that seeks to implement public policies you agree with. You can join activist groups to work toward certain public policies.

THINK ABOUT SOCIAL STUDIES

Directions: Think of a public policy that affects your life. Research online to learn whether the issue is a local, state, or federal policy. Then consider what you have learned about democratic values. Write one paragraph explaining how these values are upheld by the policy or are at risk because of the policy.

Evaluating Public Policy

In the United States, public policies are often hotly debated. You will find Americans speaking out on both sides of almost any public policy issue. Should the government implement national public policies to reduce gun ownership? Many Americans passionately argue yes: gun control will save lives. Other Americans fervently argue no: gun ownership is a right.

What about a national public policy that increases the minimum wage? Many argue that the minimum wage should be increased: people cannot live on such small incomes. But some business groups argue against an increase: companies have limited funds to spend on labor.

Name a public policy issue in the area of health, economy, education, or environment, and you will quickly find there are two or more sides to the issue. All types of public policies are subject to debate.

How do you draw a conclusion about what position to take on a public policy issue? A simple three-step process can help.

1. Make a two-column table to list the arguments used by each side. The table will help you compare the arguments.

2. Examine the evidence each side uses. Just saying something does not make it true; evidence must be used to support a position.

3. Distinguish facts from opinions. A fact can be proven. Everyone agrees on facts. They can be checked in research books. An opinion, on the other hand, is a personal viewpoint. It is based on **bias**, or personal preferences. Opinions cannot be proven. Public policy should be based on facts, not feelings.

THINK ABOUT SOCIAL STUDIES

Directions: Answer this question: Why is it important to separate facts from opinions when evaluating a public policy?

_____

_____

Vocabulary Review

Directions: Match the words and their definitions.

1. _____ accountable   A. concern
2. _____ bias   B. personal feeling
3. _____ contemporary   C. within a country
4. _____ domestic   D. responsible
5. _____ implement   E. diary
6. _____ issue   F. put into effect
7. _____ log   G. current

Directions: Read the following positions on a public policy issue. Then answer the questions.

Anne's Position

There is nothing more important than our children. Children should have a safe place to play in this community. Now they play in the street, and that's dangerous. It's only a matter of time before one of them gets hurt. I saw online that our local city council has a budget surplus this year of almost one million dollars. The city has an extra one million dollars to spend. That's a lot of money! They should use that money to build a park so our children will be safe.

Hector's Position

I agree that our children are important. But that surplus money doesn't belong to the government. It belongs to us! After all, we paid the taxes, and that's where the city got the money. Maybe our taxes should be refunded. We could all use more money! Besides, if a park was built, what then? The park would have to be maintained, and security guards might have to be hired. Where would that money come from? We would have to pay even more taxes in the future.

---

1. What public policy issue are Anne and Hector debating?

   _____

2. What facts does Anne use?

   _____

   _____

3. What facts does Hector use?

   _____

   _____

4. Which statements of Anne's are opinions?

   _____

   _____

5. Which statements of Hector's are opinions?

   _____

   _____

6. Which position do you agree with? Why?

   _____

   _____

Skill Practice

Directions: Choose the <u>one best answer</u> to each question.

1. Which is an example of public policy?

   A a. speed limit
   B. a sale at a store
   C. a young woman's decision to join the army
   D. a young man's decision to quit a job

2. The United States declares war on another country. What type of policy is this?

   A. local public policy
   B. state public policy
   C. domestic policy
   D. foreign policy

3. Which branch of the federal government influences public policies in the United States?

   A. the legislative branch
   B. the executive branch
   C. the judicial branch
   D. all of the above

4. A friend reads a news story online about a proposed city law that would allow people to bring their dogs to restaurants that have patios. He leaves a comment stating that he is opposed to the law. What is he doing?

   A. making public policy
   B. ignoring public policy
   C. attempting to influence public policy
   D. making his own policy

Writing Practice

Directions: What public policy issue do you feel passionately about? Write a journal entry in which you identify the issue, tell why you feel so strongly about it, and name at least one thing you could do to get support for your position. Be sure to use facts to support your position.

Directions: Choose the <u>one best answer</u> to each question.

<u>Question 1</u> refers to this graph.

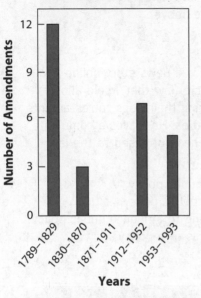

AMENDMENTS TO THE CONSTITUTION

1. Why were so many amendments passed from 1789–1829?

   A. Amendments were added to protect the United States from invasion.

   B. The Framers wanted future generations to add amendments.

   C. Before the Constitution was passed, people insisted that a Bill of Rights was necessary.

   D. The Constitution was incomplete when it was signed, so basic amendments needed to be added.

2. The Magna Carta was a document that guaranteed the basic rights of the British. What was the most important result of the signing of the Magna Carta?

   A. The king's power was limited.

   B. The first political elections were held.

   C. The monarch began to pass the throne to a son or daughter.

   D. The barons developed Parliament so they would have a representative government.

3. Which action can citizens take if they disagree with a law passed by the legislature of their state?

   A. Citizens can request a recall of the law.

   B. Citizens can vote on a referendum to repeal the law.

   C. Citizens can draft a direct initiative, or proposed law, to contradict the current law.

   D. Citizens have no formal means of challenging the law.

4. Why does the United States provide funds and resources to help developing countries?

   A. The United States is a powerful and wealthy country.

   B. UN rules require the United States to help developing countries.

   C. Providing aid helps promote democracy and US interests abroad.

   D. The United States can control the politics and culture of other countries by providing aid.

Questions 5 and 6 refer to these passages.

> We hold these truths to be self-evident, that all men are created equal, that they are endowed by their Creator with certain unalienable Rights, that among these are Life, Liberty and the pursuit of Happiness.—That to secure these rights, Governments are instituted among Men, deriving their just powers from the consent of the governed,—That whenever any Form of Government becomes destructive of these ends, it is the Right of the People to alter or to abolish it, and to institute new Government, laying its foundation on such principles and organizing its powers in such form, as to them shall seem most likely to effect their Safety and Happiness.
>
> —excerpted from the Declaration of Independence (1776)

> We hold these truths to be self-evident; that all men and women are created equal; that they are endowed by their Creator with certain inalienable rights; that among these are life, liberty, and the pursuit of happiness; that to secure these rights governments are instituted, deriving their just powers from the consent of the governed. Whenever any form of Government becomes destructive of these ends, it is the right of those who suffer from it to refuse allegiance to it, and to insist upon the institution of a new government, laying its foundation on such principles, and organizing its powers in such form as to them shall seem most likely to effect their safety and happiness.
>
> —excerpted from the Declaration of Sentiments (1848)

5. How is the Declaration of Sentiments similar to the Declaration of Independence?

   A. Both proclaim the rights and freedom of individuals.
   B. Both are about the importance of a government by and for the people.
   C. Both deal with the relationship between the United States and Great Britain.
   D. Both deal mostly with the right to vote.

6. Why does the Declaration of Sentiments closely copy the language of the Declaration of Independence?

   A. The writers hoped to declare independence from the United States.
   B. The writers used the standard format for declarations.
   C. The writers wanted to show the similarities between the colonists' and the women's struggles for rights.
   D. The writers wanted to draw on previous successful writing.

7. Why did the writers of the Constitution create two houses of Congress?

    A. They wanted Congress to be like Britain's Parliament.

    B. They wanted to distribute power fairly between large and small states.

    C. They wanted to protect from one branch of government having too little power.

    D. They wanted to make sure that Congress reflected the will of the majority of the people.

8. Why is judicial review the most important power of the Supreme Court?

    A. It allows the Supreme Court to determine whether laws and executive actions are constitutional.

    B. It allows the judicial branch to have more responsibility than any other branch of the federal government.

    C. It allows amendments to the Constitution.

    D. It allows for the Supreme Court to pass decisions about the constitutionality of state laws.

9. Which of the following influenced the people writing the US Constitution?

    A. Bill of Rights

    B. Declaration of Independence

    C. General Washington's letters

    D. Virginia Declaration of Rights

10. Which of these statements is true of public policy?

    A. Public policy is set primarily by the president.

    B. Activism has little effect on people making public policy.

    C. Citizens can best influence public policy by refusing to vote.

    D. Elected officials at all levels of government make public policy.

11. Many parties and special interest groups participate in the process of electing the US president. Why is their participation beneficial?

    A. to make sure that citizens are well informed when voting for the president of the United States

    B. to make sure that presidential candidates know all they need to know about the government and the responsibilities of the president

    C. to make sure that the select few who decide on the presidency have all the information they need to make their decision

    D. to show that the election of the president is a serious and important matter

12. In which type of government does the leader of the country have absolute power?

    A. monarchy

    B. dictatorship

    C. constitutional democracy

    D. parliamentary democracy

Review

Check Your Understanding

On the following chart, circle the number of any question you answered incorrectly. Under each lesson title, you will see the pages you can review to study the content covered in the question. Pay particular attention to reviewing those lessons in which you missed half or more of the questions.

Chapter 1 Review

Lesson	Item Number	Review Pages
Types of Modern and Historical Governments	2, 9, 12	18–25
The US Constitution	1, 7	26–31
The Executive, Legislative, and Judicial Branches of Government	8	32–37
State and Local Government	3	38–43
Political Parties and Interest Groups	11	44–47
Civil Liberties and Civil Rights	5, 6	48–53
The US Role in Global Society	4	54–59
Contemporary Public Policy	10	60–65

ESSAY WRITING PRACTICE

US Government and Civics

Directions: Write an informative or explanatory essay in response to one of the prompts below. Review Lessons 1.2, 1.4, and 1.6 for topic ideas.

INFORMATIVE ESSAY

The Constitution outlines the responsibilities of the government, tells how the government is organized, and describes the rights of US citizens. The Constitution can be amended, or changed. The first ten amendments are known as the Bill of Rights.

You are on a team that is preparing a presentation on the Constitution. Your assignment is to write about the First Amendment or the Sixth Amendment. Read these amendments online at www.archives.gov.

Write an essay describing the purpose of one of these amendments. Begin with a sentence that summarizes the amendment. Then discuss the amendment.

- If you are writing about the First Amendment, explain why freedom of speech is important today. Tell why it may be difficult to protect our freedom of speech.

- If you are writing about the Sixth Amendment, tell whether you think Americans today receive speedy public trials by an impartial jury. Explain your answer.

EXPLANATORY ESSAY

In his inauguration speech, President John F. Kennedy said, "Ask not what your country can do for you; ask what you can do for your country."

What does it mean to take your rights and your responsibilities seriously as a citizen? Following is a list of actions that can be done by concerned citizens. Choose three actions (from this list or from your own list) and explain how each action can benefit your community or the country. Organize your essay by starting with the action that you think is most important. Be sure your essay makes connections between the actions.

- Vote.

- Follow your elected officials. Keep track of how they vote and what they think about topics you consider important.

- Contact your elected officials. Let them know how you want them to vote on issues that are important to you.

- Attend a public hearing about a proposed change in the community.

- Serve on a jury.

Review

ESSAY WRITING PRACTICE

US History: Revolutionary War through the Depression

History is the study of people, places, and events in the past. Certain people, events, places, and decisions probably stand out when you think of your own past. These are all important parts of who you are today. Similarly, the United States has been shaped by people, events, and decisions throughout its history.

In this chapter, you will learn what shaped the United States from its earliest days through the Great Depression. As you read, think about events today that are similar to events of the past. How does the past help us make decisions in the present?

In this chapter you will study these topics:

Lesson 2.1: Early Democratic Traditions
Two documents written long ago in England—the Magna Carta (1215) and the English Bill of Rights (1689)—protected the people from the abuse of the king. These documents and others, such as the Mayflower Compact, provided models for the Declaration of Independence and the Articles of Confederation.

Lesson 2.2: Revolution and a New Nation
Increased taxation without representation in government led colonists to rebel against English rule. Once the colonists won their independence, they developed a new form of government. As the country grew, settlers moved west. This expansion led to conflict in territories that belonged to other nations.

Lesson 2.3: The Civil War and Reconstruction
Tension between slave states and free states led seven states to break away from the Union and form the Confederate States of America. The Civil War was fought to keep the United States whole. Eventually the war resulted in the end of slavery. After the war, the Reconstruction effort tried to rebuild what had been destroyed.

Lesson 2.4: The Progressive Era, World War I, and the Depression
Progressive politics challenged the influence of large monopolies in the late 1800s and early 1900s. The United States became a major world power after it joined the Allies in World War I and helped them to victory. The Great Depression in the 1930s began with the stock market crash of 1929. Many workers lost their jobs. As a result, people lost their homes, farms, and other property.

Goal Setting

Why is it important to study US history?

- to find out what important events helped shape the country

- to understand the causes and the effects of conflict and war

- to understand the values and principles the country was founded on

Think about the reasons people study US history.

- to pass a citizenship test

- to find out what challenges people faced in settling the United States

- to understand the reasons people came to the United States

- to learn the reasons certain heroes and holidays are celebrated in the United States

What do you hope to learn from the lessons in this chapter? List some of your ideas here. As you read this chapter, think about these goals.

_____

_____

_____

_____

_____

Early Democratic Traditions

Lesson Objectives

You will be able to

- Identify the documents that shaped US democratic traditions

- Explain the idea of social contract

- Summarize the provisions of the Articles of Confederation

Skills

- **Core Skill:** Analyze Events and Ideas

- **Reading Skill:** Summarize Ideas

Vocabulary

assembly
charter
declaration
legislature
peer
representative government
summarize

KEY CONCEPT: The government of the United States is built on a foundation of English laws and government.

You may have heard the expression "Let's not re-invent the wheel." The idea behind this saying is that we should not waste time duplicating what others have done. The wheel was invented long ago; today the question is how can we improve the wheel. For example, tires continue to be made with stronger materials and safer designs.

In the same way, when people form the government of a new nation, they often look to previous examples to see what has worked well.

Influential Documents

A series of historical documents from England and the British colonies provided ideas that shaped the government of the United States.

The English Bill of Rights

After the Magna Carta was signed in 1215, the king met regularly with the nobles. This group eventually included representatives of the common people. By the late 1300s the group became a lawmaking body, or **legislature**. It became known as Parliament. This style of governing was an early form of **representative government**—government in which people elect others to rule for them.

During the 1600s, many political struggles took place between the king, Parliament, and the people. Parliament passed the Bill of Rights in 1689. It **stipulated**, or demanded, that the rulers rule by the consent of the governed, who were represented by Parliament. It also stated that people have the right to a fair trial by a jury of their **peers**, or equals, and that people should not suffer cruel or unusual punishments.

The Mayflower Compact

The Church of England was a state church. This meant that anyone who did not belong to the church went to jail. The Pilgrims separated from the church and left England. They sailed on the *Mayflower* and arrived at what is now Plymouth, Massachusetts, in December 1620.

During the voyage, all was not peaceful among the passengers. Realizing that they needed to work together to form a system of government, they created a document known as the Mayflower **Compact**. This agreement was signed by the 41 adult males on the *Mayflower*. In the compact, they promised to follow laws and rules.

SUMMARIZE IDEAS

Writing a summary will help you to understand and remember the text you have read. When you **summarize**, you use your own words to restate the most important information. Summaries are useful when you want to review material or study for a test.

To summarize information, look for the main idea. Identify the details that support it. Look for places where the author has repeated or emphasized important ideas. A graphic organizer, such as a web or a chart, can help you organize the information.

Read the following paragraph. In a notebook, take notes as you read. Then summarize the information in the paragraph. Write one sentence that contains the most important ideas.

> (1) King John signed the Magna Carta (Great Charter) in 1215, granting rights to the people of England. (2) His barons forced the king to sign the document. (3) The rights granted can be divided into nine categories. (4) Some of the ideas and phrases in the US Constitution were taken from the Magna Carta.

Magna Carta

- signed in 1215
- gave rights to the people of England
- nine categories of rights granted
- US Constitution borrowed ideas

The Magna Carta, which was signed in 1215, granted rights to the people of England and influenced the US Constitution.

Core Skill
Analyze Events and Ideas

The genius of the Founders was their ability to take ideas they knew about and apply these ideas in a new situation. The laws and government structure of England formed a basis for how the colonies would function. Eventually they were the basis of the government in the new nation.

Today documents are written in schools, workplaces, housing developments, and other organizations to help people live and work together.

In a notebook, name one such agreement you know about. Explain how its rules encourage members to cooperate.

The Fundamental Orders of Connecticut

Later some English settlers went to nearby Connecticut. In 1639, representatives chosen from three towns in that colony met. They created a civil charter, the Fundamental Orders of Connecticut. A **charter** is a written code of rules or laws.

WRITE TO LEARN

As you read about the Mayflower Compact on page 74, identify the main idea of the section. Then write a summary of the section in your notebook.

1. Which right was guaranteed by the English Bill of Rights?

   A. the right to free speech
   B. the right to a fair trial by a jury of their peers
   C. the right to bear arms
   D. the right of freedom of religion

2. What makes the Fundamental Orders of Connecticut unique?

   A. It allowed only members of the church to vote.
   B. It applied to all the towns in the Connecticut colony.
   C. It is the only document that men consulted when writing the US Constitution.
   D. It makes no mention of a king or any other government.

One interesting feature of the Fundamental Orders of Connecticut is that the document does not mention the king of England or any existing government. Another feature is that, unlike the rules in other colonies, it extended voting rights to community members who owned land even if they were not members of the church. The Fundamental Orders of Connecticut seems to be the first constitution written to create a government. A century and a half later, those who wrote the US Constitution had a model to use.

Reading Skill
Summarize Ideas

When you summarize a passage, you restate only the most important ideas. Begin by finding the main idea, that is, the most important point in the passage. The main idea of a paragraph may be stated directly or it may be implied. Then determine which details support the main idea.

As you read the first paragraph under "Articles of Confederation," ask yourself, *What is the most important point?*

Then summarize the paragraph in your own words.

Declaration of Independence

In 1776, after the American Revolution had begun, a group of men met in Philadelphia to consider the question of independence. They began working on the document that became the Declaration of Independence. In less than a month, the document was presented to the entire **assembly**, or group. Thomas Jefferson of Virginia wrote most of the document. The **declaration**, or statement, begins by stating its purpose and defining basic rights. Next it states the charges against George III, king of England. The document ends with the declaration of freedom.

Jefferson stated that the Declaration of Independence contained no new political ideas. It borrowed the idea of a **social contract**, the idea that government is a contract between the governing authority and the people. The role of government is to protect the people's liberty, property, and lives. In return, the people give up some freedom and agree to follow the government's decisions. On July 2, 1776, twelve of the thirteen colonies voted to approve the document. Two days later, it was officially adopted.

Articles of Confederation

Following the end of the American Revolution, the new country needed a government. The first constitution, the Articles of Confederation, guided the country from 1781 to 1789. The men who wrote the Articles did not want a strong central authority. They were afraid of repeating the harshness they had endured under Great Britain. There was no president. The Articles also created a **unicameral** legislature. This means that the legislature had only one chamber, unlike Parliament, which had two chambers. The legislature had the power to control war and foreign affairs, borrow money, and control the postal service. In reality, it could not force the states to pay taxes or to send troops.

The states were not united. Every state made its own rules and printed its own money. Most states had their own navies. States taxed goods from other states, making commerce between the states difficult. People's loyalty was to their state, not to the country.

Vocabulary Review

Directions: Use these words to complete the following sentences.

assembly   charter   declaration   legislature   peers   representative government

The colonists gathered in a(n) _____ to discuss how they were going to form a government. The first order of business was making a _____ in which the freedom of the colonists was announced. The Founders wanted a _____, a document stating the laws of the new country. Most colonists wanted a _____ because they believed that the people should elect a group to rule for everyone. The group that was elected would become a _____, or lawmaking body. It was important to the colonists that people have fair trials by a jury of their _____.

Skill Review

Directions: Read the passage below. Then on a separate sheet of paper, write a brief summary of how the Founders applied ideas from the Iroquois League in a new context.

> The Iroquois League of Nations, which formed before AD 1500, linked five tribes under a single government. The Iroquois League functioned with a Grand Council of male chiefs who represented the five clans. These leaders met to discuss common issues and to reach agreements. John Rutledge of South Carolina had encountered this tradition when he was attending a congress in New York. Years later he suggested that some of its provisions become part of the government structure of the new nation.

Skill Practice

Directions: Choose the one best answer to each question.

1. Which document first guaranteed the basic rights of British people?
   A. Articles of Confederation
   B. Declaration of Independence
   C. Magna Carta
   D. Mayflower Compact

2. The Declaration of Independence contained no new political ideas. What advantage might this have given it?
   A. It would not anger the king.
   B. It contained ideas the people knew about.
   C. It would restore peace with England.
   D. It made the document confusing.

Writing Practice

Directions: The English Bill of Rights, Mayflower Compact, Declaration of Independence, and Articles of Confederation all had some ideas in common. Write a paragraph summarizing some of the main points these documents had in common. In the conclusion of your paragraph, describe how these documents became part of the government of the new nation.

Revolution and a New Nation

Lesson Objectives

You will be able to

- Understand the causes and effects of the American Revolution

- Understand how and why the Constitution was developed

- Recognize how the new nation grew geographically and economically

Skills

- **Core Skill:** Identify Cause-and-Effect Relationships

- **Reading Skill:** Understand Cause and Effect

Vocabulary

annex
cause
Constitution
effect
expansion
federal
independence
revolution
sectional

KEY CONCEPT: After defeating the British, the new United States established a democratic government. As the nation grew, conflict between regions increased.

Think about a disagreement that you have had with a friend or family member. How did you resolve the disagreement? Was the other person satisfied with the resolution?

Compromise is important in resolving disagreements. A compromise is reached when both sides find a solution that is agreeable to them. To reach a fair compromise, both sides must be flexible. When creating the new federal government, the founders compromised on several issues.

The American Revolution

In 1763, England passed several laws that resulted in new taxes for the American colonists. Among the laws were the Sugar Act, the Stamp Act, and the Tea Act. These laws angered colonists. They had no political representation in England, where the laws were passed. The colonists protested these laws by dumping tea into Boston Harbor on December 16, 1773. This event is known as the Boston Tea Party.

The English responded with the Intolerable Acts. Boston Harbor was closed until the colonists paid for the destroyed tea. In addition, colonists were forced to pay for housing English soldiers.

In response, the colonists called for a meeting of the First Continental Congress. The delegates met in 1774 to draw up a document that stated their loyalty to the king of England but also outlined their rights. They formed a plan to **boycott**, or refuse to buy, British goods.

In April 1775, British troops and American colonists fought in Massachusetts at Lexington and Concord. The battles marked the beginning of the American Revolution. A **revolution** is the overthrow of a government or ruler and replacement with another government.

The Second Continental Congress met later in 1775. It voted to establish an army, and it named George Washington as commander in chief. In July 1776, the Second Continental Congress adopted the Declaration of Independence. The Declaration established the principle that government must be based on the **consent**, or agreement, of the governed.

The colonists waged a five-year war with England. It ended in 1781 with the surrender of the British at Yorktown, Virginia. The Americans had won their **independence**; they were no longer under the control of the British government.

The American Revolution marked the first time that a European power had lost a colony to an independent movement. This influenced the successful slave revolution against the French in Haiti (1795–1803) and later struggles against Spanish rule in Latin America in the early nineteenth century.

UNDERSTAND CAUSE AND EFFECT

Writers frequently use **cause** and **effect** to show how one event causes another event to happen. For example, the introduction of a new technology can lead to greater productivity for some companies. This would be a positive effect. On the other hand, the new technology might allow machines to do much of the work that people had done in the past. This could mean that many workers will lose their jobs. This would be a negative effect.

CAUSES	EFFECTS
development of new technology	$\longrightarrow$ more productivity
machines replace people	$\longrightarrow$ increased unemployment

Identify cause-and-effect relationships by looking for key words and phrases such as *because, since, therefore, as a result, consequently, the reason was, if . . . then, led to, the outcome was, the result was, brought about, was responsible for,* and *accordingly.*

Identify the cause and the effect in this passage. Circle the phrase that signals the cause-and-effect relationship.

> The British government passed many new laws taxing the colonists. As a result, colonists boycotted British goods to avoid paying these new taxes.

Cause: The British government passed new tax laws.

Effect: Colonists boycotted British goods.

The phrase signaling the cause-and-effect relationship is *as a result.*

Research It
Identify Reliable Sources

When conducting online research, it is important to find reliable sources of information. Usually that means using websites created by educational, government, and professional institutions.

Use reliable online sources to find out more about the quest for independence in another country in the Americas or elsewhere. Identify where this revolution took place, who led it, who the revolutionists were fighting, and why the people wanted the revolution.

Take notes as you do research. Then share your findings with a partner.

You can use a two-
column chart to identify
cause-and-effect
relationships. The chart
makes it easier to
visualize how one event
is connected to another.
It can also show how
some effects may, in
turn, become causes.

Look at the example of
the two-column chart.

Causes	Effects
Articles of Confederation created a weak federal government	Interstate commerce was difficult to conduct.
Interstate commerce was difficult to conduct.	The nation was in an economic depression.

In a notebook, create a
two-column chart like
the one above. Use the
chart to identify the
causes and the effects
that resulted from the
new Constitution.

Creating the Constitution

The years after the Revolutionary War (1783–1789) were troubled times. The nation was in a serious economic depression. The Articles of Confederation were adopted in 1781. They established a weak national government with no executive branch or court system. The government had no power to tax or to regulate commerce between the states. Interstate commerce was difficult because each state could issue its own **currency** (the bills and coins used in trade) and often charged its own taxes on goods.

Meetings held in some states in 1785 and 1786 led to a call for a Constitutional Convention. The convention opened in Philadelphia in May 1787.

One of the main issues was the division of power between the central government and the states. The final **Constitution**, the document that defined the basic laws and principles of government for the United States, represented a compromise between centralized power and states' rights. The government in Washington increased its powers. It gained the right to tax, create an army and navy, control foreign trade, make treaties, and control currency. The states, however, still maintained important responsibilities. The kind of arrangement that divides power between a central government and the states is called a **federal** system.

Another compromise was reached over the issue of whether enslaved people should be counted in population totals. If they were, Southern states would have greater representation in the House of Representatives. Southern delegates argued that slaves should be counted. Northern delegates said that if enslaved people were counted for representation, they should be counted for taxation.

The Three-Fifths Compromise agreed that only three-fifths of all enslaved people would be counted in population totals. This gave slave states more power in the House of Representatives. The Constitution also protected the slave trade for at least 20 years.

The Louisiana Purchase

The new nation had gained from England most of the land east of the Mississippi River. In 1800, Spain gave France most of the Louisiana Territory. This gave France control over the Mississippi River. In 1803, President Thomas Jefferson bought the huge Louisiana Territory for $15 million. The purchase doubled the size of the United States. It also put the Mississippi River firmly under US control.

The War of 1812

The War of 1812 was fought over English interference with US merchant ships. The war ended with no clear winner. However, the War of 1812 was important for the United States for two reasons. First, it united Americans by temporarily making national interests more important than **sectional**, or local, interests. Second, it proved that the United States had a strong military. With new land open in the West and the removal of the English threat, there was opportunity to expand US territory.

THINK ABOUT SOCIAL STUDIES

Directions: Write a short response to each question.

1. What system of government did the Constitution establish?

   _____

2. Identify two effects of the War of 1812.

   _____

   _____

Westward Expansion

Expansion means "increase" or "enlargement." From 1800 to 1850, Americans believed that it was their destiny, or fate, to occupy the land from the Atlantic Ocean to the Pacific Ocean. This belief, and the policies that developed from it, came to be called **Manifest Destiny**. The United States soon obtained Florida from Spain and Texas from Mexico.

The Mexican government gave grants of land in its province of Texas to American settlers during the 1820s. Later these settlers revolted against Mexico. They declared Texas an independent republic in 1836. The brief but fierce war was famous for the battle of the Alamo in San Antonio.

In 1845, the United States **annexed**, or added on, Texas as a state. This angered many Mexicans. When US troops occupied a border region claimed by Mexico, the Mexican War began. The United States won the war. It took control of an area that now makes up the states of California, Nevada, Utah, Arizona, New Mexico, Texas, and parts of Oklahoma, Kansas, Colorado, and Wyoming. The United States also acquired the Oregon Territory from England.

THE UNITED STATES EXPANDS, 1783–1853

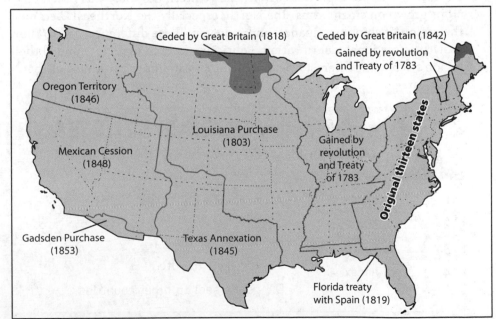

Key words and phrases
can help you identify
cause-and-effect
relationships.

As you read the
section on Economic
Development, circle the
key words and phrases
that help you identify
cause-and-effect
relationships.

WRITE TO LEARN

Think about two countries
that are currently at war
or have fought with each
other in the past. In a
notebook, write one
paragraph explaining what
caused the war. Write a
second paragraph
describing how the war
has affected the people,
lands, and culture of
those two countries.

Economic Development

Economic growth was rapid during the early 1800s. This period is called
the Industrial Revolution. The building of canals and the development
of the steamboat created a big increase in transportation by water.
That, in turn, resulted in an increase in trade. After the 1820s, building
railroads became a major economic activity. By 1860, the United States
was crisscrossed with about 30,000 miles of railroad tracks.

The cotton industry brought in more money than all other **exports**
(goods sent to another country) combined. This cotton boom began with
Eli Whitney's invention of the cotton gin in the 1790s. The cotton gin
could clean the large amounts of cotton that were needed for
manufacturing. The Industrial Revolution led to the establishment of
large mechanized mills in England and New England where cotton was
processed. The demand for Southern cotton grew. In this way, cotton
helped firmly establish slave labor as the basis for the South's economy.

Issues about democratic rights became important during Andrew
Jackson's presidency (1829–1837). Previously most states had required
people to be property owners in order to vote. Now this requirement was
dropped. All white male citizens over the age of 21 could vote. However,
Native Americans, women, and African Americans still could not vote.

More Americans wanted to **abolish**, or get rid of, slavery. These people
helped create an antislavery movement in the North and West. This
resulted in popular support for the Union position in the Civil War.

Women continued to have few rights, but they were active in early
antislavery societies. The experience of fighting for the rights of
enslaved persons helped women fight for their own rights. Women's
suffrage, or the right of women to vote, because a major cause. In
1848, Elizabeth Cady Stanton and Lucretia Mott founded the first
national women's organization at Seneca Falls, New York. Its goal
was equal rights for women.

The growth of the United States and the development of regional
economies created political problems. The Southern economy was based
on slavery and the export of cotton. The Western economy was based on
crops grown on small farms. The North, especially the Northeast, became
the region of shipping, finance, and industry. These differences led to the
growth of sectional identification. Politicians in each region defended their
region's economic interests. Sectionalism was an important cause of the
Civil War.

THINK ABOUT SOCIAL STUDIES

Directions: Match these words with their definitions.

1. _____ exports
2. _____ suffrage
3. _____ sectionalism
4. _____ annex

A. economic and political differences
among the regions of the United States

B. to add territory

C. the right to vote

D. goods sent to other countries

Vocabulary Review

Directions: Use these words to complete the following sentences.

annexed Constitution expansion federal independence Revolution sectional

1. The American _____ gave the colonists _____ from Britain.

2. The _____ established the division of power between the federal government and the states. It created a _____ system.

3. The belief in Manifest Destiny was a cause of westward _____.

4. The state of Texas was _____ by the United States in 1845.

5. Strong _____ differences existed throughout the United States.

Skill Review

Directions: Identify the cause and the effect in the passage below.

1. An unfortunate result of national growth was increasing conflict with Native Americans. The federal government's policy was to move Native Americans west of the Mississippi River. Cherokees and Creeks were forcibly moved from the Carolinas, Georgia, and Alabama to the Oklahoma Territory in the late 1830s.

   Cause: _____

   Effect: _____

Directions: Look at the chart below. Fill in the missing causes or effects.

CAUSES AND EFFECTS OF THE AMERICAN REVOLUTION

Causes	Effects
	Colonists protest the tax laws and boycott English goods.
British troops and American militia fight battles at Lexington and Concord.	
	An army is established; George Washington is named commander in chief.
In 1776 the Declaration of Independence is adopted.	
	The United States becomes an independent nation.

Directions: Choose the <u>one best answer</u> to each question. <u>Questions 1 and 2</u> refer to the map below.

SECTIONALISM AND THE VOTE IN CONGRESS ON TEXAS ANNEXATION, 1845
(vote on passage of joint resolution)

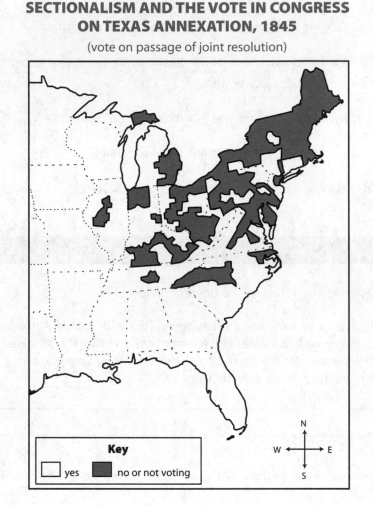

Key

☐ yes   ■ no or not voting

N   W ← → E   S

1. According to the map, in which region did most states vote no on the question of annexing Texas?

   A. South
   B. West
   C. Northeast
   D. Southeast

2. Which conclusion about the voting pattern does the map support?

   A. The Northern states were opposed to adding another Southern state in the Union.
   B. The Northern states supported Mexico's right to Texas.
   C. The Southern states preferred that Texas stay independent.
   D. The Northern states feared Texas's industrial competition.

Skill Practice (continued)

Directions: Answer the following questions. <u>Questions 3 and 4</u> refer to this excerpt from the Declaration of Independence.

"We hold these truths to be self-evident, that all men are created equal, that they are endowed by their Creator with certain unalienable Rights, that among these are Life, Liberty, and the pursuit of Happiness. That to secure these rights, Governments are instituted among Men, deriving their just powers from the consent of the governed, That whenever any Form of Government becomes destructive of these ends, it is the Right of the People to alter or abolish it, and to institute a new government, laying its foundation on such principles and organizing its powers in such form, as to them shall seem most likely to effect their Safety and Happiness."

3. Which words best describe what the founders meant by "unalienable rights"?

    A. rights that came into being when the colonies were established
    B. rights given by a monarch
    C. rights that cannot be taken away
    D. rights that exist with the president's consent

4. Why do you think the founders included the right of the people to alter or abolish the government?

    A. They wanted to be sure that the government represented the will of the people.
    B. They wanted to restore a monarchy.
    C. They wanted to be sure they would have control over the people.
    D. They wanted to give more power to the military.

5. What was the purpose of the Boston Tea Party?

    A. to entertain British soldiers
    B. to celebrate the Stamp Act
    C. to protest unfair British laws in the colonies
    D. to increase the amount of tea the colonies exported to Britain

6. What effect did the American Revolution have on other colonies and countries?

    A. Most other countries took on democratic forms of government.
    B. Some areas of Latin America rebelled against Spain's control.
    C. The English founded several new settlements in colonial America.
    D. Taxes increased in other colonies.

Writing Practice

Directions: Look at the chart you completed on page 83. Use your chart to write a short essay explaining several causes and effects of the American Revolution. Use signal words that indicate cause-and-effect relationships.

The Civil War and Reconstruction

KEY CONCEPT: The Civil War began as an attempt to preserve the Union, but it ended with the abolision of slavery in the United States.

Have you ever felt that you have been discriminated against or treated unfairly? Despite many laws that have been passed since the nation was founded, many minority groups continue to fight for equal rights and to protest unfair treatment. The Civil War ended slavery, but it did not end discrimination or sectional differences.

Lesson Objectives

You will be able to

- Identify the events and issues that led to the Civil War

- Understand the advantages and disadvantages of the North and the South during the Civil War

- Recognize how Reconstruction affected the South and the lives of newly freed African Americans

Skills

- **Reading Skill:** Recognize Persuasive Language

- **Core Skill:** Analyze Point of View

Vocabulary

abolitionist
context
point of view
poll tax
Reconstruction
secede
surrender
territory

The Problem of Slavery

Sectionalism continued to deepen the divide in the country. The economy in the North was based on industry—manufacturing, free labor, and many kinds of farming. The economy in the South was based on single-crop plantations that relied on slave labor.

The argument over slavery was at the heart of sectionalism. The divide grew sharper as the new western **territories**, land controlled by the US government, were settled. **Abolitionist**, or antislavery, forces wanted slavery banned in new territories. Proslavery forces wanted the future states to decide for themselves whether to allow slavery in their states.

Whether the western territories joined the union as free states or slave states could tip the political balance in the US Congress. Before the new states were admitted to the Union, there were 11 slave states and 11 free states. Peace was kept only through a series of compromises.

The Missouri Compromise of 1820 admitted Missouri as a slave state and Maine as a free state. In addition, it prohibited slavery in the northern part of the territory acquired in the Louisiana Purchase.

In 1849, California asked to be admitted to the Union as a free state. Again Congress was divided along sectional lines. The Compromise of 1850 attempted to give both sides something of what they wanted.

The Compromise of 1850	
Northern Compromises Won	**Southern Compromises Won**
• California admitted as a free state • slave trade outlawed in the District of Columbia	• no restrictions on slavery in the territories of Utah and New Mexico • passage of the Fugitive Slave Act, a law that helped slave owners recover runaway slaves

Although the Compromise of 1850 settled the issues in Congress, many people in the North were angry over the Fugitive Slave Act.

RECOGNIZE PERSUASIVE LANGUAGE

Writers use persuasive language to try to influence a reader's opinion on an issue or reaction to an event. The words that a writer chooses may reflect his or her feelings or beliefs about a certain topic.

Persuasive language can be used in both fiction and nonfiction. The author tries to convince the reader to agree with the **point of view**, or opinion, presented in the text. You will become aware of persuasive language if you look for strong words that show the author's bias.

Read the passage below. The author has strong feelings about one of the men she describes. Look for the persuasive words used by the author. List these words in a notebook.

> Late in the afternoon of a chilly day in February, two gentlemen were sitting alone over their wine, in a well-furnished dining parlor, in the town of P----, in Kentucky. There were no servants present, and the gentlemen, with chairs closely approaching, seemed to be discussing some subject with great **earnestness** [seriousness].
>
> For convenience sake, we have said, **hitherto** [up to this point], two gentlemen. One of the parties, however, when critically examined, did not seem, strictly speaking, to come under the species. He was a short, thick-set man, with coarse, **commonplace** [ordinary] features, and that swaggering air of **pretension** [ambition] which marks a low man who is trying to elbow his way upward in the world.
>
> —Excerpted from *Uncle Tom's Cabin*, by Harriet Beecher Stowe

Words such as "coarse," "commonplace," "pretension," and "low" convey a sense that the writer does not like the man and wants the reader to dislike him as well. This feeling is emphasized by the writer's descriptions of the man as a social climber ("trying to elbow his way upward in the world").

Research It
Locate Sources

If you want to learn more about the events described in this lesson, many sources are available. Examples:

- **Nonfiction**
  Mary Chesnut's Diary
  Team of Rivals by
    Doris Kearns Goodwin
  Memoirs by
    Ulysses S. Grant
  Battle Cry of Freedom
    by James McPherson

- **Fiction**
  Hospital Sketches by
    Louisa May Alcott
  March by Geraldine
    Brooks
  Shiloh by Shelby Foote
  North and South by
    John Jakes
  Gone with the Wind by
    Margaret Mitchell

- **Movies**
  Cold Mountain (2003)
  Gettysburg (1993)
  Shenandoah (1965)

- **Television**
  Andersonville (1996)
  The Civil War (1990)

Select one event mentioned in this lesson. Use a search engine to find a book, a movie, and a TV show about this event. Record the list in your notebook.

Frederick Douglass
was a former enslaved
person who became a
leading spokesperson
for abolition and equal
rights for African
Americans. Following is
part of a speech he gave
in April 1865.

*"I have had but one
idea for the last three
years to present to
the American people,
and the phraseology
in which I clothe it
is the old abolition
phraseology. I am for the
'immediate, unconditional,
and universal'
enfranchisement [right
to vote] of the black
man, in every State in
the Union. Without this,
his liberty is a mockery;
without this, you might
as well almost retain the
old name of slavery for
his condition; for in fact,
if he is not the slave of
the individual master, he
is the slave of society,
and holds his liberty as a
privilege, not as a right.
He is at the mercy of the
mob, and has no means
of protecting himself."*

In a notebook, write one
sentence that states
Douglass's opinion. Then
identify key words and
phrases that he uses
to emphasize his point.
Explain why you think
Douglass is (or is not)
successful in persuading
his audience.

Further events contributed to the growth of antislavery feelings:

- In 1852, Harriet Beecher Stowe published her best-selling novel *Uncle Tom's Cabin*. The book showed the harshness of slave life.

- In 1854, Senator Stephen Douglas introduced a bill to create the Kansas and Nebraska territories. In order for his bill to pass, Southern senators insisted that the Missouri Compromise be overturned and slavery be allowed in the new territories. The Kansas-Nebraska Act undid the compromise. It allowed slavery in the territories if the people who settled there voted for it.

- In the *Dred Scott* case of 1857, the Supreme Court ruled that enslaved people were not citizens. They were the property of their masters. The Court said that the Constitution protected slave owners' property rights, so Congress could make no law prohibiting slavery.

- In 1859, John Brown, a militant abolitionist, attacked the federal arsenal at Harpers Ferry (now part of West Virginia). An **arsenal** is a place where weapons are stored. Brown wanted to arm enslaved persons for rebellion. He failed and was hanged.

Founding of the Republican Party

The Kansas-Nebraska Act angered many members of both the Whig and the Democratic political parties. In 1854, antislavery members joined together to form the Republican Party. This new party was opposed to the spread of slavery. In 1860, its presidential candidate, Abraham Lincoln, won the presidential election.

THINK ABOUT **SOCIAL STUDIES**

Directions: Read the sentences below. Then number the sentences 1 to 5 to put the events in sequence.

_____ The *Dred Scott* case protects the rights of property owners.

_____ Harriet Beecher Stowe's novel *Uncle Tom's Cabin* helps build strong feelings against slavery.

_____ The Missouri Compromise limits slavery to land south of Missouri.

_____ John Brown is hanged after attacking the federal arsenal at Harpers Ferry.

_____ Republican Abraham Lincoln is elected president.

The Civil War

The South believed that the balance of power had been permanently tipped against it by the 1850s. Northern political and economic strength grew when California, Oregon, and Minnesota joined the Union. Southern leaders feared that a Republican president meant that slavery would be abolished. In late 1860 and early 1861, seven states voted to **secede**, or withdraw, from the Union. They formed the Confederate States of America.

President Lincoln, however, was unwilling to allow the Union to break up. In 1861, the Civil War began between the North and the South. Each side had certain advantages.

The Civil War	
Northern Advantages	**Southern Advantages**
• greater population • industrial resources, such as factories and shops to produce weapons and other supplies • more railroads to get supplies to troops • control of the national treasury	• strong military tradition and excellent military leaders • most of the fighting happened on Southern land • farmers could produce plenty of food

The Civil War began as an attempt by President Lincoln to save the Union. However, in 1863, Lincoln issued the **Emancipation Proclamation**, which freed the slaves living in Confederate states. Many former enslaved persons joined the Union Army as it moved through the South. This helped strengthen the Union Army.

The Battle of Gettysburg

In 1862 and 1863, Southern troops marched steadily north. They defeated the Union in battles at Fredericksburg and Chancellorsville, Virginia. On July 1, 1863, Union and Confederate forces clashed in Gettysburg, Pennsylvania. Over four days, the battle raged on. There were heavy **casualties** (deaths and injuries) on both sides. Finally Southern troops retreated to Virginia. The battle was a turning point in the war.

In November 1863, President Lincoln went to the field where the battle had taken place. Part of it was being dedicated as a military cemetery. There he gave one of his most famous speeches, the Gettysburg Address. Here are portions of his speech:

> "Four score and seven years ago our fathers brought forth on this continent a new nation, conceived in Liberty, and dedicated to the proposition that all men are created equal. . . .

> ". . . we here highly resolve that these dead shall not have died in vain—that this nation, under God, shall have a new birth of freedom—and that government of the people, by the people, for the people, shall not perish from the earth."

After four long years, the North's superiority wore down the Confederate states. General Robert E. Lee's army was defeated. It **surrendered**, or gave up the fight, in the spring of 1865.

President Lincoln was re-elected in 1864. However, he was shot and killed on April 14, 1865, by John Wilkes Booth. The nation was shocked and saddened.

Core Skill
Analyze Point of View

Point of view is the way a person looks at events or issues. For example, soneone living in the South in 1860 had one point of view about slavery, while someone living in the North might have had a different point of view. A person's experience, family, and location all affect point of view.

When reading letters, speeches, and newspaper articles, it is helpful to understand the point of view of the author. The reader must recognize the historical **context**, or situation, in which the writing was done.

As you read, ask yourself these questions:

• What was happening at this time in history?

• What is author's point of view?

• What is the purpose of the account—to persuade or simply to provide facts?

• What does the account tell you about the author?

Read the excerpt from the Gettysburg Address on this page. In a notebook, answer the questions above.

When public figures
give speeches, they are
often trying to persuade
their listeners in some
way. Listen to one of
these speeches: Martin
Luther King's "I Have
a Dream" speech
(http://archive.org/
details/MLKDream)
or Richard Nixon's
"Checkers" speech
(http://archive.org/
details/Richard
NixoncheckersSpeech).

In a notebook, answer
these questions about
the speech you listened
to. *What is the goal
of the speaker? What
persuasive words does
he use? Why do you
think this speech is
remembered today?*

WRITE TO LEARN

Pick an issue in your
community that is
important to you. Write
a paragraph about that
issue. Use persuasive
language to convince
readers of your point
of view.

THINK ABOUT SOCIAL STUDIES

Directions: Write a short response to these questions.

1. Why do you think the North's advantages were more beneficial than the South's advantages?

_____

_____

2. How did the Emancipation Proclamation affect the war?

_____

_____

Reconstruction

The time of rebuilding following the Civil War is known as the **Reconstruction** era. Abraham Lincoln's successor, President Andrew Johnson, proposed plans similar to Lincoln's to try to reunite the divided nation. His plan included these features:

- Confederate officers and politicians would be **pardoned**, or forgiven, if they took an oath of loyalty to the Union. High-level officers and officials had to ask the president for a pardon.

- Southern states had to pass new constitutions. These constitutions had to repeal secession. They also had to ratify, or approve, the Thirteenth Amendment, which abolished slavery.

- States had to refuse to pay Confederate war debts.

Once these conditions were met, the states could hold elections. Many Confederate officials returned to Southern legislatures in 1865. The legislatures passed what were called the **Black Codes**. These laws severely restricted the rights of former enslaved persons.

Radical Republicans in Congress were enraged by the actions of Southern state legislatures. They wanted protection for the rights of those people who were now free and other social changes. The Radicals were in favor of a tough policy toward the South and former Confederate officials. Their conflicts with President Johnson became so heated that they brought impeachment proceedings against him. However, the Senate did not convict Johnson of wrongdoing.

The Radicals sponsored important constitutional **amendments**, changes or additions to the Constitution. The Thirteenth Amendment (1865) abolished slavery. The Fourteenth Amendment (1868) made African Americans citizens with equal rights under the law. The Fifteenth Amendment (1870) granted African American men the right to vote.

The Radicals' Reconstruction plan temporarily forced many former Confederate officials out of office. For the first time, African Americans were elected to statewide offices and to the US Senate. In the South, the Freedmen's Bureau set up the first schools for African Americans.

Reconstruction ended in 1877 as part of a compromise between conservative Republicans and Southern Democrats. After the disputed presidential election of 1876, an agreement gave the presidency to Republican Rutherford B. Hayes. In exchange, Hayes agreed to pull US troops out of the South.

Reconstruction made few economic and social changes in the South. Large plantations still remained. The freed men had little land and no economic opportunities. Many issues of justice and equality would not be settled for another hundred years.

After Reconstruction ended, a new system of segregation destroyed any remaining hopes for racial equality. **Poll taxes**, fees paid before voting, and literacy tests denied both African American men and poor white men their right to vote. These abuses continued until the civil rights protests of the 1960s led to federal laws outlawing such practices.

THINK ABOUT SOCIAL STUDIES

Directions: Match the terms with their definitions.

_____ 1. Black Codes

_____ 2. Thirteenth Amendment

_____ 3. Fourteenth Amendment

_____ 4. Fifteenth Amendment

A. made African Americans citizens who had equal rights under the law

B. gave African American men the right to vote

C. laws passed by Southern legislators to restrict the rights of former enslaved persons

D. abolished slavery

Vocabulary Review

Directions: Use these words to complete the following sentences.

abolitionist   poll taxes   Reconstruction   secede   surrendered   territories

1. The Civil War ended when the Confederate Army _____ in the spring of 1865.

2. South Carolina was the first state to _____ after Lincoln was elected president.

3. A(n) _____ is someone who tried to bring slavery to an end.

4. The Missouri Compromise and the Compromise of 1850 tried to settle the question of slavery in new _____.

5. _____ were used to keep African Americans from voting.

6. _____ did not create permanent social changes in the South.

Directions: Underline the words or phrases that are examples of persuasive language. Then identify the point of view of the author.

1. This passage is from a newspaper editorial published after the *Dred Scott* decision.

> The three hundred and forty-seven thousand five hundred and twenty-five Slaveholders in the Republic, accomplished day before yesterday a great success—as shallow men estimate success. They converted the Supreme Court of Law and Equity of the United States of America into a propagandist of human Slavery. . . .
>
> . . . The conspiracy is nearly completed. The Legislation of the Republic is in the hands of this handful of Slaveholders. The United States Senate assures it to them. The power of the Government is theirs.

2. The following passage is from a newspaper editorial published after John Brown's failed raid on the arsenal at Harpers Ferry.

> In its immediate results this affair is a ridiculous, miserable failure. It could be nothing else. That Brown with his handful of deluded followers expected to arouse a general servile **insurrection** [uprising], overthrow existing governments, emancipate the entire body of Southern slaves, and build up a government of his own, only exhibits the pitiable plight into which the mad fanaticism of Abolition hurls its **votaries** [followers]. The culprits will attain the martyrdom which they seem to covet, and thus will end this contemptible disgraceful farce.

Skill Practice

Directions: Choose the one best answer to each question that follows. Questions 1 and 2 refer to this chart.

ECONOMIC RESOURCES IN 1860

Resources	North	South
population	71%	29%
railroad mileage	72%	28%
iron and steel	93%	7%
farm output	65%	35%

Skill Practice (continued)

1. Which resource gave the North the greatest advantage compared to the South?

   A. population
   B. railroad mileage
   C. iron and steel
   D. farm output

2. According to the chart, which conclusion can you draw?

   A. The South had a superior railroad system.
   B. Regional economic development before the Civil War was equal.
   C. The South had great agricultural wealth.
   D. The North had economic advantages over the South.

3. Which statement describes the main reason the South seceded from the Union?

   A. It underestimated Lincoln.
   B. It believed it could win the conflict.
   C. It feared a majority of free states would vote to abolish slavery.
   D. It wanted to stop abolitionists from provoking slave rebellions.

4. What effect did President Lincoln's Emancipation Proclamation have on the war?

   A. It turned the war to save the Union into a war to end slavery.
   B. It had no effect on the North's war effort.
   C. Former enslaved persons joined the Confederacy.
   D. It greatly helped the Confederacy.

5. In the years leading up to the Civil War, why was the abolition of slavery more acceptable to the North than the South?

   A. People in the North did not own slaves.
   B. The Northern economy depended on Southern cotton.
   C. There were more African Americans in the North than in the South.
   D. Northerners supported the Fugitive Slave Act.

6. What was an effect of the Black Codes passed during Reconstruction?

   A. Slavery was extended.
   B. The rights of African Americans were restricted.
   C. African American men gained the right to vote.
   D. Civil rights for African Americans were guaranteed.

Writing Practice

Directions: Write a letter home from the perspective of a soldier during the Civil War. You may be a member of the Union Army or the Confederate Army. Describe your feelings about why you are fighting in the war.

The Progressive Era, World War I, and the Depression

Lesson Objectives

You will be able to

- Understand the economic and social issues of the Progressive Era

- Evaluate the impact of World War I on the United States

- Identify the results of FDR's New Deal

Skills

- **Core Skill:** Interpret Political Cartoons

- **Reading Skill:** Interpret Graphics

Vocabulary

identify
irony
muckrakers
progressive
reforms
social

KEY CONCEPT: Industrialization, a world war, and a bust-and-boom economy led to major social and economic changes in the first half of the twentieth century.

In the first decade of the twenty-first century, major advances in technology changed the work place. The United States was involved in foreign wars, and a real estate boom fueled social and economic changes. In the first four decades of the twentieth century, the nation dealt with similar issues.

The Progressive Era 1900–1917

In the last quarter of the nineteenth century, the United States transformed from a rural farming society into an urban industrial society. By 1900 the United States had replaced Great Britain as the leading industrial producer in the world. However, many Americans were concerned about worsening social conditions brought about by industrialization and urbanization. Labor strife continued. Abuses of child labor were widespread. Living and working conditions deteriorated in the cities.

At the same time, the wealth that was generated by the new industrial economy became more concentrated in a small number of families. This concentration of economic power helped cause a serious depression in 1907. Political institutions that had been suitable for a nation of farmers and small-business people could not deal with the problems of a large-scale industrial society. The developing economic, social, and political crises led to a time known as the **Progressive** Era. *Progressive* refers to a time of moving forward. This period lasted roughly from 1900 to 1917, when the United States entered World War I.

Industrialization had created a large new class of industrial workers. It also created a large urban middle class and a very small class of wealthy industrialists and financiers. Each of these groups had its own ideas about how the country should make **reforms**, or changes, to improve society and remove abuses. Many in the middle class felt that large corporations were destroying America's free-enterprise system. This system relied on free and open competition among companies.

Radical journalists, called **muckrakers**, exposed corruption in business and politics and influenced many people. For example, in his books and articles, Lincoln Steffens exposed the corruption, poverty, and boss-run political systems in the large cities.

The growing strength of radicals and the influence of the middle class forced the Democratic and Republican parties to take reform seriously. At first, reforms were carried out at state and local levels. Local reforms included sanitation laws, building codes, and child welfare laws. But local financial resources were limited. Reformers wanted the federal government to help solve the most serious problems.

INTERPRET GRAPHICS

Sometimes a passage contains a lot of **statistics**, or information given in numbers. When this happens, it might be difficult for readers to understand. That's why writers use tables, graphs, and charts. These **illustrations**, or images, make it easier to see relationships between the numbers.

When looking at a table, graph, or chart, pay attention to the title, caption, and labels. These will tell you what information is contained in the graphic. Also, look at the key, if any. This will say what the colors indicate.

Use the bar graph below to answer these questions:

1. How were most allied and neutral ships lost?

2. When were attacks on allied and neutral ships worst?

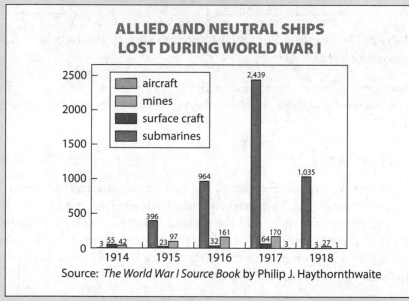

ALLIED AND NEUTRAL SHIPS LOST DURING WORLD WAR I

Key:
- aircraft
- mines
- surface craft
- submarines

Source: *The World War I Source Book* by Philip J. Haythornthwaite

For every year but 1914, the green bar is much higher than any of the others. The key shows that the green bar indicates ships lost to submarines. Thus, the answer to question 1 is "by submarine attack."

In the year 1917, all the bars are highest for all groups, so the answer to question 2 is "1917."

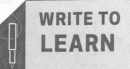

WRITE TO LEARN

Social workers and muckrakers faced the social problems of the Progressive Era head-on. They achieved considerable success in changing society.

What problems could a muckraker write about in today's society? Select a problem and write an editorial on what you think should be done to solve the problem.

Reading a cartoon is much like reading other texts. Note the title or caption. **Identify** characters; that is, figure out who is represented. Try to understand the artist's viewpoint so you can interpret the message.

Find a political cartoon in a current newspaper. Ask yourself the following questions:

- What does the title tell you?
- What do the words in the drawing explain?
- What is the artist's point of view toward the subject?

Research It
Locate Reliable Sources

During the Progressive Era, both men and women worked to point out the difficult living and working conditions of the poor and to make improvements in daily life.

Use a search engine to find information about one of the following Progressive reformers. Take notes as you read about the person.

Jane Addams
John Dewey
Florence Kelley
Upton Sinclair
Frances Willard

Then write one paragraph that introduces the reformer and tells what the person did to change the world.

Society was deeply divided over what to do. Some people supported an idea called **Social Darwinism**. Its main belief is that society is based on the survival of the fittest. To them, wealth was a symbol of survival. Nature intended for some people to succeed and others to fail. Social Darwinists did not want government to take part in social reforms.

Others believed that reforms were necessary to keep the system from falling into economic disorder. Their spokesperson was President Theodore Roosevelt. He pushed for reforms to control the worst abuses of big business. The Progressive Era produced a long list of legislative reforms. Some of these included the regulation of railroads, the establishment of the Federal Trade Commission, and child labor laws.

THINK ABOUT SOCIAL STUDIES

Directions: Write a short response to each question.

1. Why did living and working conditions in the cities improve during the Progressive Era?

   _____

2. Why did Progressive Era social reformers turn to the federal government for help?

   _____

World War I

In 1914, Archduke Francis Ferdinand, the heir to the Austro-Hungarian throne, was assassinated. This sparked a war between rival groups of European nations—the Allies and the Central Powers. The United States stayed out of the war until 1917. Then Germany stepped up its submarine attacks on US passenger and merchant ships. The United States was forced into the war on the side of the Allies.

Allies	Central Powers
Great Britain France Russia Italy United States Japan	Germany Austria-Hungary Ottoman Empire (Turkey)

By the time the United States entered the war, the warring countries were tired of fighting and neither side seemed able to win. US soldiers helped break this stalemate. On November 11, 1918, the Germans signed an armistice, or truce. Today we celebrate that date as Veterans Day.

World War I made the United States a major world power. President Woodrow Wilson proposed Fourteen Points to make a lasting peace, including free trade and open **diplomacy** (negotiations between nations). He also proposed the **League of Nations**, an international organization to help nations settle disputes. However, the other Allied leaders decided that the enemy, especially the Germans, needed to be taught a lesson. Despite Wilson's efforts, the peace treaties were harsh.

Republican leaders in the US Senate opposed Wilson's peace plans. They kept the United States from signing the peace treaties and joining the League of Nations. They feared that joining the League of Nations would force the United States to go to war if conflicts arose. The country retreated into **isolationism**, a policy of not participating in international relations. It stayed there until forced into war again in 1941.

The Roaring Twenties

Isolationism meant that world affairs were quiet for the United States in the 1920s. At home, though, a lot was happening. President Calvin Coolidge said that "the chief business of the American people is business." That certainly seemed true. Giant companies developed and expanded modern forms of production and marketing. Mass-production assembly lines produced more goods at lower prices. Americans bought telephones, radios, and automobiles.

Chain stores and department stores replaced small shops. Industrial production rose 64 percent between 1919 and 1923. Many workers' **real wages** (that is, wages adjusted for inflation) rose 24 percent. Stock dividends often increased by 100 percent. Expanding industry brought more women into the work force. The Nineteenth Amendment (1920) gave women the right to vote.

Reading Skill
Interpret Graphics

Cartoons, like photos, can be sources of historical information. Political cartoons are drawings in which the artists express their opinions about individuals, governments, businesses, and **social** conditions (that is, conditions relating to human society). Political cartoons are drawn to be humorous, or even ridiculous. Cartoonists make use of **irony**—showing things in a way that is the opposite of the way they really are.

Ask yourself the following questions when you are studying a political cartoon:

• What is the cartoon about? Does the topic help identify a period of history?

• What context clues (such as the way people are dressed) help you understand the cartoon?

• Are there labels or dialogue? Are the words familiar? What do the words tell you about the historical period?

• How does the artist use irony in the words or situation? What does this tell you about the artist's point of view?

Look at the cartoon on this page. Using the questions above, write a sentence in a notebook identifying the time period shown in the cartoon. Then write another sentence explaining context clues that help you understand the cartoon.

After reading this lesson,
think about similarities
and differences between
the early twentieth
century and today.

Use a Venn diagram like
the one below to record
your ideas.

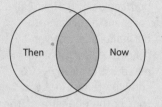

After completing the
diagram, use it to
organize and write a
short essay comparing
and contrasting
conditions in the United
States during the first
four decades of the
twentieth century with
conditions today.

African American workers continued to migrate from the South to work
in factories in the North. They could earn higher wages in the North.
The neighborhood of Harlem in New York City became home to thousands
of African Americans. This new community gave rise to the Harlem
Renaissance, a period of great artistic and cultural achievement. Harlem
Renaissance poets, writers, and jazz and swing musicians and singers
became world famous.

THINK ABOUT SOCIAL STUDIES

Directions: Write a short response to each question.

1. Why did the United States enter World War I?

   _____

2. What caused the large growth in the amount of consumer goods
   available in the 1920s?

   _____

The Great Depression

The era of economic prosperity ended suddenly with the stock market
crash of 1929. Manufacturers could not sell their goods. Farmers lost their
farms. Unemployment in some cities rose to 60 percent. People without
jobs faced losing their homes. When the Depression began, the United
States had no unemployment insurance. It had little public welfare and
no Social Security. Private relief agencies had difficulty caring for so many
people. Millions of people had no money, no work, and no hope.

World War I verterans marched on Washington, DC, to collect their
bonuses. They were driven out by the army. Organizers formed councils
for the unemployed to keep people from being evicted from their homes.

The country was on the verge of economic collapse. Franklin D. Roosevelt
was elected president in 1932. Roosevelt's New Deal programs included
Social Security and Federal Unemployment Insurance. These programs
were designed to prevent the worst features of the Great Depression from
taking place again. The Works Progress Administration (WPA) gave public
works jobs to thousands of unemployed people.

The New Deal did not get the United States out of the Depression. It did,
though, establish the idea that government is responsible for helping
people be free from economic anxiety. It did this through income support
programs and the creation of jobs. At the same time, New Deal programs
greatly increased the government's role in regulating the economy.

Labor unions made great gains during the Depression. New Deal laws
guaranteed workers the right of **collective bargaining**, or the right to
negotiate with their employers. The Congress of Industrial Organizations
(CIO), formed in 1935, unionized four million industrial workers between
1935 and 1937. The older craft-oriented American Federation of Labor
(AFL) had paid little attention to industrial workers.

Vocabulary Review

Directions: Match each word with its definition.

irony   muckrakers   progressive   reform   social

_____ 1. showing things in a way that is the opposite of how they really are

_____ 2. relating to a community

_____ 3. supporting or working for reforms

_____ 4. radical journalists who exposed corruption in business and politics

_____ 5. changes made to improve society and end abuses

Skill Review

Directions: Study this political cartoon. Then answer the questions.

A HARD NAG TO RIDE

1. What word in the title gives a clue that this is the Great Depression of the 1930s, not the recession of 2009? What might the cartoon look like if it was created today?

2. What words in the labels help you to understand the topic?

3. Do you think the artist supports government spending to help restart the economy? How does the artist express this opinion in the cartoon?

Skill Practice

Directions: Choose the <u>one best answer</u> to each question. <u>Questions 1 and 2</u> refer to the following graphs.

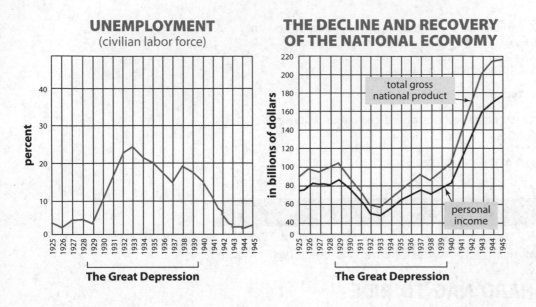

UNEMPLOYMENT
(civilian labor force)

The Great Depression

THE DECLINE AND RECOVERY
OF THE NATIONAL ECONOMY

total gross national product

personal income

The Great Depression

1. What relationship do the graphs show between unemployment in 1933 and personal income that same year?

   A. Unemployment was at a high, and so was personal income.
   B. Unemployment was low, and so was personal income.
   C. Unemployment was at its highest point in the same year that personal income was at its lowest point.
   D. There is no relationship between unemployment and personal income.

2. What do the two graphs show about unemployment?

   A. It increased from 1929 to 1933, and the gross national product declined.
   B. It decreased from 1929 to 1933, and the gross national product decreased in the same period.
   C. It declined continuously from 1933.
   D. Unemployment and the gross national product both increased in 1938.

Skill Practice (continued)

Directions: Choose the <u>one best answer</u> to each question. <u>Questions 3 and 4</u> refer to the following passage.

"Women even more than men need the ballot to protect their special interests and their right to earn a living. . . . We want a law that will prohibit home-work. . . . We hear about the sacredness of the home. What sacredness is there about a home when it is turned into a factory, where we find a mother, very often with a child at her breast, running a sewing machine? Running up thirty-seven seams for a cent. Ironing and pressing shirts seventy cents a dozen, and children making artificial flowers for one cent. . . . These women have had no chance to make laws that would protect themselves or their children.

"[Men] discriminate against the class that has no voice. Some of the men say, 'You women do not need a ballot; we will take care of you.' We have no faith in man's protection. . . . Give us the ballot, and we will protect ourselves."

—Excerpted from *Up Hill with Banners Flying*, by Inez Haynes Irwin

---

3. What is the writer's opinion in this passage?

    A. The ballot will not help the working woman.
    B. Men cannot be depended on to protect women and children.
    C. Men should protect the well-being of women and children.
    D. Giving women the right to vote will destroy the sanctity of the home.

4. The law "that will prohibit home-work" specifically refers to putting an end to what?

    A. work on one's home
    B. studying at home
    C. factory-like production at home
    D. sewing

Writing Practice

Directions: During the Progressive Era and the Great Depression, labor unions played an important role in US society and politics. What is the role of labor unions today? Think about a labor strike that you have heard about, or (if you are a union member) think about the effect your union has on your job. Write a letter to the editor for your local newspaper about an important labor union issue.

Directions: Choose the <u>one best answer</u> to each question. <u>Questions 1 and 2</u> refer to the following map.

THE UNITED STATES EXPANDS, 1783–1853

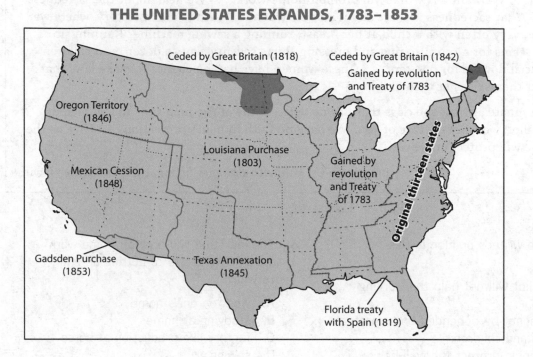

1. Which was one effect of the Mexican War?

    A. the Texas Annexation in 1845
    B. Oregon Territory gained from England
    C. the Mexican Cession in 1848
    D. the United States expanded eastward

2. Why did the United States claim the areas of land from east to west?

    A. Expansion grew westward from the original thirteen states.
    B. The United States wanted to claim land with rich natural resources.
    C. The United States wanted other countries to give it more land.
    D. The western lands were not as valuable as eastern lands.

3. Why was the Fundamental Orders of Connecticut a model for the US Constitution?

    A. It does not mention the king of England.
    B. It called for direct election of the governor.
    C. It required citizens to be church members.
    D. It was the first written constitution to create a government.

4. Which action led directly to the American Civil War?

    A. More railroads were built in Northern states than Southern states.
    B. Abraham Lincoln was elected president.
    C. John Brown attacked the US arsenal at Harpers Ferry.
    D. Lincoln issued the Emancipation Proclamation.

Review

Directions: Question 5 refers to the following chart.

ECONOMIC RESOURCES IN 1860

Resources	North	South
population	71%	29%
railroad mileage	72%	28%
iron and steel	93%	7%
farm output	65%	35%

5. Which conclusion is supported by the data?

   A. The population, railroad mileage, and iron and steel resources in the South combined are greater than the farm output in the North.
   B. The North had an advantage over the South in terms of resources.
   C. The North had the biggest advantage in railroad mileage.
   D. The South had the biggest advantage in farm output.

6. Which of the following is a reason that some people might not support Social Darwinism?

   A. They believe that the rights of the weak should be protected.
   B. They believe that government should not be involved in social reforms.
   C. They think that everyone has equal opportunities in society.
   D. They think that success should always be rewarded.

7. Which document set up the government of the United States?

   A. Articles of Confederation
   B. Declaration of Independence
   C. Magna Carta
   D. Mayflower Compact

8. What was the most important change made by the US Constitution?

   A. It set up a legislature.
   B. States could issue their own currency.
   C. The power of individual states increased.
   D. The national government gained more power.

9. What was the goal of the Missouri Compromise?

   A. to pass the Fugitive Slave Act
   B. to allow California to join the Union as a free state
   C. to maintain a balance between the number of slave states and the number of free states
   D. to keep the Southern economy based on agriculture and the Northern economy on industry

10. Which term describes John Brown, Harriet Beecher Stowe, and Frederick Douglass?

    A. abolitionists
    B. secessionists
    C. former slaves
    D. important authors

11. Which was one reason the United States did not join the League of Nations after World War I?

    A. US citizens voted against US membership in the League of Nations.
    B. Republican senators feared joining might force the United States to go to war.
    C. US leaders did not want to join a group that Germany belonged to.
    D. Democratic senators feared joining would prevent the United States from going to war.

12. Which of the following best describes the 1920s?

    A. a time of isolationism and prosperity
    B. a time of loss and hopelessness
    C. a decade of political activism and social upheaval
    D. a decade of war and political dominance

Questions 13 and 14 refer to the following passage.

> The only way whereby any one divests himself of his natural liberty, and puts on the bonds of civil society, is by agreeing with other men to join and unite into a community for their comfortable, safe, and peaceable living one amongst another, in a secure enjoyment of their properties, and a greater security against any, that are not of it. This any number of men may do, because it injures not the freedom of the rest; they are left as they were in the liberty of the state of nature. When any number of men have so consented to make one community or government, they are thereby presently incorporated, and make one body politic, wherein the majority have a right to act and conclude the rest.
>
> —*The Second Treatise of Civil Government*, by John Locke (1690)

13. Which option best describes what Locke is writing about in this passage?

    A. the best way to organize people
    B. why it is necessary to create laws
    C. how a large group of people should make decisions
    D. the social contract between the individual and the government

14. Which words from the Declaration of Independence are similar to Locke's words in this passage?

    A. "We hold these rights to be self-evident."
    B. "All men are created equal."
    C. "Governments are instituted among Men."
    D. "It is the right of the people to abolish it [a destuctive government]."

Review

Check Your Understanding

On the following chart, circle the number of any question you answered incorrectly. In the third column, you will see the pages you can review to learn the content covered in the question. Pay particular attention to reviewing those lessons in which you missed half or more of the questions.

Chapter 2 Review

Lesson	Item Number	Review Pages
Early Democratic Traditions	3, 7, 13, 14	74–77
Revolution and a New Nation	1, 2, 8	78–85
The Civil War and Reconstruction	4, 5, 9, 10	86–93
The Progressive Era, World War I, and the Depression	6, 11, 12	94–101

ESSAY WRITING PRACTICE

US History: Revolutionary War through the Depression

Directions: Write a summary in response to one of the prompts below. A summary is a general overview of the main points of a text. It is written in your own words. Organize your summary by sequence of events. Use time-order words to show how the ideas are connected.

SUMMARY OF A LESSON

Write a summary of one of the following lessons that you and others could use as a study guide:

Lesson 2.2: Revolution and a New Nation
Lesson 2.3: The Civil War and Reconstruction
Lesson 2.4: The Progressive Era, World War I, and the Depression

Use text features such as the lesson title, key concept, and subheads to determine your main points. Explain each of the main points in your own words. Include an opening sentence and a closing sentence that relate to the general idea presented in the lesson.

SUMMARY OF AN EVENT

Select a key event in US History from the Revolutionary War through the Depression. Write one paragraph summarizing the event. Then write one paragraph describing how the event has affected US history.

Review

ESSAY WRITING PRACTICE

US History: World War II through Modern Times

Throughout your life, you have had to adapt to numerous changes. As the United States has grown and developed as a nation, events within the nation and in other countries have forced the United States to adapt.

In this chapter, you will learn about US history from World War II through today. As you read, think about how events in recent history have shaped the world today. How can your actions help make the United States better in the future?

In this chapter you will study these topics:

Lesson 3.1: World War II, the Cold War, and the 1950s
In the 1930s, under Adolf Hitler's leadership, Germany conquered other European nations. This, along with the military actions of Italy and Japan, led to World War II. After World War II, the United States developed a policy that tried to stop the spread of communism.

Lesson 3.2: Protest and Politics
The 1960s were a time of great social and political change in the United States. African Americans used nonviolent protests to gain civil rights. The civil rights movement inspired women and other minorities to fight for their rights.

Lesson 3.3: US Foreign Policy in the Modern Era
From 1950 until the collapse of the Soviet Union, US foreign policy focused on stopping the spread of communism. Doing this meant that the United States became involved in conflicts around the world, in places such as Korea, Vietnam, Cuba, and Berlin. One result of the Cold War was the space race, a competition between the United States and the Soviet Union to develop space technology.

Lesson 3.4: Societal Changes
During the 1970s, the United States dealt with inflation and an energy crisis brought on by rising oil prices. President Nixon resigned because of the Watergate scandal. In the 1980s, the United States became more conservative under Presidents Reagan and Bush. In the 1990s, the economy, helped by new technologies, grew and the nation prospered.

Lesson 3.5: The United States in the Twenty-First Century
The terrorist attacks of September 11, 2001, led to US military action overseas, most notably in Afghanistan and Iraq. During the first decade of the new millenium, the United States and other nations experienced economic problems, which led to the Great Recession of 2009. In 2009, Barack Obama became the nation's first African American president.

Goal Setting

Why is it important to study modern US history?

- to find out how society has changed as a result of the Cold War
- to find out how society has developed in response to previous events in history
- to understand how recent events shape the country today

Some people who use modern US history in their jobs include

- political analysts
- economists
- community organizers
- financial planners

What do you already know about US history in the twentieth and twenty-first centuries? On the time line below, fill in information that you know.

What do you hope to learn from the lessons in this chapter? List some of your ideas here. As you read this chapter, think about these goals.

_____

_____

_____

_____

_____

World War II, the Cold War, and the 1950s

Lesson Objectives

You will be able to

- Recognize the causes and consequences of World War II

- Understand US strategies in the Cold War

- Analyze the effects of World War II on the cultural and social changes of the 1950s

Skills

- **Core Skill:** Interpret Graphics

- **Reading Skill:** Identify Implications

Vocabulary

containment
denounce
implication
isolationist
persuade
rationing
suburbs

KEY CONCEPT: The entry of the United States into World War II led to an Allied victory, a post-war Cold War, and the cultural and social changes of the 1950s.

A competition is a contest: Two or more sides come together to contest one another. Whoever wins the competition gets something, such as a prize or reward.

During the Cold War, the United States and the Soviet Union were competing for world power. This overarching competition led to smaller but significant competitions in areas such as weapons development, international alliances, and space exploration.

The Road to World War II

The entire world was gripped by the Great Depression of the 1930s. Soviet dictator Joseph Stalin tried to make the Soviet Union into an industrial power based on communism. Communism is a form of government in which goods and property are publicly owned and the means of production are state owned.

In Germany and Italy, fascist dictators rose to power. Fascism is a political belief that countries are best ruled by a **dictator**, or one ruler who has absolute power. Any opposition is forbidden.

At the same time, the Japanese military conquered Manchuria in 1931 and invaded China in 1937. Italy invaded Ethiopia in 1935. In 1936, Germany's Adolf Hitler started his march to world conquest. He took over the Rhineland, Austria, and Czechoslovakia without a fight.

Hitler signed a nonaggression pact with the Soviet Union (USSR) in 1939. When Germany attacked Poland in 1939, Great Britain and France declared war. Nations took sides as the war began.

Axis Powers	Allied Powers
Germany	France
Italy	Great Britain
Japan	United States
USSR first allied with Germany	USSR joined Allies before war's end

Germany quickly conquered most of Europe with its **blitzkrieg** ("lightning war," or a war done with great speed and force). In 1941, Hitler turned his armies toward the Soviet Union, despite the pact he had signed with Stalin.

IDENTIFY IMPLICATIONS

An **implication** is a suggestion. Often writers want the reader to understand an idea, but they do not state the idea directly. To understand a text, the reader needs to figure out what the writer is suggesting, or implying. Use information in the text and your own knowledge to figure out the message of the text.

Read the excerpt below. Then answer these questions.

(1) Where does Churchill state that the people of Great Britain will keep on fighting?

(2) Who does Churchill imply will continue fighting?

(3) Does the information given in the passage imply that British troops won or lost the Battle of Dunkirk?

> Following is an excerpt from a speech given by Winston Churchill, the prime minister of Great Britain during World War II. The speech was given June 4, 1940, after the evacuation of Dunkirk.
>
> "We shall defend our island, whatever the cost may be, we shall fight on the beaches, we shall fight on the landing grounds, we shall fight in the fields and in the streets, we shall fight in the hills; we shall never surrender."

(1) Churchill states that the British people will fight everywhere and at any cost. (2) By using the term *we*, Churchill implies that all the people of Great Britain will join in the fight. (3) The passage states that the speech was given after the evacuation of Dunkirk. Churchill's strong language and the words "we shall never surrender" imply that the British lost the Battle of Dunkirk.

Research It
Extend Your Knowledge

President Roosevelt and some influential people in the United States were internationalists. They were concerned about what was happening in Europe, Africa, and Asia. Others, including many members of Congress, favored an isolationist policy.

You can find out more about the debate between the two sides by researching on the Internet. One good place to start is the US State Department's Office of the Historian (http://history.state.gov/).

Click on "key Milestones" and select "1937–1945." Scan the topics listed for this period, looking carefully at headings and photos. Select one person or event that interests you. Then use other reliable resources to do further research about your topic.

In a notebook, take notes as you read. Compare your findings with those of other students. This will give you a broader understanding of this period in US history.

In the United States, **isolationists** wanted the country to remain neutral. Congress passed Neutrality Acts in the 1930s. The acts prevented the United States from providing support to foreign countries that were at war. However, the acts included one key exception: the United States could sell goods, except for weapons, to other nations as long as the goods were paid for immediately and the goods were transported on non-US ships.

Studying photographs can help you understand an event. Photographers uses their skill to express a point of view. They want to **persuade**, or convince, the reader to agree with their idea.

When studying a photograph, use these steps:

- Ask yourself what is happening in the photograph.

- Read the caption.

- Look at the details: what people are doing, what expressions are on their faces, and what is in the background.

In a notebook, answer these questions about the photo on this page.

- What is the little boy doing?

- What information do you learn from the caption?

- What does the expression on the boy's face tell you?

- What is the photographer's point of view about rationing?

Others, including President Roosevelt, recognized the dangers that the Axis powers posed. They worked to find ways in which the United States could help the Allies. In 1940 Congress passed the Lend-Lease Act. This act, which was based on earlier provisions in the Neutrality Acts, provided arms and support to Great Britain and many other countries. Importantly, it also kept the United States from becoming directly involved in the war.

German U-boats (submarines) began to harass and then attack US supply ships in the North Atlantic. The event that finally brought the United States into World War II, however, came from another source. The Japanese launched a sneak air attack on the US naval fleet at Pearl Harbor, Hawaii, in December 1941. Four days later, the Axis powers in Europe declared war on the United States.

World War II was truly a "world" war. Fighting raged in Europe, Asia, Africa, and the Pacific islands until 1945. Allied leaders agreed that they would fight until their enemies surrendered unconditionally.

The Home Front

At home, major industries quickly mobilized to produce war goods after the Lend-Lease Act was passed. Many men were drafted into the armed forces or joined voluntarily. As they left their jobs behind, women took their places. Women also served in the military in noncombat positions.

A system of **rationing**, limiting the availability of food and other products, was put in place. Americans planted "Victory Gardens" to grow their own fruits and vegetables. They organized scrap drives to collect and reuse paper, rubber, and metals such as copper and steel.

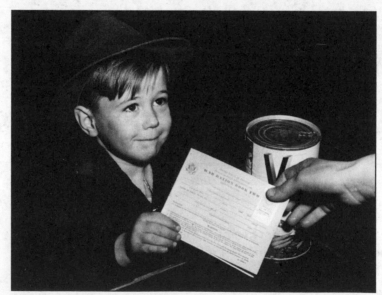

An eager school boy gets his first experience in using War Ration Book Two. With many parents engaged in war work, children are being taught the facts of point rationing so they can help out with family shopping.

Internment Camps

After Pearl Harbor, Americans of Japanese, German, and Italian descent suffered discrimination and harassment. Many were arrested, were forced to move, or had their property taken away. More than 100,000 Japanese, German, and Italian Americans were sent to **internment**, or prison, camps during the war. Most of them were American citizens.

archives.gov

The Allies invaded the European continent on June 6, 1944. The Germans were finally defeated in May 1945. The Japanese continued to fight until the United States dropped atomic bombs on the cities of Hiroshima and Nagasaki in August 1945. On August 14, 1945, Japan formally surrendered and World War II was over.

THINK ABOUT SOCIAL STUDIES

Directions: Write the numbers 1 through 4 to put these events in sequence.

_____ 1. Japan makes a sneak attack on the United States at Pearl Harbor.

_____ 2. Japan surrenders.

_____ 3. Japanese Americans are set to internment camps.

_____ 4. The United States drops two atomic bombs on Japan.

Reading Skill
Identify Implications

A writer often implies that something will happen, rather than state it directly. Readers must use clues in the text and their own knowledge understand the writer's message.

As you read "The Cold War" on this page, ask yourself what implications the writer is making.

Write answers to these questions in a notebook.

- What does the arms race imply?

- What did each side hope to gain from the production of arms?

- What do you know about whether the arms race succeeded?

The Cold War

With the signing of the peace treaties that ended World War II, the United States became one of two major world powers. The other world power was the Soviet Union.

An organization called the United Nations was formed in 1945. Its purpose was to negotiate disputes between nations. The hope was that this would lead to world peace. Great Britain, the United States, and the Soviet Union had joined together during the war to defeat Germany and Japan. However, when the war ended, Great Britain and the United States had a hostile relationship with the Soviet Union. A struggle developed between different social and economic systems in the East and the West. This period of struggle was called the Cold War. It was called a "cold" war because the two sides did not confront each other directly in war.

The Soviet Union set up Communist governments in several Eastern European countries. These countries were called satellites because they depended upon Soviet economic ties. Occupation forces kept the countries under Soviet control.

The United States used a strategy of **containment** to keep communism from spreading around the world during this period. Containment involved creating alliances with other countries to keep the power of the Soviet Union in check. An arms race between the two nations lasted for the next 40 years. Each side tried to have bigger and better weapons than the other. US weapons were kept in countries bordering the Soviet **bloc**, or satellite countries. This was meant to deter the Soviet Union from expanding into more countries.

To support containment, the United States, Canada, and the Western European countries formed a military alliance called the North Atlantic Treaty Organization (NATO). The Soviet Union and its satellites formed the Warsaw Pact military alliance.

The Marshall Plan

As a result of World War II, much of Western Europe was in ruins. Cities had been destroyed. Millions of people were homeless and starving. Secretary of State George Marshall proposed a plan to aid these countries. The Marshall Plan gave millions of dollars in cash and materials to help countries rebuild. The United States believed this aid would ensure that Europe would not turn to communism.

The Cold War at Home

Americans feared that the Communists might take over the world in the post-war era. This fear increased when Communists came to power in China in 1949. Senator Joseph McCarthy of Wisconsin and his followers led a "witch hunt" in the 1950s. This became known as McCarthyism. McCarthy and his followers accused many Americans of being Communists or Communist sympathizers. In Congress, the House Un-American Activities Committee carried out its own investigations. Thousands of Americans lost their jobs as a result of McCarthyism. In 1954, Senator McCarthy's colleagues in the US Senate **denounced** (spoke out against) him, and his committee condemned his actions.

THINK ABOUT SOCIAL STUDIES

Directions: Write a short response to the following questions in a notebook.

1. What is one strategy the United States used to support its containment policy?
2. Why did the United States approve the Marshall Plan?
3. Why did Senator McCarthy investigate Americans he suspected of being Communists or Communist sympathizers?

The 1950s

In 1944 Congress passed legislation to help veterans returning from World War II. Many soldiers had no jobs when they returned home. The GI Bill of Rights gave veterans low-interest loans to buy houses, helped them look for jobs, and provided unemployment compensation and money to go to college. Millions took advantage of the programs.

During the war, many women had worked in factories to help the war effort. When the veterans returned, those women lost their jobs even though many wanted to keep working.

Some African Americans also lost their jobs to returning veterans at the end of the war. In addition, many of the African Americans, Hispanic Americans, and other minorities who had served in the armed forces faced discrimination when they returned home.

After World War II, the nation's economy continued to grow. The standard of living grew also. A new white-collar population emerged in the 1950s. White-collar workers are professionals who are paid salaries instead of hourly wages. Many families moved out of the cities and into new housing in the **suburbs**, small communities that developed outside urban areas. New highways were built to connect the suburbs with the cities. The **baby boom**, a rapid growth in the birth rate, created a need for more schools. This helped fuel the construction industry.

Culture

Changes to life in the United States came with the growth of television. About 80 percent of families in the country had at least one TV by 1957. A new form of music, called rock 'n' roll, grew in popularity. It was a combination of African American rhythm and blues, country and western, gospel music, and jazz. Young people no longer had to work to help support their families, as they had during the Great Depression and World War II. They now had leisure time. Many had money to spend on clothes, music, and other entertainment.

Vocabulary Review

Directions: Use these words to complete the following sentences.

containment denounce isolationists rationing suburbs

1. During World War II, all Americans were subject to a system of _____, which limited the amount of food they could buy.

2. The United States followed a policy of _____ to keep communism from spreading.

3. Before the United States entered World War II, _____ wanted the nation to stay neutral.

4. In the 1950s, many Americans moved to small communities outside cities called _____.

5. To speak out against an idea you believe is wrong is to _____ the idea.

Skill Review

Directions: Read the paragraph below and answer the questions that follow.

> In 1942 the US government instituted the Bracero program to bring farmers from Mexico to the Southwest. In Spanish, *bracero* means "farmer." Thousands of workers came to the United States to help harvest crops in the Southwest. *Braceros* were considered temporary farm workers. They signed contracts written in English. These workers were often exploited, or taken advantage of.
>
> Jesús Campoya Calderón was one of these *braceros*. He describes his experience: "In the farms we would do anything, although our permit was to pick cotton only. . . . I worked four months, seven days a week, at least 12 hours every day and I took home almost $300 dollars. . . . Those were very good days. . . ."

1. What does Calderón say about the type of work he did?

_____

2. What does this passage imply about the treatment of the *braceros* by their employers?

_____

_____

3. What else does Calderón say to support this implication?

_____

_____

Directions: Read the passage and study the photograph. Then answer the questions.

During the Cold War, the Soviet Union blockaded ground supply routes to West Berlin, Germany. For ten months, supplies were airlifted into the city by the United States and Great Britain. Lt. Gail S. Halvorsen noticed children watching the planes come in. After talking with a group of these children, he began to drop tiny parachutes with candy and gum attached. Other pilots and crews soon begin dropping parachutes too. These pilots became known as the "Chocolate Flyers."

Children in Berlin cheer as a "Chocolate Flyer" flies overhead.

4. Describe the setting and the implied mood of the people in the photograph.

_____

_____

5. Do you think the photograph was effective in getting people to contribute money, candy, and gum for the airlifts? Why or why not?

_____

_____

Skill Practice

Directions: Choose the one best answer to each question. Questions 1 and 2 refer to the following map.

EUROPE AFTER WORLD WAR II

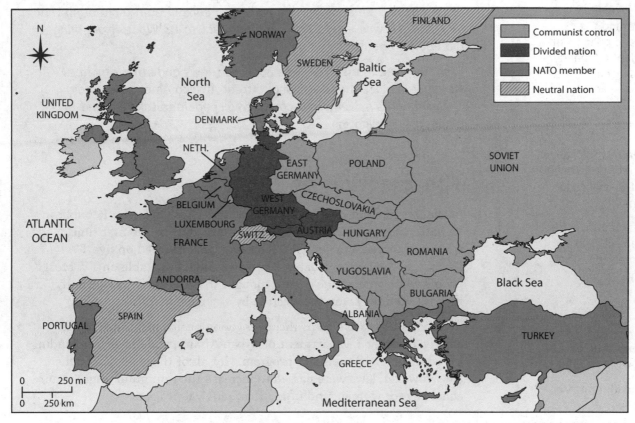

1. After World War II, the Soviet Union occupied part of Germany. Why would the Soviet Union want to keep control of this territory?

   A. It wanted to show its might and power.
   B. The Soviet Union did not have sea or ocean access without this land.
   C. Stalin wanted the Soviet Union to join NATO.
   D. Stalin wanted a base from which he could spread communism into Europe.

2. During the Cold War, the United States established military bases in Turkey. Why?

   A. to position arms closer to the Soviet Union in order to contain communism
   B. to encourage trade with Asia
   C. to build an army
   D. to have access to the Black Sea

Writing Practice

Directions: Do you think there could be a world war today? Why, or why not? Write one paragraph explaining your opinion. Support your opinion with details and facts.

Protest and Politics

KEY CONCEPT: The **1960**s and **1970**s were a time of great turmoil in the United States.

Think about a time in your life when you encountered a situation that you believed was unfair. How did you react to it? What, if anything, did you do about it?

From the time that slavery was abolished, laws and other practices were put in place that continued to treat African Americans unfairly. The civil rights movement encouraged all people to take a stand against discrimination.

Lesson Objectives

You will be able to

- Understand the domestic policies of Presidents Kennedy and Johnson

- Identify key events and leaders of the civil rights movement

- Recognize the changes in society that resulted from the civil rights movement

- Understand the effects of the civil rights movement on other minority groups

Skills

- **Reading Skill:** Relate Ideas within a Text

- **Core Skill:** Interpret Meaning

Vocabulary

boycott
civil rights movement
demonstration
discrimination
relationship
segregation
unanimous

The Election of 1960

In the presidential election of 1960, voters chose between Republican Richard Nixon and Democrat John F. Kennedy. For the first time, television played a major role. The candidates debated on live TV. Nixon was the better debater, but he was uncomfortable on TV. Most people who watched the debate thought that Kennedy had won. In the end, Kennedy won the election by a narrow margin.

Kennedy's legislative plans included giving health insurance to the elderly, creating a Department of Urban Affairs, and increasing funding for education and the space program. Not all of these plans became law. However, laws were passed to increase the minimum wage, require equal pay for women, and fund urban renewal projects.

Kennedy Assassinated On November 22, 1963, President Kennedy and his wife were riding in a motorcade in Dallas, Texas, when gunshots suddenly rang out. The president was shot twice and killed.

Johnson's Great Society

After President Kennedy's death, Vice President Lyndon Johnson was sworn in as president. Johnson announced an "**unconditional** [unlimited] war on poverty" and spoke about creating a "Great Society" that would "end poverty and racial injustice." Major reforms were passed both before and after Johnson's reelection in 1964.

RELATE IDEAS WITHIN A TEXT

It is important to identify connections, or **relationships**, between ideas when you read. Examples of relationships between ideas include cause and effect, compare and contrast, problem and solution, sequencing, and definition or description.

To identify relationships between ideas, ask yourself, *What does one idea have to do with the other?*

Read the paragraph below. Identify the important ideas. Then determine the relationship between these ideas.

> In the 1960s, the federal government set up a policy of "affirmative action." The policy required companies receiving federal money to meet certain guidelines: companies could not discriminate on the basis of race, the number of minority employees must meet a certain percentage, and companies must provide equal opportunities for workers to advance.

The ideas presented:

- Affirmative action was set up by the government in the 1960s.

- The goals of affirmative action were to prevent discrimination, to increase the number of minorities in the workforce, and to help minorities earn the promotions they deserved.

The relationship between the ideas is one of definition or description. The details to help readers understand the term *affirmative action*.

TECHNOLOGY CONNECTION

Political Debates

Go the Archive of American Television to watch an excerpt from one of the Nixon-Kennedy debates (http://www.emmytvlegends.org/interviews/kennedy-nixon-debates).

Then discuss with a partner how you felt about the candidates before the debate and after the debate. Also discuss the effect of media on today's political campaigns.

Great Society Legislation

Program Title	Explanation of Program
Economic Opportunity Act	Set up the Office of Economic Opportunity, which ran programs to help the poor
Medicare	Health insurance for people over 65
Medicaid	Health insurance for low-income families
Head Start	Preschool for children of low-income families
Clean Air and Water Quality Acts	Set standards and guidelines for air and water quality
Housing and Urban Development Act	Created a government department that oversees federal government involvement in community development and housing

Read the "Brown v.
Board of Education"
section on this page.
Identify the main idea
and the supporting
details in the text.

In a notebook identify
one example of each
of these relationships
between ideas:

• Definition or
  description

• Sequence

• Cause and effect

• Problem and solution

Research It
Expand Your Knowledge

To learn more about
Martin Luther King Jr.
and the civil rights
movement, a good place
to start is Stanford
University's King
Institute (http://mlk-
kpp01.stanford.edu/).

After learning more
about Dr. King and his
ideas, ask yourself how
the United States has
changed since the 1960s.

Then discuss these
questions with a partner:

• If Dr. King were alive
  today, what would
  please him the most?

• What would disappoint
  him the most?

Important Supreme Court cases were decided during this time. In a series of decisions, the Court ruled that the Bill of Rights applied to states as well as to the federal government. Specifically, the Supreme Court made these rulings:

• Evidence illegally collected is **inadmissible**, or not allowed, in court.

• All suspects have a right to a lawyer during police questioning and at trial.

• Police must inform people of their rights when they are arrested (the Miranda warning).

Brown v. Board of Education

One of the most important Supreme Court rulings was in the case of *Brown v. Board of Education of Topeka, Kansas*. The National Association for the Advancement of Colored People (NAACP) had been challenging **segregation** laws for decades. Segregation is the practice of separating people or groups on the basis of race. In 1954, the NAACP sued the Topeka school board on behalf of Linda Brown. Brown was forced to attend a school across town rather than the school near her house because of her race. The Supreme Court's decision was **unanimous**; that is, there was no dissent or disagreement. Racial segregation in schools was illegal. The court did not consider segregated schools to be equal under the law.

Despite the Supreme Court's ruling, segregation was a fact of life for African Americans in the South. Restaurants and movie theaters had separate sections for African Americans. They were forced to ride in the backs of buses and trains. In 1955, an African American woman named Rosa Parks sat at the front of a bus in Montgomery, Alabama. When she refused to give up her seat to a white man, she was arrested. Her actions sparked a bus **boycott**. African Americans refused to use the bus system. For over a year, they walked to work or carpooled rather than ride the bus.

The Civil Rights Movement

The bus boycott ended in 1956 when the Supreme Court ruled that segregating buses was illegal. The court ruling encouraged other protests, such as sit-ins and **demonstrations**, or public protests. Freedom Riders rode interstate buses to draw attention to continuing segregation in the South. Many African Americans faced beatings and harassment.

The movement to end **discrimination** (unfair treatment) and guarantee African Americans equal treatment was called the **civil rights movement**. A young and skillful speaker, Martin Luther King Jr. became its leader. He received widespread support for his nonviolent protests. Americans were upset by news reports showing peaceful demonstrators being attacked by police with clubs and dogs.

In 1963, President Kennedy announced a civil rights bill. The bill would ban segregation in public places and end discrimination in voting and employment. However, the bill stalled in the Senate. To pressure Congress to pass the bill, Dr. King organized a march in Washington, DC. More than 200,000 supporters joined the march. It was there that King gave his famous "I Have a Dream" speech.

Congress finally passed the civil rights bill in 1964. The Voting Rights Act was passed in 1965. It put an end to practices that denied African Americans their right to vote. As a result, hundreds of African Americans and other minorities were elected to public office. Hundreds of thousands more registered to vote for the first time.

On April 4, 1968, Dr. King was shot and killed in Memphis, Tennessee. Although the movement lost one of its most important and inspirational leaders, it continued. The civil rights movement also led women, Hispanics, Native Americans, homosexuals, and other groups to seek equal rights.

Antiwar Protests

Throughout the 1960s, the United States became more and more deeply involved in the conflict between communist and non-communist forces in Vietnam. In 1964, Congress gave President Johnson the authority to go to war.

At first, a majority of Americans supported the war. But as casualties grew, people began to protest. Images of the fighting were shown on nightly TV newscasts. For the first time, the realities of war hit home.

Statue in Washington, DC, honoring Martin Luther King Jr., leader of the civil rights movement.

There was opposition to the war for several reasons. Some people thought that the United States should not get involved in another country's civil war. Others protested the **draft** system, which required young men to serve in the armed forces. In practice, it was often men from lower-income families that were drafted and sent to fight.

President Johnson decided not to run for re-election in 1968. Democrats nominated Hubert Humphrey. The Republicans nominated Richard Nixon. Nixon's promise to end the war helped him beat Humphrey.

THINK ABOUT SOCIAL STUDIES

Directions: Choose the correct answer that completes each statement below.

1. *Brown v. Board of Education* was a Supreme Court decision banning (segregation, integration) in (private, public) schools.

2. The civil rights movement led by Dr. King favored (violent, nonviolent) means to obtain racial justice.

3. The Voting Rights Act made (discriminatory, nondiscriminatory) practices illegal.

Tom Williams/CQ-Roll Call Group/Getty Images

Core Skill
Interpret Meaning

Using what you already know about a specific time in history can help you understand new information.

Look at the photo on this page. What characteristics of Martin Luther King Jr. do you see in the statue? What do you think the artist wants you to understand about King?

You may want to go on the Internet to find out more about the King Memorial. What words are inscribed on the memorial?

In a notebook, write a paragraph describing King as he appears in the statue and explaining why King is important.

WRITE TO LEARN

Read the sections on this page about the other rights movements.

In a notebook, write a paragraph about the relationship between the civil rights movement and the struggles of other minority groups.

Other Minorities Fight for Their Rights

The civil rights movement inspired other minority groups to fight for their rights. There were over 9 million Hispanic Americans in the United States by the late 1960s. Many immigrants worked on farms, where conditions were difficult and wages were low. In response, unions such as the United Farm Workers (UFW) fought for better wages and benefits.

In the 1960s and 1970s, Native Americans also began organizing. In 1968, Congress passed a law giving Native Americans equal protection under the Bill of Rights. In the 1970s, they won court cases that gave them greater control over reservations and money owed to them by the government.

During and after World War II, more women joined the workforce. But only certain jobs were offered to women, and their pay was not equal to the pay men received. Using their experience with civil rights, women began to protest. As a result, these legislative reforms were enacted:

- 1963: Equal Pay Act makes it illegal to pay men more than women for the same job

- 1964: Civil Rights Act, Title VII, outlaws job discrimination on the basis of race, color, religion, national origin, and gender

- 1972: Educational Amendments, Title IX, makes it illegal for any school receiving federal funds to discriminate on the basis of gender

Vocabulary Review

Directions: Use these words to complete the following sentences.

boycott   civil rights movement   demonstrations   discrimination   segregation   unanimously

The goal of the _____ was to end _____ against African Americans. One of the first major events was the arrest of Rosa Parks for refusing to give up her seat on a bus. Her arrest led to a bus _____ that lasted more than a year. The Supreme Court _____ ruled that _____ was illegal, but it was still practiced. Only after many years of _____ were laws passed that guaranteed African Americans equal rights.

Skill Review

Directions: Read the passage and answer the question that follows.

Betty Friedan was an author and a leader of the modern women's rights movement. After graduating from Smith College in 1942, she became a writer and political activist. Her most famous book, *The Feminine Mystique*, was published in 1963. The book grew out of surveys that she had taken of her classmates from Smith. These surveys showed that despite their education and subsequent successes, the women were unhappy with their lives. The book became a best seller. In 1966, Friedan and other feminists formed the National Organization for Women (NOW). NOW worked to get women equal access to education and pay that was equal to the pay of men.

Skill Review (continued)

1. List one cause-and-effect relationship in the passage about Betty Friedan?

_____

Directions: Study the photo. Then answer the question.

2. Apply what you know about Martin Luther King Jr. and this time period to explain the importance of what is being shown in the photo.

_____

_____

Skill Practice

Directions: Choose the one best answer to each question.

1. Which statement describes one possible result of the bus boycott in Montgomery, Alabama?

   A. African Americans were happy not to have to ride the buses anymore.
   B. The bus system suffered financial loss.
   C. People were not aware of the bus boycotts.
   D. More people began taking the bus.

2. Which statement might be a reason King believed nonviolent protests were the best way to fight for social change?

   A. Nonviolent protests are easy to start.
   B. People get into less trouble in nonviolent protests.
   C. People naturally don't like fighting.
   D. People are against bloodshed, regardless of the cause.

Writing Practice

Directions: Select one of the laws or court cases mentioned in this lesson. Write a journal entry describing how it has affected your life.

US Foreign Policy in the Modern Era

Lesson Objectives

You will be able to

- Understand how communism affected foreign policy for the second half of the twentieth century

- Analyze the different strategies used toward the Soviet Union

- Evaluate the impact of the Vietnam War on US foreign policy

Skills

- **Reading Skill:** Read Charts

- **Core Skill:** Interpret Graphics

Vocabulary

administration
brinksmanship
chart
détente
repression
succeed
trend

KEY CONCEPT: The Cold War and the spread of communism dominated the focus of US foreign policy from the end of World War II until the fall of the Soviet Union in the 1990s.

Every day we interact with many people. Depending on the situation, we may act differently toward different people.

A president's foreign policy is shaped by the president's political viewpoint, but the issues and events happening in the world also make a difference. Different policies may be more or less successful depending on what is happening around the world.

Foreign Policy from 1950–1993

In the half-century following World War II, the presidency changed eight times. Both Republicans and Democrats came to power. Each **administration**—that is, the president and those working with him in the executive branch—had its own position on foreign policy. Until the 1990s, the primary focus of US foreign policy was the containment of communism. After the collapse of the Soviet Union, the focus of US foreign policy shifted to Latin America and the Middle East.

The Korean War

After World War II ended, Japan was forced out of its colony in Korea. The Soviet Union occupied the northern part of Korea, and the United States occupied the southern part. Both countries eventually withdrew their troops, but very different governments were left behind. In the south, elections were held and a democratic government was formed. In the north, a communist government was formed.

In June 1950, communist forces from the north invaded South Korea. President Truman did not ask Congress to declare war, but he did take action. The United Nations, at Truman's request, agreed to send troops to defend South Korea. The majority of the troops were from the United States.

By the time troops arrived, North Korean forces had taken over most of South Korea. Over the next several months, UN forces pushed them back beyond the 38th parallel, the line of latitude that was considered the border between the two countries.

Dwight Eisenhower, 1953–1961

Dwight Eisenhower was a World War II hero, a Republican, and a political conservative. During his presidential campaign, he promised to end the war in Korea. **Negotiations** (discussions to end a dispute) had been going on since 1951. Finally, in July 1953, a cease-fire agreement was reached. The agreement created a **demilitarized zone** around the 38th parallel. In this area, no military troops were allowed.

READ CHARTS

Writers use visuals to make information clear to the reader. **Charts** are visuals that organize information so it will be easier to understand. Charts can be used to compare data and summarize information.

When you come across a chart, read the title. Study the column headings. Then look at the information in the chart. Make comparisons. Look for differences. Use information in the chart to draw conclusions.

Study the chart and then answer these questions.

- What comparisons can you make by using the data in the chart?
- Between which years was there the biggest decline in the number of troops? Why do you think this was so?

TROOPS IN VIETNAM

Year	Number of Troops
1963	15,620
1964	17,280
1965	129,611
1966	317,007
1967	451,752
1968	537,377
1969	510,054
1970	390,278
1971	212,925
1972	35,292
1973	265

The data helps you compare the number of troops in Vietnam from year to year. The biggest drop in the number of troops was between 1971 and 1972. This was probably because the war, or at least the major fighting, ended in 1972.

REAL WORLD
CONNECTION

Research Data

Not all interactions with foreign countries are on battlefields. The United States gives millions of dollars of foreign aid to countries all around the world.

Use the Internet to find current information about foreign aid. Then make a two-column table. In the first column, list ten countries that received foreign aid in one year. In the second column, show the amounts they received in one year.

You might want to round the amounts to millions of dollars. For example, $331,825,000 would be written $332M.

Give your chart a title. Be sure to label the columns.

The Korean War showed the Soviet Union that the United States was willing to fight to stop the spread of communism. However, despite his commitment to ending the war, Eisenhower continued the arms race with the Soviet Union. A new form of political strategy called **brinkmanship** began. Brinkmanship pushed each side to the brink, or edge, of war.

Charts are a good way to organize information as you read. Creating a chart can help you understand and remember what you read.

In a notebook, make a three-column chart. Label the columns Event, United States, and Soviet Union. In the Event column, list important events, beginning with the space race.

Then ask yourself which country—the United States or the Soviet Union—made the event happen. In that country's column, write the date of the event. Continue to fill in the chart as you read through the lesson.

After the chart is complete, write one sentence that states what conclusion you can draw from your chart.

The United States continued its policy of containment. When the French left Vietnam in 1954, Vietnam was divided in two. North Vietnam was a Communist country led by Ho Chi Minh. It sponsored **guerrilla** (independent armed forces) activity in South Vietnam. The United States sent aid to South Vietnam so the Communists would not take over.

Space Race The Soviet Union launched its first space satellite in 1957, during Eisenhower's second term in office. This began a "space race" between the Soviet Union and the United States that lasted for the next 40 years. Each nation wanted to be the most advanced in space exploration. The first US venture into space was the launching of the *Explorer* in 1958. Then, in 1961, the Soviet Union put the first human into space. The space race would continue until the fall of the Soviet Union almost 20 years later.

John F. Kennedy, 1961–1963

The United States put its first human into space in 1962, during the presidency of John F. Kennedy. Kennedy was a Democrat. He was the youngest president ever elected. He inherited a continuing Cold War, an arms race, and the first communist takeover in the Western Hemisphere: Cuba. Fidel Castro, a Communist, seized power in Cuba in 1959. Thousands of Cubans took refuge in the United States. In 1961, Kennedy approved a CIA plan to invade Cuba by using the Cuban refugees as soldiers. This invasion, called the Bay of Pigs after the soldier's landing spot in Cuba, was a failure.

Berlin Wall After World War II, Germany had been divided into two sections: West Germany and East Germany. East Germany was under Soviet control. Even though Berlin, the capital, was well within East Germany, it was also divided into East and West. Great Britain, the United States, and France merged their occupied zones to form West Germany. West Germany, including West Berlin, was controlled by the Germans.

Soviet Premier Nikita Khrushchev demanded that the West sign a treaty, a written agreement between countries, giving all of Berlin to the Soviet bloc. In August 1961, the Soviets began to build a wall between East and West Berlin. The intent was to keep people in East Germany from escaping to the West. The wall became a symbol of communist **repression**, or control by force. Anyone caught climbing over the wall was killed. East Germans who tried other means of escaping were imprisoned.

Cuban Missile Crisis In October 1962, a US spy plane found signs of Soviet nuclear missile bases in Cuba. President Kennedy began a US naval blockade of Cuba. The **blockade** attempted to cut off all communications and supplies moving to and from Cuba. Kennedy warned that if the Soviets launched any missiles from the Cuban bases, the United States would strike back with an attack on the Soviet Union.

When the Soviets were shown US photographs of the Cuban bases, they agreed to negotiate. Ultimately the Soviet Union agreed to withdraw the missiles and tear down its bases in Cuba. In turn, the United States ended its blockade and agreed not to invade Cuba. The United States also agreed to remove missiles it had in Turkey, near the border of the Soviet Union.

THINK ABOUT SOCIAL STUDIES

Directions: Choose the <u>one best answer</u> to the question.

1. Why did the United States send aid to South Vietnam?
   A. to keep communists from taking over the country
   B. because of the destruction caused by the Korean War
   C. because the United States wanted to fight North Vietnam
   D. to support guerilla forces fighting in South Vietnam

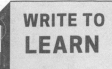

WRITE TO LEARN

This lesson describes US foreign policy in the second half of the twentieth century. US policies affected other countries. How do you think those countries felt about US policies?

Look for information in print or on the Internet about the opinions and responses of other countries. Then imagine you are the leader of one of these countries. Write a letter to the US president telling him what you think of his policies.

Lyndon Johnson, 1963–1969

Lyndon Johnson came to the presidency after the assassination of John F. Kennedy. He inherited all the Cold War issues that Kennedy had been dealing with, including increasing tensions in Vietnam. In August 1964, Congress passed the Gulf of Tonkin resolution. The resolution gave Johnson the go-ahead to send troops to Vietnam. Soon after, North Vietnamese forces attacked US bases in South Vietnam.

Vietnam War US troop strength in Vietnam reached more than 537,000 by 1968. More tons of bombs were dropped by air on North Vietnam than had been dropped on Germany, Italy, and Japan during World War II. It did little good. The North Vietnamese could not be defeated.

Richard Nixon, 1969–1974

Richard Nixon was a Republican conservative and an anticommunist. However, he had won the presidency in part because he promised to end the Vietnam War. In 1973, the United States signed the Paris Peace Agreement and pulled out of Vietnam. Two years later, the communists united Vietnam under their leadership. All the military and economic support had not worked to contain communism.

Another of Nixon's important achievements was his policy of **détente**. *Détente* is a French word that means "relaxing." In politics, it signifies easing the tensions between nations. Nixon's policy called for peaceful cooperation between the United States and the Soviet Union.

Nixon Visits China The United States did not **recognize**, or acknowledge, China as an independent nation after the communists took over that country in 1949. But Nixon visited China and re-established our relationship. He then turned his attention toward the Soviet Union. Nixon traveled to Moscow and met with Soviet premier Leonid Brezhnev. They signed the Strategic Arms Limitation Treaty (SALT I). This treaty agreed to limit nuclear weapons. It was the first step toward ending the Cold War.

Space Race Continues The space race continued during the Nixon years. In 1969, American Neil Armstrong became the first person to land on the Moon. The Soviet Union never tried to land a man on the Moon. Instead, in 1971 it placed the first space station into orbit.

Gerald Ford, 1974–1977

In 1973, Nixon's vice president Spiro Agnew had been forced to resign. Nixon chose Gerald Ford, the Republican leader of the House of Representatives, to fill the position. When Nixon was forced to resign in 1974 over the Watergate scandal, Ford became president. During his two-year term, Ford followed Nixon's policy of détente.

Jimmy Carter, 1977–1981

Jimmy Carter was a little-known Democratic governor from Georgia when he defeated Ford. He based his foreign policy on his concept of right and wrong. He was a strong advocate for human rights.

Camp David Accords The creation of Israel after World War II led to continuing tensions in the Middle East. Several small wars broke out between Arab nations (such as Egypt, Syria, and Jordan) and the Israelis. Israel usually won. In 1978 President Carter invited the prime ministers of Israel and Egypt to meet with him at Camp David to talk about peace. In 1979, they signed a formal treaty called the Camp David Accords.

Iran Hostage Crisis In 1978–1979, there was a revolution in Iran. The **shah**, the Persian term for *king*, was overthrown. The United States had supported the shah, hoping to keep Islamic religious leaders from coming to power. Later in 1979, the US embassy in Iran was invaded. Fifty-two Americans were taken hostage. Failure to gain the release of the hostages led to Carter's defeat in the election of 1980.

Ronald Reagan, 1981–1989

Conservative Republican Ronald Reagan felt the way to deter communist threats was to support guerrillas fighting against communist regimes. This policy was called the Reagan Doctrine. In 1979, the Soviet Union invaded Afghanistan. Reagan sent aid to the Afghan guerrilla forces. The Soviets pulled out of Afghanistan in 1988 after being unable to defeat the guerrillas.

In 1985, Mikhail Gorbachev came to power in the Soviet Union. He encouraged reforms to the Soviet system. Reagan and Gorbachev agreed to new arms-control treaties. Relations between the two superpowers improved.

TOTAL ECONOMIC ASSISTANCE (in millions of dollars)				
	1960	1970	1980	1990
Cambodia	128.7	0.0	86.2	0.1
Colombia	63.8	579.8	52.1	31.0
Israel	314.2	181.8	1,769.5	1,758.1
South Korea	1,229.1	622.3	69.3	0.1
Vietnam	1,035.0	2,108.4	(less than $50,000)	0.1

George H. W. Bush, 1989–1993

George H. W. Bush was Reagan's vice-president. Bush **succeeded**, or came after, Reagan. During Bush's administration, the Berlin Wall was torn down, and Germany was reunited. Within two years, the Soviet Union broke into 15 independent republics. Communism survived in only a few countries, such as North Korea and China. Market economies—economies based on goods and services exchanged in free markets—were introduced in nearly every former communist country. The Cold War was over.

Persian Gulf War In 1990, Iraqi dictator Saddam Hussein invaded Kuwait. The UN demanded that Iraq withdraw by a set date. Hussein refused. UN forces launched air and ground attacks. Only 100 hours later, the war was over. Iraqi forces withdrew and accepted the UN cease-fire agreement.

While communism was breaking up, other problems arose that required the attention of the United States. Fighting broke out in Yugoslavia, which split into several independent countries. Many African countries faced hunger, economic decline, and heavy debt. The Middle East continued to be a battleground. Acts of terrorism occurred all around the world. As the United States moved toward the twenty-first century, it faced a vast assortment of political, social, and environmental issues.

WRITE TO LEARN

Look at the chart on page 128. Then think about what you have read so far in this lesson.

In a notebook, write a few sentences answering the following question: Why do you think aid to South Korea decreased after 1960?

THINK ABOUT SOCIAL STUDIES

Directions: Complete these sentences.

1. President _____ established a policy of détente with China and met with Soviet leaders.

2. President Carter negotiated the _____, a historic peace agreement between Egypt and Israel.

3. After the collapse of the Soviet Union, most former satellite countries set up _____.

Vocabulary Review

Directions: Match these words with their definitions.

administration brinksmanship détente repression succeed

_____ 1. to follow or come after

_____ 2. the relaxing or easing of tensions between nations

_____ 3. the president and people appointed to work with him

_____ 4. to push each side to the edge of war

_____ 5. control by force

Directions: Study these charts related to gross domestic product (GDP) per capita. GDP per capita is the total value of all goods and services produced in a country in one year divided by the number of people in that country. Then answer the questions that follow.

China GDP per Capita (in current US dollars)	
1970	112
1975	176
1980	193
1985	292
1990	314
1995	604
2000	949
2005	1,731
2010	4,333

World Average GDP per Capita (in current US dollars)	
1970	785
1975	1,428
1980	2,479
1985	2,570
1990	4,151
1995	5,212
2000	5,285
2005	7,029
2010	9,166

1. What was China's GDP per capita in 1970? How does it compare to the world average for 1970?

_____

2. Between 1980 and 1985, which GDP per capita increased more: China's or the world average?

_____

3. What was China's GDP per capita in 2010? How does it compare to the world average for 2010?

_____

4. What trend applies to both sets of data?

_____

5. How would you describe the trend that the data shows when you compare China's GDP per capita to the world average?

_____

_____

6. What prediction can you make based on the trends you have identified?

_____

_____

Skill Practice

Directions: Choose the one best answer to each question. Questions 1 and 2 refer to the following map.

THE CUBAN MISSILE CRISIS

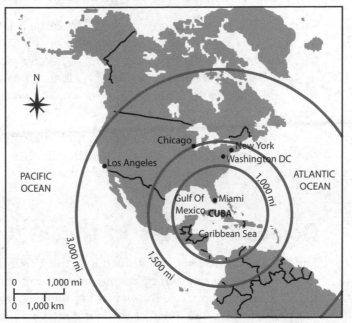

The rings shown in the map indicate the distances that the missiles could reach.

1. Many of the missiles installed in Cuba had a range of approximately 1,000 miles. If the missiles were launched from Cuba, which US city could they hit?

   A. Los Angeles
   B. Chicago
   C. Washington, DC
   D. Miami

2. On the basis of the map and your knowledge of the cold war, which statement summarizes why the Soviet Union would be interested in building bases in Cuba?

   A. The Soviet Union and Cuba were historic allies.
   B. Missiles launched from Cuba could hit the United States.
   C. Cuba could easily launch naval ships to target South America.
   D. The United States could not launch missiles in response to a Cuban threat.

Writing Practice

Directions: What is the main problem that you think the next US president should focus on? In a notebook, draft a short letter to him or her identifying and explaining that issue. Be sure to make your point of view clear.

Societal Changes

Lesson Objectives

You will be able to

- Identify US domestic issues from the 1970s through the 2000s

- Understand the issues and events important to the early environmental movement

- Learn about the technological revolution

Skills

- **Reading Skill:** Get Meaning from Context

- **Core Skill:** Interpret Graphics

Vocabulary

conservative
conserve
definition
emissions
example
liberal
technology

KEY CONCEPT: From the **1970s** through the **2000s**, the United States faced difficult economic and environmental issues. Many of these issues continue to challenge the United States today.

Many people are not aware of a problem in their lives until there are obvious signs of it. However, the problem may have been developing for some time. For example, individuals often have to deal with difficult health problems or personal budget issues that began before they realized it. Once a person is aware of the problem, steps can be taken to fix it.

A country's economic or environmental problems often come about in the same way. Existing conditions build until they become noticeable. Then the country must work to fix the problem.

Domestic Issues in the 1970s

The turmoil of the 1960s continued into the 1970s. Despite the progress made by the civil rights movement, minorities were still fighting for social justice. The war in Vietnam was winding down, but problems in other areas of the world affected the US economy.

Watergate Before the 1972 election, Nixon and his staff were worried about Nixon's chances of winning. In June, five men broke into the Democratic Party's national headquarters in Washington, DC. They were caught and arrested. It soon was revealed that one of the men worked for the Committee to Re-elect the President. Nixon denied knowing anything about the break-in.

After his re-election, a Senate committee continued to investigate the break-in. Information came out proving that Nixon had ordered a cover-up. He had also told the Central Intelligence Agency (CIA) to stop their investigation of the break-in. Facing impeachment, Nixon resigned on August 9, 1974.

Inflation and the Energy Crisis New federal government programs of the 1960s put large amounts of money into the economy. This led to **inflation**, which is a rise in the cost of goods and services. Energy costs were also rising. The United States depended on cheap oil **imports**, goods brought from a foreign country. A war in the Middle East caused oil prices to rise quickly. At one point, the Organization of Petroleum Exporting Countries (OPEC) stopped shipping fuel to the United States. When shipping resumed, prices continued to rise.

GET MEANING FROM CONTEXT

When you read, you might come across an unfamiliar word. When that happens, you can use a dictionary to find the word's meaning. Another way to find the meaning of an unfamiliar word is to look for clues in the context. Words that appear near the unfamiliar word are the context.

Two common types of context clues are **definitions** and **examples**.

A definition is a statement of the word's meaning. Sometimes the definition is surrounded by commas or appears inside parentheses.

> A <u>liberal</u> is someone who believes government regulations protect citizens.
>
> A <u>conservative</u>, someone who believes in limited government, is unlikely to support raising taxes.

An example provides a sample that helps the reader understand what a group of something is like. The words *for example, such as,* and *like* often signal example-type context clues.

> <u>Imports</u> such as oil, cars, and computers that are shipped into a country are important to a healthy economy.
>
> <u>Logos</u> like elephants and donkeys are associated with political parties.

Read the following sentence. Identify types of context clues provided for the underlined word.

> An <u>emission</u> is a substance, such as carbon dioxide or lead, that is released into the air. Common sources of emissions are power plants, factories, and automobiles that emit pollutants in their exhaust.

The first sentence defines the word *emission* as "a substance that is released into the air." The phrase *such as* introduces an example-type context clue. The second sentence gives examples of where emissions come from.

Reading Skill
Get Meaning
from Context

Sometimes the meaning of a word can be discovered through surrounding words or phrases. In these cases, it might be unnecessary to look up the word in a glossary or dictionary.

As you read the text on this page, circle words that are unfamiliar to you. Then look for context clues that provide examples or definitions of those words. Underline the context clues.

Conservation and Alternative Energy

Presidents Ford and Carter encouraged people to **conserve** energy. To *conserve* means to "prevent waste or overuse." People started looking into alternative energy sources. The first commercial nuclear power plant in the United States opened in 1957. The industry grew rapidly in the 1960s and 1970s. Nuclear energy is relatively cheap to produce, but it also has risks. An malfunction or accident in a plant can release radiation into the environment. Such an accident happened at the Three Mile Island plant in Pennsylvania in 1979.

When you "read" a political cartoon, look carefully at both the art and the words.

Study the cartoon on this page. Ask yourself these questions:

• Who is pictured in the cartoon?

• What does the text say?

The cartoon shows three drawings of the same person. The artist is telling the reader there are many opinions about this person. As a reader, you must interpret, or think about, the author's opinion about this person.

Write one sentence in your notebook stating the artist's opinion.

WRITE TO LEARN

In a notebook, write a paragraph comparing (describing similarities) and contrasting (describing differences) Presidents Ronald Reagan, George H. W. Bush, and Bill Clinton. Discuss their political parties, the positives or negatives resulting from their presidencies, and the state of the country when they left office.

The Reagan Years

Toward the end of the 1970s, the United States was becoming more conservative. In 1980, Republican Ronald Reagan was elected president. Many Americans supported his plans to cut taxes and increase defense spending. They also agreed with his conservative political philosophy. **Conservatives** generally want to limit government's role in regulating the economy and solving social problems.

To help the economy, Reagan and Congress passed a 25 percent tax cut. Major cuts were made to spending on social programs to keep the budget **deficit**, or shortage, under control. Reagan eliminated many government **regulations**, or rules, especially in the transportation, energy, and banking industries. The economy began to recover and Reagan won re-election in 1984. In 1988, his vice president, George H. W. Bush, was the Republican candidate. He, too, was elected.

relative size...

As the nation now sees him →

As conservative Republicans see him →

Reagan actual size—as we knew him ↓

* space does not allow halo to be shown

ED FISCHER

Urbanization

America continued to become a more urban nation. In 1970, more than 149 million people lived in urban areas. In 1990, that number had risen to more than 187 million people. Not everyone who lived in an urban area lived in the heart of a city. Many suburbs had grown so much that they were big enough to be considered urban areas themselves. This caused problems known **collectively** (as a whole) as "urban sprawl." Traffic and commuting times increased.

Smog, a form of air pollution, caused air quality to decline in many areas. Studies showed that car exhaust and other pollution sources caused health and environmental problems.

To control growing air pollution, the government began to regulate **emissions**, substances released into the air. The Clean Air Act of 1970 provided for state and federal regulation of emissions and for enforcement of those regulations. In the same year, the US Environmental Protection Agency (EPA) was established. It was the EPA's job to make sure that these regulations were created and put into practice.

Into the 1990s

George H. W. Bush, 1989–1993 The economy had grown throughout Reagan's presidency. In 1990, however, foreign and domestic problems led the nation into a recession. US businesses **downsized**, or cut back, in order to be more efficient. The rising national deficit also hurt the economy. The government had to borrow money to pay the interest on the national **debt**, which is the money owed by the national government. Despite a campaign promise, Bush was forced to raise taxes. Once again, many Americans were unhappy with the government and the direction of the nation. In the presidential election of 1992, Bush was defeated by Democratic candidate Bill Clinton.

William Jefferson Clinton, 1993–2001 Bill Clinton campaigned as a new kind of Democrat. In general, Democrats are considered **liberals**. Liberals believe that government should regulate industries in order to protect citizens. They also believe in strong government social programs. Clinton promised to cut government spending and taxes. He also promised to reform health care and government welfare programs.

Clinton believed that the key to economic growth was to lower interest rates. To do this, he had to reduce the budget deficit. Even though he had promised to cut taxes, he and Congress passed tax increases. They also agreed on legislation that required a balanced budget. The economy began to turn around. A boom began that turned out to be the longest period of economic growth in US history.

During Clinton's first term, an independent investigator was appointed to look into some business deals that Clinton was involved in as governor of Arkansas. Investigator Kenneth Starr later also examined whether the president had lied under oath when asked about his relationship with a White House intern. Starr's report led to impeachment hearings. The House of Representatives passed two articles of impeachment. However, the Senate vote was short of the two-thirds majority needed to impeach.

The Technological Revolution The economic boom was helped by the development of new technologies. **Technologies** are the machines and equipment developed from advances in scientific knowledge. The size, cost, and speed of computers was continually improving. In the late 1970s, companies such as Apple and IBM introduced new computers that were meant to be used at home.

In the 1990s, advances continued. Computers became faster and more powerful. The Internet connected computers all over the world. E-mail allowed people to communicate instantly. Cell phones became small and inexpensive enough for many people to use regularly. These new technologies made businesses more productive. Companies began selling products and services online. Some businesses, such as Amazon, exist only online.

Research It
Find Reliable Sources

Use online and print sources to learn more about alternative energy. Look for reliable information to answer these questions:

- What kinds of alternative energy exist?

- What are their benefits?

- What are their drawbacks?

In a notebook, write a short essay arguing for or against US investment in alternative energy forms.

THINK ABOUT
SOCIAL STUDIES

Directions: Write short responses to the following questions.

1. What are some beliefs that you can determine that most liberals may have in common?

   _____

2. What helped boost economic growth during former President Clinton's administration? _____

   _____

3. How does the Internet help businesses be more productive? _____

   _____

Vocabulary Review

Directions: Use these words to complete the following sentences.

conservatives   conserve   emissions   liberals   technologies

Both _____ and _____ have worked to solve the country's environmental issues. For example, President Nixon passed the Clean Air Act. This legislation regulated the _____ that cars and factories could produce. Presidents Ford and Carter encouraged all Americans to _____ energy. In the past several years, both Republican and Democratic presidential administrations have encouraged the development of new _____ to help the United States become energy independent.

Skill Review

Directions: Read the passage below and answer the questions in a notebook.

> The Nashua's pollution grew up with America. For more than a century, wood, wool, shoe, cotton, and paper mills had dumped waste into its quiet flow. . . . Because of dumped dyes, people used to bet on whether it was going to be red, orange, blue, green, or white the next day. Then a woman named Marion Stoddart started a campaign to restore the Nashua and its tributaries. It's been called a one-woman crusade, but in many ways it worked because it wasn't. . . .
>
> —Michael Parfit, *National Geographic*, November 1993

1. The passage does not tell you what the Nashua is. From context clues, what do you think the Nashua is?

2. Which context clues helped you determine what the Nashua is?

Directions: Look at the cartoons below. Then answer the question.

3. What comparisons and contrasts can you make about the two cartoons?

Skill Practice

Directions: Choose the <u>one best answer</u> to each question. <u>Questions 1 and 2</u> refer to the following graph.

US NATIONAL DEBT, 1940–2010

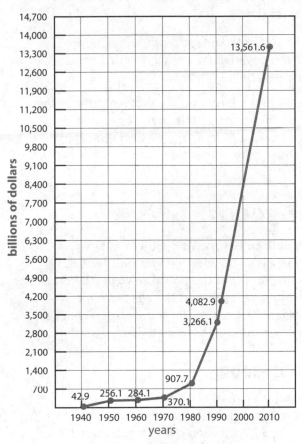

Source: *American Almanac 2010*

1. During which 10-year period did the national debt show the largest dollar increase?

   A. 1940–1950
   B. 1960–1970
   C. 1970–1980
   D. 1990–2000

2. What was the difference in the national debt between 1970 and 1960?

   A. $538 billion
   B. $213 billion
   C. $86 billion
   D. $28 billion

3. Which statement provides a cause for President Nixon's impeachment?

   A. He wanted to win the reelection.
   B. He ordered a cover-up of the Watergate break-in.
   C. He tampered with the voting process.
   D. He broke into the Democratic National Committee offices.

4. Which was a cause of increased urbanization?

   A. a decrease in air pollution
   B. an increase in suburban population
   C. a decrease in commuting times
   D. an increase in industrial jobs

Writing Practice

Directions: Taxes are a big issue in every political election. Although most people would like to pay lower taxes, most people want more government services and benefits. Write an essay describing some of the benefits you receive from the government. Think about all aspects of your life—health, travel, recreation, voting privileges, as well as cash benefits such as unemployment insurance.

The United States in the Twenty-First Century

KEY CONCEPT: In the first decade of the twenty-first century, the United States experienced a terrorist attack, elected its first African American president, and suffered its largest economic decline since the Great Depression.

Think about an issue that has affected you recently. How did it change your daily life? Did the government do anything to respond to the issue? Did that have any effect on you?

The first decade of the twenty-first century was a turbulent time in the United States. Many important historical events occurred, events that affected people's priorities and way of life. These events also affected what people expected from their government.

The Election of 2000

In the election of 2000, Republican George W. Bush ran against Vice President Al Gore. The result of the election was not decided for more than a month. Although Gore won the **popular vote** (the total of all votes cast across the country), Bush won the electoral vote. A presidential candidate needs 270 votes to win the electoral college vote. In the end, Bush had 271 votes, and Gore had 267.

George W. Bush, 2001–2009

Bush was a conservative Republican. Early in his first term, the economy was slowing. To turn it around, Congress passed spending cuts that were expected to save $1.35 trillion over 10 years. In 2003, Congress passed a bill adding prescription drug benefits to Medicare. They also passed education reform laws that were intended to increase the **accountability**, or responsibility, of schools and teachers and to set a standard for education across the country.

Bush was more of an isolationist than previous presidents. He ended talks with North Korea that aimed to keep North Korea from developing nuclear weapons. Bush insisted that other nations (South Korea, Japan, and Russia) be involved before restarting talks.

In spite of Bush's tendency toward isolationism, he announced a major new initiative in his State of the Union address in 2003. He asked Congress to provide $15 billion to battle AIDS, tuberculosis, malaria, and other diseases in Africa and the Caribbean.

IDENTIFY AUTHOR'S BIAS

A **bias** is a belief, preference, or prejudice. Not all writers express their bias when writing, but sometimes writers use their bias to influence readers. One way to investigate author's bias is to see whether the author's statements can be proven.

When you read, look for words that express strong opinions and positive or negative feelings. Read between the lines.

Read the passage below and then answer these questions:

- Is the author for or against the war in Iraq?
- What words does the author use that express bias?
- Is the author trying to convince the reader that the war positively or negatively impacted the United States?
- Does the author back up the argument with facts?

> President Obama has pledged that by August 31, 2010 . . . all combat troops will be out of Iraq and by the end of 2011 all American troops will be gone.
>
> For a badly overstretched American military it will certainly be time to go. Repeated deployments have taken a huge toll on soldiers and their families. The Iraq war—an unnecessary war— has **diverted** [directed] critically needed resources away from Afghanistan, the real front in the war on terrorism.
>
> —*New York Times* Editorial page, June 29, 2009

The passage begins by stating a fact: President Obama has promised to remove all US troops from Iraq by the end of 2011. The tone and language used in the second paragraph indicate that the author is against the war in Iraq. Phrases like "badly overstretched," "huge toll," and "unnecessary war" show the author's bias. The author is trying to convince the reader that the war negatively impacted the United States. The author does not provide any facts to support that opinion.

REAL WORLD
CONNECTION

Remember the Event

As you read about the events described in this lesson, recall where you were and what you were doing as each event occurrred. Make notes about what you remember.

When you have finished reading, choose one event and write a journal entry about how it affected your life, both at the time of the event and later.

September 11, 2001

On the morning of September 11, 2001, Bush's view of the world changed. **Terrorists**, people who use fear and violence for political gain, attacked the United States. Two commercial airliners were flown into the World Trade Center in New York City. Another plane targeted the Pentagon in Washington, DC. A fourth plane, flying over Pennsylvania, crashed when passengers fought back against the terrorists on board. More than 3,000 people died in the September 11, 2001 attacks, including many first responders.

A group known as al-Qaeda claimed responsibility for the attacks. Al-Qaeda is an Islamic **fundamentalist** group. Fundamentalists believe in strict traditional interpretation of religious beliefs or principles. Al-Qaeda has claimed responsibility for attacks worldwide.

Global War on Terror

On September 20, 2001, Bush said, "Our war on terror begins with al-Qaeda. . . . It will not end until every terrorist group of global reach has been found, stopped and defeated." Afghanistan was run by the Taliban, a fundamentalist group that allowed al-Qaeda to operate in the country. Al-Qaeda had terrorist training bases there. In October 2001, US troops were sent to overthrow the Taliban and destroy al-Qaeda.

Iraq War

In 2002, the Bush administration was fairly certain that Iraq had **weapons of mass destruction** (WMDs). WMDs are chemical, biological, and nuclear weapons. In 2003, US troops, along with forces from several other nations, invaded Iraq. The Iraqi army was quickly defeated, and Iraqi dictator Saddam Hussein was captured. Unfortunately Hussein's removal left the country without a government. **Insurgents**, or armed rebels, resisted change. Even after a new constitution was written and a new government formed, Iraq remained unstable.

In 2007, costs were continuing to rise and the war was becoming increasingly unpopular with Americans. In an effort to stop the violence, Bush sent about 30,000 additional troops. The "**surge**" (rush), as it became known, helped reduce the instability.

The Election of 2008

In 2008, many Americans were angry about the continuing war in Iraq and discouraged by the decline in the economy. The 2008 election featured two firsts: an African American man (Senator Barack Obama) and a woman (Senator Hillary Clinton) were serious contenders for the Democratic nomination. After a long primary season, Obama won the Democratic nomination for presidency. He ran against Republican Senator John McCain.

Barack Obama, 2009–2016

Barack Obama was the first African American elected to the presidency and the third African American to win the Nobel Peace Prize. He promised to withdraw US troops from Iraq, cut taxes for middle class families, and reform health care. One of Obama's first acts as president was to submit an **economic stimulus** package. An economic stimulus is a program of government spending designed to boost the economy. In March 2010, Obama signed into law the Affordable Care Act. This law ensures all Americans access to health insurance.

The Iraq war ended in August 2010; however, US troops went on fighting in Afghanistan. In addition, the war on terror continued. On May 2, 2011, US forces attacked a compound in Pakistan, killing the al-Qaeda leader, Osama bin Laden.

Challenges for the Twenty-First Century

As the second decade of the twenty-first century began, the United States faced several continuing challenges.

Economic Issues

In 2007–2008, a recession led to a rapid economic decline in housing, banks, auto manufacturers, and many other areas. Unemployment rose to almost 10 percent in 2009. By 2013, unemployment had dropped below 8 percent. The globalization of financial institutions meant that trouble in one country affected the rest of the world. Many US companies opened offices and factories overseas, moving jobs to countries where hiring workers was less expensive.

Environmental Issues

Americans were becoming increasingly aware of environmental issues. Drastic climate change, also known as **global warming** was a great concern. This concern grew in 2012, as heat waves and storms, like Hurricane Sandy, affected much of the United States. The need to develop renewable energy resources became more urgent. Automobile companies worked to develop cars that ran on biologically-based fuels other than gasoline. Other companies created new materials and technologies that generated power from sustainable energy sources such as wind, the Sun, and heat deep in the ground.

Mienny Photography/Getty Images

Foreign Policy

Great challenges existed for the United States in foreign policy as well. These were some of the problems:

- the rise of China as a world power
- continuing instability in North Africa and the Middle East
- North Korea's isolation and nuclear capacity
- hostility and nuclear ambitions in Iran

Core Skill
Analyze Point of View

Both written texts and visuals can express point of view. As you read written texts and study photographs and cartoons, ask yourself whether the writer or artist is for or against an issue.

Read "Environmental Issues" and ask yourself why the photograph has been included with the text. What is the author's point of view about the topic? Ask yourself these questions:

- Is the author concerned about environmental issues?

- Or does the author think people should worry more about other matters?

- Or is the author unbiased—that is, do you think the author does not have a strong opinion about this topic?

In your notebook, write one sentence expressing the author's point of view as it relates to the photograph.

THINK ABOUT SOCIAL STUDIES

Directions: Write short responses to the following questions in a notebook.

1. What made the presidential election of 2008 historic?

2. Which twenty-first century challenge facing the United States do you think will be most difficult to overcome? Why do you think this?

Vocabulary Review

Directions: Match these words with their definitions.

accountability   economic stimulus   impact   insurgent   surge

_____ 1. government spending to help the economy

_____ 2. the rapid build-up of troops to stop violence

_____ 3. force or effect

_____ 4. armed rebel

_____ 5. responsibility

Skill Review

Directions: Read the opinion passage below. Answer the questions that follow in a notebook.

The idea that global warming is a fact is absurd! There is no reliable technology that can predict long-term climate change. Most weather technology can't even correctly predict tomorrow's weather. If the world's temperature is meant to rise, then what does human activity have to do with it? Even if there is an increase in climate temperature, there would not be much difference when the increase is spread out over hundreds of years. Meanwhile, attention and resources are being used to fight this "issue" when they should be fighting real issues like poverty and nuclear weapons.

1. What is the author's opinion?

2. Which words and phrases show the author's bias?

Directions: Examine the photograph below. Answer the questions that follow in a notebook.

3. What do you think the photo shows?

4. What can you interpret is the photographer's opinion may be about the issue portrayed in the photo?

Skill Practice

Directions: Directions: Choose the <u>one best answer</u> to each question. <u>Questions 1 and 2</u> refer to the following text.

> The politicians pushed it through Congress even though "we the people" were clearly opposed to it. We took it to the Supreme Court, but even the justices sided with those spendthrift liberals in the White House and Congress. Now we're stuck with Obamacare. Now we all have to buy health insurance, whether we want it or not—and whether we can afford it or not. If we don't buy it, we have to pay anyway because they'll fine us. What's more, Obamacare is too expensive. It's going to mean more government spending and more government debt. The Affordable Care Act isn't affordable for Americans, and it's not affordable for America either.

1. Which assumption does the writer make about government?

   A. Having three branches of government provides a good system of checks and balances.
   B. Government debt is higher than it has ever been.
   C. All the branches of government side against the people.
   D. The government wants the people to pay off the US debt.

3. Which statement shows the relationship between the surge of troops to Iraq in 2007 and the level of violence?

   A. The surge led to increased violence.
   B. The surge led to decreased violence.
   C. The level of violence was not affected by the surge.
   D. The level of violence rose when the surge ended.

2. Which statement is most likely true about the writer?

   A. The author believes the US economy is strong.
   B. The author feels Obamacare should be done away with.
   C. The author has faith in the Affordable Care Act.
   D. The author believes no one should have health insurance.

4. How can government spending help reverse economic decline in the United States?

   A. Providing people and industries with money encourages them to spend money. This keeps the economy moving.
   B. People's salaries will increase.
   C. The government will create new industries and new products.
   D. If people see the government spending money, they will want to spend as well.

Writing Practice

Directions: What qualities does the president of the United States need? Write a job posting advertisement for a new president.

Directions: Choose the <u>one best answer</u> to each question. <u>Questions 1 and 2</u> refer to the passage below.

> American military leaders did not want to get involved in direct action in Bosnia-Herzegovina, a country in southeastern Europe, during the early 1990s. They knew the American public would not support direct military action. High-level US Defense Department sources reported that military leaders were well aware of the unpopularity of the Vietnam War. In that war, about 58,000 Americans were killed and some 153,000 were wounded. The war cost more than $140 billion. Because of the lack of public support for the Vietnam War, US military leadership urged the administration to be cautious about direct military involvement in Bosnia-Herzegovina.

1. According to the passage, why were US military leaders reluctant to urge involvement in Bosnia-Herzegovina?

   A. They did not believe that the public would support military action.
   B. They were worried about the training needed for US troops.
   C. They believed that neighboring countries would not support US troops.
   D. They did not have enough information about the conflict in Bosnia-Herzegovina.

2. How does a foreign policy of isolationism support this passage?

   A. Nations should not get involved in the conflicts of other nations.
   B. The number of deaths caused by war should be reduced.
   C. Nations are most successful when they fight their own wars.
   D. Americans do not like people in other countries.

3. Why was the space race important to the United States and the Soviet Union?

   A. Space exploration and discovery would provide huge sources of information about outer space.
   B. The space race heightened the tension already existing between the two countries.
   C. Advancements in space exploration would be helpful in the development of nations around the world.
   D. Competition is a healthy way for nations to interact with each other.

4. Why did the United States become involved in the global war on terror?

   A. Many other countries were already fighting against al-Qaeda terrorists.
   B. The terrorist attacks in the United States on September 11, 2001, led to US involvement.
   C. The United States was not directly involved in the war on terrorism, but it supported other countries that were.
   D. Terrorism affects all countries, so the United Nations required all countries to get involved.

5. President Lyndon Johnson's Great Society programs included Medicaid, the Office of Economic Opportunity, and Head Start. Which group was intended to benefit the most from his programs?

   A. the poor
   B. the elderly
   C. the young
   D. the wealthy

6. The United States entered World War II three years after it started. Why did the United States wait?

   A. The United States did not have the finances to join the war.
   B. Public opinion was not in favor of joining the fight.
   C. German submarine attacks led to the loss of US lives.
   D. The United States decided it would lose its status as a powerful nation if it joined the war.

7. Which new technology greatly influenced the 1960 presidential election?

   A. radio
   B. e-mail
   C. television
   D. the Internet

8. What was the primary goal of US military actions in Korea and Vietnam?

   A. to eradicate terrorism
   B. to liberate East Germany
   C. to defeat Nazi Germany and its allies
   D. to prevent the spread of communism

9. Which of the following is a direct effect of urban sprawl?

   A. traffic
   B. inflation
   C. high gas prices
   D. alternative energy

10. What cause did the Freedom Riders draw attention to?

    A. the draft
    B. segregation
    C. poverty
    D. unequal pay for women

11. How did President Truman affect relations between North and South Korea?

    A. He asked Congress to declare war and sent US troops to defend South Korea.
    B. He helped negotiate peace between the two countries.
    C. He asked the UN to send troops to defend South Korea.
    D. He helped South Korea establish an alliance with the Soviet Union.

12. In which way was President Barack Obama unique?

    A. He involved the United States in wars in the Middle East.
    B. He was the first president to focus on health care.
    C. He was the first African American to become president.
    D. He was the first president to face a global economic crisis.

13. Which of these trends had the greatest effect on the way that Americans communicate with one another?

    A. The desire to conserve energy led to a decrease in the manufacturing of writing insruments.
    B. Urban sprawl meant that people were living outside the heart of major cities.
    C. Worry over carbon emissions kept people from traveling to see friends and family.
    D. Smaller, cheaper technology allowed more people to have home computers.

14. What did the United Farm Workers fight for in the 1960s?

    A. equal pay for women and men
    B. a ban on job discrimination based on race, color, religion, national origin, or gender
    C. a ban for gender-based discrimination in publicly funded schools
    D. improvements in wages and benefits for workers

Review

Check Your Understanding

On the following chart, circle the number of any question you answered incorrectly. In the third column, you will see the pages you can review to study the content covered in the question. Pay particular attention to reviewing those lessons in which you missed half or more of the questions.

Chapter 3 Review

Lesson	Item Number	Review Pages
World War II, the Cold War, and the 1950s	1, 2, 6	110–117
Protest and Politics	5, 7, 10, 14	118–123
US Foreign Policy in the Modern Era	3, 8, 11	124–131
Societal Changes	9	132–137
The United States in the Twenty-First Century	4, 12, 13	138–143

ESSAY WRITING PRACTICE

US History: World War II through Modern Times

Directions: You are preparing a study guide to help students use this history chapter. It is up to you to decide which six events since World War II have been the most significant in US history. First, select those six events. Then, make a time line showing these events. Finally, write an essay in response to the prompt below. Look at the chapter opener to review time lines. Review Lessons 3.1, 3.2, 3.3, 3.4, and 3.5 to identify major events.

TIME LINE

A time line is a quick way to see the big picture for a given period of time. It includes important events that occurred over the time period. The events are shown in order. The year is labeled, and a short phrase describes each event.

Show your six major US history events since World War II on a time line similar to this one.

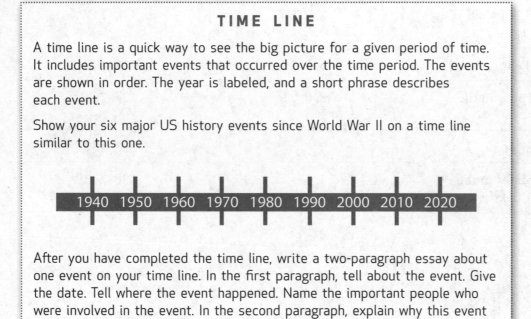

1940 1950 1960 1970 1980 1990 2000 2010 2020

After you have completed the time line, write a two-paragraph essay about one event on your time line. In the first paragraph, tell about the event. Give the date. Tell where the event happened. Name the important people who were involved in the event. In the second paragraph, explain why this event is important in modern US history.

UNIT 2

Global Connections

World History and Political Systems

Have you ever met people from another state or another country? Perhaps you had an interesting discussion with those people, comparing and contrasting where you live with where they live. You may have noticed that despite some differences, there were things you had in common. In a similar way, the study of the history and culture of other nations shows the scope of human activity. It can give you a clearer idea of how civilizations have formed and changed throughout time.

In this chapter, you will learn how urbanization changed the way people live. You will see how technological changes have enabled people around the world to work together. You will understand how population growth can lead to a scarcity of natural resources.

In this chapter you will study these topics:

Lesson 4.1: Political Theories and Systems in World History
Governments make and enforce their country's laws. In a monarchy or a dictatorship, a single ruler controls the government. In an oligarchy, a small group controls the government. In a democracy, the citizens control the government. No matter how governments are structured, they must interact with one another.

Lesson 4.2: International Organizations
The United Nations, the world's largest diplomatic organization, was set up to keep peace between nations. Other international organizations have been formed for economic or military reasons.

Lesson 4.3: International Relations
The US government forms relationships with other nations around the world. The president generally takes the lead in setting foreign policy goals. The president appoints ambassadors to other countries and is the commander in chief of the armed forces.

Lesson 4.4: The World in the Twenty-First Century
Technology has led to globalization, which has been beneficial in many ways to the world's economies. However, the world is challenged by increased population, the overuse of nonrenewable energy resources, and terrorism.

Goal Setting

Why is it important to study world history?

- to find out what events shaped the development of various civilizations

- to understand how countries interact

- to understand the progression of ideas and technology

Think about the reasons people study world history.

- to understand different cultures

- to understand why cities and countries formed as they did

- to understand how cities and countries change over time to meet the needs of their citizens

- to find out what challenges people and how people respond to these challenges

- to understand how new ideas and technology are used worldwide

What do you hope to learn from the lessons in this chapter? List some of your ideas here. As you read this chapter, think about these goals.

_____

_____

_____

_____

_____

Political Theories and Systems in World History

KEY CONCEPT: Governments are classified by who leads the government and how citizens participate in the government. The United States is a representative democracy.

Think of a situation where you were told what to do. How willingly did you perform the duty assigned to you? In contrast, think of a situation where you were asked for suggestions about how to handle a particular task. In this case, you probably had more enthusiasm for doing your duty.

In some countries, people do not have a say in the decisions made by the government. Resentment and unrest can grow under this type of government. In democracies, however, the people run the government. They may do so directly or through elected representatives.

What Is Government?

A **government** is the body that makes and **administers**, or manages, society's laws. Most governments promote the general welfare of their people in the areas of health, safety, education, and aid to the needy. The police and the courts maintain order. The armed forces provide security against attack.

Political science is the study of governments and how they work. Political scientists study governmental structure and policy making, political parties, interest groups, and international relations.

A political system is an **institution**, or organization, that shapes the power relationships in a society. People have created a wide variety of political systems. The earliest systems had no formal structure. Important decisions were often made by one person or by a council. As societies became more complex, people created more complicated forms of government.

Functions of Government

All governments perform these three necessary functions:

- executive (administer the government and carry out the laws)
- legislative (make the laws)
- judicial (interpret the laws)

All governments possess the power to make decisions and carry them out. Some governments rule by direct force or by the threat of force against their citizens. Others rule with the support of their citizens.

UNDERSTAND THE AUTHOR'S PURPOSE

Everything you read is written for a reason. This reason is called the author's **purpose**. The basic reasons for writing are to inform, to entertain, and to persuade. Identifying the author's purpose will help you understand a passage.

When the author's purpose is to inform, the author provides information about a topic. If the author's purpose is to entertain, the writing will be funny or interesting. Finally, if the purpose is to persuade, the author might present only one side of an argument or only a few facts because the author want to convince you to share his or her opinion.

To identify the author's purpose, ask yourself these questions: *What is the author writing about? Is the author offering factual information? Is the author writing to entertain? Is the author trying to persuade me to think a certain way?*

Read the following paragraph and identify the author's purpose.

> Without government, who would take responsibility for building highways, certifying teachers, protecting the environment, and all the other tasks that government does? Private companies might take on these projects, but they would have to be paid. Where would the money come from? As much as people complain about government, most would agree that it is necessary.

This passage states the opinion that government is necessary. The author supports this argument by identifying the important work of the government. The author implies that it would be too expensive if private companies did this work. The author's purpose is to persuade the reader that people need government.

Reading Skill
Understand the Author's Purpose

An author's purpose is usually to inform, to entertain, or to persuade. To figure out an author's purpose, ask yourself these questions:

- Does the author offer factual information?

- Is this passage fun to read?

- Does the author express an opinion?

Find a newspaper article on a topic that interests you. Read the article. Then write one sentence in your notebook identifying the author's purpose for writing the article. Use the questions above to help you figure out that purpose.

When the people believe that the government is not working in their interest, governmental authority can break down. If a government uses force against the people, the struggle can **escalate**, or increase. Some governments have been overthrown by revolution. A good example is the American colonists' fight against the British government. Governments may also be overthrown by a small group rather than by a popular uprising. This kind of action is called a **coup d'état**, which means "a blow against the state."

WRITE TO LEARN

In the United States, the executive branch of government is headed by the president. Write one paragraph telling what you know about the current president of the United States.

Most illustrations reflect the artist's viewpoint about a subject. For example, a photographer who is unhappy with a particular president may try to catch a shot of the president looking angry or bored.

Similarly, political cartoonists express their personal opinions about an issue when they address that issue in a cartoon. When you figure out the cartoon's main message, you can usually tell how the artist feels about the issue.

Study the cartoon on this page. Use a dictionary to look up any words in the cartoon that are unfamiliar.

In a notebook, identify the topic of the cartoon. Then write a few sentences saying what you believe the artist's opinion is about this topic.

Types of Governments

There are four main types of government. They are monarchy, democracy, oligarchy, and dictatorship.

Monarchy

Monarchy is one of the oldest forms of government. In a monarchy, a king or a queen is the head of the government. Queen Elizabeth II of Great Britain and King Harald V of Norway are monarchs.

Countries that have both constitutions and monarchs are called **constitutional monarchies**. Great Britain is a constitutional monarchy. The queen's tasks are chiefly ceremonial. She reigns, but she does not rule. Instead, Great Britain has a prime minister, a cabinet, and a permanent civil service. These officials carry out the day-to-day job of governing. They do so according to laws passed by Parliament, which is the legislative branch. In Britain, one house of Parliament is popularly elected.

Countries where the monarch's word is the law are called **absolute monarchies**. King Abdullah II of Saudi Arabia is an absolute monarch. The country has no constitution, no parliament, and no political parties. Sometimes absolute monarchs claim to rule by **divine right**. This means that they believe their right to rule comes from God.

England, France, and Russia used to be absolute monarchies, but the people overthrew Charles I in 1649, King Louis XVI during the French Revolution in 1792, and Tsar Nicholas II in the Russian Revolution of 1917.

Democracy

A second type of government is **democracy**. The power to rule in a democracy comes from the people. (In Greek, *demos* means "people," and *cracy* means "power" or "form of government.") The United States is a democracy in which the people take part in the government. Some other countries, such as France and India, are also democracies.

Democracy has deep roots in Western political tradition. It can take a variety of forms. In ancient Greek city-states, it took the form of a direct democracy. Greek citizens participated directly in running the government. In contrast, the United States has a **representative democracy**. The country is too large for everyone to gather to discuss and vote on laws as they did in ancient Greece. Instead, the people elect representatives to carry out their wishes according to the Constitution. In a representative democracy, all people over a certain age have the right to vote. The decisions that guide the government, however, are made by elected representatives rather than by the citizens themselves. The largest representative democracy in today's world is India, with a population of more than 1.2 billion.

Representative democracy reflects ideas expressed during the 1600s and 1700s. At that time, Enlightenment thinkers wrote about a social contract in which those in power rule through the consent of the governed.

Slane, Chris/CartoonStock.com

Oligarchy

A third type of government is **oligarchy**, which is government controlled by a few. Before the Industrial Revolution, England was considered an oligarchy. Even though it had a monarch whose powers had been limited, the real power was in the hands of a few members of Parliament. Voting was limited to people with a certain income. Therefore, the aristocracy and rich merchants controlled the government.

Some of the ancient Greek city-states were oligarchies ruled by a few leading families. The seafaring Republic of Venice was ruled by the most elite merchants. The rest of the people had no say in the government. Some countries today might be considered oligarchies even though they would not call themselves that. Certain developing countries, particularly in Latin America, have long been ruled by leading families who control the economies of these countries.

Dictatorship

Throughout history, many countries have struggled under a form of government known as **dictatorship**. A dictator rules like an absolute monarch but does not use royal titles such as *king* or *emperor*. In modern times, dictators have become totalitarian rulers. Under **totalitarianism**, all parts of life are under the complete control of one ruler who has all the power. Joseph Stalin of the Soviet Union and Adolf Hitler of Germany were totalitarian dictators. Both kept control through a secret police that terrorized people so they could not oppose the government. The Communist Party in the Soviet Union had this role from 1918 to 1990. The Nazi Party in Germany supported Hitler from 1933 until 1945, when the Allied victory in World War II ended his rule.

At the present time, a few developing countries are dictatorships, particularly in Africa and Asia. North Korea is one of the last Communist dictatorships. Although countries with dictators often have constitutions and legislative bodies, the wishes of the dictators are always carried out over the wishes of the people.

> ### Research It
> Compare and Contrast
>
> In the United States, people take freedom of speech for granted, but this freedom is not guaranteed in every country.
>
> With a partner, conduct research to identify three countries where citizens have freedom of speech and three countries where they do not. Find out what type of government each of the countries has.
>
> With your partner, discuss how freedom of speech is affected by the type of government that a country has.

A Global Perspective

Thanks to modern systems of transportation, communications, and marketing, people in one part of the world are more connected to other parts of the world than they have been in the past. These connections can affect government.

These connections can also affect political relationships between countries. For instance, conflicts between France and Germany led to two world wars in the twentieth century. Today, however, these two countries both belong to the European Union. Their use of a shared currency and their common economic goals have led to a peaceful relationship.

>
> ### THINK ABOUT SOCIAL STUDIES
>
> **Directions:** Match each type of government with a country where it is found.
>
> 1. dictatorship
> 2. absolute monarchy
> 3. constitutional monarchy
> 4. representative democracy
>
> A. India
> B. Great Britain
> C. North Korea
> D. Saudi Arabia

Vocabulary Review

Directions: Use these words to complete the following sentences.

administering   democracy   escalate   governments   institutions

1. Governments are responsible for making and _____ the laws of the country.

2. All _____ have executive, legislative, and judicial functions.

3. In one form of _____, the people are represented by the leaders they elect.

4. Political scientists study how the _____ of government work.

5. Tensions between the government and its people may _____ if issues are not resolved.

Skill Review

Directions: Write your answers on the lines.

1. Use these terms to identify the author's purpose for writing each of these articles.

   to inform   to entertain   to persuade

   _____ A. editorial in a national newspaper

   _____ B. campaign ad for a person running for Congress

   _____ C. government brochure entitled "How to Vote"

   _____ D. political cartoon

   _____ E. short story in a magazine

Directions: Using the photograph and the information in this lesson, answer the following questions.

North Korean leader Kim Jong-un (seated, in dark coat)

Skill Review (continued)

2. Describe the people in the photo and tell what they are doing.

_____

3. What viewpoint do you think the photographer has of Kim Jong-un—positive, negative, or unbiased? Explain your answer.

_____

_____

4. When looking at this photo, what opinion do you have of Kim Jong-un? Explain your answer.

_____

_____

5. What opinion do you think North Koreans would have of Kim Jong-un when they look at this photo. Explain your answer.

_____

_____

Skill Practice

Directions: Choose the one best answer to each question.

1. Which conclusion could be made about an oligarchy?

   A. Most people are happy because the government provides for them.
   B. Oligarchies have existed for a long time, so they must be a good form of government.
   C. Control of the government by the upper class means the beliefs of that class have great influence on the laws.
   D. Even though only a few people control government, the views of most of the people are represented.

2. Which is a function of all governments?

   A. making laws
   B. forming political parties
   C. avoiding revolution
   D. controlling the economy

3. Which statement best explains the difference between a dictatorship and a totalitarian dictatorship?

   A. In a dictatorship, a small group controls the government. In a totalitarian dictatorship, only one person controls the government.
   B. In a dictatorship, one person controls the government. In a totalitarian dictatorship, one person controls everything except political, social, and economic matters.
   C. In a dictatorship, the majority rules. In a totalitarian dictatorship, every person has input in government matters.
   D. In a dictatorship, one person controls the government. In a totalitarian dictatorship, one person controls not only the government but also all political, social, and economic matters.

Writing Practice

Directions: Research a government leader who is often in the news. Then use your research to write two newspaper editorials—one in favor of the person and the other one against the person.

International Organizations

KEY CONCEPT: International organizations are made up of members from two or more nations. They are formed for diplomatic, economic, or military reasons.

Have you ever heard the expression "there's safety in numbers" or "there's strength in numbers"? These expressions mean that when people join together, they can help to keep one another safe. A group of people facing danger stands a better chance of survival than one lone person does.

The United States and many other countries agree with this idea. They have formed international organizations—organizations whose members come from a variety of nations—to improve the well-being of people around the world.

International Organizations

International organizations have played an increasingly important role in foreign policy. **Foreign policy** is the plan a country has for interacting with other countries. One of the most important roles played by any international organization is the prevention of war and other forms of global conflict. International organizations fall into three categories: diplomatic, economic, and military.

Diplomatic Organizations To be **diplomatic** means to be involved with managing relations between countries. Diplomatic organizations promote understanding between nations and work to prevent serious conflicts. Two important diplomatic organizations in recent history are the League of Nations (1919–1939) and the United Nations (UN) (1945–present). The League of Nations was formed after World War I. It was an organization of 65 countries that joined together to try to stop such a war from ever happening again. The United States never joined the League. Many Americans believed joining the organization would threaten US independence. In addition, Americans wished to return to a policy of isolationism. **Isolationism** is the unwillingness to become involved in the affairs of the world.

The League of Nations lacked any power to enforce its decisions. It finally collapsed with the beginning of World War II.

The UN was formed at the end of World War II. US leaders realized the need for an international peacekeeping organization. World War II showed them that isolationism was no longer in the best interests of the country. Instead, the United States became increasingly involved in world affairs. Due to this new outlook, the United States was the first nation to **ratify**, or sign, the UN charter in 1945.

The UN was **established**, or set up, to keep peace among nations and to encourage friendly interaction among all the nations of the world. The UN helps countries cooperate to solve economic and social problems. As of 2013, the UN is composed of 193 members. Their goal is to promote basic human rights throughout the world.

UNDERSTAND THE MAIN IDEA

Everything you read has a main idea. Finding the main idea will help you understand what you read.

Often the main idea of a passage is stated in the first sentence. However, the main idea can appear anywhere within a passage. Sometimes it may not be stated as a single sentence. Instead, you may need to summarize several key points to understand the main idea.

To understand the main idea, ask yourself these questions: *What is the paragraph about? What is the author's most important idea?*

Read this passage. Then identify the main idea in the passage.

---

(1) The United Nations (UN) is headed by a secretary-general. (2) The secretary-general is elected by the members of the UN General Assembly, which includes a representative from each member country. (3) The secretary-general serves for five years. (4) At the end of this time, he or she can be re-elected to another term. (5) There have been eight secretaries-general since the UN was established. (6) The current secretary-general is from South Korea.

Sentence 1 states the main idea: the UN is headed by a secretary-general. Sentences 2 through 6 provide details about the office of the secretary-general.

Core Skill
Determine
Central Ideas

Writers support their main ideas with details. These **supporting details** expand on the main idea or make it clearer. For example, when discussing international organizations, the writer might include such details as the names, history, and purpose of important organizations.

Read the passage below from *Encyclopedia Brittanica*. Then, in a notebook, list the details that describe the functions of international organizations.

"International organizations serve many diverse functions, including collecting information and monitoring trends . . . , delivering services and aid . . . , and providing forums for bargaining . . . and settling disputes. . . . By providing political institutions through which states can work together to achieve common objectives, international organizations can help to foster cooperative behaviour."

The General Assembly of the UN is made up of one representative from each member nation. These representatives vote on questions of world peace and other issues. Most of the UN's real decision-making power, however, resides in the powerful Security Council. It consists of 15 members, five of which are permanent: the United States, the United Kingdom, China, Russia, and France. The Security Council investigates disagreements that might threaten world peace. The General Assembly and the Security Council together choose the UN secretary-general. The secretary-general is the organization's spokesperson and leader.

The UN provides a way for nations to air their disagreements and for diplomats to communicate with one another. The UN also organizes international peacekeeping forces to oversee the settlement of disputes. To accomplish its peacekeeping goals, the UN undertakes military operations around the world. More than 100 countries contribute troops to these peacekeeping operations.

The UN includes many important agencies. The World Health Organization (WHO) promotes better health for the people of the world. The Food and Agricultural Organization (FAO) works to increase food production and improve distribution of food. The Educational, Scientific, and Cultural Organization (UNESCO) provides education about people and cultures, and the United Nations Children's Fund (UNICEF) provides assistance to children in developing countries.

Economic Organizations International economic organizations encourage world trade, find loans for economic development, and **obtain**, or get, better markets for exports. Economic organizations also provide **forums**, or meetings, for settling trade disagreements between countries.

The Organization of Petroleum Exporting Countries (OPEC) was formed to regulate the oil production of member countries in order to control world oil prices. The organization was founded in 1960 by five oil-producing countries: Iran, Iraq, Kuwait, Saudi Arabia, and Venezuela. Today the group has 12 members, which produce about 40 percent of the world's oil supply.

The European Union (EU) is an organization of 27 nations from both Western and Eastern Europe. These countries have joined together to formulate common economic, social, and security policies. The organization has taken many steps to unify Europe. For example, the EU has its own currency: the euro. Major decisions for the union are made by the Council of Ministers. This group is composed of an ever-changing membership, depending on the issue under discussion.

THINK ABOUT SOCIAL STUDIES

Directions: Match the words with the descriptions.

1. _____ euro

2. _____ OPEC

3. _____ Security Council

A. organization regulating oil production

B. UN decision-making body

C. EU currency

Military Alliances Military alliances are formed to provide countries with with defense and security. An **alliance** is a formal agreement that establishes an association between nations. The North Atlantic Treaty Organization (NATO) is a military alliance made up of the United States, Canada, and 26 European nations. It was established in 1949. The United States entered into several international alliances following World War II with the goal of preventing future aggression from the Soviet Union.

MILITARY ALLIANCES AFTER WORLD WAR II

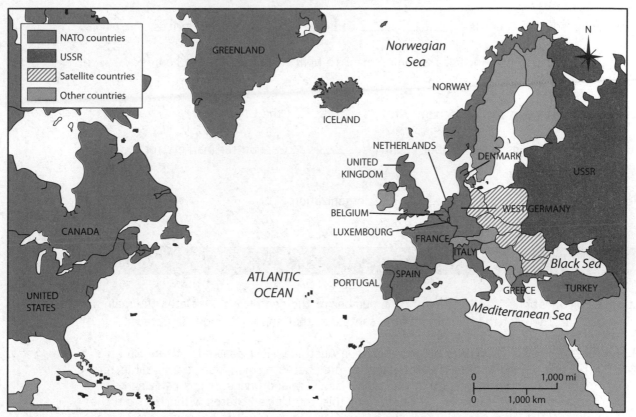

Members of NATO have agreed to settle disputes peacefully and to support each other in the event of attack from another country. This idea is set out in the North Atlantic Treaty, which states that "an armed attack against one or more of them in Europe or in North America shall be considered an attack against them all."

Other international security alliances begun after World War II include the ANZUS Pact (which includes Australia, New Zealand, and the United States) and the Inter-American Treaty of Reciprocal Assistance (the Rio Pact), which joins the United States, Canada, and much of Latin America.

THINK ABOUT SOCIAL STUDIES

Directions: Write a short response to the following questions in a notebook.

1. Why do you think countries ally themselves with other countries?

2. What do you think causes the relationships between countries to change over time?

Vocabulary Review

Directions: Use these words to complete the following sentences.

alliances   diplomatic   established   foreign policy   obtain   ratify

1. The United States entered into several military _____ in the years following World War II as a way to discourage any nation from attacking a member country.

2. Several oil-producing countries _____ OPEC to regulate world oil prices.

3. Today US _____ includes a commitment to fight terrorism both at home and abroad.

4. The United States was the first country to _____ the UN charter.

5. Economic organizations help member countries _____ better markets for their exports.

6. The UN is the world's largest _____ organization.

Skill Review

Directions: For <u>questions 1 and 2</u>, identify the number of the sentence that states the main idea the passage. Then list the numbers of the sentences that supply supporting details.

1. (1) The ANZUS Pact is a security alliance between Australia, New Zealand and the United States. (2) It was signed in 1951. (3) The name of the pact is formed from the initial letters of each member country's name. (4) In the 1980s, New Zealand banned ships carrying nuclear arms from using its ports. (5) Because of this, the United States withdrew from the pact. (6) The ANZUS Pact formally remains in force, but in reality it is no longer functioning.

_____

2. (1) NATO was first formed to help guard against aggression from the Soviet Union. (2) However, the relationship between NATO and the former Soviet Union has changed over time. (3) Since the collapse of the Soviet Union in 1991, several nations that were once part of the Soviet Union have joined NATO. (4) It was hoped that their membership in NATO would help them remain outside Russia's influence. (5) By the twenty-first century, Russia was no longer considered a major threat to NATO nations. (6) Russia and NATO began to cooperate in several areas, including terrorism and arms control.

_____

3. According to the passage in the sidebar box on page 159 and the persuasive essay you wrote, what is the most important reason for a country to join an international organization such as the United Nations?

_____

_____

Skill Practice

Directions: Choose the <u>one best answer</u> to each question. <u>Question 1</u> refers to the following passage.

> The United Nations is an international organization. This is underscored by the fact that the land and building of the UN headquarters belong to all the member states of the UN, even though the property is located in New York City. In addition, the UN has its own postage stamps and police force. The United Nations has six official languages: Arabic, Chinese, English, French, Russian, and Spanish. The UN building includes many pieces of fine art that have been contributed by member states.

1. Which statement best illustrates the main idea of the passage?

   A. The UN is an international organization.
   B. The UN has its own postage stamps and police force.
   C. The UN has six official languages.
   D. The UN headquarters belongs to its member states.

2. How do economic organizations help prevent future wars?

   A. by making laws against war
   B. by helping to stabilize the economies of all nations
   C. by diverting the attention of leaders away from war and toward economic issues
   D. by making the economic decisions for all their members

3. Which part of the UN has the most influence over world affairs?

   A. Security Council
   B. General Assembly
   C. office of the secretary-general
   D. UNICEF

4. The United Nations was formed as a reaction to World War II. What other international organization was formed as a result of this conflict?

   A. OPEC
   B. NATO
   C. World Health Organization
   D. EU

Writing Practice

Directions: Despite the fact that the League of Nations failed in its primary goal of preventing another world war, Americans were willing to join the United Nations following World War II. Write a paragraph explaining why you think the outlook of Americans had changed.

International Relations

Lesson Objectives

You will be able to

- Identify the role of the president in foreign affairs

- Understand the responsibilities of the State Department

- Describe the role of Congress in foreign affairs

Skills

- **Reading Skill:** Make Comparisons

- **Core Skill:** Analyze Events and Ideas

Vocabulary

alike
authorization
different
executive agreement
implement
negotiate
quota
treaty

KEY CONCEPT: In a global society, the relationships between nations are extremely important. The US government uses many tools and policies to direct these international relations.

You have many relationships in your life. At times, balancing all these relationships can be tricky. For example, your mother may expect you to help her on the same day that your boss wants you to work extra hours. If everyone involved is reasonable, a compromise may be worked out. At times, however, someone may make compromise difficult.

In international relations, governments must often compromise to find an acceptable solution to the many challenges that arise. When compromise is not possible, the consequences can be serious. Failure to find compromise can lead to war.

US Roles in International Relations

Today's turbulent world has made the field of international relations more important than ever. Various branches of the federal government play important roles in making and **implementing**, or carrying out, foreign policy. The main goal of US foreign policy is to protect the country and its citizens. The United States also tries to promote US interests abroad and spread democracy when possible.

The President's Role in International Relations

The Constitution grants the president four important foreign policy responsibilities: the power to make treaties and executive agreements, the power of diplomatic recognition, the power to act as commander in chief of the armed forces, and the power to appoint ambassadors.

Treaties and Executive Agreements A **treaty** is a formal agreement between two or more nations. The president can **negotiate**, or work out, treaties with other countries. These treaties, however, must be approved by the Senate before the president can ratify the treaty. Once a treaty has been ratified, it is like a law passed by Congress; it must be followed by later presidents.

The president can also make executive agreements with other nations. An **executive agreement**, like a treaty, is an agreement between the United States and another country. Unlike a treaty, however, an executive agreement does not require Senate approval. Agreements pledge the word of a particular president, but later presidents are not bound to follow the agreement. Since 1940, presidents have used executive agreements much more frequently than treaties.

Diplomatic Recognition Presidents can extend diplomatic recognition to new governments or nations. This is the formal acceptance of a country as a legal entity. It recognizes the laws of the country and offers the country an equal place among nations in the world.

MAKE COMPARISONS

When you think about how two or more things are **alike** (the same) and **different** (not the same), you are making comparisons. Writers often use comparisons to make their writing interesting and to help readers visualize what they are reading about.

In some texts, comparisons are made by describing the details of one item and then describing the details of the second item. In other texts, one feature of both items is compared and then a second feature is compared.

To compare and contrast, ask yourself these questions: *How are these two people, places, events, ideas, or things alike? How are they different?*

Read the following paragraph and determine what is being compared. How are these two events alike and different?

---

(1) World War I was fought from 1914 to 1918, and World War II from 1939 to 1945. (2) Both were international conflicts, but there were major differences between the two wars. (3) While sixteen countries were directly involved in World War I, twenty-seven were involved in World War II. (4) Whereas World War I lasted a little more than four years, World War II lasted almost six years. (5) The cost of World War I—about $200 billion—is dwarfed by the $2 trillion spent on World War II.

Sentence 1 introduces the topic of the paragraph. Sentence 2 describes one similarity between the wars—both were international in scope. Sentences 3 through 5 explain some major differences between the two world wars.

Notice the text structure of this paragraph. In sentences 3 through 5, one feature of each war (number of countries involved, length of the war, and cost) is contrasted. The writer goes back and forth from World War I to World War II.

Reading Skill
Make Comparisons

When you make a comparison, be sure you are comparing similar things. For example, you cannot compare war with a soldier, but you can compare a soldier with a diplomat (someone who serves as the president's representative).

After reading the section about ambassadors on page 166, write a paragraph in which you compare ambassadors and military personnel. Consider their duties, qualifications, and benefits.

Organize your paragraph like the comparison on this page between World War I and World War II.

WRITE TO LEARN

One way to think critically about what you have read is to compare and contrast.

As you read about treaties and executive agreements, note their similarities and differences. Then write a paragraph in a notebook that compares and contrasts executive agreements and treaties.

When analyzing events
or ideas, it can be useful
to look for comparisons
(similarities) and
contrasts (differences).

There are many ways to
compare and contrast.
For example, you can do
so in a paragraph, in an
outline, or in a diagram.
A **Venn diagram** is
particularly useful
when comparing and
contrasting.

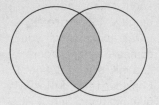

The information in the
overlapping part of the
circles lists similarities.
The information in the
outside sections of the
circles lists differences.

Study the Venn
diagram below. Then,
in a notebook, create
a Venn diagram that
compares and contrasts
presidential powers and
congressional powers in
the field of international
relations.

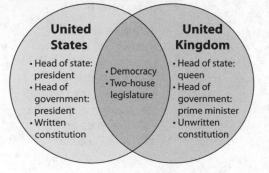

United States		United Kingdom
• Head of state: president	• Democracy	• Head of state: queen
• Head of government: president	• Two-house legislature	• Head of government: prime minister
• Written constitution		• Unwritten constitution

In some cases, presidents have withheld diplomatic recognition to show
disapproval of a nation's system of government. For example, the United
States withheld recognition of the former Soviet Union for 16 years. On
the other hand, presidents have also extended recognition to new nations
to give them support and help them to survive in their early days. In
1948, for example, President Harry Truman recognized Israel on the same
day that the nation was created.

Commander in Chief The president is commander in chief of the armed
forces. Sometimes presidents have used this power to order military action
without a formal declaration of war by Congress. Without congressional
authorization, or approval, for example, President Truman sent troops
into Korea in 1950. During the 1960s, Presidents Kennedy and Johnson
sent troops to Vietnam. President Clinton sent troops to the Balkans in
1995 and 1999.

Many people believe the president should not have the power to involve
the country in an undeclared war. To restrain the president, Congress
passed the War Powers Act in 1973. This act limits the president's ability
to send troops into combat when Congress has not declared war.

Ambassadors Ambassadors are the highest-ranking diplomats
representing the United States. An ambassador is sent to a particular
country to conduct international relations. The president appoints
ambassadors, but the appointments must be approved by the Senate.
Some ambassadors are people who gave large amounts of money to a
presidential campaign. Others are career diplomats. In either case, it is
best if an ambassador has a good understanding of the culture, politics,
and history of the country where he or she is stationed.

THINK ABOUT SOCIAL STUDIES

Directions: Answer the questions in a notebook.

1. Does being commander in chief allow the president to declare
   war on another country? Explain.

2. Do you think awarding ambassador posts to those who
   contributed to a presidential campaign is a good way to
   appoint ambassors? Why?

The State Department

The US Department of State is the section of the executive branch
directly responsible for foreign affairs and the US diplomatic
service. This department supports the president in negotiating
treaties and making agreements with other countries. Its other
responsibilities include representing the United States at the
UN, analyzing US relations with other countries, and promoting
human rights.

The head of this department is the secretary of state. Secretaries of state represent the president. They can play an influential role in foreign affairs. The president nominates the secretary of state. This choice must also be approved by the Senate.

Congress and Foreign Relations

Congress exerts its influence in foreign policy through its ability to approve or disapprove **appropriations** (money set aside for a particular purpose), treaties, and ambassadors and by exercising its sole right to declare war. Only Congress can raise and support an army and a navy. Many of the bills that Congress considers—including tariffs, immigration policies, and import **quotas** (quantities that establish limits)—can have far-reaching international effects. For example, following the terrorists attacks of September 11, 2001, Congress created the Department of Homeland Security. The duty of this department is to protect the nation against terrorist attacks. It has wide authority in the areas of border control and immigration.

THINK ABOUT SOCIAL STUDIES

Directions: Write a sentence explaining the role of each of these people.

1. commander in chief of the armed forces
2. ambassador
3. secretary of state

REAL WORLD CONNECTION

Explore the World

Many countries, including the United States, encourage cultural exchanges with other nations. They hope that knowledge of other nations will bring about peace and understanding. The US Bureau of Education and Cultural Affairs offers programs for people of various ages and experience. Many schools, religious organizations, and service groups also offer exchange or study-abroad programs.

Research cultural exchanges between countries. Think about people you know who have gone to other countries or people who have visited the United States on exchange programs.

In a notebook, write two paragraphs describing a cultural exchange you know about or have read about. Discuss how cultural exchanges affect people's understanding of the world.

Vocabulary Review

Directions: Use these words to complete the following sentences.

authorize executive agreement implementing
negotiate quotas treaties

1. Because the president felt certain that the Senate would not _____ a treaty with Iraq, he chose to issue a(n) _____.

2. The president has the power to _____ _____ with other countries, but they must then be approved by the Senate.

3. The State Department is the section of the executive branch most responsible for _____ the foreign policy goals of the president.

4. Congress can set limits, or _____, on immigration.

Directions: Read the paragraph. Then fill in the chart to outline similarities and differences.

What is the difference between international affairs and domestic affairs? Both have political, economic, and social aspects. Both are important in every presidential administration. Both are the subject of laws passed by Congress. International affairs, however, involve other countries. Domestic affairs, on the other hand, involve only the United States. International affairs include matters such as foreign aid, wars, and trade relationships. Domestic affairs include health-care reform and tax cuts. International affairs are dealt with mainly at the national level, while domestic affairs affect national, state, and local levels of government.

1.

International Affairs	Both	Domestic Affairs

Directions: Review the information in the chart below. Then answer the question that follows.

Diplomatic Recognition of Countries	
Recognition Withheld	**Recognition Granted**
Country's laws are not considered valid.	Country's laws are considered valid.
Country cannot join international organizations.	Country is granted all the rights and privileges of other diplomatically recognized countries.

2. When a new nation is formed, the president can decide whether the United States should grant diplomatic recognition to that nation. Explain why the president might decide for or against recognizing a new nation.

_____

_____

_____

_____

_____

_____

Skill Practice

Directions: Choose the one best answer to each question.

1. Which role is the most important responsibility of an ambassador?

   A. to advise the president on foreign policy issues

   B. to protect the United States against terrorism

   C. to represent the United States in another country

   D. to allow foreign representatives to meet with the president

2. In July 2009, President Obama signed the UN Convention on the Rights of Persons with Disabilities treaty. Under the US Constitution, what must happen before the treaty can become law?

   A. It must be ratified by the UN.

   B. It must be ratified by the Senate.

   C. It must be ratified by the US Congress.

   D. Once the president has signed the treaty, it becomes law.

3. How is a treaty different from an executive agreement?

   A. A treaty does not need to be approved by Congress.

   B. A treaty does not need to be upheld by the next president.

   C. A treaty is unlikely to be approved by Congress.

   D. A treaty is more likely to affect foreign policy for years after it is agreed on.

4. How does the Constitution separate the war powers between the executive and legislative branches?

   A. The president has all war powers, but Congress has all law-making powers.

   B. The president can declare war, but Congress must approve that action.

   C. The president can order a draft, while Congress commands the army.

   D. The president is commander in chief, but only Congress can declare war.

Writing Practice

Directions: Write a paragraph defining the terms *politician* and *diplomat*. In your paragraph, explain how politicians are similar to diplomats and how they are different. Use terms such as *both* and *in contrast*.

The World in the Twenty-First Century

Lesson Objectives

You will be able to

- Explain the new global culture and economy
- Determine the effects of recent wars on the world
- Evaluate the results of terrorist attacks

Skills

- **Core Skill:** Evaluate Evidence
- **Reading Skill:** Predict Outcomes

Vocabulary

ethnic cleansing
fossil fuels
global culture
judge
outcome
terrorism

KEY CONCEPT: Major changes in the world's culture, economy, and political scene are shaping the twenty-first century.

Have you ever moved to a new town or a new state? If so, you may have felt disoriented as you tried to find your way around.

Life in the twenty-first century has changed so drastically that some people feel they are living in new place. The effects of a more global culture and economy as well as the results of terrorism have changed the world.

Global Culture, Global Economy

In many ways the world has become a much smaller place since World War II. High-speed trains, superhighways, and jet planes have made travel much faster. As a result of fax machines, e-mail, cell phones, video conferencing, and the Internet, communication happens instantly. The world—once rich in clearly distinct cultures—is increasingly becoming one **global culture**, or a common worldwide culture. People around the world eat similar fast foods, play the same computer games, and use the same business technologies.

Global culture arose from the growing global market. Western Europeans saw how free trade between states benefited the United States. In the past, a businessperson in France could not trade with someone just a few miles away in Belgium or Spain without facing trade barriers, taxes, and currency (money) exchange. People in Western Europe wanted a market similar to the one between states in the United States.

In 1957, six nations formed the European Common Market. The goal of the Common Market was to reduce the barriers to trade and boost economic growth. Later other nations joined, and the Common Market was replaced by the **European Union** (EU). The EU also expanded its goals. It pledged to aid its weaker members and promote peace, equality, and a greener environment. In 2013, the EU had 27 member nations, all with democratic governments. It represented more than 500 million people. Other countries have applied for membership.

Europeans also adopted a single currency, the euro, to replace various national currencies such as the French franc and the German mark. Before that time, separate currencies had to be exchanged when merchandise moved across borders. To adopt the euro, EU member nations must meet a set of conditions. About two-thirds of member nations have done so. Denmark and Britain have not adopted the euro.

PREDICT OUTCOMES

An **outcome** is the result. When you predict the outcome of an event, you are making a logical guess about what will happen next. We do this in our lives all the time. We predict the outcome of movies, television programs, and sporting events. We also predict the outcome of job interviews and elections. In the same way, we can predict outcomes as we read.

Read the following paragraph. Then answer the question.

> One type of tax imposed by the federal government is a tariff. **Tariffs** are taxes on imported goods, that is, on goods that come from another country. The companies that import the goods pay the tax. Then, to make up for the extra expense, they raise the price of the goods. By adding tariffs to foreign-made goods, the price of US–made products may seem more reasonable.

If the US government signs an agreement to lift (end) tariffs on goods from Central America, what do you predict will happen to consumer prices for those goods?

A. Prices would fall.

B. Prices would rise.

C. Prices would fall and then rise.

D. Prices would rise and then fall.

The correct option is (A). You can predict that prices will fall if tariffs are lifted from imported goods. Consumers will be happy to see goods for sale at lower prices.

Core Skill
Evaluate Evidence

When you look for evidence to support an idea, you must **judge**, or evaluate, whether the information is relevant to your topic. No matter how fascinating the information is, if it does support your main idea or answer your question, it is not relevant.

Your assignment is to answer the question "What are the causes of increasing globalization?"

As you read "Global Culture, Global Economy," highlight information that is relevant to the question.

In your notebook, answer the question.

THINK ABOUT SOCIAL STUDIES

Directions: Write a short response to the following questions.

1. How and why did the European Union form?

   _____

   _____

2. What are some of the benefits of using the euro?

   _____

   _____

TECHNOLOGY CONNECTION ▶

Make Contacts

Forms of communication are changing rapidly. In addition to smartphones and e-mail, people communicate by text message, social media sites, blogs, vlogs, and microblogs.

In a notebook, write a paragraph about how advancements in social media affect your life. Include both positive and negative aspects.

WRITE TO LEARN

In North America, the United States, Canada, and Mexico eliminated trade barriers when they signed the North American Free Trade Agreement (NAFTA) in 1994. A second trade agreement, the Dominican Republic–Central America–US Free Trade Agreement (CAFTA-DR), took effect in 2006. Under CAFTA-DR, all **tariffs** are to be removed within 20 years. Tariffs increase the price of imported goods because the tax is passed on to the consumer.

While the world is more united in many ways, in other ways it remains divided. Ethnic conflicts continue to affect many regions of the world. During the 1990s, for example, Yugoslavia broke into several smaller nations based on ethnicity, culture, and religion. In the process, certain groups practiced **ethnic cleansing**, killing members of other ethnic groups. An estimated 200,000 people perished. Similar conflicts have happened in recent years in Rwanda, Somalia, Indonesia, Myanmar, and other places. Internal conflicts have also troubled many of the nations in Central and South America.

Concerns in the Twenty-First Century

One major concern is global population growth. At the beginning of the twentieth century, the world's population was about 1.6 billion. By the end of the century, more than 6 billion people lived on the planet. Medical and technological advances have made it possible for people to live longer. However, those advances meant there were almost four times as many people to feed in 2000 as there had been in 1900. Technology has made it possible to feed most of these people. However, there is uncertainty about how long technology can keep up with population growth.

Another problem is damage to the environment. Human activity has polluted much of the land, water, and air. Oxygen-producing rain forests are cut down to make way for farms. Global warming and melting polar ice caps also trouble scientists. A warmer environment will affect our ability to grow food, and it may cause mass plant and animal extinctions. In 2006, an island off the coast of India disappeared because of rising sea levels. The 10,000 people who had lived there had to relocate. Other island nations and cities built near coasts may also be in danger.

The use of **fossil fuels**, such as oil, coal, and natural gas, is another key issue. Because fossil fuels are a limited resource, interest in renewable energy sources and "green" technology is growing. In 2008, investment in clean technology exceeded investment in fossil fuels for the first time. Solar, water, and wind energy are renewable energy sources. They do not have negative effects on the environment.

Alternative energy sources such as biofuels are attracting more interest. Biofuels are created by converting plant matter into liquid fuels. Corn and soybeans can be used to create biofuels, but using food crops in this way can increase food prices. Vegetable oils and animal fats can be used to create biodiesel or added to regular diesel fuel to make it cleaner.

The United States is the world's largest consumer of energy. However, countries such as India and China are rapidly developing. The growing populations and economies in these countries have increasing demand for energy. This will further strain the world's limited resources.

The HIV/AIDS crisis is another major problem in the twenty-first century. The first known cases of AIDS were reported in 1981. The World Health Organization (WHO) estimated that about 34 million people were living with HIV in 2011. About 1.7 million people around the world died from AIDS that year. Caribbean nations and the sub-Saharan nations of Africa are most critically affected. Although only about 10 percent of the world's people live in sub-Saharan Africa, about 70 percent of those infected with HIV live there. No place on the globe is immune. New drugs make it possible for people with the disease to live, but efforts to prevent the spread of the disease have not been effective so far.

ADULTS LIVING WITH HIV, 2011

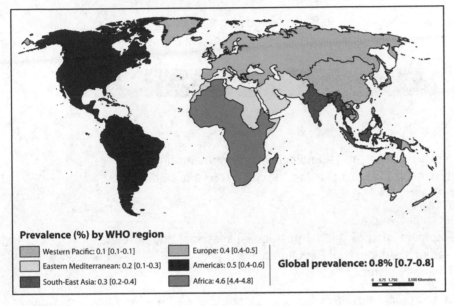

Prevalence (%) by WHO region

- Western Pacific: 0.1 [0.1-0.1]
- Eastern Mediterranean: 0.2 [0.1-0.3]
- South-East Asia: 0.3 [0.2-0.4]
- Europe: 0.4 [0.4-0.5]
- Americas: 0.5 [0.4-0.6]
- Africa: 4.6 [4.4-4.8]

Global prevalence: 0.8% [0.7-0.8]

0   0.75   1,750   3,500 Kilometers

Terrorism

On September 11, 2001, a group of religious fundamentalists and terrorists coordinated a series of attacks against the United States. More than 3,000 people died.

This was not the first attack against the United States. A car bomb exploded in 1993 at the World Trade Center. In 2000, a boat carrying explosives deliberately rammed the USS *Cole*, an American military ship, while it was in port in Yemen.

Some political groups use **terrorism** (violence and fear) to advance their causes. Some of these groups are supported by foreign governments. Others are independent. Terrorist attacks have occurred all over the world. Israel, the Philippines, Ireland, Spain, India, Pakistan, and Greece are some of the countries that have recently experienced attacks.

Vocabulary Review

Directions: Use these terms to complete the following sentences.

ethnic cleansing   fossil fuels   global culture   terrorism

1. The use of _____ has created the problem of global warming.

2. The events of September 11, 2001, are associated with _____.

3. Being able to buy Kentucky Fried Chicken in Asia is an example of _____.

4. _____ has eliminimated large populations in Rwanda and Yugoslavia.

Skill Review

Directions: Read and answer the questions below.

1. You have been asked to write a research paper on technological developments in the twenty-first century. Which source is most likely to provide the most relevant evidence for your report?

   A. a 1960 pamphlet from a Ford automotive plant
   B. a magazine article on the development of GPS (global positioning systems) and satellites
   C. an encyclopedia article on causes of the Industrial Revolution
   D. a 1985 biography of inventor Thomas Edison

2. How can you determine whether a source is relevant?

   _____

   _____

Directions: Read the following paragraph and answer the questions below.

> The CAFTA-DR free trade agreement will eventually eliminate tariffs and other trade barriers between the United States, Central America (the countries of Costa Rica, El Salvador, Guatemala, Honduras, and Nicaragua), and the Dominican Republic. According to the Government Accountability Office (GAO), Central America and the Dominican Republic currently make up the second-largest export market for US goods and services. Tariffs on information-technology products, construction equipment, paper products, cotton, wheat, soybeans, and some fruits and vegetables were removed immediately.

3. How would the prices of construction equipment and paper products have changed when the tariffs were removed?

   _____

4. What effect would the change in prices have on the amount of goods exported?

   _____

Skill Practice

Directions: Choose the <u>one best answer</u> to each question. <u>Questions 1 through 3</u> refer to the following chart.

Selected Statistics of Developing and Developed Nations						
Nation	Average Income (GNI per capita, dollars)	Infant Mortality Rate (deaths per 1,000 births)	Fertility Rate (births per woman)	Telephones (per 100 people; not include cell phones)	Cell Phone Subscribers (per 100 people)	Internet Users (per 100 people)
Angola	$2,829	86	6	2	71	15
Bangladesh	$1,998	49	3	1	54	5
Cambodia	$2,116	54	3	4	68	3
China	$6,193	16	2	21	74	38
Peru	$5,594	21	2	11	99	36
Germany	$30,150	4	1	55	128	83
Italy	$29,414	3	1	37	141	57
US	$41,557	6	2	49	91	78

1. What comparison can you make between the number of cell phone subscribers and the number of telephones in each country?

   A. There are fewer cell phone subscribers than telephones.
   B. There are more cell phone subscribers than telephones.
   C. Each country differs—some have more cell phone subscribers, others have more telephones.
   D. The number of cell phone subscribers and telephones is about the same in all countries.

2. Which nations have an infant mortality rate lower than that of the United States?

   A. China and Peru
   B. Angola and Bangladesh
   C. Angola and Cambodia
   D. Germany and Italy

3. Which nation has the highest fertility rate?

   A. Germany
   B. Bangladesh
   C. Angola
   D. United States

Writing Practice

Directions: Look at the statistics about telephones and Internet use in the chart above. On the basis of these statistics, what outcomes can you predict about the role of technology around the world? Write one paragraph explaining your predictions.

Directions: Choose the <u>one best answer</u> to each question. <u>Questions 1–3</u> refer to the following passage.

> The United States should change its form of government to a direct democracy. New technology has made direct democracy possible, even through the nation's population is now more than 300 million. Almost everyone has access to the Internet at home, at work, or at a local public library. Using this technology, every interested citizen can vote directly on proposed laws. This would be much closer to a true democracy because everyone's input would count equally.

1. How is a direct democracy different from a representative democracy?

   In a direct democracy,

   A. people vote only on the issues or laws that are important to them
   B. people vote on proposed laws rather than elect officials to vote on laws
   C. fewer people will need to vote on proposed laws in order to pass them
   D. more people will have Internet access

2. Which statement best supports the idea that a direct democracy would be better for the United States?

   A. Almost everyone has Internet access.
   B. The nation's population is more than 300 million.
   C. Because of the Internet, everyone would vote.
   D. Everyone's input would count equally.

3. According to the passage, what could cause the switch to direct democracy?

   A. new technology
   B. population growth
   C. need for laws to pass more quickly
   D. direct input from citizens

4. What is the difference between an executive agreement and a treaty?

   A. An executive agreement must be approved by the Senate; a treaty does not need approval.
   B. A treaty must be approved by the Senate; an executive agreement does not need approval.
   C. There is no difference between the two.
   D. An executive agreement is proposed by the president; a treaty is proposed by Congress.

5. Why might a country join an international economic organization?

   A. to control prices on imports
   B. to increase trade and gain a larger market for exported goods
   C. to outlaw war
   D. to encourage all govenments to be democratic

6. Which statement identifies an effect of globalization?

   A. It is increasingly difficult for people around the globe to communicate.
   B. Ethnic conflicts are increasing.
   C. The United States has increased its consumption of fossil fuels.
   D. Individual cultures are becoming less distinct.

7. In the twenty-first century, why are people and governments investing in alternative energy sources?

   A. We have run out of oil and natural gas.
   B. Biofuels are damaging the environment.
   C. They want to make money on new technologies.
   D. Solar, water, and wind energy do not cost money to use.

8. Which statement illustrates the difference between foreign aid and trade agreements?

   A. Foreign aid is the sharing of goods and resources between two countries; trade agreements are the documents that promise foreign aid.
   B. Foreign aid allows two countries to develop an economic partnership; trade agreements involve political and economic partnerships.
   C. Foreign aid is an unofficial way of trading goods between nations; trade agreements are official contracts.
   D. Foreign aid is the offering of various resources to countries in need; trade agreements are contracts made between two countries that want to trade goods.

9. After World War I, the United States did not join the League of Nations, but after World War II, it was the first country to ratify the UN charter.

   Why did the US reverse its policy on joining an international diplomatic organization?

   A. US leaders feared that the alliances formed through the League of Nations might lead to another war, but they recognized that the UN would enforce peace.
   B. In 1919 the United States wanted to protect its independence and return to a policy of isolationism, but by 1945 US leaders realized that isolationism was no longer in the country's best interests.
   C. Americans did not want to join the League of Nations because it was too large for the United States to control; the UN, on the other hand, was smaller, so US leaders felt they could dominate it more easily.
   D. The League of Nations was a militaristic organization, and Americans were tired of war after World War I; in contrast, the UN's goal was to keep peace among all nations, so Americans favored membership.

10. What role do monarchs typically play in a constitutional monarchy?

    A. Their role is to rule by divine right.
    B. Their role is to represent their electors.
    C. Their role is to hold absolute power.
    D. Their role is mainly ceremonial.

11. Which is one goal of the United Nations international agencies?

    A. to promote a unified currency through Europe
    B. to provide assistance to children in developing countries
    C. to prevent the spread of communism
    D. to regulate oil production and pricing

12. Which is one way that an absolute monarchy is similar to a dictatorship?

    A. The rulers have absolute control.
    B. The rulers use royal titles, such as *king* or *emperor*.
    C. The rulers are mostly ceremonial, with real power in the hands of an elected body.
    D. The rulers usually give in to the wishes of the people.

13. Which was a driving force behind the formation of NATO?

    A. The success of the UN led other countries to form small alliances with specific groups of nations.
    B. The members of NATO wanted to model themselves after ANZUS.
    C. The members of NATO wanted to prevent future aggression from the Soviet Union.
    D. The United States wanted to ensure that the European Union did not become too strong.

14. How are US ambassadors appointed?

    A. They are voted in by the people in a direct election.
    B. They are nominated by the president, and then they pay a large contribution to the president.
    C. They are nominated by the president and approved by Senate.
    D. They are chosen by the government of the country where they will serve.

15. Which statement best illustrates the relationship between the United States and the European Union?

    A. The United States is one of the leading members of the European Union.
    B. Easy trade between US states was an inspiration for the European Union.
    C. The European Union was formed to compete with the United States.
    D. The United States has pledged to protect all members of the European Union from threats.

Review

Check Your Understanding

On the following chart, circle the number of any question you answered incorrectly. In the third column, you will see the pages you can review to study the content covered in the question. Pay particular attention to reviewing those lessons in which you missed half or more of the questions.

Chapter 4 Review

Lesson	Item Number	Review Pages
Political Theories and Systems in World History	1, 2, 3, 10, 12	152–157
International Organizations	5, 9, 11, 13	158–163
International Relations	4, 14	164–169
The World in the Twenty-First Century	6, 7, 8, 15	170–175

ESSAY WRITING PRACTICE

World History and Political Systems

Directions: Write an essay in response to one of the prompts below. Review Lessons 4.1, 4.2, 4.3, and 4.4 to identify facts you can use to support your argument.

PERSUASIVE ESSAY

A persuasive essay is a way to share your opinion and to convince others to agree with you. When writing a persuasive essay, state your opinion in the introductory paragraph. In the body of the essay, support your opinion with facts and other evidence. Finally, restate your opinion in the concluding paragraph.

On an upcoming class trip to Washington, DC, you will meet with one of your state's senators. In preparation for the trip, each student will write a persuasive essay discussing the responsibilities that the United States should have toward one foreign country.

Select one country that you are familiar with or interested in. Do research to learn how the United States helps that country in three ways. You may consider issues such as medical aid, economic development, food aid, military support, and education assistance. Your persuasive essay should be five paragraphs long.

EXPLANATORY ESSAY

An explanatory essay is an opportunity to educate your readers. You present information about a situation or an event so your subject can be easily understood. Do not include your opinions. Instead, your writing should present unbiased facts. In your opening paragraph, tell what you are going to explain. Use the three paragraphs in the body of your essay to explain three key ideas. Reinforce your main idea in the concluding paragraph.

Your class will visit the exhibit *Our Neighbors, Our World*. It has been set up to show the cultural backgrounds of immigrants to your city.

Select one country that you are familiar with or interested in. Do research to learn about the living conditions and the political system in that country. Identify three key points that would help people understand the culture and background of immigrants from that country. Your explanatory essay should be five paragraphs long.

UNIT 3

Economics

Economic Foundations

As a child, you might have traded something you had for something a friend had. Each of you probably believed that the thing you gained was worth more than what you gave away. Both of you thought you were better off because of the trade.

In this chapter, you will learn how goods and services are bartered or sold and how economic systems are formed. As you read, consider how your daily economic choices impact the greater economy.

In this chapter you will study these topics:

Lesson 5.1: Basic Economic Concepts

In any economic system, limited resources force people to make choices. People cannot have everything they want. The study of economics helps us analyze the best way to use our limited resources.

Lesson 5.2: The Role of the Market

A market is anywhere a buyer and a seller freely choose to exchange one thing for another. The laws of supply and demand help companies figure out how many goods to make and how much to charge for them.

Lesson 5.3: The Role of Government

Until the 1930s, government had little role in the economy. This changed during the Great Depression when the government provided jobs for millions of unemployed workers and developed the Social Security system. Taxation pays for government programs.

Lesson 5.4: Money and Financial Institutions

Money is used as a medium of exchange, as a standard of value, and as a way to store value. Today US banks insure the money deposited in their accounts. The country's central bank is the Federal Reserve.

Lesson 5.5: Monopoly and Competition

In a monopoly, one seller controls the market for a particular good or service. When there are many sellers providing similar goods or services, there is competition. Competition often leads to innovation.

Lesson 5.6: Profit

To make a profit, a company must consider the factors of production (land, labor, and capital). It must also be concerned about incentive and morale.

Lesson 5.7: Productivity and Interdependence

For a company to be productive, it must operate efficiently. Its profits are influenced by the cost of its supplies and by the price customers are willing to pay. This interdependence has increased due to technologies like computers and the Internet.

Lesson 5.8: Fiscal and Monetary Policy

The federal government plays two important roles in the US economy. First, it makes decisions about collecting and spending money (fiscal policy). Second, through the Federal Reserve System, it controls the money supply and interest rates (monetary policy).

Lesson 5.9: Credit, Savings, and Banking

Various economic tools allow individuals to manage their money. These include checking accounts, savings accounts, and credit cards.

Goal Setting

Why is it important to understand economics?

- to understand how the laws of supply and demand affect the market

- to understand how money is used

- to understand how countries trade with one another

- to understand how to make appropriate economic choices with a given income and specific needs

Some of the people who use economics in their jobs include

- stock traders

- manufacturers

- business owners

- bankers

- international aid officers

- real estate owners

What do you already know about economics? In the middle column of the chart below, explain the terms you are already familiar with. When you finish reading the chapter, fill in the last column.

Economic Terms	Explanation of terms you already know	Explanation of terms you learned about in these lessons
goods		
services		
demand		
supply		
recession		
tax		
monopoly		
profit		
productivity		
money supply		
credit score		

Basic Economic Concepts

Lesson Objectives

You will be able to

- Explain how scarcity requires people to make economic choices

- Recognize that economic choices have costs

- Analyze a production possibilities curve

Skills

- **Core Skill:** Interpret Graphics

- **Reading Skill:** Recognize Supporting Details

Vocabulary

factor of production
opportunity cost
production possibilities
   curve
scarcity
table

KEY CONCEPT: Scarcity, which is a universal economic problem, requires individuals and societies to make choices about how to use their limited resources.

Suppose your best friend called you, hoping to meet you at the mall on Saturday afternoon. You may have already planned to run errands during that time, however. You can't do both activities at the same time. Because your time is limited, you have to choose to do one activity and not the other.

The economic choices people make operate in a similar way. Resources, such as time, are limited—but there are many ways these resources can be used. Individuals, businesses, the government, and others must choose which resources will best meet their wants and needs.

Scarcity and Choice

Sometimes people ask why we bother studying economics. There are many possible answers to this question. Most economists say that we study economics so we can learn how to deal with the problem of scarcity. **Scarcity** is the shortage of goods. It occurs because people have unlimited wants or needs, but they have limited resources for satisfying those wants and needs. To put it more simply, we cannot have everything we may want. Scarcity is often called the universal economic problem because people in every society, past and present, have faced scarcity.

People have tried to overcome scarcity by improving the ways goods and services are produced. For example, during the Industrial Revolution, manufacturing was changed from small-scale **cottage industries** (people working at home to produce goods) to mass production in large factories. These factories also transformed how the factors of production were used. The **factors of production** are the key resources used to produce goods and services. The three main factors of production are natural resources (land), human resources (labor), and capital goods (capital).

Factors of Production	Definition	Examples
Natural Resources (land)	natural features or materials	oceans, wild animals, forests, minerals
Human Resources (labor)	the time and effort of workers	factory workers, doctors, teachers, farmers
Capital Goods (capital)	items designed to produce other goods	tractors, computers, office and factory buildings

RECOGNIZE SUPPORTING DETAILS

Good writers clearly state their main idea. Then they support the main idea with details. Supporting details can be examples, statistics, or expert opinions. A writer will use a variety of supporting details to explain a topic, strengthen an argument, or defend a viewpoint.

To identify the supporting details, ask yourself, *What evidence helps me understand the author's viewpoint?*

Read the following paragraph. In a notebook, list the main idea and two supporting details.

> The US **economy** (the production and use of goods and services) is by far the largest economy in the world. The most widely used measure of the size of an economy is the gross domestic product (GDP). The GDP is the market value of all goods and services produced by a country in one year. The US GDP was more than $15 trillion in 2012. This was roughly double the GDP of China, which had the world's second-largest GDP. The US economy produced about one-quarter of all goods and services produced in the world in 2012.

The main idea is that the US economy is the largest economy in the world. The two supporting details are (1) the US GDP is about twice as large as the GDP of China, the second-largest economy and (2) the United States produces about 25 percent of global goods and services.

Unfortunately, changes that occurred during the Industrial Revolution did not mean workers and their families had easier lives. In fact, large factories often became sweatshops. Laborers were forced to work long hours under unpleasant and dangerous conditions for little pay. Technology had made production more **efficient** (productive without being wasteful) and had increased output, but scarcity was not eliminated.

Core Skill
Interpret Graphics

An author can present information and data in lists, graphs, diagrams, or tables. A **table** organizes information in horizontal rows and vertical columns. You use tables in your studies and in daily life.

The table on page 184 identifies the three main factors of production. The cell that defines *capital goods* tells you that capital goods are items designed to produce other goods. The cell that provides examples of capital goods lists tractors, computers, and buildings.

Visit a local business to learn about factors of production. Make a table to show what you learn. In a notebook, copy the first two columns from the table. Then fill in the Examples column with the natural resources, human resources, and capital goods that the company uses to produce its product. Give your table a title.

Reading Skill
Recognize Supporting Details

Supporting details explain the main point of a passage.

Read "Choices Involve Costs." The main idea of this section is that people must choose how to use their resources. The details provide examples of the choices made by people and businesses.

With a partner, discuss times you have made choices because of your limited time or money. Determine the opportunity cost of your decisions. Evaluate your choices.

21st Century Skills
Life and Career Skills

A budget is a plan for how to spend money. Companies and governments have budgets. Many individuals find it helpful to make a budget.

In your notebook, write a personal budget for one month. Begin with your net income, or the amount you earn after taxes and other deductions. Subtract necessary expenses such as housing, food, and transportation. Then set aside a certain amount for savings. Finally, make decisions about how you will spend the remaining amount. Your optional spending may include items like entertainment and clothing.

Scarcity forces us to make choices about how to use limited resources. When a business has a scarcity of one or more of the factors of production, the business may have difficulty producing its product.

People also face scarcity. For instance, you may want to see a new movie, shop for shoes, and go out to dinner. However, you have only enough money to do one of these things. Your scarce resource is money. You will not be able to do everything you would like to do; you'll have to choose which activity is the most important or the most necessary.

THINK ABOUT SOCIAL STUDIES

Directions: Write a short response to the following questions in a notebook.

1. What is scarcity?
2. Why is scarcity considered the universal economic problem?
3. Why does scarcity force people to make economic choices?

Choices Involve Costs

When we think about the cost of something, we normally think about the price of items we purchase. For example, if you choose to buy a coat, the "cost" to you is the price you paid for the coat.

Economists tend to look at cost in a different way. They measure the true cost by what a consumer did not buy, by what a business did not produce, or by what goods or services the government did not provide. This is called the **opportunity cost**. It is the item or service that was not purchased.

Consumer Choices

Suppose Janet has $20 to spend on Saturday night. Janet narrows her plans to two choices. She can buy a movie ticket and treats at the theater, or she can buy a large pizza. If Janet buys the pizza, the opportunity cost is what she gave up, in this case, the movie ticket and treats.

Business Choices

Similarly, businesses face opportunity costs when they decide what items to produce. Suppose Clara's Clothing Outlet can produce two types of clothing—T-shirts and sweatshirts. Because of the size of the business and the number of available workers and machinery, Clara's Clothing can produce 1,000 T-shirts per day or 500 sweatshirts per day. If the business chooses to produce the 1,000 T-shirts, the opportunity cost is the 500 sweatshirts that were not produced.

Government Choices

Even the government confronts opportunity cost. Suppose your town needs to upgrade local schools and also needs to upgrade the water-treatment plant. Each project will cost $10 million. However, the town has only $10 million to spend. If your town spends its scarce financial resources ($10 million) to upgrade local schools, the opportunity cost is the improvement of the water-treatment plant.

Graphing Opportunity Cost

Graphs organize data to show trends and relationships. The **production possibilities curve** (PPC) is a graph that shows all possible combinations of two products that suppliers might produce. If the supplier produces more of one product, it will have to cut back on the production of the other product. This is because the supplier's resources are limited. Economists assume that available resources are being used efficiently. The suppliers of products could be businesses, government, or the entire economy.

Production Possibilities Table

Clara's Clothing Outlet can produce 1,000 T-shirts *or* 500 sweatshirts per day, but not 1,000 T-shirts *and* 500 sweatshirts. The business can also choose to produce some T-shirts and some sweatshirts. The following table shows some of the combinations of T-shirts and sweatshirts the business can make.

Production Possibilities (Daily)				
Product	**Points**			
	A	**B**	**C**	**D**
T-shirts	1,000	800	500	0
Sweatshirts	0	200	400	500

Notice option A—if the firm produces 1,000 T-shirts, 0 sweatshirts are produced. This is the case when all of the firm's resources are used to produce T-shirts. With option B, however, some of the firm's resources are switched from the production of T-shirts to the production of sweatshirts, so the firm can produce 800 T-shirts and 200 sweatshirts. With option D, all of the firm's resources are used to produce 500 sweatshirts, and no resources are available to produce any T-shirts.

Production Possibilities Curve

A PPC plots the numbers from the production possibilities table on a graph. This graph shows how the increased production of one item (sweatshirts) causes a drop in the production of a second item (T-shirts).

The vertical axis of the PPC shows how many T-shirts Clara's Clothing Outlet might produce in a single day. As you can see, the firm could produce from 0 to 1,000 T-shirts. The horizontal axis of the PPC shows how many sweatshirts the firm might choose to produce, which ranges from 0 to 500.

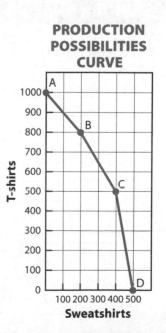

PRODUCTION POSSIBILITIES CURVE

Using the PPC to Show Opportunity Costs

Economists draw PPCs to identify the opportunity cost of a supplier's production decision. Take a look at points A and D on the PPC graph shown on page 187. These are the extremes. At point A, 1,000 T-shirts are produced. What is the opportunity cost to the business at point A? It is the 500 sweatshirts that were *not* produced. Similarly, at the other extreme, point D, the business uses all its resources to produce 500 sweatshirts. Thus, at point D, the opportunity cost is the 1,000 T-shirts the firm chose *not* to produce.

Finally, take a look at point B. At point B, the business produces 800 T-shirts and 200 sweatshirts. To figure the opportunity costs at point B, you must determine how many of each item were *not* produced. The opportunity costs at point B:

- 200 T-shirts (the firm could have produced 1,000 T-shirts) and

- 300 sweatshirts (the firm could produce 500 sweatshirts)

Vocabulary Review

Directions: Use these terms to complete the following sentences.

factors of production   opportunity cost   production possibilities curve   scarcity

1. Business firms use the _____ to produce goods and services.

2. The universal economic problem of _____ exists because people have limited resources but nearly unlimited wants and needs.

3. If a consumer has $500 and chooses to buy a television set rather than a $500 mountain bike, the mountain bike is the _____ of the buyer's decision.

4. The graph used to illustrate how much of one product must be given up to produce more of a second product is called a _____.

Skill Review

Directions: Find three supporting details in the passage below. List the details in the space provided.

News about large businesses grabs most of the headlines. However, small businesses are an important part of the US economy. Generally speaking, a small business is a firm that employs fewer than 500 workers. In 2008, more than 99 percent of US businesses were small businesses. These small firms created about two-thirds of all new jobs. They also produced more than half of the country's output of nonfarm goods and services. Keeping small businesses healthy is important for US economic prosperity.

1. A. _____

   B. _____

   C. _____

Directions: Use the production possibilities table and production possibilities curve to answer these questions. Write your answers in a notebook.

Sam can produce subs (grinders) or sandwiches in his deli. With his current resources, his daily production of subs and sandwiches is shown in the table.

Production Possibilities (Daily)

Product	Points				
	A	**B**	**C**	**D**	**E**
Sandwiches	450	400	300	150	0
Subs	0	100	200	300	350

PRODUCTION POSSIBILITIES CURVE

2. How many sandwiches could Sam produce if all his resources are used to make sandwiches? On the PPC, which point shows this?

3. At point D, how many sandwiches could Sam's Deli produce? How many subs?

4. What is the opportunity cost at point B, stated in terms of sandwiches?

5. What is the opportunity cost at point C, stated in terms of subs?

Skill Practice

Directions: Choose the one best answer to each question.

1. Why does the economic problem of scarcity exist?

   A. The Industrial Revolution created sweatshop working conditions.
   B. Societies have created different types of economic systems.
   C. Businesses, consumers, and governments face opportunity costs.
   D. People have limited resources but unlimited wants and needs.

2. What does a production possibilities curve demonstrate?

   A. Consumers must make choices between competing goods.
   B. When suppliers produce more of one item, they must determine how much of each item to produce.
   C. Governments do not face opportunity cost because tax dollars are used to supply needed services.
   D. Scarcity applies to modern economies but did not apply to ancient economies.

Writing Practice

Directions: Look again at the production possibility table for Sam's Deli. If you worked for Sam, what advice would you give him about the production of sandwiches and subs? In a notebook, draft a letter to Sam proposing a plan for the production of sandwiches and subs. Support your ideas with details from the production possibility table.

The Role of the Market

KEY CONCEPT: The forces of demand and supply create market prices for most products and resources in the US economy.

Have you ever used a store coupon or manufacturer's coupon to buy groceries, clothing, or a pizza? Coupons might offer you "$5 off" the price of an item or the chance to "buy 1 and get 1 free." Because coupons make items less expensive, they send buyers an invisible signal to purchase more of the item.

The functioning of markets in the US economy is based on invisible signals, many of which offer people incentives to buy or to produce certain goods. Price is perhaps the most important signal that influences people's economic behaviors.

Lesson Objectives

You will be able to

- Explain *demand* and understand a demand curve

- Explain *supply* and understand a supply curve

- Analyze a market-equilibrium graph for a product

Skills

- **Reading Skill:** Understand the Implied Main Idea

- **Core Skill:** Make Inferences

Vocabulary

demand
implied main idea
market
market equilibrium
money
supply

Markets

A **market** is any situation in which a buyer and a seller freely choose to exchange one thing for another. Markets have two sides: a demand side (buyers or consumers) and a supply side (producers).

Markets have operated in different ways over time. Some ancient societies used barter as the method of exchange. **Barter** is the direct exchange of one product for another product. As civilizations grew, they often developed a form of money to make exchanges easier. **Money** is anything people will accept in payment for products. People have used precious metals, paper, shells, and stones as money.

Money helps set a price for products. When you shop, price helps you compare the value of products. For example, at a bakery the price of a donut may be $1, while the price of a Danish may be $2. This tells you that the value of the Danish is double the value of the donut. Where does the price of a product come from? To answer this question, we must examine the forces that create most prices in a market economy— the forces of demand and supply.

Demand and the Law of Demand

Demand is the amount of a product people are willing and able to buy at a specific price within a certain time. This definition may sound complicated but demand is really just common sense. The **law of demand** tells us that when the price of a product increases, the quantity we will buy falls. The reverse is also true. That is, when the price of a good decreases, the quantity we will buy goes up.

Demand Schedule and Demand Curve

Economists illustrate the law of demand in two ways: a demand schedule and a demand curve. A **demand schedule** is a table that shows how price impacts the quantity of a product that is demanded. The demand schedule for pizza slices is shown on page 192. As the price of a pizza slice increases, the quantity demanded falls.

UNDERSTAND THE IMPLIED MAIN IDEA

Everything you read has a main idea. Sometimes the main idea is stated directly in the passage. At other times the main idea is implied. An **implied main idea** is an idea that is suggested by the information in the paragraph but not directly stated. A passage that expresses an opinion, such as an editorial, may have an implied main idea about a necessary reform, a course of action, or needed policy change.

The main idea is the most important idea the author wants you to understand. To figure out the main idea when the author does not state it directly, you must draw a conclusion about what the author wants you to remember after reading the passage.

To find the main idea of a passage, ask yourself these questions: *What is this passage about? Does the author state the main idea directly? If not, what conclusion can I make about the author's main idea?*

Read the following passage. In a notebook, write one sentence stating the implied main idea.

> In 2012, another study found that sugary drinks can kill you. There is even a number in this study: 180,000 deaths worldwide in 2010. The more sugar you drink, the more likely you are to die from diabetes, heart disease, or cancer. Despite these findings, advertisers keep showing us images of healthy, active people guzzling sodas and energy drinks. In response, we willingly cram our shopping carts with bottle after bottle, lining the pockets of those drink producers. If the ads told us how much sugar is in the drinks, would we still rush out to buy them?

The implied main idea is that advertisers of sugary drinks should be required to state the sugar content of their drinks in order to safeguard people's health.

21st Century Skill
Critical Thinking and Problem Solving

The value of a good or service is not necessarily the same as its price. In fact, a product's **perceived value** depends on how much the buyer wants or needs the product. A buyer considers not only the cost but also the benefit of a product. If people can't afford the product, they won't buy it. But no matter how low the price, people won't buy a product if they don't want it or need it.

Write a paragraph about a time you wanted something but did not buy it because you thought it was too expensive. Describe how the price would have had to change before you would have considered buying the product.

THINK ABOUT SOCIAL STUDIES

Directions: Match the words with their definitions.

_____ 1. money

_____ 2. price

_____ 3. barter

_____ 4. market

A. direct exchange of one good for another

B. stated value of a good

C. a voluntary exchange of one good for another

D. anything accepted in payment for goods

If the writer does not
directly state the main
idea of a passage, you
must figure out the
implied main idea. Ask
yourself, *What does
the writer want me to
understand?*

Read the paragraph
below the Demand
Schedule chart and
graph. This paragraph
implies, or hints, that
producers do not always
think the same way
consumers think.

Then use the
information in the
paragraph to answer
these questions in a
notebook:

- How might producers
  (businesses) use the
  law of demand?

- Why would producers
  lower or raise prices
  for their products?

- Can producers charge
  any price they want
  for their products?

A **demand curve** plots the numbers from the demand schedule onto a graph. The graph consists of two axes: the price axis (vertical) and the quantity-demanded axis (horizontal). The points show the number of slices people will buy at each price. For example, point E shows that people will buy 100 slices of pizza at $1 per slice. On the other hand, at point A (where pizza costs $5 per slice), people will only buy 20 slices.

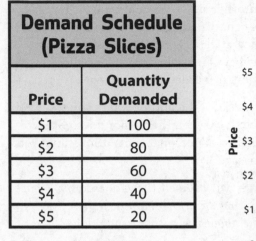

Demand Schedule (Pizza Slices)	
Price	Quantity Demanded
$1	100
$2	80
$3	60
$4	40
$5	20

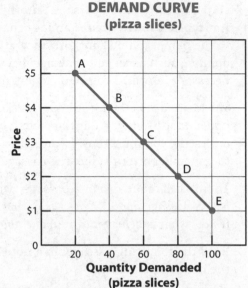

DEMAND CURVE
(pizza slices)

The demand curve slopes downward to reflect the law of demand. The demand curve shows just one side of a market—the side of the consumer, or buyer. Looking at the demand curve, you can see that the lower the price, the more pizza consumers will buy. Producers, or suppliers, have a different perspective on how much of a product they should supply and at what price.

Supply and the Law of Supply

Supply is the amount of a product businesses are willing and able to produce at a specific price in a certain time. When products are profitable, businesses are willing to produce more of them. The law of supply contrasts with the law of demand (which focuses on how much of a product a consumer is willing to buy). The law of supply says that when the price of a product increases, the supplier will increase production. Conversely, when the price decreases, the supplier will produce less.

Supply Schedule and Supply Curve

Economists illustrate the law of supply in two ways: a supply schedule and a supply curve. A **supply schedule** is a table that shows the impact of price on the quantity of a product supplied. The supply schedule shown on page 193 is for pizza slices. Note that as the price of pizza slices increases, the supplier is willing to increase the supply.

A **supply curve** plots the numbers from the supply schedule onto a graph. Price is on the vertical axis, and quantity supplied is on the horizontal axis. At point V, the producer will supply 20 pizza slices at $1 per slice. At point Z, in contrast, the producer is willing to supply 100 pizza slices because of the high price.

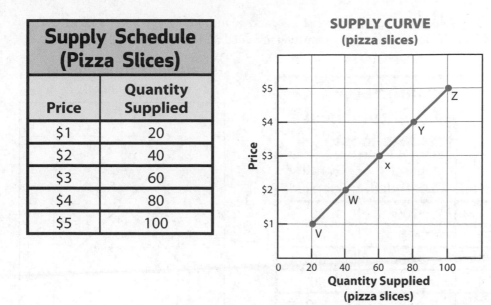

Supply Schedule (Pizza Slices)	
Price	Quantity Supplied
$1	20
$2	40
$3	60
$4	80
$5	100

SUPPLY CURVE
(pizza slices)

The supply curve slopes upward to reflect the law of supply. The supply curve shows just one side of a market—the side of the producer and seller of goods and services. The producer would like to produce a lot of pizza slices at the high price of $5 per slice. However, buyers would like to buy a lot of pizza slices at the low price of $1 per slice. To arrive at a fair compromise between these two opposing views, the demand curve and the supply curve must appear on the same graph.

THINK ABOUT SOCIAL STUDIES

Directions: Write a short response to the following questions in a notebook.

1. Why does the demand curve for products typically slope downward?

2. Why does the supply curve for products typically slope upward?

3. Whose viewpoint is expressed by the demand curve? By the supply curve?

Market Equilibrium

The **market equilibrium** is the point where the demand is equal to the supply. It is the best compromise between the interests of the consumer and the interests of the producer.

To visualize market equilibrium, the demand curve and the supply curve must be placed on the same graph. What is the market equilibrium price and quantity for pizza slices? To answer this question, the data for both curves—the demand curve and the supply curve—are plotted on one graph, which is shown on page 194.

WRITE TO LEARN

A written analysis is a statement that examines evidence and offers a conclusion about a topic. For instance, when a meteorologist analyzes atmospheric conditions, the conclusion is a weather report. Similarly business people can draw conclusions and make predictions based on economic data.

Read "Market Equilibrium." Then consider what would happen if the pizza producer insists on producing 100 pizza slices and charging $5 per slice.

Write an analysis of this situation. Draw a conclusion about the producer's decision.

You make an inference when you use clues in a passage to figure out something that the author does not tell you.

Read "Government Intervention." Then think about price floors and price ceilings. Answer one of these questions in a notebook:

- If the minimum wage is increased, what effect might that have on employers and employees?

- In some cities, rent controls are not changed for long periods of time. What effect does that have on apartments, apartment owners, and renters?

In the graph, price is on the vertical axis, and quantity is on the horizontal axis. This graph title indicates that quantity demanded and quantity supplied are both included in the graph.

Demand/Supply Schedules combined (pizza slices)		
Price	Quantity Demanded	Quantity Supplied
$1	100	20
$2	80	40
$3	60	60
$4	40	80
$5	20	100

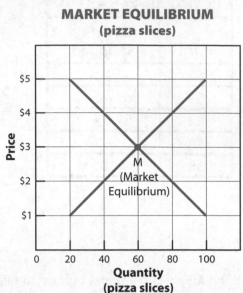

MARKET EQUILIBRIUM
(pizza slices)

The intersection (or crossing) of the demand curve and the supply curve shows the price and quantity at market equilibrium. This is at point M on the graph. The market equilibrium price is $3, and the market equilibrium quantity is 60 pizza slices. Keep in mind that demand and supply determine prices in a market economy.

Government Intervention

The government sometimes steps in to set the price for goods or services. Price setting by the government is often called **price control**. There are two types of price controls: price floors and price ceilings. A **price floor** occurs when the government creates a minimum (lowest) price for a good, service, or resource. For example, the minimum wage is a price floor because it sets the minimum price (hourly wage) that an employer can pay workers. A **price ceiling** occurs when the government creates a maximum (highest) price for a product. For example, rent control on apartments is a price ceiling because it sets the maximum price (monthly rent payment) that the apartment owner can charge tenants.

Vocabulary Review

Directions: Use these words to complete the following sentences.

demand   market   market equilibrium   money   supply

1. The best compromise between the interests of the consumer and the producer of a good is called the _____.

2. The _____ reflects the producer's willingness and ability to make a product at a certain price. The consumers' willingness and ability to buy a product at a certain price is reflected in the _____ for the product.

3. Throughout history, people have accepted many kinds of _____ for products exchanged in a _____.

Directions: Read the following chart and passage. In a notebook, write a short response to the questions below.

Poverty continues to be a serious problem in the United States. In 2009, the number of poor people living in the United States was nearly 43 million. This was more than 14 percent of the population. Opportunities for the poor to advance in society are limited by several factors. One of the main factors is the lack of education. Is it acceptable for one of the world's most prosperous countries to allow so many people to remain in poverty?

Income of Households and Level of Education, 2010

Level of Education	Median Annual Income
Less than 9th grade	$21,635
9th to 12th grade (no diploma)	$25,604
High school graduate	$39,647
Some college (no degree)	$48,413
Associate's degree	$56,789
Bachelor's degree or more	$82,722

Statistical Abstract of the US: 2012, US Census Bureau

1. What government policy or action does the author imply the United States should pursue?

2. What would happen if the government did nothing? Use the data to explain your response.

3. Does the information imply that poverty can be completely eliminated? Explain.

Skill Practice

Directions: Choose the <u>one best answer</u> to each question.

1. What is the market equilibrium of a product?
   A. the most profitable point for the business
   B. the equal balance of price and supply of the product
   C. the shortage of the product
   D. the surplus of the product

2. According to the law of demand, what relationship exists between the price of a product and the quantity demanded of the product?
   A. When price increases, the quantity demanded increases.
   B. When quantity demanded decreases, the price increases.
   C. When price decreases, the quantity demanded increases.
   D. When quantity demanded is constant, the price increases.

Writing Practice

Directions: American consumers like to shop at sales. Write a paragraph describing how you (or someone you know) shops for sale prices. Explain how sale prices affect the demand. Consider why it is not always good for the consumer to shop at sales. Draw a conclusion about why store owners offer low prices, even when these low prices reduce their profits.

The Role of Government

KEY CONCEPT: The role of government in the US economy has increased dramatically during the past century.

The family is the most basic social unit. In families, parents or guardians use household income to provide for the family's needs. These heads of household also create household rules to protect the health and safety of the family.

Similarly, the government at all levels—local, state, and federal—provides for society's needs. Government programs are financed by taxing the people. Government also creates rules and regulations to guide the economic behavior of individuals and firms and to protect the overall health of the economy.

Government's Role in the Economy

The role of government in the US economy has expanded over the past century. The average American in the early 1900s would be astounded by the new roles that have been taken over by government.

Laissez-Faire Capitalism

Laissez-faire is a French term that means "let do" or "let be." In economics, **laissez-faire capitalism** is an economic system run without government interference. The laissez-faire doctrine dominated the US economy from the early twentieth century until the start of the Great Depression in the 1930s.

The Great Depression and New Deal

The Great Depression was a severe decline in the US economy during the 1930s. In November 1932, Franklin D. Roosevelt was elected president. Assisted by a worried Congress, Roosevelt launched the New Deal in March 1933. It vastly expanded the role of government in the US economy. The New Deal included these achievements:

- put millions of unemployed people to work in government programs such as the Civilian Conservation Corps (CCC) and Works Progress Administration (WPA)

- created the Social Security system

- created new regulations to monitor business practices and strengthen banks, including the Federal Deposit Insurance Corporation (FDIC) to protect bank deposits

- created the Fair Labor Standards Act to guarantee workers a minimum wage, a 44-hour work week, and overtime pay

ANALYZE INFORMATION

Analyzing information is the process of identifying and evaluating information. The ability to **analyze**, or break information into parts, can help you make better economic decisions.

Analyzing information involves a few steps.

- First, identify the main idea. What is the author's most important point?

- Second, identify evidence that is used to defend the author's viewpoint.

- Third, evaluate the evidence. Is it reliable? Is it unbiased? Does it relate to the topic?

- Finally, form a conclusion based on your analysis.

Analyze this paragraph by following the steps above. Write answers to the questions in your notebook.

> The growth in federal spending on health insurance programs has risen dramatically in recent years. The federal government's spending on Medicare, the health insurance program mainly for the elderly and disabled, more than doubled from 1997 to 2007 (rising from $210 billion to $431 billion), according to the US Department of Health and Human Services (HHS). HHS reported similar growth in Medicaid, the health insurance program for the poor. Medicaid benefits given out by the federal government grew from $95 billion to $186 billion during the same 10-year period. HHS predicted that the growth in federal spending for Medicare and Medicaid would far outpace growth in the overall economy from 2008 to 2018.

The main idea is _____.
Is the author's position valid? Explain your position.

WRITE TO LEARN

Analyzing information in a text or a passage involves evaluating the evidence provided and forming conclusions based on that evidence.

Read "The Great Depression and New Deal" on page 196. As you read, evaluate the reasons that the New Deal came about and the kinds of programs that were developed. Ask yourself, *Why did the role of government in the US economy change during the 1930s?*

In your notebook, write an analysis of government's changing role.

From 1946 through the 1980s

Immediately after World War II, Congress passed the Employment Act of 1946, which was designed to help stablize the economy. The government would now be expected to create policies that would promote economic growth, full employment, and stable prices if the US economy faltered.

1. What is laissez-faire capitalism?

_____

2. Why was the New Deal of the 1930s a turning point in the role of government in the economy?

_____

Authors sometimes construct arguments using **faulty logic**, or arguments in which the reasoning does not make sense. When you evaluate the author's reasoning, ask yourself whether the author has drawn a logical conclusion.

As you read the following paragraph, think about the author's conclusion.

Studies show that the most shark bites occur in the months with the highest ice cream sales. If the new ice cream parlor opens in town, we will have increased risk of shark bites.

This paragraph shows faulty logic.

In your notebook, explain why the author's conclusion is illogical.

During President John F. Kennedy's administration (1961–1963), the government cut taxes. Soon after that, President Lyndon B. Johnson (1963–1968) and Congress enacted the Great Society programs. These programs expanded aid to the needy. Medicare provided health insurance for the elderly, and Medicaid did the same for the poor.

Some attempts were made to reign in government involvement in the 1980s. During President Ronald Reagan's administration (1981–1989), policies to eliminate business regulations and tax cuts were enacted.

From 2007 to the Present

A serious recession from 2007–2009 brought another wave of government interventions in the economy. A **recession** is an economic downturn in which business activity slows, unemployment rises, and investment decreases. In 2008, near the end of George W. Bush's presidency (2001–2009), the government provided hundreds of billions of dollars to rescue ailing financial institutions. The Bush administration also supported a large tax rebate. A tax rebate is similar to a tax refund. The goal was to bring about economic recovery by encouraging people to buy more goods.

Under the Barack Obama administration (2009–2016), hundreds of billions of additional dollars were pumped into an "economic stimulus package." The stimulus package was intended to create jobs and to encourage economic growth.

The Four Roles of Government

One of the most important features of the US economic system is **limited government**. However, the role of government has expanded over time. Today government has four roles in our economy. It regulates businesses, provides public goods, promotes the well-being of the people, and stabilizes the overall economy. People generally support some government involvement in these areas. Still, there is debate about how involved the government should be in the country's economy.

Regulating Business Activity

The government creates laws that govern businesses. For instance, laws prohibit monopolies from forming. This is to promote competition, which should provide consumers with more options and better prices.

In addition, over time the government has created numerous federal agencies to guide business behavior. The Federal Trade Commission (FTC) protects people from dishonest or misleading advertising. The Consumer Product Safety Commission (CPSC) protects consumers from dangerous products. The Securities and Exchange Commission (SEC) protects investors from investment fraud. The Occupational Safety and Health Administration (OSHA) protects workers from unsafe working conditions.

Providing Public Goods

Government at all levels—local, state, and national—provide public goods. **Public goods** are goods that the government provides for all people to use.

But why does government, rather than private businesses, produce public goods? The answer is that individuals and businesses are not willing to produce all the public goods needed to satisfy people. For example, a business needs highways so it can sell its products in cities across the country. But it is not willing to build the highways. In fact, other businesses also need the highways, and private citizens would use the highways for work or recreation. Over time the government recognized the need for highways. To spread the cost of these roads among all possible users, the government collected taxes to build those highways.

Promoting the Well-Being of the People

The government promotes well-being mainly through transfer payments. A **transfer payment** is money used to help people in need. The two types of transfer payments are social insurance programs and public assistance programs.

Social insurance programs give benefits to people who have made regular financial contributions to the program. The largest social insurance programs are Social Security and Medicare. Working people and their employers pay into these two programs. Upon retirement these people receive income and health benefits from the government.

Public assistance programs give benefits to people who have not made financial contributions to the program. Payments to the poor under Temporary Assistance to Needy Families (TANF) and health insurance through Medicaid are examples of public assistance programs.

Stabilizing the Economy

The government stabilizes the economy by trying to ease economic downturns and other economic problems. Traditionally, the two main types of government policies used to stabilize the economy are fiscal policy and monetary policy.

Fiscal policy is the use of taxation and government spending to deal with economic problems. During times of recession, when business activity is slow, Congress and the president might decrease taxes and increase government spending. More money circulating in the economy creates more demand for goods, more production, and more jobs. To fight **inflation** (a general rise in prices), the government might increase taxes and decrease government spending.

Monetary policy is under the control of the Federal Reserve System (the Fed), the central bank of the United States. The Fed's most important monetary tool is open-market operations. Open-market operations occur when the Fed buys or sells government securities, such as bonds. To fight recession, the Fed buys back its securities from investors. This adds cash to the economy so business activity will increase. To fight inflation, the Fed sells additional securities to investors. This removes excess cash from the system and slows the rise of prices.

Core Skill
Evaluate Reasoning

Authors try to create logical arguments by using solid evidence, making reasonable assumptions, and drawing conclusions based on the evidence.

In "Providing Public Goods," the author states that public works such as highways are necessary. Work with a partner to think of other public goods provided by the government.

Then select one of the public goods you have thought of. Write a paragraph answering the following questions. Use evidence and logical reasoning to support your ideas.

- Why does the government provide this public good?

- If this public good were not provided by government, who would provide it?

- What is the advantage or disadvantage of the government's providing this public goods?

To analyze information you must evaluate the evidence and then form a conclusion about the writer's main point. You are evaluating whether the writer has made a convincing argument.

Read the information on this page about various types of taxes. Some people claim that lower-income groups in the United States pay the highest taxes. To analyze this claim, ask yourself the following questions:

• Which taxes are aimed mainly at lower-income groups?

• Which taxes are aimed mainly at higher-income groups?

• Does the evidence support the claim that lower-income groups pay the highest taxes?

Taxation: Paying for Government Programs

A **tax** is a **mandatory**, or required, payment people make to the government. Individuals and businesses pay taxes to the local, state, and federal government.

Local Taxes Local taxes are used mainly to take care of local needs such as education and public safety. The property tax is the most important local tax because it raises the most money for towns or cities. A property tax requires people with major assets—mainly their homes—to pay a tax on these assets each year.

State Taxes State taxes are used to take care of state and local needs such as highways, education, and the criminal justice system. Most state tax revenues come from three taxes: state income tax, state sales tax, and excise taxes. State income taxes vary. Typically, the tax consists of a percent of the worker's wage. The state sales tax requires people who purchase certain goods to pay a percent of the purchase price as a tax. Some states exempt items such as food and medication from the sales tax so that the tax is less of a burden on the poor. The excise tax is a tax on a specific item. Many states impose excise taxes on cigarettes, alcohol, and gasoline.

Federal Taxes Federal taxes are used mainly to pay for major federal programs, such as national defense, Social Security benefits, and Medicare and Medicaid programs. Most federal revenues come from three taxes: the personal income tax, social insurance taxes, and corporate income tax. The personal income tax raises the most money for the federal government. It is a progressive tax, which means that people with higher incomes pay a higher percent of their income in taxes. Social insurance taxes, such as the Social Security and Medicare tax, take a percent from wage earners' paychecks. The corporate income tax takes a portion of corporation profits.

Vocabulary Review

Directions: Use these words to complete the following sentences.

limited government   public goods   recession   tax   transfer payments

1. The government provides _____ to people when it is clear that neither individuals nor businesses are willing to provide these goods and services.

2. A _____ is a payment that an individual or a company must make to the government.

3. The concept of _____ has expanded greatly over the past century, but it is still a basic principle of the US economy.

4. _____ are used to help people in need.

5. A country is in a _____ when business activity slows and unemployment rises.

Directions: Read the following passage. Answer the question in a notebook.

> In the election of 1928, Herbert Hoover, a Republican, was elected president of the United States. He was sworn in as president in March 1929. In the fall of 1929, the New York Stock Exchange, the largest stock market in the United States, crashed, and many investors lost money. Soon the United States dipped into a depression. Unemployment rose and national output declined during President Hoover's term of office (1929–1933). Factories were idle, and unemployed workers sank into despair. Many people could not make their monthly mortgage payments, and thousands of families were evicted from their homes. Shantytowns, sometimes called Hoovervilles, sprung up all over the country. One thing is clear: President Herbert Hoover was solely responsible for the collapse of the US economy in 1929.

1. Is the author's logic sound or faulty? Give evidence to support your reasoning.

Directions: Read the passage below. Answer the questions that follow in a notebook.

> The following is an excerpt from President Franklin D. Roosevelt's Inaugural Address, delivered to the American people on March 4, 1933, at the height of the Great Depression.
>
> "Our greatest primary task is to put people to work. This is no unsolvable problem if we face it wisely and courageously. It can be accomplished in part by direct recruitment by the Government itself, treating the task as we would treat the emergency of a war, but at the same time, through this employment, accomplishing greatly needed projects to stimulate and reorganize the use of our natural resources.
>
> ". . . There are many ways in which it [the economy] can be helped, but it can never be helped merely by talking about it. We must act and act quickly."

2. What are the main economic benefits that Roosevelt sees if his ideas are turned into action?

3. What course of action is not acceptable to FDR?

Skill Practice

Directions: Choose the one best answer to each question.

1. Which situation was most responsible for the end of laissez-faire capitalism in the United States?

   A. the severity of the Great Depression
   B. the US entry into World War II
   C. the Great Society programs for the needy
   D. the severity of the 2007–2009 recession

2. Which strategy deals specifically with regulating business activity?

   A. using fiscal policy
   B. building highways and schools
   C. granting transfer payments
   D. creating the Securities and Exchange Commission

Writing Practice

Directions: Write a blog entry identifying a public program—such as college loans or free clinics—that promotes the well-being of the people. Give your opinion about why the program should be provided by the government. Support your arguments with sound reasoning.

Money and Financial Institutions

Lesson Objectives

You will be able to

- Identify the functions of money and types of money

- Recognize the components of the US money supply

- Describe the role of banks and other financial institutions in the US economy

- Explain how the US government regulates the banking system

Skills

- **Core Skill:** Evaluate Evidence

- **Reading Skill:** Distinguish Fact from Opinion

Vocabulary

adequate
commercial bank
credit union
Federal Reserve System
fiat money
money supply
savings institution

KEY CONCEPT: Banks and other financial institutions connect people who want to save money with people who want to borrow money in a regulated US financial system.

At some point, you have probably borrowed money from a family member or a close friend. You likely promised to repay the money in the near future. The core of this agreement is that the lender, in this case your relative or friend, trusted you to repay the debt.

Banks and other firms that lend money operate in a similar way. Banks accept deposits from savers and grant loans to borrowers—usually individuals or businesses. A bank makes a loan only if it believes the borrower will repay the loan with interest.

Money and Its Uses

Money is anything that people generally accept in exchange for goods or services. Money has been used for thousands of years. It has taken many forms, including coins, paper currency, shells, cacao, even stones.

Functions of Money Money has three main functions.

- Money is a medium of exchange. People use and accept "money" to buy goods or repay debts.

- Money is a standard of value. Each item offered for sale has a monetary value, or price. The price of an item tells its value compared to other items.

- Money is a store of value. Money holds its value over time. If a society's form of money quickly lost its value, people would not accept money in payment for goods or services.

Types of Money Today the US currency is **fiat money**. Fiat money is money that has value because the government says it has value. Note the words that are printed on US paper currency: "This note is legal tender for all debts public and private." This means that businesses in the United States must accept the currency in payment for goods or services.

In the past, two other types of money have been used in the United States: commodity money and representative money. Commodity money is a form of money that is valuable in itself. Bales of cotton and tobacco were used as money in some parts of America during the colonial era. Representative money is backed by something valuable, such as gold. For much of US history, our paper currency was backed by gold or silver.

DISTINGUISH FACT FROM OPINION

We get information from television, radio, newspapers, magazines, books, Internet blogs, and conversations with friends and family. People collect and process information in a variety of ways. In doing so, they form different viewpoints on problems, issues, and events.

To understand a topic, you need to be able to distinguish facts from opinions. A **fact** is a statement that can be verified, or proven. A fact could be a historical date, a statistic, a specific action, or other information that can be objectively tested or researched. An **opinion** is a person's viewpoint or judgment about an issue, event, or other topic. Opinions can be stated directly or implied. Editorials and other types of writing combine fact and opinion to convey an author's point of view.

How do you separate facts from opinions? Ask yourself these questions: *Can I objectively test a piece of information to see if it is true? Can I find this information in a reference text? Does the author make a judgment about something? Is this a statement that people might disagree with?*

Read the following passage. Identify each sentence as a fact or an opinion.

---

(1) Today the Federal Deposit Insurance Corporation (FDIC) insures bank deposits up to $250,000 per account. (2) The FDIC was created during the 1930s. (3) Originally the FDIC protected deposits up to $2,500 per account. (4) Before the FDIC was created, there was no federal program to protect people's savings in US banks. (5) The FDIC was the most important economic reform that came from the Great Depression era. (6) We should raise FDIC insurance protection to $500,000 per account.

Sentences 1–4 are facts. The information can be verified by looking up the FDIC in a reference book. Sentences 5 and 6 are opinions. They express the author's point of view.

THINK ABOUT SOCIAL STUDIES

Directions: Match these terms with their definitions.

_____ 1. representative money

_____ 2. fiat money

_____ 3. money

_____ 4. commodity money

A. any item that is accepted as a medium of exchange

B. money that has value in itself

C. money that has value due to government decree

D. money backed by gold or silver

A fact is information that can be objectively tested and proven to be true. Authors use facts to explain a topic or defend a viewpoint. At times, you may find that the facts presented are true but not **adequate**, that is, they do not provide enough evidence to prove a point or to support a conclusion. At other times, the facts may be taken from unreliable sources, so the evidence provided is not trustworthy.

Study "Financial Institutions." Then read the following sentences. In your notebook, tell which statements are adequately supported by the facts in the passage.

1. Commercial banks and most savings institutions make more profits than credit unions.

2. Credit unions limit who can put money into their savings accounts.

3. Everyone can borrow money from large commercial banks.

The Money Supply

The **money supply** is the amount of money available for use at any one time. Economists have several ways to measure the amount of money in our economy.

The most common measure of our money supply is called the M1. The M1 consists of currency (bills and coins), traveler's checks, and checkable deposits (money held in people's checking and savings accounts). A summary table of M1 is shown here.

The US Money Supply (M1)	
Components of M1	**Dollar Amount ($ billions)***
Currency	$2,000
Traveler's checks	$4
Checkable deposits	$451
Total M1	**$2,460**

Source: *Federal Reserve System, Statistical Release, Table 1: Money Stock Measures, March 21, 2013.* *some rounding

Financial Institutions

We normally think of banks when we discuss saving or borrowing money. However, a bank is just one type of financial institution that provides financial services to people. Other financial institutions are savings institutions and credit unions. Financial institutions collect deposits and extend loans. They also provide a wide variety of financial services.

Commercial Banks A **commercial bank** is a for-profit firm that provides many financial services to people. Commercial banks accept deposits and make loans to businesses and individuals.

Savings Institutions **Savings institutions**, or "thrifts," focus on making loans to individuals rather than to businesses. The two main types of savings institutions are savings and loan associations (S&Ls) and savings banks. These institutions extend mortgage loans so people can buy homes. They also make small personal loans to consumers for purchasing cars and making home repairs. Most savings institutions are for-profit.

Credit Unions **Credit unions** are owned by their members. They give home mortgage and personal loans to members. Credit unions are not designed to earn profits. As a result, they typically offer higher interest rates on members' savings deposits. They may also offer lower interest rates on money that members borrow.

Government Oversight of Financial Institutions

Over the past century, the federal government has become more active in monitoring and strengthening the US banking and financial system. Two of the most important watchdogs are the Federal Deposit Insurance Corporation and the Federal Reserve System. These agencies often assist each other in safeguarding the country's financial well-being.

Federal Deposit Insurance Corporation The FDIC was created in 1933 to provide federal insurance for bank deposits. Thousands of US banks had collapsed during the early years of the Great Depression. The FDIC and other government actions reassured Americans. Almost overnight, "panic runs" to withdraw money from the banks stopped.

The FDIC was created as an independent agency of the federal government. It receives no tax dollars to support its work. Instead, it raises funds by collecting premiums from banks and savings institutions. Other revenues are earned from FDIC investments. This money is used to stabilize the banking system and to support the FDIC operations.

The main responsibilities of the FDIC are to supervise banks and savings institutions and to resolve financial problems when they arise. If a bank fails, the FDIC helps negotiate the sale of the failed bank to a stronger bank. Some FDIC money may be needed to complete the sale. However, in most cases, banking functions at these failed banks continue without interruption.

The Federal Reserve System The **Federal Reserve System**, often called the Fed, is the central bank of the United States. It was created by the Federal Reserve Act in 1913. As our central bank, the Fed supervises the banking system and provides services to strengthen the financial system. The Fed also creates monetary policy to stabilize the entire economy.

The creation of the Fed followed a series of financial crises. The most serious of these crises was the Panic of 1907, a time when people feared large-scale bank failures. Worried depositors made panic runs on the banks. This threatened the country's entire banking system because the government was unable to stop the panic. Banking giant J. P. Morgan and other major bankers restored order by loaning money to weak banks.

The Fed was created as an independent agency of the federal government. Like the FDIC, the Fed does not rely on tax dollars. Instead, it earns revenues from fees paid by banks, interest earned on its investments, and other transactions.

How does the Fed monitor and strengthen the US banking system? One way is by supervising the nation's banks. Supervision ensures that banks follow laws and rules. The Fed also provides some financial services. For instance, technologies used by the Fed help the government process Social Security checks, help people pay bills electronically, and help banks clear checks. The Fed also makes sure that banks have enough money to meet their needs. The ability to quickly supply money to banks helps create confidence among savers and prevent panic runs.

Other Agencies While the FDIC and the Fed are the largest government watchdogs, other federal agencies also help monitor and protect the financial system. The National Credit Union Administration (NCUA) oversees thousands of credit unions. It also administers the National Credit Union Share Insurance Fund (NCUSIF), which provides insurance protection for people who deposit their savings in credit unions. The Office of Thrift Supervision (OTS) helps regulate savings institutions such as S&Ls and savings banks.

WRITE TO LEARN

Social scientists study cause-and-effect relationships. A cause is an event that creates a response. The response is the effect. For example:

Cause: Bank accounts are insured.

Effect: People are confident their money is safe in savings accounts.

Read "Government Oversight of Financial Institutions." Find the events (causes) that led to the creation of the FDIC and the Fed (effects).

Write a paragraph that explains this cause-and-effect relationship. Use signal words such as *because* and *therefore*.

Reading Skill
Distinguish Fact from Opinion

A fact is information that can be proven. An opinion is a judgment.

Use online resources to learn about one commercial bank, one savings institution, and one credit union in your community.

In your notebook, write one fact and one opinion that you find about each of these financial institutions.

Vocabulary Review

Directions: Use these terms to complete the following sentences.

**commercial bank   credit union   Federal Reserve System   fiat money
money supply   savings institution**

1. A _____ is a nonprofit financial institution that provides financial services
to its members.

2. Currency that is backed by a government order is called _____.

3. A _____ is a for-profit institution that gives loans to businesses and individuals.

4. The US central bank, called the _____, helps supervise our banking and
financial system.

5. A savings and loan association is a type of _____ that makes home mortgage
loans and personal loans to individuals.

6. The _____ is the amount of money available for use at any one time.

Skill Review

Directions: In the passages shown below, identify the statements that are facts and the
statements that are opinions.

1. (1) The Social Security System should be abolished because it fails to meet the needs of
twenty-first century Americans. (2) The Social Security System was created in 1935, during
the Great Depression. (3) In the 1960s, Medicare, the health insurance program for retired
workers, was created. (4) Today the combined Social Security tax and Medicare tax takes
more than 7 percent from most workers' wages each payday. (5) Employers must match this
amount and send the money to the government. (6) The present Social Security tax and
Medicare tax are unfair and unnecessary. (7) People should be able to save money for their
own retirement and not rely on government programs.

Facts: _____

Opinions: _____

2. (1) A stock market provides a way for investors to buy or sell stocks of a corporation.
(2) On the basis of the number of stocks bought and sold, the NASDAQ Stock Market is
the largest stock market in the world. (3) The NASDAQ Stock Market is made up of a
complex network of investors and investment companies that are linked by computers.
(4) The New York Stock Exchange (NYSE) is the second-largest stock market. (5) The way
stocks are traded at the NYSE is old fashioned, so it should close its doors. (6) Companies
currently listed on the NYSE should switch to the more modern NASDAQ Stock Market.
(7) In addition, the US government should extend FDIC insurance protection to investors
to guarantee that investors don't lose money on their stocks.

Facts: _____

Opinions: _____

Skill Review (continued)

Directions: Read the statements below. If the facts in the statement are adequate to prove the author's point, write "A" for adequate. If the facts are not adequate, write "NA" for not adequate.

_____ **3.** Last month Joe lost his job at the local auto manufacturing plant. Two months earlier Jane lost her teaching job due to budget cuts in her school district. This shows the economy is in a recession.

_____ **4.** The FDIC insures bank deposits up to $250,000 and supervises the business practices of banks across the country. Because of these reforms, bank failures today are impossible.

_____ **5.** Social Security payments are linked to the cost of living, so payments to recipients change each year. The number of Social Security recipients will grow by millions in the coming years. As a result, the federal government will have to spend more money on Social Security benefits in the future.

Skill Practice

Directions: Choose the one best answer to each question.

1. Jin earns $500 each week from his job. He saves $50 per week in a bank. Within a year he hopes to have enough money to buy a used car. Jin is confident that the value of his money will not fall during the coming year. His decision to save money for a future purchase best illustrates which function of money?

A. medium of exchange
B. store of value
C. standard of value
D. opportunity cost

2. Regina owns a business and needs to borrow $1 million to expand it. At which financial institution will Regina apply for a business loan?

A. savings and loan association
B. credit union
C. savings bank
D. commercial bank

3. FDIC insurance directly protects which group in the US economy?

A. savers
B. investors
C. workers
D. consumers

Writing Practice

Directions: Write an essay comparing the benefits of commercial banks with the benefits of credit unions. In the first paragraph, compare and contrast the two institutions. In the second paragraph, write your opinion of which type of institution you would prefer to use. Be sure to support your opinion with clear reasons and evidence.

Monopoly and Competition

KEY CONCEPT: When only one seller offers a product, the seller determines the price and the level of service. When two or more sellers provide the same product to the same group of customers, the sellers must take customers' wants and needs into account.

Suppose there's one laundromat in your neighborhood. Although its machines don't always work, it is the only place nearby to do your wash. A second laundromat with brand-new machines opens. The first laundromat soon offers free soap. What's behind this "laundry war"? To attract the same group of customers, each laundromat must show why it is the better choice. Customers benefit from the improved service.

Monopolies and Competition

A **market** is any place where buyers and sellers can do business. The market can be real, like a shopping mall, or it can be virtual, like an online seller. **Market structure** describes how a market is organized. Factors that determine the market structure include the number of companies selling a product, the number of buyers for a product, and the number of similar products available. Two types of market structures are monopoly and competition.

Monopoly exists where there is only one seller that provides a product or service. In practice, a pure monopoly does not exist. Instead, the word *monopoly* has come to mean that one seller controls most of the market. One kind of monopoly is a utility company, such as a supplier of electricity. All residents in an area must buy their electricity from one company.

A company may become a monopoly by setting up a **barrier to entry**—that is, a condition that prevents competition. For example, a company may patent a drug so no other company can make and sell that medication. A company that has the only access to a diamond mine can prevent other companies from mining diamonds in an area. Patents and access to natural resources are two examples of barriers to entry.

Competition is the opposite of monopoly. Competition is created when many businesses provide a similar product. Competing suppliers do research to determine what customers want, and then they develop products to meet those desires. Competing companies set prices that attract customers and provide good service.

Competition leads to **innovation**, or original and creative changes. An example is the auto industry, which regularly develops new vehicle models. Buyers compare products, prices, and services. In the mind of customers, competition is often linked with freedom and prosperity. Having many sellers, a wide choice of products, and interested buyers can lead to economic growth and job creation.

DETERMINE CENTRAL IDEA

The central idea is the most important idea that the author wants you to understand. A paragraph has a central idea, a longer passage has a central idea, and an entire book has a central idea.

Often the author states the central idea at the beginning of the passage. Sometimes the title can help you determine the central idea.

Read the following passage about market structure. What is the central idea that the author wants you to remember?

How Market Structure Affects Prices

Competition in the market affects the price of goods and services. The price of an item changes in response to either the **supply** (the number of products available for sale) or the **demand** (the interest customers have in buying the product or service). This is especially noticeable during a crisis. Because of the heavy damage caused by Hurricane Sandy in 2012, consumers in New England saw a sharp rise in the cost of electrical generators and gasoline as well as the price of hotel rooms and nonperishable food.

Even in noncrisis situations, an increase or decrease in demand and an increase or decrease in supply affect the price of goods and services. These **fluctuations**, or changes, can drive prices up or down.

In a competitive market structure, buyers and sellers have many choices. For example, a buyer may choose to buy a less-expensive product if the original item is too costly. Sellers may try to lure customers by reducing prices or adding services. Both the buyer and the seller affect the price of goods and services.

By contrast, in monopolies, the single producer or seller can control the price. The buyer in a monopoly situation has little choice, and demand has little effect on the price. The seller in a monopoly will set a price as high as possible. However, if prices rise too high, consumers will search for other ways to cut their costs.

An example of how customers control costs can be found in what customers do when utility rates increase. Some customers use less power, use more energy-efficient appliances, or use appliances at night when rates are lower. None of these consumer strategies will lower the utility rates. However, by altering their energy use, consumers may reduce their own costs and cut into the profits of the utility company.

The central idea of the passage is stated in the first sentence of the passage: "Competition in the market affects the price of goods and services." Details in the passage help you understand this idea.

Reading Skill
Determine Central Idea

Finding the central idea, or main idea, of a passage helps you understand what you are reading. Then you will be able to see how the facts in the text fit together to support that central idea.

Ask yourself these questions to determine the central idea of a passage:

- What does the title tell me about the topic of the passage?

- What idea does the writer state in the topic sentence (often the first sentence in a paragraph or a section)?

Read "Monopolies and Competition." Then, in a notebook, write answers to these questions:

- What is the central idea of the passage?

- How does the title relate to the central idea?

In the passage about AT&T, you will find some **multiple-meaning words**. These are words that have more than one meaning. To figure out the meaning of a multiple-meaning word, look at the context—that is, look for clues in the text surrounding the multiple-meaning word.

Read the following sentences and look at the underlined word or phrase. Circle context clues that help you figure out the meaning of that word or phrase as it relates to economics.

1. AT&T had a monopoly on the <u>market</u> for telephones and telephone service.

2. After Bell's patents expired, the <u>barriers to entry</u> were lowered for anyone who wished to compete with AT&T.

3. The company had to consider <u>demand</u>. It had to attract customers by providing the types of service customers wanted.

4. <u>Competition</u> and new phone technology drove down the price of long-distance service.

Directions: Read the following passage about the development and breakup of the telephone company AT&T, which has been a monopoly during much of its existence. Then write one reason why this monopoly has been good for our economy and one reason why it has been bad.

AT&T Reinvents Itself

The story of AT&T is a history of adapting to changing times and advances in technology. In the mid-1870s, Alexander Graham Bell completed his most famous invention, the telephone. Bell obtained US patents for the telephone in 1876 and 1877. With the patents in hand, Bell and two investors formed the Bell Telephone Company to produce and sell his invention. By 1885, the company was known as the American Telephone and Telegraph Company (AT&T).

Because AT&T held the patents, only AT&T could manufacture telephones and operate telephone systems in the United States. The company licensed the service providers that brought local telephone service to most of the country's major cities and towns. AT&T had a monopoly on the market for telephones and telephone service.

After Bell's patents expired, the barriers to entry were lowered for anyone who wished to compete with AT&T. Thousands of new telephone companies formed in the United States. However, because these companies were not connected to one another, the customers of one company could not talk to customers of other companies. AT&T provided the long-distance service that linked the independent phone companies.

By 1939, more than 80 percent of US phone service was controlled by AT&T. The company was the dominant provider of phone equipment as well as service. Because there was little competition, AT&T put its innovative efforts into services and products that the company thought were important. However, these innovations were not necessarily what customers wanted.

THINK ABOUT SOCIAL STUDIES

Directions: Fill in the chart to compare the market structures of monopoly and competition.

Monopoly	Competition
Pricing:	Pricing:
Barriers to entry (high or low):	Barriers to entry (high or low):
Number of suppliers:	Number of suppliers:

While AT&T was a monopoly, it did make many technological advances. It pioneered the use of undersea cables to carry telephone calls between the United States and Europe, and it placed the world's first commercial communications satellite into orbit.

The US Justice Department grew concerned about AT&T's control of the market. Twice the Justice Department sued AT&T to restrict the monopoly. The first lawsuit led to the signing of a consent decree between AT&T and the Justice Department in 1956. The decree restricted AT&T's activities to working on the national telephone system and working for the government. The second lawsuit started in 1974 and was settled in January 1982. In 1984, as a result of the lawsuit, AT&T gave up the regional phone companies that provided local phone service.

Although AT&T no longer supplied local phone service, it was still the country's largest provider of long-distance phone service. But AT&T did have competition in the long-distance market. Therefore, the company had to consider demand. It had to attract customers by providing the types of service that customers wanted.

Competition and new phone technology drove down the price of long-distance service. The use of long-distance telephone service soared, partly because of the need to carry data over the Internet. By 2000, there was more data traffic than voice traffic on the AT&T network.

AT&T has reinvented itself many times. It went from being a provider of local telephone service to being a long-distance phone service provider. Now it is a company that provides a mix of voice and data communication.

THINK ABOUT SOCIAL STUDIES

Directions: Answer the following questions, using AT&T as an example.

To determine demand, many companies do R&D, or research and development. Companies ask customers about their wants and then develop products to fulfill those wants.

1. In what ways did AT&T use R&D to improve telephone service?

   _____

   _____

2. Describe how companies providing phone service today research customer demands and adapt their services.

   _____

   _____

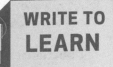

WRITE TO LEARN

Write a journal entry in which you tell about a personal experience you have had comparing the prices and features of two or more similar products. What factors most affected your final decision about which product to buy?

WORKPLACE CONNECTION

Find a Temp Agency

Today many employers hire temporary help instead of permanent employees. This trend has increased the number of temp agencies. As the competition between these agencies increases, many temp agencies are offering employee benefits, such as paid holidays, to the temp workers they send out to local companies.

If you plan to work for a temp agency, you will want to find the agency that offers you the best job possibilities and the best benefits.

In a notebook, make a list of the questions you would ask the person interviewing you at a temp agency so you can compare the benefits offered by various temp staffing agencies.

Vocabulary Review

Directions: Use these terms to complete the following sentences.

barrier to entry   competition   demand   innovation   market structure   monopoly

1. When a company changes a product to make it more attractive to buyers, the new feature or service is called an _____.

2. Customer desire for a particular product is known as _____.

3. The way a market is organized for the sale of particular goods or services is the _____.

4. Companies that sell the same product or service are in _____ with one another.

5. A company that has a _____ is able to set whatever price it wants for its goods or services.

6. Having the patent to make a product, such as the telephone, is a _____ to others who might also want to make that product.

Skill Review

Directions: Choose the <u>one best answer</u> for each question.

1. When you compare and contrast the features of monopoly and competition, what do you discover?

   A. They both promote innovation.
   B. They are each the sole supplier of certain goods or services.
   C. They are both driven by consumer demand.
   D. They are the opposite of each other.

2. What is the relationship between consumer demand and prices?

   A. When consumer demand decreases, prices increase.
   B. When consumer demand decreases, innovation may increase.
   C. When consumer demand increases, prices may increase.
   D. When the government steps in to control prices, consumer demand decreases.

3. During the early days of AT&T, which of the following was a barrier to companies that wanted to enter the telephone industry?

   A. There were thousands of independent telephone companies.
   B. Alexander Graham Bell had the patent to produce the telephone.
   C. A lawsuit challenged AT&T's monopoly.
   D. The invention of the Internet meant that much of AT&T's network was used to transmit data.

Skill Review (continued)

Directions: Write a description of a service you would like to provide in your community. Tell how you could make your service better than what is offered now, and explain why there would be a demand for the service.

4. _____

_____

_____

_____

Skill Practice

Directions: Read this 1984 cartoon and answer the questions that follow.

1. Which historical event does the cartoon refer to?

_____

2. What is the meaning of "competitive market" in the second frame of the comic?

_____

Writing Practice

Directions: Reread the passage about AT&T, or identify another monopoly—even a local one, such as a business in your neighborhood. Why is this business a monopoly? In your opinion, should this business remain a monopoly? Give reasons for your answer.

Profit

KEY CONCEPT: The possibility of increased profits encourages business owners to take risks, to expand, and to try various strategies that will increase productivity.

In the last two months, Mike's cab business has not turned a profit. He had a costly car repair. Road construction has created detours around the business district where he picks up most of his fares. Even with the risks, Mike enjoys being in business for himself. To increase profits, Mike decides to broaden his operations. He begins to advertise that he will deliver packages and do small moving jobs.

Making a Profit

In a capitalist economy, businesses exist to make a **profit**. Profit is the income left after subtracting expenses. To make a profit, a business must do a good job of managing the land, labor, and **capital** needed to make a product. Economists refer to these elements as the factors of production. *Land* refers to the land and all the natural resources used. *Labor* includes all the physical effort, skills, and knowledge of the workers. *Capital* is the physical materials—such as buildings, machines, and supplies—needed to run the business. Income must be greater than the cost of land, labor, and capital to make a profit.

One way to keep expenses down is to increase **productivity**, or output. Productivity is usually measured by how many goods are produced for each hour of labor. For example, a group of workers produces 60 cars per hour. Together they are paid $1,000 per hour. If the workers could make 120 cars per hour, they would increase their productivity by 100 percent. Then, if they are still paid $1,000, the business owner has reduced the cost of labor. By increasing productivity, the owner has reduced the cost of one of the factors of production.

Decreasing any factor of production should increase profit. Businesses can reduce their electrical costs by replacing old light bulbs with more efficient CFLs. They can cut mailing costs by relying on e-mail. They can ask vendors to provide bids, helping the business buy goods and services at lower costs. Some businesses lower their costs by moving production to a foreign country.

Another important way for a company to increase profits is to increase sales. Advertising is one way to sell more of a product. A business may also raise the price of its goods and services so it will have a greater profit.

The Role of Incentive in Making a Profit

Incentive, or motivation, plays a role in every aspect of business. People respond to both positive and negative incentives when making business decisions. This is true of people running a company, employees working for a company, and customers buying the company's products.

DETERMINE THE CENTRAL IDEA

The central idea is the idea that the author wants you to remember. Often you will find the central idea stated at the beginning of a passage and also at the end. The author does this to emphasize the most important idea.

Read the following passage. Then determine its central idea. Underline the sentences that help you figure out the central idea.

> When workers are happy on the job, their high **morale**, or confidence and enthusiasm, filters through the entire company. Employee morale affects every aspect of job performance. Employees with high morale take pride and satisfaction in their jobs and their companies. Satisfied employees are more productive, miss fewer days of work, and put extra time and effort into their jobs. There is less employee turnover in a company with high morale. This saves the company money and increases productivity.
>
> Dissatisfied employees, on the other hand, are costly. They miss more days of work, are less productive when they are at work, and may even damage company property. Their low morale affects the morale of others.
>
> Managers who value their employees' contributions want to keep those employees. They look for ways to boost morale through recognition, involvement, and rewards. They encourage employees to set their own job goals and identify ways of working more efficiently. Because labor is one of the factors of production, efforts to develop and reward good employees can go a long way toward creating high morale—which will, in turn, improve profits.

The central idea of this passage is that employees with high morale help the company. The first sentence in the passage and the last sentence state this idea.

Profit is an important incentive for taking the risk of starting and running a business. People will spend their savings, take out loans, and work nonstop to build up a new business. The chance to make more money is part of what motivates them.

Wages, plus bonuses and tips, are also a powerful incentive for workers. Yet money is not the only incentive for working hard. When employees rate their job satisfaction, their paycheck is just one factor in what makes them happy on the job.

What other factors are incentives for workers? Good working conditions are important. It is hard to focus on work in a space that is noisy, crowded, or too hot or too cold. Employers must make sure their workers feel safe and comfortable on the job. A good employer also thinks of the emotional needs of employees. Company policies, workloads, and the attitude of coworkers all affect the emotional environment of the work place.

Incentive also plays a role for customers. It is the job of the marketing staff to study what customers want and then to come up with ads that encourage customers to buy a particular product. The ads must show how the product will benefit buyers in some way. Good marketing increases sales, which in turn increases profits.

Reading Skill
Determine the Central Idea

The central idea is the main point the writer wants you to understand. All the details in the passage help you understand this main point.

The central idea is often stated in the first sentence of a short text or in the first paragraph of a longer text. The central idea is often restated at the end of the text.

Determine the central idea in "The Role of Incentive." In a notebook, write the central idea and three key details.

WRITE TO LEARN

Business magazines and professional groups make lists each year of the best companies to work for. Do research online to find one of these lists.

Read the description of three companies that appear on the list. What benefits do these companies offer to their employees?

Write one paragraph describing two benefits that you think are important. Explain how providing these benefits might help the company to raise its profits.

Text structure is the organization of ideas in a text. Headings, bullet points, and boldfaced type can help you figure out how the writing is organized. Understanding how a text is structured makes it easier to **interpret**, or explain, the meaning of the text.

One text structure often found in nonfiction writing is cause and effect. This text structure is used to explain why something happened. The effect is what happened. The cause is the reason it happened. Words such as *if, then, because, since, therefore,* and *so* help you identify a cause-and-effect structure.

Read an article in a magazine or newspaper that describes a business. Then in a notebook, write at least one cause-and-effect sentence you found in the article.

THINK ABOUT SOCIAL STUDIES

Directions: Answers these questions.

1. List three factors that raise employee morale. Which factor do you think is most important? Explain your answer.

   _____

   _____

   _____

2. Explain the relationship between incentive and morale.

   _____

   _____

   _____

Vocabulary Review

Directions: Match each word with its definition.

1. _____ capital
2. _____ incentive
3. _____ interpret
4. _____ morale
5. _____ productivity
6. _____ profit

A. money that remains after expenses are paid

B. promise of a reward

C. equipment used to create a product

D. the pace at which work is completed

E. explain

F. confidence and enthusiasm

Directions: For each workplace condition listed below, write *high morale* or *low morale* to describe how the condition would contribute to the workplace.

1. _____ Managers provide on-the-spot bonuses for work well done.

2. _____ Job goals are set by employees.

3. _____ Employees can sign up for training classes through a company website.

4. _____ An employee breaks a copy machine on purpose.

5. _____ A new policy requires all workers to arrive one-half hour early on Fridays.

6. _____ The families of employees are invited to the annual company picnic.

Skill Practice

Directions: Read the description of the ABC Widget Factory. Then answer the questions that follow.

> The ABC Widget Factory makes widgets, useful gadgets that help customers open jar lids. Recently the factory outsourced the production of one part of the widget to another country. This step reduced the cost of labor and increased profits. However, some workers were laid off, so morale in the factory fell. In response, the president of the company hired new directors of production and marketing. These two new directors have been given the task of raising morale and increasing profits.

1. What was a positive effect of reducing the cost of labor? What was a negative effect?

   _____

   _____

2. What are three actions the new director of production can take to raise morale?

   _____

   _____

   _____

3. What action can the new director of marketing take to increase profits?

   _____

   _____

Writing Practice

Directions: You want to help your manager make improvements to your workplace. Write one paragraph giving suggestions on how to improve the workplace, increase worker productivity, and lower costs in order to increase company profits.

Productivity and Interdependence

KEY CONCEPT: Productivity and interdependence are fundamental economic concepts. Both productivity and interdependence have a direct effect on the US economy and on the economies of countries around the world.

Have you ever had a day when you felt good because you got so much done? Perhaps you mailed a package to your brother, got your lawnmower repaired, bought groceries, and cleaned up the garage. To get some of these tasks done, you were dependent on the help of others.

Production and Products

The root of the word *production* is *produce*, which means "to make or create." In economics, something that is created, or produced, is called a **product**. The process of making the product is called *production*.

The production process may take place in a variety of locations. Factories, offices, medical clinics, and barbershops are all production facilities.

There are two types of products: goods and services.

- **Goods** are physical objects, such as shirts, smartphones, loaves of bread, and motorcycles.

- **Services** are actions or activities that individuals provide for others, such as cutting hair, giving a flu shot, fixing the plumbing, and painting a house.

If you have ever had a car repaired and were charged for "parts and labor," you understand the difference between goods and services. The parts are the goods, and the labor is the service.

INTERPRET WORDS AND PHRASES IN TEXT

All readers come across words that are new to them. Often you can figure out the meaning of unfamiliar words by looking at the context. Writers sometimes define words they think readers will not understand. At other times, they provide hints about a word's meaning. Occasionally you must use a dictionary to understand the meaning of a word that is important to the text.

Read the following passage. Find two words that are unfamiliar to you. Interpret the meaning of these words by looking at the context.

When people talk about **productivity**, they mean that a lot has been accomplished. In the study of economics, the word has a special meaning. Productivity refers to how **efficiently** a company does its work. Working efficiently means that products are made with the least cost and effort.

Think about cars, which use fuel to move. A car that has good fuel efficiency uses less gas to go the same distance than a car with poor fuel efficiency. You could say that the more efficient car operates with greater productivity.

The "fuel" that makes a business function is everything needed to create a product. All that goes into making a product is the **input**. The final product is the **output**. Suppose the output of a factory is a shawl. The input includes materials (cloth and thread), machinery (sewing machines), and labor (workers who make the shawls). Another important part of the input is the money that a business uses to buy materials, rent sewing machines, and pay workers.

Productivity is the relationship between the input and the output. If the owner of the shawl-making company can find a way to produce the same number of shawls with fewer workers (perhaps by using better sewing machines), she has increased productivity. A business that maintains its output while decreasing its input is more efficient; that is, the business has increased its productivity. Fewer workers mean lower expenses—and greater profit. This is why business owners are constantly searching for ways to increase productivity.

You know that profit is one goal of business. To make a profit, expenses must be kept as low as possible. Working efficiently— that is, increasing productivity—helps lower expenses. This increases the business's profit margin. The **profit margin** is a measurement of how much money a business keeps out of every dollar of its sales.

Perhaps the words *function* and *shawl* are unfamiliar to you. *Function* means "work." A shawl is a piece of clothing.

Reading Skill
Interpret Words and Phrases in Text

When reading, you may come across words or phrases that are new to you or words that are being used in a new way. Take time to **interpret** these words, or figure out their meaning.

When you are not sure what a word means, follow these steps:

1. Look for a definition provided by the writer. In this book, **boldfaced** words are defined in the text.

2. Look for context clues. The context is the words and sentences surrounding the unfamiliar word. Often the context will give you hints or clues to help you interpret what a word means.

3. Reread the sentence and substitute a familiar word whose meaning you know for the unfamiliar word. If the substituted word does not make sense, try another word.

Read an article in a newspaper or magazine about a topic that interests you. Find three words in the article that are unfamiliar. Figure out the meaning of these words and write their meanings in a notebook. Writing down the words and their meanings will help you remember them.

Research It
Follow Production

Select a common, everyday object from your classroom, home, or workplace. Your job is to research the interdependence behind that common object.

Conduct online research to find out how the product was made. What raw materials were used? Where did these materials come from? Where was the product manufactured? How was it shipped?

Make a list of the jobs and companies involved in creating that product and delivering it to you. On a world map, mark all the locations involved in creating and selling the product.

Interdependence in Economics

Understanding the concept of interdependence is fundamental to understanding economics. *Inter* means "between." *Dependence* means "relying on someone or something else." Therefore, **interdependence** means "relying on one another." Good friends are interdependent—they count on each other.

To appreciate how important interdependence is in economics, think about something as simple as a trip to a corner store. The store was built by a local construction company. The building owner rents the space to the store owner. The store owner hires the clerk. The clerk uses a cash register that was designed by an engineer in Korea. You buy a candy bar that was made from cocoa beans grown in Ghana that were shipped by a British transportation company to the United States. The candy was manufactured in Pennsylvania and brought to the store by a trucking company. You hand the clerk a dollar bill printed by the US government. The coins given to you as change are made from metals mined in Canada. You toss the wrapper into a trash bin that will be emptied by a city employee—who is paid money you and others paid in taxes.

Think of all the people, businesses, and organizations that relied on one another for that simple economic transaction (exchange) of buying a candy bar. Not any one of them could have provided the candy bar by itself. Because these people and businesses were interdependent, the candy bar was made, sold, and eaten. The economic transaction was successful.

Now think of the *trillions* of economic transactions that take place every day around the world. Each one is the result of interdependence. Interdependence has always been part of economics, but it is growing more important all the time. People, businesses, and governments are becoming more interdependent because of computers and the Internet.

WRITE TO LEARN

Read the passage on page 221 about Adam Smith and the division of labor. Then write one paragraph telling how the division of labor and specialization are used where you work or at a workplace you are familiar with.

Tell what product is being created or service is being offered. Describe the steps completed by various workers.

THINK ABOUT SOCIAL STUDIES

Choose a recent economic transaction that you participated in, similar to the purchase of a candy bar described in the text. In a notebook, write one paragraph telling about the interdependent steps that occurred during that transaction.

_____

_____

_____

_____

Productivity and Interdependence

Adam Smith is sometimes called the father of modern economics. In his book *The Wealth of Nations* (1776), Smith described a pin factory that employed ten pin makers. Smith wrote that if each pin maker made pins alone, each pin maker could produce 20 pins a day. In total, all ten workers could make 200 pins in a day. However, if the pin makers divided the work—with one worker unrolling and straightening the wire, another cutting the wire, a third grinding the tip, and so on—they could make more pins. A lot more pins. Instead of 200 pins a day, the same number of workers could produce 48,000 pins in the same amount of time.

Smith was describing the advantages of **division of labor** and **specialization**. With division of labor, the work of creating the pins was *divided* among the workers. Each worker *specialized* in one task. The increase in productivity is astounding. In fact, the wealth of material goods in the modern world has been made possible largely because of the productivity gains brought about by the division of labor and specialization.

Just as interdependence makes it possible to buy a candy bar, the interdependence of specialized workers dividing the work among themselves makes vast feats of production possible.

Scottish philosopher and economist Adam Smith (1723–1790). His concept of the division of labor changed the way products are manufactured.

Core Skill
Interpret Meaning

Notice how the word *interdependence* is explained on page 220 by breaking the word into parts and defining each part. This is a good way to interpret the meaning of new terms.

The word *economy* comes from the Greek words *oikos*, meaning "household," and *nomos*, meaning "laws." *Economy* meant "management of a household." This management included a sense of being thrifty.

Use a dictionary or other online resource to interpret the following words. Breaking the words into parts will help you understand the words.

construction
exchange
manufacture
specialization

In a notebook, write the separate parts of each word. Then write the word's meaning.

Vocabulary Review

Directions: Match each word with its meaning.

1. _____ division of labor
2. _____ efficiently
3. _____ input
4. _____ interdependence
5. _____ output
6. _____ productivity
7. _____ specialization

A. end product
B. how efficiently work is done
C. focus on one task
D. something put into a process
E. mutual assistance
F. accomplished with the least effort
G. sharing work tasks among several workers

Directions: Write *goods* or *service* to identify the following products.

_____ 1. magazine

_____ 2. eye exam

_____ 3. car

_____ 4. manicure

_____ 5. tutoring

_____ 6. laptop

_____ 7. mail delivery

_____ 8. sandwich

Directions: Choose the <u>one best answer</u> to questions 9 and 10.

9. Which of these is a service?

   A. a shoe
   B. a shoebox
   C. a shoeshine
   D. a shoelace

10. Which are the *input* for a laundromat?

   A. soap, laundry carts
   B. electricity, water
   C. washing machines, dryers
   D. all of the above

Directions: Read the dictionary entries. Then answer the question.

> **ec·o·nom·ic** (adjective) relating to the economy or to business
>
> **trans-** (prefix) across, through, or with
>
> **ac·tion** (noun) the process of doing something

11. What is an economic transaction? Give an example of an economic transaction you made today.

_____

_____

_____

Skill Practice

Directions: Read the text below. Then answer the question that follows.

> Three friends have opened a sandwich shop. They work together to manage and run the shop. Each person takes orders, makes sandwiches, and rings up sales. Customers compliment the managers on the food, but they complain about slow service.

1. How can the three sandwich shop owners improve their productivity?

_____

_____

_____

Directions: Choose the one best answer to each question.

2. Which is the best synonym for *productivity*?

   A. production
   B. output
   C. efficiency
   D. interdependence

3. In an economic transaction, which people are interdependent?

   A. the manufacturer and seller
   B. the buyer and manufacturer
   C. the seller and buyer
   D. all of the above

Writing Practice

Directions: Write a paragraph in which you define *division of labor* and *specialization*. Describe a real-world example where both are present.

Fiscal and Monetary Policy

Lesson Objectives

You will be able to
- Define *fiscal policy*
- Define *monetary policy*
- Explain how fiscal and monetary policies help manage the economy

Skills

- **Reading Skill:** Interpret Graphics
- **Core Skill:** Conduct Research Projects

Vocabulary

circulation
expenditures
fiscal policy
inflation
interest rate
monetary policy
national debt
revenue

KEY CONCEPT: The federal government uses fiscal policies and monetary policies to manage the economy.

Whether you watch the news on television or read the news online, you have heard about government spending, taxes, and the economy. How the federal government responds to the US economy directly affects your job and your paycheck. It pays for you to understand economic policy.

Federal Revenue and Expenditures

The US government is a massive organization with millions of employees. To pay for itself, the government collects taxes. The government spends that money to do its business. The term **fiscal policy** refers to the government's taxing and spending policies. Congress and the president determine US fiscal policy.

The word *fiscal* comes from an old Latin word that means "basket." It refers to a basket that was used to hold money. Associating the word *fiscal* with a basket is a good way to understand fiscal policy. Like individuals and private businesses, the federal government has income and expenses: it earns money and it spends money. Think of money going into and coming out of the federal government's basket.

Government income, or **revenue**, is received mostly in the form of taxes. This is money going into the basket. Income taxes (paid by people and by businesses) make up almost half of the federal government's revenue. A similar amount is raised through payroll taxes—Social Security and Medicare taxes that are deducted from every employee's paycheck. Other taxes make up a much smaller percentage of federal income. Each year the federal government collects about $2.5 trillion; that is $2,500,000,000,000!

The federal government also takes money out of that basket. Government **expenditures** are the money that is paid out. The federal government spends money for a wide variety of reasons. It buys aircraft carriers and builds office buildings. It finances weather research and bridge repairs. In addition, it pays the salaries of nearly 5 million government employees (including members of the armed services).

FEDERAL GOVERNMENT EXPENDITURES BY PERCENTAGE: FISCAL YEAR 2012

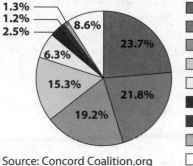

1.3%
1.2%
2.5%
8.6%
23.7%
6.3%
15.3%
21.8%
19.2%

- ■ Health
- ■ Social Security
- ■ Defense
- ▨ Income Security
- □ Interest
- ■ Education
- ■ Environment
- ▨ International Affairs
- □ All Other

Source: Concord Coalition.org

FEDERAL REVENUES BY PERCENTAGE: FISCAL YEAR 2012

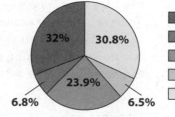

32%
30.8%
23.9%
6.8%
6.5%

- ■ Individual Income Taxes
- ■ Corporate Income Taxes
- ▨ Social Insurance Taxes
- ▨ Other Taxes
- □ Deficit

Source: Concord Coalition.org

Fiscal Policies

Because the government collects and spends so much money, its fiscal policies have a great influence on the economy. These policies also affect the way people behave.

Federal tax policies not only raise the money that the government needs, they also attempt to change the way people and businesses spend money. Many **economists** (people who study the economy) believe businesses and individuals will spend more money if they pay less taxes. When people buy more goods and services, there is more economic activity and more jobs are created. This, in turn, increases the amount of taxes collected.

Tax policy is also used to discourage behavior. For example, the federal government has increased the taxes on tobacco products as a means of discouraging smoking.

Federal spending policy is a powerful tool as well. By buying hundreds of billions of dollars' worth of goods and services from private businesses, the federal government helps the economy. Often the government increases its expenditures in bad economic times in order to increase economic activity. For example, the federal government may provide additional benefits to people who lose their jobs so these people can continue to spend money and keep the economy moving.

For many years, the federal government has spent billions of dollars more than it has taken in. To cover its costs, it has borrowed large sums of money. The money that the federal government owes is called the **national debt**. Interest payments on the national debt are a major expenditure. This is a subject of concern to some economists.

A research project is a great way to learn about new and important topics. Follow these basic steps to organize your research project:

1. Choose a topic. For this research project, your topic will be the federal American Recovery and Reinvestment Act.

2. Search for sources. Use the Internet and library tools (and a librarian's help) to locate books and articles about your topic.

3. Scan the sources you have located to identify the most helpful information. Read these sources and take notes.

4. Produce your project.

Write one paragraph describing the American Recovery and Resource Act. Your paragraph should explain the law to someone who has never heard of it.

Monetary Policy

Another tool the federal government uses to manage the economy is **monetary policy**. Monetary policy is the federal government's control of the money supply and interest rates.

The **money supply** is the total amount of money in the economy. It includes funds deposited in banks and money in **circulation**, or in use. To have a healthy economy, the amount of money in circulation must be in balance. When the economy grows—that is, when people and businesses are earning more money and spending more money—that increased economic activity requires more money in circulation.

Having too little money in circulation can slow economic activity. However, too much money in circulation can lead to **inflation**, or a general rise in prices. If the economy slows, the government may put more money into circulation. If the economy is suffering from inflation, the government may take money out of circulation.

Just as the federal government controls the money supply to manage the economy, it also adjusts interest rates for the same purpose. The **interest rate** is the payment that a lender charges when someone borrows money. Interest rates are calculated as a percentage. For example, if you borrow $100 at a 5 percent interest rate, you would have to pay back $105 after one year.

To manage the economy, the federal government sometimes varies interest rates. If the economy is weak, the government may lower interest rates. This makes it easier for individuals and businesses to get loans to start or expand businesses and purchase goods. If the economy is growing too rapidly, the government may increase interest rates in order to slow economic activity and fight inflation.

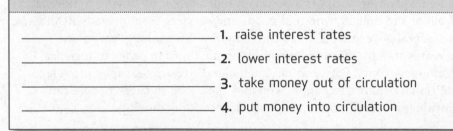

THINK ABOUT SOCIAL STUDIES

Directions: Write *help economy grow* or *fight inflation* to identify why the federal government would take each action.

_____ 1. raise interest rates

_____ 2. lower interest rates

_____ 3. take money out of circulation

_____ 4. put money into circulation

The Federal Reserve System

In the United States, monetary policy is the responsibility of the **Federal Reserve System**. "The Fed," which is the central bank of the United States, has more freedom to act independently than most other government agencies. It was created by Congress in 1913 to achieve a number of economic goals.

The Fed is a complex organization that includes 12 Federal Reserve banks, private banks, and government officials. This organization performs a variety of important tasks. It serves the banking needs of the federal government. It holds government funds, makes government loans, and places money into circulation. It also serves the banking needs of private banks—it is "the banks' bank"—and helps monitor these private banks.

Perhaps the most important role of the Federal Reserve is to help manage the US economy. The goal of the Fed is to encourage economic growth, control inflation, and promote employment.

The Federal Reserve System is administered by its board of governors. Members of the board are appointed by the president, with the consent of the Senate. This board then works on its own to make decisions about monetary policy.

By influencing interest rates and the money supply, the Fed's actions can have a major impact on the US economy. Because the economy of the United States is so large, the Fed can even affect the world's economy. The Federal Reserve System is an enormously powerful organization.

Directions: Read the passage below about the payroll tax holiday. With a partner, create a presentation about this policy. Evaluate how it affected you and your family members. Discuss whether the tax holiday helped or harmed the US economy. Tell whether you think there should be another tax holiday. Be sure to explain your opinions in your presentation.

> In 2010 the Federal government enacted a payroll tax holiday. It dropped the payroll tax from 6.2 percent to 4.2 percent. The policy decreased the part of a worker's payroll tax that helps pay for Social Security. The law was meant to help the economy by giving workers more money in each paycheck. The payroll tax holiday expired at the end of 2012. Then workers saw 2 percent less income in their paychecks. The payroll tax holiday cost the government nearly $240 billion in tax revenue, which added to the national debt.

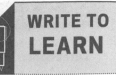

WRITE TO LEARN

When the Fed raises interest rates, consumers pay more for car loans and **mortgages**, which are loans used to buy homes.

Write one paragraph that explains how higher interest rates might affect your budget.

WORKPLACE CONNECTION

Understand Your Paycheck

Your paycheck usually comes with a "pay stub" telling you how much money you earned during the last pay period. This is your "gross pay." It also tells how much was deducted for taxes, insurance, and savings.

In your notebook, write your gross pay. Then write the amount you paid for federal and state income taxes, Social Security tax, Medicare tax, health insurance, and retirement savings. The amount of money you actually receive after all the deductions is your "net pay."

If you do not understand some of the terms or abbreviations on your pay stub, ask someone in your Human Resources Department for an explanation.

Vocabulary Review

Directions: Match each word with its definition.

1. _____ circulation
2. _____ expenditures
3. _____ fiscal policy
4. _____ interest rate
5. _____ monetary policy
6. _____ national debt
7. _____ revenue

A. decisions about money supply and interest rates

B. decisions about taxing and spending

C. money spent for something

D. money owed by the US government

E. income

F. fee paid to borrow money

G. movement of money from one person to another

Skill Review

Directions: Conduct a short research project to identify the person who is chair of the Federal Reserve System (or one of the people who has been chair of the Fed in the past). Describe one decision made by that person and tell how that decision has been important to the US economy.

To complete your project, follow the steps below.

1. Choose your topic. Decide who you will write about.

_____

2. Search for sources. List three sources you have found on the Internet or in a library.

_____

_____

_____

3. Scan the sources to identify the information that is most useful. Write your notes here.

_____

_____

_____

_____

4. Produce your project. Use your notes to write a paragraph introducing one person who has been chair of the Fed and explaining how that person's work has been important.

_____

_____

_____

_____

Skill Practice

Directions: Choose the <u>one best answer</u> to each question.

1. Which of the following is an accurate statement?

   A. To keep the economy from growing too rapidly, the federal government may raise interest rates.

   B. To discourage certain behaviors, the federal government may lower taxes on some products.

   C. To help a weak economy, the federal government may raise interest rates.

   D. To slow inflation, the federal government may put more money in circulation.

2. Which would be most likely to add to the national debt?

   A. a decrease in federal expenditures

   B. a decrease in federal taxes

   C. a decrease in jobless benefits

   D. all of the above

3. Which of the following policies would help the economy grow?

   A. increase federal expenditures

   B. decrease federal taxes

   C. lower the interest rate

   D. all of the above

4. In which case would the Fed be most likely to increase the money supply?

   A. Federal revenues decrease.

   B. Inflation is increasing.

   C. The economy is growing.

   D. The president orders the Fed to do this.

Writing Practice

Directions: Write one paragraph stating the measures you would take as chair of the Federal Reserve to help a weak economy. Explain why you think your plan is the best approach.

Credit, Savings, and Banking

Lesson Objectives

You will be able to

- Describe how to use a bank

- Recognize the importance of saving

- Explain the concept of credit and credit scores

Skills

- **Reading Skill:** Integrate Visual Information

- **Core Skill:** Interpret Meaning

Vocabulary

checking account
credit score
deposit
financial planning
savings account
withdraw

KEY CONCEPT: Personal financial management is a vital life skill.

Would you like to have more money than you do? Do you worry about your financial future? These are probably the easiest questions you will ever be asked! Of course, everyone could use more money, and no one wants to worry about the future. One key to a brighter financial future is furthering your education. Another is learning about personal finance.

Personal Finance

Personal finance refers to the financial affairs of an individual or a family (rather than the finances of a business or the government). *Finance* means "anything to do with money." Personal finance includes your income, bills, and savings.

Money has a big influence on your plans for the future. Whether you are making short-term goals like going to a movie and buying new pants or making longer-term goals like going to college and opening a business, you need to have money. Achieving your goals requires **financial planning**. This type of planning lays out organized steps to guide you in spending money, saving money, and paying back any debts you may have.

Setting up a **personal budget**, or an outline for spending and saving, is a useful financial planning tool. A budget shows how your monthly income will be used for expenses such as rent, food, taxes, insurance, education, transportation, debt repayment, and entertainment. Sample budget forms can be downloaded from the Internet, along with suggestions for creating your budget. Professional financial planners can also be helpful to you, particularly in planning how to pay back large debts.

Banks and Checking Accounts

There are banks in every town and city in the country. Banks are private businesses that provide money-related services. Although some banks are called "state banks" or "national banks," these banks are not run by the state or national government. These terms tell whether the bank is operating under state or federal (national) laws.

Banks make money by charging their customers for services. Before you open a bank account, ask about service charges. Often you can limit what you pay the bank by knowing why the bank charges fees. Sometimes you can even avoid paying bank charges.

Most banks are commercial banks. A **commercial bank** is a large financial institution that offers a wide variety of services. Credit unions are another important type of bank. A **credit union** is owned and run by its members. Credit unions offer the same services that commercial banks offer, but credit union fees are often less than commercial bank fees.

Most people use banks in order to have a checking account. A **checking account** is a bank account that lets account holders write checks and use an automated teller machine (ATM) card to get cash. Account holders **deposit**, or place, money into their accounts. They **withdraw**, or take out, money by writing checks or using an ATM card.

Typically people deposit their paychecks into their checking accounts and then write checks to pay for their rent, utilities, and other bills. Many employers will deposit paychecks directly into their employees' accounts. The US government will deposit Social Security checks and tax refunds directly into checking accounts.

It is important to record every deposit and withdrawal from your account. This lets you calculate your current account balance. The **account balance** is the amount of money in the account. Writing a check for more than the account balance can cause a lot of problems. The bank will charge you a fee if you do not have enough money in your account to pay for the check. If you do this often, the bank may close your account. In addition, you will probably be charged a fee by the business you wrote the check to.

Reading Skill
Integrate Visual Information

A table can help you understand ideas presented in a text. To visualize a personal financial plan, you can make a chart.

For one week, record the items you purchase that are not necessities. (Necessities would include grocery items, medications, school supplies, and gasoline.) For example, do not enter *loaf of bread $2.70*, but do enter *deli sandwich $6.00*. Other items might include *movie $7.50, e-book $10.99, music downloads $6.50*.

After one week, total the amount spent, and then answer the questions below.

Day	Items	Price
		Total

What items could you have gone without? How much money would you have saved?

How much would you save in one year—52 weeks— if you saved that much money each week? Keep in mind that interest in a savings account would add to your total.

Reread the first sentence in the second, third, and fourth paragraphs on this page. Notice that each of these paragraphs begins with a question.

These questions are called *rhetorical questions*. You are not expected to answer them. They are designed to get readers or listeners thinking about the subject.

Reread the paragraphs that start with a question. Notice that each paragraph provides the answer to the question. When you read, keep an eye out for rhetorical questions—and look for the answers that follow.

In a notebook, write two rhetorical questions that you might add to the text about banking on page 231. Be sure the text answers your questions.

Saving for Your Future

Keeping money instead of spending it is called saving. There are many reasons to save, and there are many ways to do it.

Why should you save? People save money so they can purchase an expensive item like a car or a house. They save for major expenses like community college tuition. They also save for unexpected emergencies like medical bills.

How do you save? There is an old saying "Pay yourself first." This means that the first payment you make every month should be a deposit into your **savings account**. A savings account is a bank account where you store money.

Where should you keep your savings? Saving cash is not a good idea. Cash can easily be lost or stolen. The best place to keep your saved money is in a savings account at a commercial bank or credit union. Savings accounts pay interest. Earning interest is the key to making your savings grow.

Suppose you save $25 a week, or $100 a month. In a year, you would have saved $1,200. If your savings account pays 5 percent interest, you will have $1,227.89 at the end of the year. That extra $27.89 might not sound like a lot, but you did no work to earn it. The next year, you will earn interest on the money you put into the account and on the interest you already earned. After five years of saving $100 a month, your savings will total $6,000 without interest—or $6,861 with interest. You can see the long-term benefit of putting money into a savings account that earns interest!

THINK ABOUT SOCIAL STUDIES

Directions: Place a check mark (✓) in each box to complete the table.

	Checking Accounts	Savings Accounts
Accounts located at a bank		
Bank charges fees		
Use account to pay monthly bills		
Can withdraw money to pay for major purchases		
Bank pays interest		
Money in account belongs to you		

Understanding Credit

You can buy things with cash, or you can buy them with credit. Using **credit** is a way of taking ownership of something before you pay for it. The word *credit* comes from an old Latin word that means "trust." When a company sells you an item on credit, it is trusting you to pay the bill.

You probably know how a credit card works. When you charge an item to the credit card, the seller gets the money from your credit card company. You are responsible for paying the credit card company. In addition to paying for the item, you may also have to pay interest. Every time you use a credit card, you are taking out a loan from the credit card company.

There are some advantages to using credit cards. You do not need to carry a lot of cash. You can make purchases online or over the telephone. Items bought on credit may also be easier to return if you decide you do not want them.

Using credit wisely and paying your credit card bill on time will help you build your credit score. Your **credit score** is a report of how well you pay your bills. Banks and other institutions report your bill-paying habits (for example, whether you pay bills late) to credit agencies. Credit agencies determine your credit score. This score is available to companies that you want to borrow money from. If you want to take out a car loan, a good credit score will help you get the loan and let you pay a lower interest rate. A bad credit score can mean that the loan will be denied or that you will pay a higher interest rate.

One disadvantage of using credit cards is the temptation to buy more things than you can afford. Interest rates on credit cards can be very high, and late payment fees are costly. Many people go into debt by using their credit cards unwisely, and then they struggle for years to pay off the debt.

WRITE TO LEARN

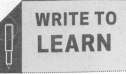

Write a journal entry in which you reflect on your personal finances. What do you need to learn about managing money? Are you saving for your future? Are you using a credit card wisely?

Then write three steps you can take to improve your financial situation.

REAL-WORLD CONNECTION

Understand Interest

To understand the real cost of using a credit card, study your monthly credit card statement. Find your annual percentage rate (APR). This is the rate of interest you must pay if you do not pay your full monthly bill on time.

Think of a luxury item you would like to buy. In your notebook, calculate the real cost of that item if you pay the bill over one year. To find the interest charges, multiply the price times the APR ($500 × .24). Then add the price of the item and the interest charges to find the real cost of using your credit card.

Vocabulary Review

Directions: Match each term with its definition.

1. _____ checking account
2. _____ credit score
3. _____ deposit
4. _____ savings account
5. _____ withdraw

A. rating of how well you pay bills

B. to take money out of a bank account

C. to put money into a bank account

D. account that lets you write checks and use ATMs

E. account used to earn interest

Skill Review

Directions: Read the information in the box. The main idea of this text is that you should get a copy of your credit report. After reading the text, complete the activity below.

> **Q:** Why do I want a copy of my credit report?
>
> **A:** Your credit report has information that affects whether you can get a loan—and how much you will have to pay to borrow money. You want a copy of your credit report to:
>
> • make sure the information is accurate, complete, and up-to-date before you apply for a loan for a major purchase like a house or car, buy insurance, or apply for a job.
>
> • help guard against identity theft. That's when someone uses your personal information—like your name, your Social Security number, or your credit card number—to commit fraud. Identity thieves may use your information to open a new credit card account in your name. Then, when they don't pay the bills, the delinquent account is reported on your credit report. Inaccurate information like that could affect your ability to get credit, insurance, or even a job.
>
> —US Federal Trade Commission

Directions: Write one paragraph identifying three ways that an inaccurate credit report might affect you.

_____

_____

_____

_____

_____

Skill Practice

Directions: Choose the <u>one best answer</u> to each question.

1. Which phrase best describes banks?

   A. consumer protectors
   B. government agencies
   C. for-profit businesses
   D. credit agencies

2. How do commercial banks differ from credit unions?

   A. Commercial banks have branch banks that are more conveniently located.
   B. Credit unions are owned by their members.
   C. Credit unions always offer better services.
   D. all of the above

3. Which should you use to pay monthly bills?

   A. checking account
   B. savings account
   C. credit card
   D. credit report

4. Who is likely to pay a higher interest rate on a car loan?

   A. someone who pays his or her electric bill on time
   B. someone who has successfully repaid a car loan in the past
   C. someone who is late in making rent payments
   D. someone who has had a steady job for several years

Writing Practice

Directions: Write one paragraph in which you discuss your experience with using a credit card. Do you feel that you have used your credit card wisely? Have you purchased items on credit that you did not need, simply because a credit card purchase was so easy? Has your credit card company charged you interest on your account? End your paragraph with a one-sentence conclusion summarizing your opinion of credit card use.

Directions: Choose the <u>one best answer</u> to each question.

<u>Questions 1 and 2</u> refer to the following passage.

> This passage is from *The Wealth of Nations*, an economics book written by Adam Smith in 1776. It deals with how business activity takes place.
>
> "It is not from the benevolence [kindness] of the butcher, the brewer, or the baker, that we expect our dinner, but from their regard to their own self interest. We address ourselves, not to their humanity but to their self-love, and never talk to them of our own necessities but of their advantages."

1. What economic value is most apparent in this excerpt?

   A. Government will set the prices of goods and the wages of workers.
   B. Businesses will make products that they can sell for a profit.
   C. Consumers will be forced to buy whatever firms produce.
   D. Businesses will put the interests of society over their own interests.

2. When Smith describes the self-interest of the butcher, brewer, and baker, what is he referring to?

   A. their desire to make a profit
   B. their incentive to increase morale
   C. the need for equilibrium
   D. the need for increased productivity

<u>Questions 3 and 4</u> refer to the following diagram.

ECONOMIC RECOVERY, GREAT DEPRESSION

FDR and Congress create millions of jobs through New Deal programs (WPA, PWA, CCC).

→ Workers receive wages and spend money on food, clothing, shelter, and other products.

↓ Because of higher consumer demand for products, businesses hire more workers and produce more products.

↓ Economic recovery begins.

3. What was the first cause of the economic recovery during the Great Depression?

   A. Workers received higher wages.
   B. There was higher consumer demand for products.
   C. Workers spent more money.
   D. FDR and Congress created millions of new jobs.

4. Which headline would go best with the diagram?

   A. "Depression Deepens with No End in Sight"
   B. "President Roosevelt Blames Congress for Economic Mess"
   C. "FDR Plans Job Creation Program to Save the Economy"
   D. "Government Accepts Blame for Economic Downturn"

Review

5. How is *economy* best defined?

- **A.** a system for exchanging goods and services
- **B.** a system for producing goods and services
- **C.** a system for producing, distributing, and consuming goods and services
- **D.** a system for producing goods and guiding government policy

6. Within the context of economics, what is a *market*?

- **A.** a store that sells household goods and food
- **B.** anywhere buyers and sellers do business
- **C.** a group of stalls selling fresh fruits and vegetables
- **D.** an outdoor area where sellers offer arts, crafts, and foods

7. During most holiday seasons, one toy becomes especially popular. As quickly as a shipment arrives in the store, it is sold out. Many customers are willing to pay much more than the regular price to get this toy. What would an economist say about this situation?

- **A.** A surplus of toys causes prices to increase.
- **B.** A shortage of toys causes prices to decrease.
- **C.** A surplus of toys causes prices to decrease.
- **D.** A shortage of toys causes prices to increase.

8. If the country were in a recession and the Federal Reserve wanted to help the economy grow, what might it do?

- **A.** increase the money supply
- **B.** reduce the money supply
- **C.** require banks to keep more cash on deposit
- **D.** increase interest rates

9. How do consumers pay for the goods and services provided by government?

- **A.** by paying taxes
- **B.** by paying interest
- **C.** with monthly bill payments
- **D.** through annual subscriptions

10. Which of the following best describes the money used in the US today?

- **A.** commodity money
- **B.** fiat money
- **C.** paper money
- **D.** representative money

11. Which of the following best explains the difference between monopoly and competition?

   A. Monopoly is characterized by innovation, while competition is characterized by barriers to entry.
   B. Competition leads to product scarcity and higher prices, while monopoly keeps prices low through high production levels.
   C. Monopoly offers consumers a range of products and prices, while competition forces consumers to compete for a limited supply of one product at one price.
   D. Competition is characterized by a variety of sellers offering similar products or services, and monopoly is characterized by one seller controlling most of the market.

12. What is the main motivation for US companies that move their production to another country?

   A. to lower their production costs
   B. to take advantage of favorable exchange rates
   C. to provide their employees with better working conditions
   D. to offer their customers lower prices for higher quality goods

13. Why do companies offer their employees the chance to learn new job skills?

   A. to boost employee morale
   B. to decrease their production costs
   C. to avoid having to hire more workers
   D. to encourage them to look for other jobs

14. If the economy is suffering from inflation, what action will the government probable take?

   A. It will lower interest rates and place more money in circulation.
   B. It will lower interest rates and take money out of circulation.
   C. It will raise interest rates and place more money in circulation.
   D. It will raise interest rates and take money out of circulation.

15. In the United States, who is responsible for monetary policy?

   A. Congress
   B. the president
   C. the treasury secretary
   D. the Federal Reserve System

16. Which statement about credit card use is true?

   A. Using a credit card is cheaper than using cash.
   B. Using a credit card is more expensive than using cash.
   C. When you buy something using a credit card, the credit card company is giving you a loan.
   D. When you buy something using a credit card, you will have to pay late fees and a high rate of interest.

17. When a company gets a report on your credit score, what do they learn about you?

   A. how much you owe
   B. whether you pay bills on time
   C. what you buy regularly
   D. where you have used your credit cards

18. A large company builds a new factory in a small town. Soon new restaurants and other businesses open near the factory. The town widens and improves roads near the factory to accommodate deliveries, shipping, and other traffic. People move to the town to find work. New schools open, and a shopping mall is built.

What best explains all this growth and change?

A. fiscal policy
B. productivity
C. specialization
D. interdependence

19. Which of the following best defines *profit margin*?

A. how much money a business receives from its sales
B. how much of its income a business has left after paying its expenses
C. how much money a business spends to produce its goods or services
D. how much of its income a business has to spend on its input and output combined

Check Your Understanding

On the following chart, circle the number of any question you answered incorrectly. In the third column, you will see the pages you can review to study the content covered in the question. Pay particular attention to reviewing those lessons in which you missed half or more of the questions.

Chapter 5 Review

Lesson	Item Number	Review Pages
Basic Economic Concepts	5	184–189
The Role of the Market	1, 2, 6, 7	190–195
The Role of Government	3, 4, 8	196–201
Money and Financial Institutions	10	202–207
Monopoly and Competition	11	208–213
Profit	12, 13	214–217
Productivity and Interdependence	18, 19	218–223
Fiscal and Monetary Policy	9, 14, 15	224–229
Credit, Savings, and Banking	16, 17	230–235

ESSAY WRITING PRACTICE

Economic Foundations

Directions: Write an essay in response to one of the prompts below. You may wish to reread Lesson 5.9 to review credit, savings, and banking.

PAMPHLET ON BORROWING MONEY

A local bank has asked you to write a pamphlet about borrowing money. Write a three-paragraph essay in which you describe the reasons people borrow money, explain how they can borrow, and tell about the cost of borrowing money. Give examples of the fees. Your pamphlet should make it clear that borrowing money increases the cost of items purchased.

PAMPHLET ON USING CREDIT CARDS

Write a pamphlet that will be mailed to first-time credit card holders. Write a three-paragraph essay in which you describe how to use credit cards responsibly. The essay should discuss minimum monthly payments, rising interest rates, and credit card security. Your pamphlet should make it clear that using a credit card may increase the cost of what you buy.

Review

ESSAY WRITING PRACTICE

Economic Events in History

Looking back at your life, you may see patterns. For example, the cycle of seasons affects your life in many ways. In the long nights and cold days of winter, you choose different clothing and entertainment than in the long, hot days of summer. Another pattern relates to experience. You learn a new skill, and soon you find yourself moving on to more complicated skills. Children learn to walk, soon they run, and before long they can balance themselves on bicycles. Experience increases what we can do.

There are also patterns in economic history. Some are cyclical like the seasons. Others are cumulative, with one event building upon the last. New discoveries become the accepted basis for further research and innovation. This chapter examines some of these patterns.

In this chapter you will study these topics:

Lesson 6.1: Major Economic Events
Economies experience ups and downs. This pattern of boom and bust is called the business cycle. At the low point in the cycle, the economy may enter a recession or even a depression. During the Great Depression of the 1930s, the US government drew on the ideas of economist John Maynard Keynes to develop policies that would help the country.

Lesson 6.2: Industrialization and Imperialism
After the Civil War, the United States became more industrialized. Cities grew rapidly, and the economy boomed. In addition, the country tried to expand its foreign trade and increase its influence by taking over territories outside the continental United States.

Lesson 6.3: Scientific and Industrial Revolutions
Economic cycles are often fueled by advances in science. For instance, in the sixteenth and seventeenth centuries, discoveries and ideas in astronomy, chemistry, physics, and other fields provided new knowledge about our world. People used this knowldege to invent new machines and processes. This progress drove the Industrial Revolution and the Transportation Revolution of the eighteenth and nineteenth centuries. Scientific discoveries have continued to affect the economy. A good example is today's Digital Revolution.

Goal Setting

Why is it important to study economic history?

- to understand economic patterns

- to analyze current economic events

- to understand the relationship between science and the economy

Who uses economic history in their job?

- government leaders

- manufacturers

- business owners

- managers

- bankers

- farmers

- realtors

What do you hope to learn from the lessons in this chapter? As you read through this chapter, use the chart below to define words and concepts related to economic patterns and events in history.

Economic History	
Business cycle	
Great Depression	
Great Recession	
Imperialism	
Industrial Revolution	
Scientific Revolution	
Digital Revolution	

Major Economic Events

KEY CONCEPT: Understanding the business cycle and government spending will help you understand your own finances.

Have you had times when you were doing well financially? Have you gone through some tough financial times? Everyone has ups and downs. Like individuals, the US economy has its ups and downs. Whether individuals are doing well often depends on whether the US economy as a whole is doing well.

Lesson Objectives

You will be able to

• Identify the parts of the business cycle

• Describe the Great Depression

• Explain Keynesian economics

Skills

• **Core Skill:** Integrate Content Presented in Different Ways

• **Reading Skill:** Infer

Vocabulary

business cycle
contraction
depression
expansion
Great Depression
gross domestic product (GDP)
peak
recession
trough

Gross Domestic Product

The term *gross domestic product* (GDP) is an important part of all discussions about the economy. *Gross* means "total." *Domestic* in this context means "within the country." *Product* means "goods and services." Therefore, the **gross domestic product** is the total value of goods and services produced in a country in one year. You can think of GDP as the total output of an economy. The GDP of the United States is about $15 trillion. China, the next largest economy in the world, has a GDP that is half the size of the US GDP.

GDP is one way that economists measure the health of an economy. Another useful measurement is GDP per capita. **Per capita** means "for each person." GDP per capita is simply the GDP divided by the number of people in a country. In the United States, GDP per capita is about $50,000. This means that the United States is one of the ten richest countries in the world. In very poor counties, like the African countries of Zimbabwe and Congo, the GDP per capita is less than $1,000.

In most countries, the population increases each year. The economy, as measured by the GDP, needs to grow along with the population. What happens if the population rises faster than the GDP? The GDP per capita goes down—the country is poorer. That's why economic growth, or an increase in the GDP, is so important.

Yet economic growth can be hard to maintain. Sometimes the economy seems to have a life of its own—a life of ups and downs.

The Business Cycle

During good economic times, businesses do well and it is relatively easy to find a job. In bad economic times, business slows down and it is hard to find a job. Good economic times are called *booms*, and bad times are called *busts*. Over time, the economy goes from boom to bust and back again. This boom-to-bust movement is called the **business cycle**.

On this graph of the business cycle, the vertical line represents GDP. The horizontal line represents time. The graph has no numbers or dates because it represents the business cycles in general.

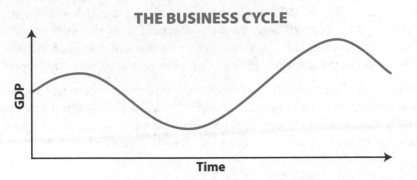

THE BUSINESS CYCLE

When the line is rising, GDP is growing. This is a boom period. It is called an **expansion** because the economy is growing. Eventually economic growth reaches a high point, or **peak**. Then inflation (a general increase in prices) sets in. Consumer demand slows, and business costs rise.

Then the line goes down. GDP is shrinking. This is a bust period. It is called a **contraction** because the economy is getting smaller. People spend less, so there is less profit. Some companies go out of business, and other companies lay off workers. When the economy reaches its low point, it is said to have reached a **trough**.

A deep trough is called a **recession**. During a recession, unemployment is high. Consumers cannot afford to buy as many goods and services, so some businesses fail. If the trough is very severe and lasts a long time, the trough is called a **depression**. A depression that occurred almost a century ago changed the country forever—and it affects you today.

Core Skill
Integrate Content Presented in Different Ways

Content refers to information in a text. Content may be words in a book, pictures on a website, or data in a chart. When you integrate content presented in different ways, you are combining information from different formats. Reading a text, looking at photos, and studying a chart all help you understand a topic.

Practice integrating content by rereading the description of the business cycle. In a notebook, draw the graph shown on this page. Then use the words below to label the graph. You will use some of the terms more than once.

Labels:
    expansion
    peak
    contraction
    trough

THINK ABOUT SOCIAL STUDIES

Directions: Study the table below. Then fill in the right column. A country's GDP is calculated by multiplying the GDP per capita times the population. You may use a calculator.

Country	Population in 2012 (rounded to nearest 100,000)	GDP per Person (rounded to the nearest $1,000)	GDP
Canada	34,300,000	$41,000	
Egypt	81,300,000	$6,000	
Japan	127,400,000	$35,000	

Source: CIA World Factbook

When you infer, you figure out an idea that was not directly stated in a text. When you think about the information you are reading and then use your prior knowledge to expand the information, you are making an inference.

The last sentence on page 245 is "A depression that occurred almost a century ago changed the country forever—and it affects you today."

The last two sentences in "The Great Depression" are "The Great Depression seemed endless. Then entered an economist named John Maynard Keynes."

In a notebook, write one sentence stating what you might infer when you combine the information from these three sentences.

The Great Depression

The single worst economic event in US history was a deep trough in the business cycle, or a depression. Today it is remembered as the **Great Depression** of the 1930s. (*Great* does not always mean "good." Here it means "huge" or "enormous.")

The Great Depression was a period of tremendous economic pain for the country. The GDP in 1932 was only about half of what it had been at its peak in 1929. About 25 percent of US workers found themselves without jobs. In many areas, the unemployment rate was much higher. Banks failed, and people lost their life savings. Homelessness was widespread.

Today unemployed people may receive unemployment benefit checks. They can use Electronic Benefit Transfer (EBT) cards to obtain cash and food. Some of them receive Social Security benefits. In the early 1930s, however, these programs did not exist. People depended on family, friends, and charity.

What did government officials do about the Great Depression? Initially, they did nothing. Most economists believed that the business cycle was self-correcting—that is, they thought the trough would fix itself. During previous economic contractions, workers who had lost their jobs were willing to take jobs that paid lower wages. Businesses hired them. Production increased, and an economic expansion began.

Yet the Great Depression dragged on. Millions of Americans were miserable. A major problem was that businesses would not hire anyone, even if the workers were willing to work for nothing but food. Business owners felt there was no point in hiring more workers because there was little demand for goods and services. People were buying very little. The Great Depression seemed endless.

Then entered an economist named John Maynard Keynes.

Keynesian Economics and the New Deal

John Maynard Keynes (1883–1946) was a British economist. During the Great Depression, he wrote a book stating that governments should use their powers to manage economies. Economists had previously argued that government should stay out of economic affairs. Their approach, called *laissez faire* [less´-ay fair´], is French for "let it be."

John Maynard Keynes proposed increased government spending as a way to ease the hardships of the Great Depression.

©Bettmann/Corbis

Keynes believed that recessions and depressions were caused by a lack of demand. Not enough people had money to buy goods and services from businesses. Keynes thought that government spending could provide the demand for businesses. This would stimulate economic activity and thereby end the depression. These ideas are called Keynesian economics.

In the United States, President Franklin Delano Roosevelt created policies that used Keynes's ideas. President Roosevelt's programs and federal actions designed to counter the hardships of the Great Depression were called the **New Deal**.

The New Deal included the Works Progress Administration (WPA), which employed people in construction and the arts. Employees of the Public Works Administration (PWA) built public works, like bridges. The Federal Deposit Insurance Corporation (FDIC) protected people's savings when banks failed. The Social Security Act, a key part of the New Deal, provided income to elderly and disabled Americans.

Never before had the federal government played such a direct role in the economy or in the lives of individual citizens. Since the New Deal, the power of the federal government and its role in public and private affairs has grown tremendously.

In 2008, the United States fell into the worst economic trough since the Great Depression. Called the "Great Recession," this economic contraction devastated tens of millions of Americans. In response, President Barack Obama pressed for passage of the American Recovery and Reinvestment Act of 2009, a large government spending program to help revitalize the economy.

WRITE TO LEARN

In a notebook, write one paragraph explaining why you agree or disagree with this statement:

In hard economic times, the government should take care of people who do not have jobs.

Research It
Understand History

Use the Internet to compare the Great Depression to other times in US history.

Make a table showing unemployment rates for several years (for example, 1933, 1945, 1980, 2010, today). In column 1 of your table, list the years you have researched. In column 2, list the unemployment rates. Give your table a title.

Vocabulary Review

Directions: Match each word with its definition.

1. _____ business cycle
2. _____ contraction
3. _____ depression
4. _____ expansion
5. _____ Great Depression
6. _____ gross domestic product (GDP)
7. _____ peak
8. _____ recession
9. _____ trough

A. trough in the business cycle

B. total production of a nation's economy

C. severe economic downturn of the 1930s

D. low point of the business cycle

E. increase in GDP

F. high point of the business cycle

G. especially deep trough in the business cycle

H. decrease in GDP

I. alternating periods of boom and bust

Directions: Read the following text from a government website. It describes the government's plan for recovering from the 2008 recession. Then use this information to make inferences in order to answer the questions.

On February 13, 2009, in direct response to the economic crisis and at the urging of President Obama, Congress passed the American Recovery and Reinvestment Act of 2009—commonly referred to as the "stimulus." . . . The President signed the Recovery Act into law. The three immediate goals of the Recovery Act are

- Create new jobs and save existing ones

- Spur economic activity and invest in long-term growth

- Foster unprecedented levels of accountability and transparency in government spending

The Recovery Act intended to achieve those goals by providing $787 billion in

- Tax cuts and benefits for millions of working families and businesses

- Funding for entitlement programs, such as unemployment benefits

- Funding for federal contracts, grants and loans

In 2011, the original expenditure estimate of $787 billion was increased to $840 billion to be in line with the President's 2012 budget and with scoring changes made by the Congressional Budget Office since the enactment of the Recovery Act.

—US Recovery Accountability and Transparency Board

1. How was the stimulus expected to affect the business cycle?

_____

_____

_____

2. How did President Obama think government spending would affect employment?

_____

_____

_____

3. How would the government recover the money it spent to stimulate the economy?

_____

_____

_____

Skill Practice

Directions: Choose the <u>one best answer</u> to each question.

1. Four countries have the same GDP. The population of these four countries is listed here. Which country has the highest GDP per capita?

   A. Country A, 22 million people
   B. Country B, 32 million people
   C. Country C, 42 million people
   D. Country D, 52 million people

2. Which of the following is least like the others?

   A. recession
   B. depression
   C. expansion
   D. trough

3. What did the Great Depression lead to?

   A. widespread suffering
   B. the New Deal
   C. the application of Keynesian economics
   D. all of the above

4. Why was the period beginning in 2008 called the Great Recession?

   A. It was an economic boom.
   B. It was an economic downturn.
   C. It was a historic economic expansion.
   D. It led to the acceptance of *laissez faire* economics.

Writing Practice

Directions: Reread the text about Keynesian Economics and the New Deal. Choose one of the New Deal programs established to help people through the hardships of the Great Depression. Research that program online. Then write one paragraph in which you evaluate that program's impact on the Great Depression.

KEY CONCEPT: After the Civil War, the United States rapidly became an urban, industrial society. Then it wanted to expand its power by building a colonial empire.

Most jobs require workers to have certain skills. Within a company, a worker who acquires new skills may be promoted to a job with a higher salary. Once a worker has a higher job level, that worker might have more power within the company.

Industrialization is the development of large-scale industries and mass-production techniques. After the Civil War, industrialization allowed the United States to gain economic power in the world. The United States also increased its power by acquiring more land that could be used to develop the country's economy.

Changes in Society

From 1865 to 1900, great changes occurred. The foundations of modern America were built in the factories, mills, mines, and cities of the Midwest and the East. Businessmen in the Northeast had gained wealth and experience from the Civil War. After the war, they changed the way goods were produced. In doing so, they put the United States on the road to **industrialization**. This is the process of changing the country from an agricultural society to an industrial society. Large industry became the most important factor in economic growth.

Inventions revolutionized all areas of life. The national railroad system expanded greatly. The telegraph established nationwide communication. The invention of new processing techniques led to the creation of a giant steel industry. New coalfields opened, and oil-well drilling developed. An electrical generator capable of delivering the large amount of power needed for industry was invented.

Industrialization caused huge growth in the population of cities and towns. Americans moved so they would be where the jobs were. The population shift from rural areas to cities is called **urbanization**. In addition, large numbers of people moved west to settle in new states and territories.

Industry centered around sources of raw materials, energy sources, and good transportation. New industry was needed to build housing and transportation for the new urban areas. A boom in immigration from Europe helped US cities grow. About 25 million Europeans were **recruited**, or enlisted, to work in US mines, mills, and forges. Many of these immigrants had faced hard economic times and political problems in their homelands. They came to the United States to find a better life. However, the new immigrants often faced poverty and discrimination in their new homeland.

UNDERSTAND THE MAIN IDEA

The **main idea** is the most important information in a passage. The details in the passage support, or explain, the main idea. Understanding the main idea can help you understand what you are reading.

The main idea is often—but not always—stated in the first sentence of a passage. To find the main idea, read the passage and then ask yourself, *What is the most important idea the writer wants me to understand?*

Read the following paragraph and underline the main idea.

> (1) The Mississippi River has always been important to the growth of the US economy. (2) The river has supplied water to the people and industries in nearby cities. (3) Trading with the surrounding area has been made easier because the river could be used for transportation.

Sentence 1 states the main idea. Sentences 2 and 3 give examples of ways that the Mississippi River has been important.

Core Skill
Analyze Events and Ideas

Values are ideas or beliefs that people consider important in life. However, not everyone shares the same values. Some people value having a good career, and some value having close ties with family. Others value helping people or saving the environment.

Look at the cartoon about John D. Rockefeller. Analyze, or examine carefully, the ideas expressed in this cartoon. Then, in your notebook, write one sentence describing the values portrayed in the cartoon.

A powerful group of businessmen developed during this period of industrialization. Andrew Carnegie, John D. Rockefeller, J. P. Morgan, Cornelius Vanderbilt, and others controlled giant companies that ruled the US economy. They created **monopolies**, businesses that owned nearly all of the market for one particular type of goods or services. The power of these business leaders was often misused to keep prices high and wages of their workers low. Because they controlled large sectors of US industry, these business owners were able to influence politics so laws would be passed that were favorable to their businesses.

John D. Rockefeller was the cofounder of Standard Oil Company.

© Bettmann/CORBIS

Reading Skill
Understand the
Main Idea

The main idea is
the most important
information in a passage.
The main idea may
be stated in the text.
However, sometimes you
must use the details in
the passage to infer, or
figure out, the main idea.

Read the first paragraph
on this page. Then ask
yourself, "What is the
author's most important
point?" In a notebook,
state the main idea of
the paragraph.

Workers and Farmers Respond

Workers and farmers saw very little of the new riches that resulted from rapid industrialization. Factory, rail, and mine workers often worked more than 12 hours each day for extremely low pay. In reaction to these conditions, workers began to organize. The Knights of Labor was the first national federation of trade unions.

Union organizers, however, were only mildly successful. A few unions made up of skilled workers survived to form the American Federation of Labor (AFL), but most attempts to organize unskilled and semiskilled laborers failed. Meanwhile, high credit costs and steep railroad freight rates led to protests throughout rural areas. **Mechanization** (the use of machinery) had increased farm production. However, the bankers and the monopolies were the ones profiting from this increased production. Across the country, farmers organized Farmers' Alliances to fight for their interests.

Protests against the power of the monopolies led to the passage of the Interstate Commerce Act (1887) and the Sherman Anti-Trust Act (1890). Nevertheless, the influence of the monopolies was great. The **antitrust**, or anti-monopoly, law was enforced more frequently against unions and farmers than against the monopolies.

The failure of reform laws such as the Sherman Act led to strong public support for the Populists (People's) Party in the 1890s. This third-party movement wanted government to have greater control over monopolies. The Populist Party won more than a million votes in 1892. In 1896, its demands were added to the Democratic Party platform. However, Republican candidate William McKinley, who was supported by big business, defeated Democrat William Jennings Bryan. Later many of the Populists' ideas were adopted by both parties.

In the last 30 years of the nineteenth century, industrialization and urbanization changed America. The social and political problems created by these changes were not solved. They would come up again in conflicts during the twentieth century.

THINK ABOUT SOCIAL STUDIES

Directions: Choose the one best answer to each question.

1. What was the Populists' goal?

   A. to establish more monopolies

   B. to protect the rights of Native Americans

   C. to control the power of unions

   D. to help in the struggle against big business

2. Why did workers try to become unionized?

   A. They were working 12-hour days.

   B. They received good pay.

   C. They wanted to increase the rate of industrialization.

   D. They wanted to protest the low cost of credit.

Imperialism

The Monroe Doctrine of 1823 declared that the United States would not tolerate any new European colonization or interference in the Western Hemisphere. At that time, though, the United States was not very interested in foreign affairs, so the policy was not enforced.

By 1890, when the West was largely settled, European countries were building up large colonial empires in Africa and Asia. The United States did not want to be left out, and Americans became interested in taking over lands outside the United States. The country began a policy of **imperialism**, a plan to increase power by taking over foreign land.

Spanish-American War

Beginning in 1895, Cuba fought a violent war against Spanish rule. The US press published newspaper articles describing the horrors of the war. Some of the articles were exaggerated, showing only the Cuban point of view. This style of one-sided reporting is called **yellow journalism**. It encouraged Americans to support the fight against Spain. The Cuban struggle for independence from Spain gave US imperialists the opportunity they wanted. In 1898, the United States decided to help Cuba in its fight against Spain. US troops fought a three-month war in Cuba. However, the first battle between US and Spanish forces occurred in the Philippines, another Spanish colony that wanted its independence. At the end of the war, Cuba became independent, but it was under US control for a number of years. The Philippines were surrendered to the United States. The Spanish colonies of Puerto Rico and Guam both became US territories.

Hawaiian Islands, Latin America, China, and the Caribbean

In 1898, the United States took over the Hawaiian Islands. After 1900, the United States helped Panama become independent from Colombia in exchange for the right to build and control a canal across Panama. During the next few years, US troops were sent to Mexico, Nicaragua, the Dominican Republic, and Haiti. Americans believed these actions were necessary to protect US interests.

After acquiring Hawaii, the Philippines, and Guam, the United States became interested in China. In the late 1890s, a weakened China was overtaken by foreign powers that had **spheres of influence**, or control over parts of China. The United States, which had no sphere of influence, wanted to tap into China's vast natural resources, but US leaders were worried that the nations occupying China might shut them out. Secretary of State John Hay proposed the Open Door policy in 1899. This policy would require all spheres of influence in China to keep trading with other nations. This ultimately prevented one foreign power from having too many advantages within the occupied territory.

In 1904, President Theodore Roosevelt was concerned that political problems in the Caribbean would cause European forces to intervene in Latin America. Roosevelt introduced a policy known as the Roosevelt Corollary. A **corollary** is a follow-up to something. In this case, the corollary was a follow-up to the Monroe Doctrine. In the Roosevelt Corollary, the United States asserted its right to intervene in the affairs of Latin American nations in times of economic or political crisis.

21st Century Skill
Understand Current Events

After you read "Imperialism," look for information about territories that currently belong to the United States: American Samoa, Guam, Northern Mariana Islands, US Virgin Islands, and Puerto Rico.

Write a brief report about one of these territories. Describe where the territory is located (or draw a map). Explain how and when the United States acquired the territory and what rights the people in the territory have.

WRITE TO LEARN

Throughout history, countries have occupied other countries. Use the information about imperialism in this lesson and your own knowledge about current events to write a blog about having your country taken over by another nation.

Describe how your government has changed, how a different culture is changing your way of life, and different values are affecting you.

Directions: Use these words to complete the following sentences.

corollary   imperialism   industrialization   monopolies

1. The _____ of America marked a major change in the country's economy.

2. A _____ of the Monroe Doctrine stated that the United States could intervene in the troubled affairs of Latin America.

3. The United States took part in _____ by building up colonies in foreign lands.

4. Large companies formed powerful _____ that prevented smaller companies from competing with them.

Skill Review

Directions: Find and underline the main idea in each passage below.

1. (1) Large areas of the South were still characterized by the old agricultural system of sharecropping. (2) Sharecropping was much like the old plantation system because tenant farmer sharecroppers did not own the land. (3) They had to pay part of their crop as rent. (4) The sharecroppers were in constant debt to the large landowners.

2. (1) Some Americans opposed imperialism. (2) They wanted more foreign trade, but they did not want the United States to have colonies. (3) These Americans founded the Anti-Imperialist League. (4) Writer Mark Twain was one of its most outspoken members.

Directions: Read this passage on imperialism and answer the following questions.

Imperialism is the right of any powerful country. To stay powerful, a country must expand its land and area of control. It is important for a powerful country to keep its power. Countries like the United States must find ways to access raw materials in other countries. Imperialism helps the United States defend itself because it builds up military forces abroad. By establishing colonies in foreign lands, the United States helps the people in those lands maintain order.

3. Which statement best expresses the values of the author?

   A. The United States should respect foreign lands and people.
   B. Imperialism is a sign of weakness.
   C. Imperialism is a helpful and necessary means of survival.
   D. The United States should have stricter trading rules.

4. According to the passage, which activity is considered the most important?

   A. adding to a country's power
   B. trading within a country
   C. establishing a strong industrial economy
   D. communicating well with other countries

Skill Practice

Directions: Choose the <u>one best answer</u> to each question. <u>Questions 1 and 2</u> refer to the maps below.

THE SPANISH-AMERICAN WAR

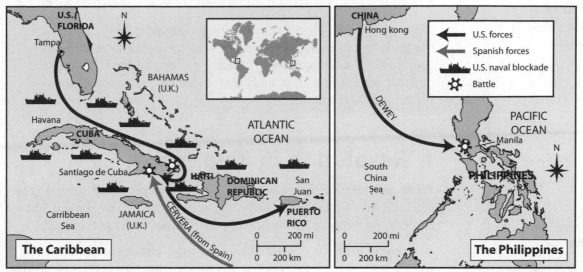

1. According to the two maps, which statement is correct?

   A. More battles took place in the Caribbean than in the Philippines.

   B. US forces had an easier route to the Caribbean.

   C. There was an equal number of US naval blockades in the Caribbean and the Philippines.

   D. Spanish forces traveled from China to the Philippines.

2. Where did US forces land in the Caribbean?

   A. Haiti and the Dominican Republic

   B. Jamaica and Haiti

   C. Cuba and Jamaica

   D. Cuba and Puerto Rico

Writing Practice

Directions: A new business in your community wants to create a monopoly on a particular product. Write one paragraph explaining why the monopoly might be good for the business owner but bad for consumers. You may wish to name a specific product in your essay.

Scientific and Industrial Revolutions

Lesson Objectives

You will be able to

• Describe the Scientific and Industrial Revolutions

• Describe the Digital and Transportation Revolutions

• Identify the current impact of these revolutions

Skills

• **Reading Skill:** Sequence Events

• **Core Skill:** Analyze Events and Ideas

Vocabulary

analyze
Digital Revolution
era
fundamental
Industrial Revolution
revolution
Scientific Revolution
theory
Transportation Revolution

KEY CONCEPT: Today's world has been shaped by the technological advances of the Scientific Revolution, the Industrial Revolution, the Transportation Revolution, and the Digital Revolution.

Which technology product do you rely on the most? Perhaps it is a computer if you enjoy keeping up with social media. Or it might be your music player if you enjoy listening to songs. Maybe it is your phone if you make a lot of calls. Or it could be your smartphone—for all of those reasons.

A Revolution in Your Hand

When you watch a movie or TV show that was produced several years ago, you may find yourself laughing, even if the film or show is not a comedy. Sometimes the technology being used looks old and silly.

In a movie from the 1970s, a character might be desperately looking for coins to use in a pay phone. In a movie from the 1980s, someone might be carrying around a "portable phone" as big as a brick. Even movies that are only a few years old look out of date if the characters are using out-of-date cell phones or are typing on typewriters instead of computers. Often *futuristic* films made only a decade ago include computer graphics that are already old-fashioned.

The reason that movies look out-of-date so quickly is that you live in an **era**, or period of time, of remarkable change. If someone told you that you are living in the middle of a **revolution** (a sudden and dramatic change), would you believe that? What if you were told that the tools and gadgets you use in your everyday life are the result of two revolutions? Or three? Or even four? You might find that hard to believe.

As you read about the revolutions that are changing your life, keep a smartphone in your hand or in your mind. You will soon see it as a revolutionary device.

The Scientific Revolution

Most people understand that science has a lot to do with the many technologies available to us today. Without science, we would not have computers, telephones, music players—or all three of these pieces of equipment wrapped up in a smartphone.

Science is a method of learning about the natural world. Scientists 1) make careful observations, 2) use experiments to identify facts, and 3) organize facts into theories. A **theory** is a general statement that explains the facts observed by scientists. Theories are tested, often by many scientists in a variety of places. Scientists continue to observe, to **analyze** (or examine carefully), and to experiment—a process leading to new theories that better explain the facts.

The **Scientific Revolution** is the name given to an era that lasted from the late 1500s to the early 1600s. During that time, scientists developed many new theories about how the world worked.

A good way to understand the Scientific Revolution is to think about the solar system. For centuries, people had had a **fundamental**, or basic, belief about the solar system: they thought the Sun and the other planets revolved around Earth. In 1543, however, the Polish astronomer Nicolaus Copernicus (1473–1543) *proposed the theory* that Earth and the other planets revolved in circular orbits around the Sun.

Later, other astronomers actually observed the orbit of planets. Danish astronomer Tycho Brahe (1546–1601) carefully *measured* the movements of objects in the night sky. Galileo Galilei (1564–1642), an Italian, observed the orbit of moons around Jupiter. Then the German astronomer Johannes Kepler (1571–1630) analyzed Brahe's measurements to *calculate* that the planets' orbits were not circular but oval in shape. The observations and experiments of these astronomers later led Englishman Isaac Newton (1642–1727) to propose the theory that the Sun and planets exert gravity on objects that orbit them.

Over the centuries, scientists have used scientific theory, observation, experimentation, measurement, and calculation to advance human knowledge. Through these scientific methods, scientists have achieved a long **sequence**, or series, of advances—not only in astronomy, but also in chemistry, geology, physics, meteorology, and biology. Such scientific advances eventually enabled inventors to create the smartphone and other modern marvels.

Reading Skill
Sequence Events

When you read, you often encounter passages having to do with time. Sometimes specific days or years are mentioned. At other times, the passage of time is marked by words and phrases such as *later*, *then*, *before*, or *after a while*.

As you read, look for words and phrases that refer to time. Doing so will help you understand the sequence, or order, of events.

Reread this page. Look for dates and time words. In a notebook, create a time line showing the sequence of the events mentioned here.

In social studies texts, you read about many people, places, events, and ideas. Analyzing them often means making the connections between them. When you analyze an event, ask yourself, "Why did that happen?"

Think about the connections between the events and ideas described on this page. In a notebook, answer these questions:

- When the Industrial Revolution took place in Britain's textile-manufacturing industry, where were the first mills built?

- Why were the mills built in those locations?

- What effect did the large textile mills have on the surrounding area?

WORKPLACE CONNECTION

Compare Tasks

Think of one task that you do at work, such as receive payment from customers. In your notebook, brainstorm to develop of list of ways that your job might have been done differently in the past. For example, consider the equipment you use, your source of energy, and the time it takes to do your job.

The Industrial Revolution

It is clear that a modern smartphone would not exist without the Scientific Revolution. The Scientific Revolution alone, however, did not put a smartphone in your hand. For that, you needed another revolution: the Industrial Revolution.

The **Industrial Revolution**, which took place in the late 1700s and early 1800s, was a fundamental change in the way goods are made. Before the Industrial Revolution, most goods in Europe and North America were made by hand, in homes in rural settings. After the Industrial Revolution, most goods were made by machines, in factories in urban settings, using the power of water or steam. The Industrial Revolution began in Europe and spread to the United States. It has now reached all the developed countries in the world.

The Industrial Revolution started in Britain's textile (cloth) industry. Inventors created spinning and weaving machines that made cloth much more quickly than people had been able to do by hand. At first, these new machines were powered by flowing water. The water in streams turned waterwheels, and the waterwheels turned the gears in the machines. Later the steam engine was invented. Steam-powered machinery could turn out miles of cloth in short periods of time. Textile company owners built mills to house the machines, and towns grew up around the mills.

The sequence of manufacturing changes in the textile industry was repeated in industry after industry in Britain and the United States. Improvements in iron- and steel-making industries provided a reliable source of metal for manufacturing factory machinery and new consumer goods. The population shift from rural areas to cities increased as thousands of men and women moved away from farms to work long hours in urban factories.

The Transportation Revolution

Steel and the steam engine combined to make steam locomotives and steamships possible. These mighty machines, along with the building of canals and railroads, led to the **Transportation Revolution**, which opened up new trade routes. Trains and steamboats carried the ever-increasing number of manufactured goods to a widespread network of markets. This led to the growth of cities such as Chicago. Soon railroads opened up the American West to settlement and industry.

The Digital Revolution

The Scientific Revolution led to a basic method of learning that enabled people to invent the smartphone. The Industrial Revolution led to methods of manufacturing that allow factories to produce lots of smartphones. The Transportation Revolution led to technologies that make it possible to ship smartphones all over the world. One final revolution, however, made the technology of smartphones possible.

The **Digital Revolution** refers to the ever-increasing number, types, and applications of digital devices found in business and in everyday life. The Digital Revolution began about 1980, and it is still going on today. The digital devices that make up this revolution are electronic instruments that use information coded in *digits*, or numbers.

Computers seem smart, but if you were to analyze a computer, you would find it is really just a collection of switches, each with an *on* and *off* position. When you use digits to represent these two positions, you use 0 and 1. Using lots of switches, computers record huge amounts of information, always using just the numbers 0 and 1. For example, to a computer the letter *A* is 01000001, where each 0 represents a switch in the *off* position and each 1 represents a switch in the *on* position. The switches are called *transistors*. Two million transistors could fit on the period at the end of this sentence.

Digital devices are everywhere today. Tiny computers are used in cars, kitchen appliances, satellites, TVs, electronic toys, all types of industrial machines—the list goes on and on. Your smartphone is a result of the Digital Revolution—and the other revolutions as well.

WRITE TO LEARN

How have the revolutions described in this lesson affected your life at home or in the workplace? Choose one digital device that is part of your life. It can be something you own, like a music player, or something you use, like the digital TV display of a bus schedule or the computer at your workstation.

Go online and research how developments in each of the revolutions described in this chapter—Scientific, Industrial, Transportation, and Digital—have played a part in bringing that device into your life.

In a notebook, write a two-paragraph essay that summarizes the impact of these revolutions on your chosen device.

THINK ABOUT SOCIAL STUDIES

Directions: Draw a line from each historical event to its most closely related idea or invention.

Scientific Revolution	steam engine
Industrial Revolution	transistor
Transportation Revolution	locomotive
Digital Revolution	theory

Vocabulary Review

Directions: Match each word with its definition.

1. _____ Digital Revolution
2. _____ era
3. _____ fundamental
4. _____ Industrial Revolution
5. _____ revolution
6. _____ Scientific Revolution
7. _____ theory
8. _____ Transportation Revolution

A. sudden and dramatic change

B. period of time

C. idea that explains observations

D. change in ways of moving

E. growth of digital devices

F. development of science

G. basic

H. change in ways of manufacturing

Skill Review

Directions: Write the number 1, 2, 3, or 4 next to each event to show the sequence in which the events occurred, with 1 being first and 4 being last.

_____ Digital Revolution

_____ Industrial Revolution

_____ Transportation Revolution

_____ Scientific Revolution

Directions: Answer these questions.

2. Observation and experimentation were methods first used in which revolution?
   A. Digital Revolution
   B. Transportation Revolution
   C. Industrial Revolution
   D. Scientific Revolution

3. How did astronomer Johannes Kepler's theory about the solar system differ from Nicolaus Copernicus's theory? What scientific observation allowed Kepler to arrive at his theory?

_____

_____

_____

_____

Skill Practice

Directions: Choose the <u>one best answer</u> to each question.

1. Which best describes the Scientific Revolution?

   A. the creation of astronomy
   B. the development of a method of learning
   C. the application of ideas to industry
   D. the invention of powered machinery

2. What did the Industrial Revolution affect?

   A. where goods were made
   B. how goods were made
   C. how many goods were made
   D. all of the above

3. Which was most likely a result of the Industrial Revolution?

   A. an increase in rural population
   B. an increase in the availability of goods
   C. a decrease in mining activity
   D. a decrease in factory production

4. Which of the following was invented in the Digital Revolution?

   A. a ship
   B. a book
   C. an airplane
   D. the Internet

Writing Practice

Directions: Write one paragraph about a revolution you read about in this lesson. Which one do you think is the most important for you to know about? Defend your answer.

Directions: Choose the <u>one best answer</u> to each question. <u>Question 2</u> refers to the photograph.

1. Which of the following explains why business owners and industrialists created monopolies?

   A. to lower prices
   B. to keep control of business
   C. to produce the best-quality products
   D. to introduce new products to the market

2. Which of the following summarizes the photographer's view of labor conditions?

   A. Workers should not be allowed time off to strike.
   B. Employers should offer health benefits.
   C. Unions disrupt the workplace.
   D. Wages should permit workers to care for their families.

Review

3. Where did the Industrial Revolution begin?

   A. Britain
   B. China
   C. Poland
   D. United States

4. How did the transportation revolution help the United States expand?

   A. by shipping smartphones long distances
   B. by moving settlers and goods across the country
   C. by helping people get to cities to look for jobs
   D. by using steam technology and modern engineering

5. Which of the following best describes the business cycle?

   A. the expansion of a country's economy
   B. movement from boom to bust and back again
   C. the relationship between the GDP of various countries
   D. interaction between a country's population and its economy

6. How were the economic policies of Barack Obama like those of Franklin Roosevelt?

   A. Both presidents had to contend with the Great Depression.
   B. Both presidents worked to limit the power of trusts and monopolies.
   C. Both sets of policies drew on the economic principles of John Maynard Keynes.
   D. Both sets of policies introduced social security and health care for elderly Americans.

7. What happened as a result of the Spanish-American War?

   A. Cuba and the Philippines won their independence.
   B. Secretary of State John Hay proposed an Open Door policy.
   C. Mexico gave some of its territories to the United States.
   D. The United States became an imperial power by acquiring territories abroad.

8. Which statement best describes Keynesian Economics?

   A. An economy in recession will repair itself.
   B. The government should make efforts to repair a troubled economy.
   C. Increased industry will support an economic expansion.
   D. Troughs in the economy are a normal part of the business cycle.

9. "Where trade unions are most firmly organized, there are the rights of the people most respected."

   Which statement best supports the point of view of the speaker?

   A. The importance of people's rights depends on location.
   B. Strong unions help protect people.
   C. Unions depend on how interested people are in them.
   D. People should not support unions.

10. How did the Populist Party feel about monopolies?

    A. It wanted to reorganize monopolies.
    B. It ignored monopolies to focus on other issues.
    C. It worked to limit the power of monopolies.
    D. It supported monopolies.

11. Which revolution allowed companies to ship products to other parts of the world?

    A. the Scientific Revolution
    B. the Industrial Revolution
    C. the Transportation Revolution
    D. the Digital Revolution

Review

Check Your Understanding

On the following chart, circle the number of any question you answered incorrectly. In the third column, you will see the pages you can review to study the content covered in the question. Pay particular attention to reviewing those lessons in which you missed half or more of the questions.

Chapter 6 Review

Lesson	Item Number	Review Pages
Major Economic Events	5, 6, 8	244–249
Industrialization and Imperialism	1, 2, 7, 9, 10	250–255
Scientific and Industrial Revolutions	3, 4, 11	256–261

ESSAY WRITING PRACTICE

Economic Events in History

Directions: Write a summary in response to one of the prompts below. When you write a summary, you restate the main ideas of what you read. A summary is a useful way to review what you've read, because you are identifying the main ideas and explaining them in your own words.

SUMMARY OF MAJOR EVENTS IN US ECONOMIC HISTORY

The US economy has undergone major changes over the course of the nation's history. These changes have affected how and where people live and how they earn a living. They have also affected the actions of the government.

Identify and summarize the major events in US economic history. Explain the role of government in shaping the US economy. Base your summary on Lesson 6.1. Your summary should be four paragraphs long.

SUMMARY OF THE EFFECTS OF INDUSTRIALIZATION AND SCIENTIFIC INNOVATIONS ON THE US ECONOMY

Industrialization brought sweeping changes to the US economy. Modern scientific innovations have changed not only the economy but also the structure of the workforce, the way goods are produced and distributed, and the use of resources.

Summarize the information in Lessons 6.2 and 6.3 about the effects of industrialization and scientific innovations on the US economy. Your summary should be four paragraphs long.

Review

ESSAY WRITING PRACTICE

Economics in the Twenty-First Century

Think about all the things you do in an average day. You get dressed and perhaps drive to school or work, use a computer, watch television, and cook your meals. You might be surprised to learn how many of the things you use in a day has been imported from another country. Oil, cars, and medicines, as well as cell phones, computers, and other electronic equipment are all leading imports in the United States.

In this chapter, you will learn about how economies work on a national and international scale. As you read, think about how much of what you buy is imported from other countries and why we import so many products.

In this chapter you will study these topics:

Lesson 7.1: National Economic Performance

A number of indicators can show a country's economic health. These include the unemployment rate, the gross domestic product, and the rate of inflation or deflation. Economic growth is based on efficient use of natural resources, labor, and capital goods.

Lesson 7.2: Global Markets

Greater economic globalization has meant more companies and workers are involved in the exchange of goods and services between countries. The pace of globalization has increased with new technologies. Global institutions such as the World Bank, the International Monetary Fund, the World Trade Organization, and the United Nations help maintain the global economy.

Goal Setting

Why is it important to study economics in the twenty-first century?

- to understand how the United States and other countries evaluate economic health

- to understand how countries trade with one another

- to understand the impact of imports and exports on the national economy

Think about the reasons people study modern economics.

- to understand world news

- to understand how a country's economy works and how it can be affected

- to understand how one country's economy can affect the economies of other countries

- to learn how other people live in other countries

What do you hope to learn from the lessons in this chapter? List some of your ideas here. As you read this chapter, think about these goals.

_____

_____

_____

_____

_____

_____

National Economic Performance

KEY CONCEPT: The US economy is considered healthy when it achieves full employment, price stability, and economic growth.

A healthy person has certain characteristics, such as a normal body temperature and the absence of symptoms like coughing, sneezing, and fatigue. When you catch a cold, you may develop a fever and you might start experiencing uncomfortable symptoms.

Similarly, when economists determine the overall health of the economy, they look at certain characteristics, for instance, positive or negative changes in the unemployment rate, price levels, and economic growth rate. These factors help economists evaluate how well our economy is performing.

A Healthy Economy

The Employment Act of 1946 expanded the US government's role in the economy. It focused on three key goals: achieving full employment, stabilizing prices, and growing the economy.

Full Employment

Full employment is achieved when about 5 percent of the labor force are without work and 95 percent have jobs. It might seem strange that our economy achieves full employment when the unemployment rate is 5 percent. However, some unemployment occurs naturally in an economy. For example, *frictional unemployment* occurs when people are between jobs. These workers may be receiving job training, or they may be seeking a better position. Frictional unemployment is a normal and healthy part of an economy. Seasonal unemployment is another normal type of unemployment. *Seasonal employment* results from expected changes in the economy. For example, jobs are sometimes created or lost during different seasons. Fewer ski instructors are employed in July, and fewer lifeguards are employed in December.

Economists are more concerned about two other types of unemployment: structural unemployment and cyclical unemployment. *Structural unemployment* results from changes in the structure of the economy. For example, new technology creates some jobs but eliminates others. Today we need many workers to make and service computers and software. However, not many workers are needed to make or repair typewriters.

Cyclical employment results from changes in the nation's **business cycle**. A business cycle has two main parts, or phases. The expansion phase occurs when the **gross domestic product** (GDP; the total market value of goods and services produced by a country in a single year) rises over time. The contraction phase occurs when the GDP falls over time. Cyclical unemployment happens mainly during contraction. Firms produce fewer goods, so workers are laid off.

USE CONTEXT CLUES TO UNDERSTAND MEANING

The **meaning** of a word or phrase is the message that the word expresses or conveys. Sometimes you can figure out the meaning of a word or a phrase by looking at other words around it. The context (surrounding text) of an unfamiliar term often gives clues or hints about the word's meaning. Context clues can help you understand what you read.

To identify a context clue, see if the unfamiliar word is paired with more familiar words. The familiar words are the clues. A passage might use the word *pragmatic* and follow this word with a synonym such as *practical* or *sensible*. Sometimes opposites are used as context clues. If the unfamiliar word is *compassionate*, the passage might contrast it with *cruel* or *harsh*.

To understand the meaning of unfamiliar words, look for hints about the meaning of words or ideas. Ask yourself these questions: *Which words in the passage give me hints about the meaning of unfamiliar words or ideas? Are there hints in photographs, diagrams, charts, or captions that help me understand the passage?*

Read the following paragraph. Use context clues to explain the meaning of the terms *redundancy employment* and *lethargic*.

> Redundancy employment was a major problem in Poland during the 1980s. During that time the communist government insisted that state-owned businesses hire additional workers even when there was no work for them to do. One worker often did the required work and others simply watched or wasted time until the workday was done. Under these conditions the work force grew lethargic. What the economy really needed, however, was an energetic and industrious labor supply.

The context clues "major problem," "additional workers," and "no work" help you understand what the term *redundancy employment* means. The word *however* in the last sentence helps you understand that *lethargic* is the opposite of "energetic and industrious."

Core Skill
Analyze Events and Ideas

Interdependence is an important factor in the economy. An event that occurs in one part of the world often affects people in another part of the world. Likewise, a change in one industry can affect the workers in other industries.

Read "Full Employment." Then identify a new piece of technology that has changed a business you are familiar with. Write one paragraph explaining the effect that change is having on a related industry and on the labor force.

21st Century Skill
Global Awareness

Today interdependence reaches beyond national borders. Even companies that are not international often have partners, suppliers, or customers abroad.

Think about how changes in the US economy might affect the economies of countries that the United States trades with. Write a paragraph explaining your ideas.

THINK ABOUT SOCIAL STUDIES

Directions: In a notebook, give an example of each kind of unemployment.

1. structural unemployment
2. frictional unemployment
3. cyclical unemployment
4. seasonal unemployment

WRITE TO LEARN

Inflation and Deflation

Price instability is the upswing or downswing in the prices of goods we buy. There are two types of price instability: inflation and deflation. Inflation is more common than deflation.

Inflation occurs when the overall price level for goods and services increases over time. The **inflation rate** is the percentage of price increases. The inflation rate shows the overall price increase for all products, not for a specific item such as an MP3 player or a car.

Economists debate the causes of inflation. It could be caused by too much demand: too much money is available for purchasing too few goods. This results in people "bidding up" the price of goods. Inflation might also be caused by increased costs. Higher wages, more expensive energy, or other increased costs could force firms to charge higher prices for their output.

An inflation rate of 2 or 3 percent per year is considered normal. When the inflation rate rises above 10 percent, it is viewed as a serious problem. A high inflation rate reduces the value of our money. The purchasing power of each dollar falls. This makes it difficult for businesses, government, and people to plan how to use scarce resources.

Deflation occurs when the overall price for goods and services decreases over time. This might seem positive because consumers like lower prices. But deflation is a serious problem. Even a small percent decline in price level sends negative signals to businesses. When businesses sense there is a deflation, they tend to decrease production and lay off workers.

Economic Growth

Economic growth is another way economists assess the nation's economic performance. **Economic growth** occurs when the **real GDP** (the size of the economy adjusted for inflation) increases over a significant period of time. To determine whether our economy is growing, economists look at long-term trends. There have been many brief contractions and two severe depressions over the past century or so. Overall, however, the expansions have outweighed the brief contractions. Therefore, the long-term trend in the US economy has been one of economic growth.

Causes of Economic Growth Economic growth is the result of a wise use of society's resources, or factors of production.

- Natural resources: Good soil and fresh water support agriculture. Deep-water harbors support trade. Supplies of oil and minerals support mining industries and fuel the economy.

- Human resources (labor): Education, job training, and health care build a skilled and healthy labor force. Support for entrepreneurs helps create new businesses, products, and services.

- Capital goods: Capital goods—such as buildings, vehicles, and computers—are the human-made items needed to make products.

Other factors support the wise use of resources. For example, government must be honest and must enforce fair rules. This provides incentives for people to work hard and for firms to produce efficiently.

Vocabulary Review

Directions: Use these terms to complete the following sentences.

business cycle   deflation   full employment   inflation

1. A decline in price levels in an economy is called _____.

2. Expansion and contraction are the two phases of an economy's _____.

3. If about 5 percent of workers have no job, the economy has achieved _____.

4. _____ reduces the purchasing power of money in an economy.

Skill Review

Directions: Read the passage. Use context clues to answer the questions in a notebook.

> One of the most important engines of economic growth is entrepreneurship. Entrepreneurs are the innovators and risk-takers in an economy. They invent new products, find new ways to provide services, and start new businesses. In 1976, Steve Jobs and Steve Wosniak invented one of the first personal home computers. Instead of inventing new products, some entrepreneurs invent new ways to produce an existing product. Henry Ford did not invent the automobile. Instead, he introduced the moving assembly line to mass-produce automobiles. This innovation enabled Ford Motor Company to dominate the US auto industry in the early twentieth century. Entrepreneurs are not content with the status quo. Instead, they seek innovation, progress, and positive change in the economy.

1. Using context clues from the passage above, define the term *entrepreneurship*.

2. Define the term *status quo*. What context clues helped you figure out your definition?

Skill Practice

Directions: Choose the one best answer to each question.

1. Which phrase best summarizes US economic performance over the past century?

   A. mostly uncontrolled inflation
   B. mostly economic growth
   C. mostly massive unemployment
   D. mostly declines in gross domestic product

2. "US Unemployment Rate Drops to 5 Percent of Labor Force." What does this headline say about the US economy?

   A. It has achieved full employment.
   B. It has entered a cycle of contraction.
   C. It should expect an increase in inflation.
   D. It has no frictional unemployment.

Writing Practice

Directions: Reread the paragraph above about entrepreneurship. Then think about someone who has started a small business in your community. Write a paragraph describing how this entrepreneur has affected the economy.

Global Markets

KEY CONCEPT: Globalization creates more integrated and interdependent global markets. However, it can have negative effects on workers and on the environment.

A school relies on many people to provide the best possible learning experience for its students. Teachers, administrators, librarians, custodians, and cafeteria workers all contribute to the process of educating children.

Similarly, many people, businesses, and institutions around the world help one another. They combine their efforts to support businesses, health care, and education. Globalization benefits billions of people around the world, but it does not always lead to prosperity.

Lesson Objectives

You will be able to

- Explain the main components of economic globalization

- Identify institutions that support globalization

- Recognize the potential benefits and costs of globalization

Skills

- **Core Skill:** Interpret Graphics

- **Reading Skill:** Recognize Unstated Assumptions

Vocabulary

assumption
foreign direct investment
globalization
stabilize

Economic Globalization

Economic **globalization** is the process of creating an economy that connects countries on a worldwide scale. Economic globalization creates commercial links between people, businesses, and governments around the world. The global economy has many parts.

International Trade The cross-border flow of goods and services is called international trade. Buyers and sellers around the world are linked by these trade relationships.

Foreign Direct Investment The investment that a company makes in a foreign country is **foreign direct investment** (FDI). A US company building a factory in Mexico is an example of FDI. FDI creates commercial ties between two countries. These ties can bring jobs and other benefits to the second country.

Foreign Exchange Cross-border flows of money link investors from different countries. Computer networks allow investors to buy and sell securities in stock markets around the globe. Currencies such as the US dollar and the Japanese yen are traded.

Other Exchanges Other cross-border flows, such as the flow of workers from one country to another, are also a part of globalization. For example, every year millions of workers cross national borders in search of jobs and a better life. New ideas and technologies increase productivity across the globe.

Institutions of Globalization

Globalization is supported by many international organizations. These institutions work to create and maintain positive economic relations between nations. The policies and actions of these organizations are often controversial. The table to the right summarizes the roles of some key international organizations.

RECOGNIZE UNSTATED ASSUMPTIONS

An **assumption** is an idea that an author believes to be true; however, this idea has not been proven. Economists make assumptions all the time. For instance, the law of demand says that people will buy more of a good if the price falls. This economic principle is usually correct. The underlying assumption is that buyers will act logically—they will buy more of a good when it is cheaper and less of the good when it is more expensive.

When assumptions are stated, the author might begin by saying, "Let's assume . . ." or "Suppose . . ." However, sometimes the author does not warn the reader that a statement is unproven. An unstated assumption forces the reader to analyze the author's argument.

To recognize an unstated assumption, ask yourself these questions: *What is the author's main point? What evidence is offered to support this view? What line of reasoning led to this conclusion? Which parts of the argument are proven and which are unproven?*

Read the paragraph. Then write the unstated assumption made by the author.

> International trade is based on the principle of mutual benefit. That is, both parties in the exchange are better off after the exchange takes place. International trade encourages countries to specialize in the production of goods best suited to their resources. When countries specialize, they use their resources more efficiently, and the global output of goods and services increases. This benefits buyers and sellers in all trading countries. International trade helps create a more prosperous global economy.

The unstated assumption is that there is a demand for the specialized output that every country produces and that countries will be paid a fair price for their products.

WRITE TO LEARN

A code is a written list of rules, regulations, or laws that guides behavior. Sometimes codes are meant to guide the behaviors of individuals. At other times, they guide the behaviors of organizations or businesses.

Suppose you work for a global corporation. Write a code of conduct to guide your company's business behaviors in its plants around the world. In your code, address the needs of both workers and managers.

Global Institution	Purpose
World Bank	Gives loans and grants to poorer countries to help them develop their economies
International Monetary Fund (IMF)	Gives loans, advice, and supervision to poorer countries to **stabilize** (hold steady) currencies, financial institutions, and trading relations with other countries
World Trade Organization (WTO)	Establishes and enforces rules to guide and encourage free trade
United Nations (UN)	Establishes a forum to discuss and promote global security, economic development, and social progress

Core Skill
Interpret Graphics

Some authors use visual documents such as cartoons to convey a message to their readers.

Read "Institutions of Globalization" and study the political cartoon. Answer these questions in a notebook:

- What is the topic of the cartoon?

- What do the characters represent?

- What message do the title, caption, words, and symbols convey?

- What is the author implying about the WTO?

THINK ABOUT SOCIAL STUDIES

Directions: Write a short response to the following question in a notebook.

Why do you think the actions of institutions that support globalization are often controversial?

Reading Skill
Recognize Unstated Assumptions

Read "Benefits and Costs of Globalization." Discuss these questions with a partner:

- What assumptions do supporters of globalization make about the behavior of foreign companies that operate in poorer countries?

- What assumptions do opponents of globalization make about these business behaviors?

- How do assumptions sometimes influence people's judgments about a topic?

Benefits and Costs of Globalization

The pace of globalization has increased in recent decades. New technologies have helped this growth. Advanced information and communications systems support the flow of services, money, and ideas. Modern transportation systems make it easier for people and goods to move from one country to another.

Supporters argue that globalization creates prosperity. Global trade, for example, enables countries to become more efficient by specializing in the production of goods best suited to their resources. In turn, efficient production encourages countries to export goods for profit. In addition, FDI brings modern machines and equipment, technology, and business skills into poorer regions of the world. Trade and FDI also bring more money into poorer economies by creating jobs. Countries collect more tax revenue when their economies grow. This means better public services can be provided. Finally, by opening national borders, immigrant and migrant workers have access to jobs and other opportunities. Therefore, supporters argue that globalization improves living standards.

Globalization also has its opponents. Globalization, they say, leads to the exploitation of people and the environment. They note that the profits earned through trade and investment benefit mainly the rich—the stockholders in far-away lands and the privileged classes in the poorer host countries. This widens the income gap between rich and poor. In addition, the pursuit of profit can blind companies to the harm they are doing in a host country. Issues include the unjust treatment of workers and the abuse of the environment.

Finally, opponents of globalization point to the negative effects globalization can have on employment in richer countries. When a US company moves its production abroad, for example, the workers in US factories lose their jobs and many supporting businesses close.

Vocabulary Review

Directions: Use these terms to complete the following sentences.

foreign direct investment   **globalization**   **stabilize**

1. _____ is an investment a company makes in a foreign country.

2. _____ is the process of integrating the economies of the world.

3. The IMF works to help _____ the economies of poorer countries.

Skill Review

Directions: Read the statement and answer the question.

Free trade will lead to prosperity for the peoples of the world.

1. The unstated assumption made is that the wealth gained through free trade will be

   A. shared widely by ordinary people
   B. held mainly by the rich
   C. taxed heavily by the government
   D. lost due to corruption

Skill Practice

Directions: Choose the one best answer to each question.

1. Which best describes the main function of the World Bank?

   A. It stabilizes national currencies.
   B. It provides development loans.
   C. It distributes foreign aid.
   D. It regulates international trade.

2. According to the opponents of globalization, which group would least likely be hurt by globalization?

   A. workers in poorer countries
   B. small businesses in poorer countries
   C. people who lack modern information technologies
   D. stockholders of major international companies

Writing Practice

Directions: Do you think that globalization is beneficial? In a notebook, write a journal entry giving your opinion. Support your ideas with details from the lesson, other reading, and your own experience.

Directions: Choose the <u>one best answer</u> to each question. <u>Questions 1–3</u> refer to the chart below.

Selected Leading Economic Indicators	Explanation	Signals of an Expansion	Signals of a Contraction
number of building permits issued	indicates construction of new homes and businesses	many permits issued	few permits issued
orders for large consumer goods	indicates level of consumer demand in the economy	many orders	few orders
performance of stocks on New York Stock Exchange	indicates level of investor confidence in the economy	stock values rise	stock values decline
number of business start-ups	indicates level of business confidence in the economy	many business start-ups	few business start-ups

1. Which result might be the consequence of an expansion?

   A. fewer businesses in operation
   B. a stronger recession
   C. an overabundance of workers
   D. a stronger economy

2. A clothing manufacturer lays off 20 percent of its work force. What does this indicator signal?

   A. Businesses are expanding.
   B. The economy is contracting.
   C. Stock prices are declining.
   D. Consumer demand is increasing.

3. Why might economists use economic indicators to make predictions?

   A. Economic indicators accurately predict the state of the economy in future years.
   B. Economic indicators show how the economy has behaved in the past.
   C. Economic indicators reflect how strong or weak the economy is.
   D. Economic indicators determine the price of stocks.

4. "IMF Builds Assembly Plant in India." What is described in this headline?

   A. foreign exchange market
   B. international trade
   C. foreign direct investment
   D. regional trade agreements

5. How are the World Bank and the International Monetary Fund similar?

   A. Both offer trading and economic advice to Western nations.
   B. Both give financial support to developing countries.
   C. Both help promote global security.
   D. Both offer banking services.

6. Which statement describes the most likely result of a prolonged drop in prices of consumer goods?

   A. The economy will grow quickly.
   B. The economy will experience inflation in the near future.
   C. The number of business start-ups will rise.
   D. Businesses will reduce production.

Directions: <u>Questions 7–9</u> refer to the passage below.

Since the end of World War II, the world has moved steadily toward free trade. Free trade opposes the use of trade barriers, such as tariffs and import quotas. In 1947, the General Agreement on Tariffs and Trade (GATT) brought leading economies together to begin reducing tariffs on goods traded between nations. Since this time, GATT and its successor organization, the World Trade Organization (WTO), have led the move toward free trade in the global economy.

---

7. Which statement describes the direction leading world economies took after World War II?

   A. They moved toward free trade with other nations.
   B. They moved toward free trade within each nation.
   C. They began working to prevent economic depressions.
   D. They increased their use of tariffs and import quotas.

8. What is the importance of the World Trade Organization?

   A. It allows nations to share information regarding their political structures.
   B. It helps nations improve their economies through easier trade.
   C. It allows nations to be isolationist.
   D. It helps nations expand the number of jobs available to its citizens.

9. Which is an example of a trade barrier?

   A. fences between countries
   B. organizations that improve international trade
   C. building codes that control factory construction
   D. taxes on imported goods

Directions: Questions 10 and 11 refer to the graph below.

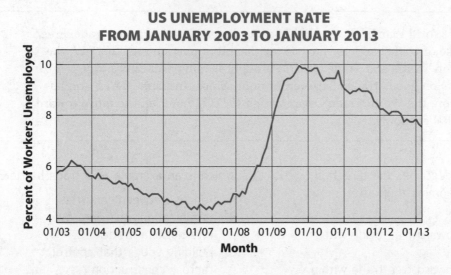

**US UNEMPLOYMENT RATE
FROM JANUARY 2003 TO JANUARY 2013**

10. According to the graph, when did the United States experience full employment?

   A. at the end of 2009
   B. throughout the decade
   C. during 2006 and 2007
   D. at no time during that decade

11. What is a possible explanation for the changes in the unemployment rate after January 2008?

   A. cyclical unemployment
   B. frictional unemployment
   C. normal unemployment
   D. seasonal unemployment

12. Which of the following might lead to a rise in structural unemployment?

   A. stores letting workers go at the end of the holiday season
   B. layoffs in the automobile industry as a result of reduced demand
   C. more companies outsourcing production and service to other countries
   D. workers choosing to quit their jobs to attend college-degree programs

Review

Directions: Question 13 refers to the following text.

> Globalization is a mixed blessing. Of course, it provides poorer countries with useful technology and skills so they can make better use of their resources. It relocates jobs from countries with high labor and production costs to countries where these costs are low. This boosts company profits. It also helps the workers who get the outsourced jobs, as well as their governments, whose tax revenues rise. Globalization also makes it easier for workers to move from poor countries to richer ones in hope of finding greater prosperity and opportunity. However, this leads to an intriguing question: When those workers arrive looking for jobs, where will those jobs be?

13. What possible problem with globalization is the writer pointing out?
    A. In rich countries, companies may have to contend with high production costs.
    B. Poor countries do not have the technology and equipment to thrive economically.
    C. The profits brought to poor countries by globalization will end up in government pockets.
    D. People coming to rich countries for work may find many jobs have been outsourced.

Check Your Understanding

On the following chart, circle the number of any question you answered incorrectly. Under each lesson title, you will see the pages you can review to study the content covered in the question. Pay particular attention to reviewing those lessons in which you missed half or more of the questions.

Chapter 7 Review

Lesson	Item Number	Review Pages
National Economic Performance	1, 2, 3, 6, 10, 11, 12	270–273
Global Markets	4, 5, 7, 8, 9, 13	274–277

ESSAY WRITING PRACTICE

Economics in the Twenty-First Century

Directions: When you analyze an issue, you break it down into smaller parts, show how the parts affect one another, and then present your conclusion. Write an essay analyzing an issue in response to one of the prompts below.

ANALYSIS OF THE EFFECTS OF PRICE STABILITY

Price stability affects the health of the US economy. It can also have an effect on average American families. When prices rise (inflation), a family can buy fewer goods. When prices fall (deflation), people with small businesses may have lower incomes.

Write an essay analyzing the effect of inflation and deflation on the US economy and on an average American family such as your own.

ANALYSIS OF GLOBAL MARKETS

China, the United States, and Japan are the top automobile manufacturers countries in the world. In an essay, discuss how sharing the global car market benefits the US economy and how competing with foreign manufacturers creates disadvantages for US carmakers.

UNIT 4

Geography

CHAPTER 8
Geography and People

Geography and People

Most of us have ancestors who came to the United States from somewhere else. One reason people move to different countries or regions is to get away from poor physical conditions such as drought, lack of farmland, or weather that is too hot or too cold.

Geography is the study of Earth and its features. Geographers study natural features of our world, such as climate, soil, mountains, and waterways. They also study how human populations use Earth. Recognizing differences in geography can help you understand how people adapt to the land where they live and how they change the land. Maps are one of the tools geographers use to represent information about natural features and human populations. As you read, consider how humans have interacted with the world and changed it.

In this chapter you will study these topics:

Lesson 8.1: Physical and Cultural Landscapes
Throughout history, the features of the landscape have influenced how people use land for settlements, farming, fishing, and other purposes. As the world's population density increases and new technologies are developed, people are changing the environment more and more.

Lesson 8.2: Physical Systems
The physical systems of Earth include natural resources such as land, water, plants, animals, and minerals. Earth has seven continents, five oceans, and thousands of ecosystems. Each of these ecosystems is affected by global warming.

Lesson 8.3: Human Systems
Demography is the study of people on the planet. Social scientists collect information about population growth, death rates, and birthrates. They also study migration, urban growth, and the mixing of cultures.

Lesson 8.4: Nationhood and Statehood
The world is not naturally divided into nations and states. Changing borders reflect the conflicts and the cooperation that have occurred between groups of people throughout history.

Lesson 8.5: Sustainability
Increasing population and economic development place a huge strain on Earth's natural resources. The burning of fossil fuels sends carbon dioxide into the atmosphere. This adds to the greenhouse effect and increases global warming. People and governments are investigating ways of dealing with these problems through sustainable development.

Lesson 8.6: Natural and Cultural Diversity
Just as Earth has many landforms, climates, and ecosystems, it is also home to a wide variety of human cultures. Within a culture, the people share certain traits, such as language, values, and behaviors.

Goal Setting

Think about the reasons geography can be useful.

- to use maps showing trends or patterns of how people live

- to understand how the systems of the world are interconnected

- to understand how Earth's features affect culture and civilization

Some people who use geography in their jobs include

- truck drivers

- farmers

- fishers

- oil, gas, and mine workers

- demographers

- city planners

- historians

Think about what you know about geography and what you would like to learn. Fill in the first two columns of the table below. When you have completed the chapter, fill in the last column.

What I already know about geography	What I want to learn about geography	What I learned about geography

Physical and Cultural Landscapes

KEY CONCEPT: From the beginning of time, humans have adapted to their physical environment. At the same time, however, the physical environment has been changed by humans.

Have you seen a new apartment building or road built in your area? These are examples of people changing places. The people in some ancient cultures farmed because they lived where good soil and water were plentiful. Other people hunted and gathered because good soil and plentiful water were lacking in their area. These are examples of places changing people.

Physical Geography Affects People

In the early years of civilization, the physical environment had a major impact on people's lives. The **environment** is the surroundings in a particular area. If an area did not have a source of fresh water, people did not settle there. If a particular region was too cold or too mountainous, people usually looked for an easier place to live.

In ancient times, people also learned to **adapt**, or adjust, to their environment. Early Americans in the Southwest deserts, for example, learned to grow crops that needed little rain, and they built sprawling **irrigation systems**. These ditches or canals brought water to dry areas. The people built houses using bricks that they cut from the clay soil and dried in the sun. When a **drought** (a long period without rain) hit, these people abandoned their villages in search of a more suitable environment.

ANNUAL PRECIPITATION, ARIZONA

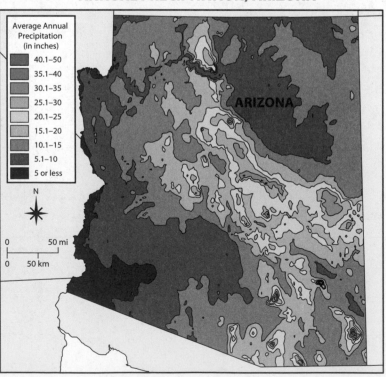

Average Annual Precipitation (in inches)

- 40.1–50
- 35.1–40
- 30.1–35
- 25.1–30
- 20.1–25
- 15.1–20
- 10.1–15
- 5.1–10
- 5 or less

ARIZONA

0   50 mi
0   50 km

USE A MAP KEY

Most maps have a key or legend. A map key uses symbols and colors or shading to represent features of the real world. Symbols are used for cities, rivers, highways, boundaries, and capitals. Colors or shading may show climate regions, altitude, or rainfall.

To use a map key, look at each item in the key. Read the label to determine what the symbol represents. Then look for those symbols on the map itself.

Look at the map below. Who would use this map? What features on the map help you figure out the purpose of the map?

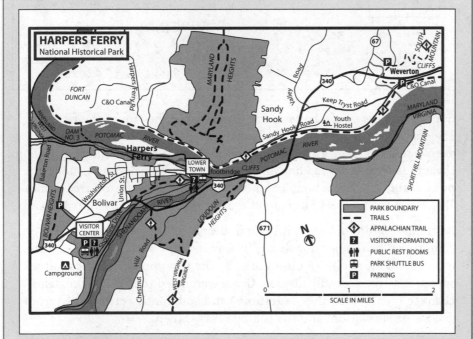

This map is for visitors to Harpers Ferry National Historical Park. The key tells you that the map can help visitors find parking, shuttle buses, rest rooms, information desks, and trails. It also identifies roads that lead to the park.

Reading Skill
Use a Map Key

Map keys often use color or shading to **convey**, or communicate, information on a map. The key explains what the color represents.

Look at the maps on pages 286 and 288. Then answer these questions in a notebook: *How are the keys alike? How are they different? What do the maps tell you about the difference between Arizona and Virginia?*

Research It
Discover Change

Our environment changes over time. Photographs keep a record of these changes. Some libraries, such as the San Francisco Public Library's Historical Photograph Collection (sfpl.org), have photo collections that document such change.

Find a library, museum, or online site that has a collection of historical photographs. Look for several photos of one location. Ask yourself these questions: *What is responsible for the changes? How would the changes have affected humans living in the area?*

Write your observations in a notebook.

Maps can be used to explore countless features. For example, a population density map shows how many people live in a certain area. By looking at population density maps of China and Australia, you can compare and contrast the population density of these two countries. You could also compare population density between two areas within one of these countries.

Use an atlas or an online search engine to find a map of your state showing annual precipitation. Compare that map to the map on page 286 or 288.

In a notebook, compare the average annual precipitation in your state to that of Arizona or Virginia.

Other Effects of Geography

Geography continually influences the world. When European colonists arrived in North America, geography guided their choice of where to build the first towns. The English, Spanish, and others who set up colonies looked for access to the sea and fresh water. They also looked for land that was flat enough to farm and land that offered materials for building.

ANNUAL PRECIPITATION, VIRGINIA

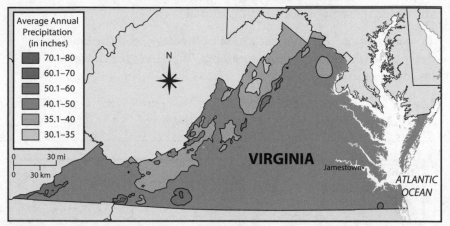

English settlers chose Jamestown, Virginia, for the site of their colony. They believed the area's geography made it a good place to settle because deep water ran right up to the shore. This meant ships could be pulled up close to land for easy loading and unloading. In addition, the site was a **peninsula**, which is a body of land surrounded by water on three sides. This made the area easy to defend against enemies approaching by land.

As time went on, however, it became clear that the geography of Jamestown had major drawbacks. It was swampy and humid. The water was unhealthy, and mosquitoes bred by the thousands. The mosquitoes spread malaria, a deadly disease. Crops were hard to grow in the damp **climate** (general weather conditions) and soil. Many settlers died from disease or starvation, and the colony nearly failed.

Geography again proved important when the colonists rose up against the British in the American Revolution. Because the British government was so far from its colonies, supplies took weeks to reach the British troops. In addition, because the war spread along the entire North Atlantic coast, the British found their resources stretched too thin. These factors contributed to the success of the American uprising.

THINK ABOUT SOCIAL STUDIES

Directions: Write a short response to the following question.

What geographic elements did early settlers from Europe look for when setting up their North American colonies?

People Affect Geography

As the population of the original 13 states grew, more food was needed. Not enough farmland existed near the coasts, so people began moving west in search of good farm land. Because of this, the United States expanded.

At the same time people are adapting to their environment, often they are also changing that environment. Settlers cleared forests and planted crops. They built roads and bridges. In the 1860s, workers laid thousands of miles of railroad track across the country, altering the physical geography of the United States as they did so. When the steel plow was invented, farmers tilled acres of grassland. All of this activity disturbed the environment of the Great Plains and led to massive dust storms in the 1930s. Because of the growing industrialization, people flocked to the cities to work. High-rise apartments were built to house these workers.

PERCENT OF POPULATION LIVING IN METROPOLITAN AREAS

1910

2010

Percent of population in metropolitan areas

- 75 or more
- 50 to 75
- Less than 50
- Not applicable

As technology advances, people have more and more control over their environment. Irrigation systems bring water to the desert, engineers blast through mountains and drain wetlands. Tunnels bored beneath Earth's surface are used by thousands of motorists every day. Phone and cable lines are strung along nearly every road and highway in the country. Humans have even altered the environment above Earth by sending satellites and space stations into orbit.

All of this activity has important benefits. Improved transportation and communications and a more varied food supply are among the most signficant benefits. These changes come with a cost, however. Altering the physical geography of Earth can have disastrous results. Human activity causes air and water pollution. Growing cities in desert areas have strained water supplies. The clearing of the rain forests in Brazil and other tropical areas has had far-reaching consequences, including the loss of plant and animal life, flooding, and climate change.

THINK ABOUT SOCIAL STUDIES

Directions: Write a short response to the following question.

How did population growth and the invention of the steel plow affect the geography of the Great Plains?

Vocabulary Review

Directions: Use these words to complete the following sentences.

adapt   climate   drought   environment   irrigation systems   peninsula

1. People's lives were threatened when _____ struck an area in ancient times.

2. Modern _____ allow the desert to bloom.

3. Land access from the mainland to a _____ is from one direction only.

4. The _____ of the Jamestown colony was one reason the colony nearly failed.

5. When humans alter the physical _____, there are both positive and negative consequences.

6. Settlers must _____ to the conditions of their environment.

Skill Review

Directions: Look at the map below. In a notebook, answer questions 1 through 3.

IMMIGRANTS, 1870–1900

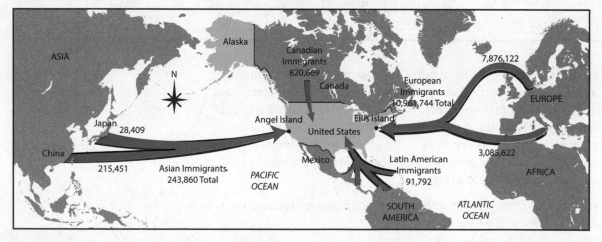

1. How many immigrants came from Canada? How many from Europe?

_____

2. How does the number of Asian immigrants compare to the number of Latin American immigrants? _____

3. How does the number of immigrants from Europe compare to the total number of immigrants from all other places? How does this information help you understand the current population of the United States?

_____

_____

Skill Review (continued)

Directions: Study the map. Then answer questions 4 through 6.

4. What do the black arrows show? _____

5. Where did the Dust Bowl migrants end up? _____

6. Which states lost population from 1930 to 1940? _____

THE DUST BOWL, 1930s

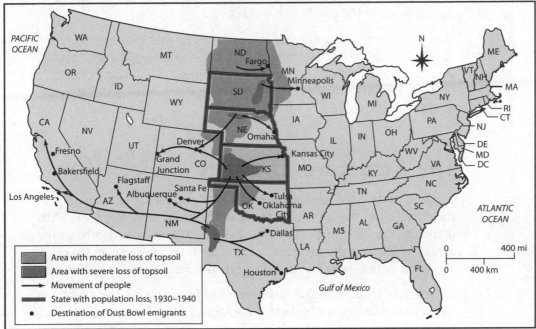

Skill Practice

Directions: Choose the one best answer to each question.

1. What was the link between the environment and the abandonment of early villages in the Southwest?

   A. geography
   B. irrigation
   C. distance to the ocean
   D. population

2. Which shows an example of people changing the geography of a place?

   A. Because Greece has little area for farming, the ancient Greeks grew crops that required little space.
   B. Fill is dumped in the marshes around the city of Boston to create the South End district.
   C. Native Americans in the Southwest built their homes from dried clay bricks.
   D. War breaks out in the Middle East over the rights to water in the Euphrates River.

Writing Practice

Directions: Use information from the map above to explain the Dust Bowl of the 1930s. What changes to the environment occurred? How were people living in area affected? How did they react?

Physical Systems

Lesson Objectives

You will be able to

- Understand that natural resources are distributed and utilized in various ways

- Recognize the many ecosystems on Earth

- Consider weather and climate systems

Skills

- **Core Skill:** Integrate Content Presented in Different Ways

- **Reading Skill:** Use Maps, Graphs, and Charts

Vocabulary

data
ecosystem
global warming
greenhouse effect
natural resource
region

KEY CONCEPT: The world around us is made up of many interconnecting parts. Land, air, water, plants, animals, and weather are just some of the physical systems of the planet Earth.

Physical changes to Earth happen all around us. You may notice seasonal changes—the cycle of warming and cooling temperatures and changes in the plants and animals.

Over millions of years, our planet has undergone a never-ending series of transformations. These changes are still happening, though they usually occur so slowly that we cannot see them. Most come about through natural processes. Some, however, are caused by the activities of the human race.

The Structure of Earth

Earth is made up of four major layers. The outside layer is called the crust. Below the crust lies the mantle, which is mostly rock. This is the thickest part of Earth—it is about 1,800 miles in depth. At the center of Earth is the core, made up of an outer core and an inner core. The outer core is very hot liquid metal. The inner core is solid metal.

A variety of landforms and waterways are found on Earth's crust. Examples of landforms include mountains, hills, **plateaus** (flat areas raised above nearby land), **plains** (large areas of level land), river valleys, peninsulas, **isthmuses** (narrow strips of land connecting two larger land areas), and deserts. Examples of water forms include oceans, seas, rivers, lakes, streams, and ponds.

Regions of the World

There are seven **continents**, or large land masses, in the world. They are Asia, Africa, North America, South America, Europe, Australia, and Antarctica. The continents are **distributed**, or spread out, unevenly over Earth's surface. More than 65 percent of the land area is in the Northern Hemisphere. The Southern Hemisphere is mostly ocean; only about 11 percent of the Southern Hemisphere is land.

To make the study of geography easier, geographers often write about **regions**. A region is an area that has a number of common elements. Regions have no uniform size. Some are small, and others are quite large. Regions may be defined by physical elements (such as climate or soil) or by elements related to people (such as language or religion).

When regions are defined by the kind of people who live there, they are called **cultural regions**. For example, two large cultural regions in the Western Hemisphere are the English-speaking region and the Spanish-speaking region. Some continents, such as Asia and Africa, are home to many regions because the people living on those continents have widely differing cultures.

USE MAPS, GRAPHS, AND CHARTS

Maps, graphs, and charts are useful ways to show information in a visual way. The information in a map, chart, or graph is called **data**. A large amount of data can be quickly understood when it is presented in a map, chart, or graph. Seeing data organized visually makes it easier to recognize trends and changes over time.

To use a map, graph, or chart, begin by reading the title. Then look at headings, labels, and keys. Finally, read the data.

Look at this circle graph. In a notebook, explain why it can be difficult to find drinking water, even though Earth is mostly covered in water.

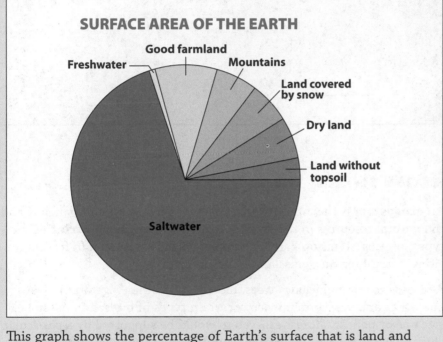

SURFACE AREA OF THE EARTH

- Freshwater
- Good farmland
- Mountains
- Land covered by snow
- Dry land
- Land without topsoil
- Saltwater

This graph shows the percentage of Earth's surface that is land and water. It further breaks down water into saltwater and freshwater. Although water covers about 70 percent of Earth's surface, most of that water is not drinkable. The graph shows that only a very small percent of the water on Earth's surface is freshwater.

TECHNOLOGY CONNECTION ▶

Mapping Data

A Geographic Information System (GIS) is a computer system that collects and analyzes data from various sources and displays that information on a map.

For example, a GIS can create maps showing the location, strength, and frequency of earthquakes. Governments and scientists use these maps to plan for emergencies and to establish building codes for areas where earthquakes frequently occur.

You can read more about GIS on the US Geological Survey website (egsc.usgs.gov /isb/pubs/gis_poster/). As you read, think about how GIS might be used by your state or local government. Discuss your ideas with a partner.

Natural Resources

Natural resources are the raw materials that occur naturally in the environment. They include land, water, air, minerals (such as copper, coal, and petroleum), energy, plants, and animals.

Natural resources are necessary for our survival. Renewable resources are resources that the environment replaces quickly (this includes many types of plants and animals) and resources that are available in unlimited amounts (such as air). Nonrenewable resources are resources that take millions of years to form. Fossil fuels (coal, oil, and gas) are nonrenewable resources.

Maps show features of a place, such rivers or political boundaries. When you link information from a map with information in your reading, you are integrating information presented in different ways.

Consider what you have read about the location of cities. Then study the map on this page.

In a notebook, describe the population distribution in Asia.

Humans use resources at an amazing rate. Because of this, there is concern that nonrenewable resources (for example, oil) will run out. In addition, even renewable resources are endangered. Deforestation has destroyed many plant and animal species. This can create a imbalance in an ecosystem. Water is a potential crisis. Some regions face the possibility of water shortages as their populations grow.

LARGEST CITIES IN ASIA

Ecosystems

An **ecosystem** is the interaction between a community of organisms and the natural resources in the environment. There are many **varieties**, or types, of ecosystems on Earth. Examples include tropical rain forests, cities, coastal regions, grasslands, and deserts.

A forest ecosystem includes trees, mosses, and other vegetation; deer and other animals; certain insects; certain types of birds; and possibly streams or ponds. A forest ecosystem would be supported by a particular climate, while a desert ecosystem would have a completely different type of climate.

Research It
Historical Maps

People have always made and used maps to help them locate things. Hunters living thousands of years ago drew maps on cave walls so they could return to good hunting grounds. Columbus and other sailors used maps to find stars, ocean currents, and landmarks.

To find maps from other eras, do an online search for "historical maps." Examine maps of the same regions from different time periods. How do they differ? Share the maps you found with another student, and discuss your ideas about how and why maps have changed over time.

THINK ABOUT SOCIAL STUDIES

Directions: Write a short response to the following questions in a notebook.

1. What is the difference between renewable resources and nonrenewable resources?

2. What is an ecosystem?

Weather and Climate Systems

A region's climate is determined by the type of weather patterns the area experiences over a long period of time. One important factor of climate is temperature. A region's distance from the equator can determine its average temperatures. Areas closer to the equator have hot climates. Those farther away from the equator have cold climates. Climate is also influenced by elevation. Higher elevations are colder than lower elevations. Elevation is a strong influence on climate. High mountains are snow covered even when they are near the equator.

The amount of **precipitation** (rain, hail, snow, or other forms of water falling in the atmosphere) a region receives is part of its climate. Some areas are wetter than others. Most areas receive a majority of their precipitation during certain months of the year.

Global Warming

In recent years, researchers have become concerned about a phenomenon called global warming. **Global warming** is the rise of Earth's temperature. Scientists have studied global warming for a long time, but they do not agree about its causes, extent, or possible long-term effects.

To understand global warming, you need to understand the **greenhouse effect**. Earth is surrounded by an atmosphere that traps the heat of the Sun in order to warm the planet. This keeps Earth from being too cold for human life. Because people are using fossil fuels in greater quantities, the atmosphere is trapping carbon dioxide, the gas that is produced by burning fossil fuels. This trapped gas appears to be raising Earth's temperature.

Some researchers worry that without action to reduce greenhouse gases, sea levels could rise as polar ice caps melt. Other possible effects include drought and flooding. Some people believe that changes in Earth's temperature are due to natural forces, not to the use of fossil fuels.

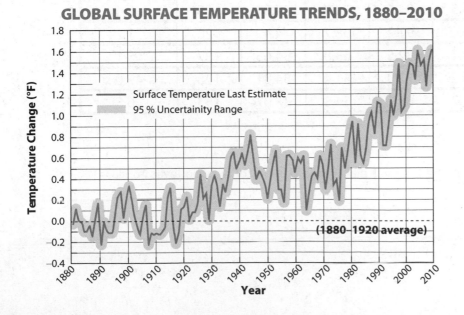

GLOBAL SURFACE TEMPERATURE TRENDS, 1880–2010

WRITE TO LEARN

A persuasive essay presents evidence to support an opinion. The purpose of the essay is to convince others to agree with you.

Use the graph on this page to write an essay supporting or opposing the development of renewable energy sources. State your opinion clearly. Provide evidence to support your point of view.

Reading Skill
Use Maps, Graphs, and Charts

Graphs have an x-axis (horizontal) and a y-axis (vertical). If data is being shown over time, the x-axis will usually show units of time. The y-axis will show a range of values. By following across the graph, you can see how a value changes over time.

Study the graph on this page. Then answer these questions in a notebook:

- What do the numbers along the x-axis represent?

- What do the numbers along the y-axis represent?

- What can I learn from the graph?

Vocabulary Review

Directions: Use these words to complete the following sentences.

ecosystem   global warming   greenhouse effect   natural resources   region

1. Earth's atmosphere traps the Sun's heat, creating a _____.

2. We must use nonrenewable _____ wisely to ensure that they are not used up.

3. The Western Hemisphere is a _____ on Earth.

4. Scientists have shown that the polar ice caps are melting, probably due to _____.

5. A coastal _____ might include beaches, sea gulls, and grasses.

Skill Review

Directions: Study the chart below. Then answer the questions in a notebook.

Climate of Select US Cities							
City	**Average monthly temperature (°F)**				**Rainfall**		**Snowfall**
	Jan.	**April**	**July**	**Oct.**	**Average annual**		Average annual (in.)
					(in.)	**(days)**	
Atlanta, GA	42.7	61.6	80.0	62.8	50.20	115	2.1
Boston, MA	29.3	48.3	73.9	54.1	42.53	127	42.8
Chicago, IL	22.0	47.8	73.3	52.1	36.27	125	38.0
Detroit, MI	24.5	48.1	73.5	51.9	32.89	135	41.3
Fairbanks, AK	−9.7	31.7	62.4	23.5	10.34	106	67.7
Houston, TX	51.8	68.5	83.6	70.4	47.84	105	0.4
Las Vegas, NV	47.0	66.0	91.2	68.7	4.49	26	1.2
Memphis, TN	39.9	62.1	82.5	63.8	54.65	107	5.1
Milwaukee, WI	20.7	45.2	72.0	51.4	34.81	125	47.0
Portland, OR	39.9	51.2	68.1	54.3	37.07	153	6.5

1. What climate information is given in the chart?

2. Which city shown in the chart would be the best place for a person to live who loves to ski?

Skill Review (continued)

Directions: Study the map. In a notebook, answer the following questions.

3. Which two continents produce the greatest amounts of carbon dioxide?

4. Which continent produces the smallest amount of carbon dioxide? What does this fact tell you about that continent?

ANNUAL CO₂ EMISSIONS, 2011
(expressed in metric tons per capita of carbon)

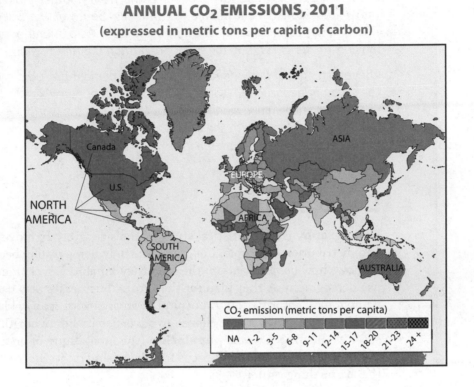

Skill Practice

Directions: Choose the one best answer to each question.

1. What is the climate like at a location far from the equator and high in elevation?
   A. mild and dry
   B. tropical and wet
   C. cold and snowy
   D. humid and warm

2. Which of these would be an ecosystem?
   A. the Florida Everglades
   B. the city of New York
   C. French-speaking Canada
   D. small towns in Maine

Writing Practice

Directions: What region of the United States do you live in? What sort of terrain does it have? What is its climate like? What natural resources are there? Write a paragraph describing your region. (You may need to do some research before writing your paragraph.)

Human Systems

Lesson Objectives

You will be able to

- Understand what is meant by the study of demography

- Recognize that population growth, migration, and settlement patterns tell a great deal about how humans interact with their environment

- Explain the general trend toward urban growth in the United States

Skills

- **Reading Skill:** Find Details

- **Core Skill:** Analyze Events and Ideas

Vocabulary

demography
describe
fertility rate
migration
mortality rate
population

KEY CONCEPT: As active inhabitants of Earth, humans are closely connected with the physical environment around them.

Do you live in a city, in a suburb, or in a rural area? Have you always lived there, or did you move to your home from another place? In the United States, most people live in cities. South of the Sahara, in Africa, most people live in rural areas. In East Asia, many people are moving to the cities, but the rural population is still growing.

These facts about human movement and settlement patterns are part of the study of geography. Your personal decision about where to live may not seem to have much significance to the rest of the world. When your decision is combined with the choices of millions of others, however, it takes on a much greater meaning.

Demography

Demography is the statistical study of the size, growth, movement, and distribution of people. Geographers study demography because it shows how people relate to the land they inhabit. Governments use demography as they plan for the future. Businesses also use demographic information. A hospital in an area with many elderly people, for example, might choose to advertise its home health services. In an area where **population** (the inhabitants of an area) is younger, a hospital might focus its advertising on its state-of-the-art birthing center.

Demographic data are gathered by many groups. The federal government conducts a nationwide census every ten years. State and local agencies also gather information on births, deaths, marriages, divorces, immigration, occupations, and family income. Demographers often use maps and graphs to analyze their findings.

Population Growth

The population of the world has grown dramatically. Since 1900, world population has grown from 1.6 billion to more than 7 billion in 2013. This rapid growth is called the **population explosion**.

Great increases in population growth are usually due to two reasons: reduction in **mortality rates** (death rates), particularly of women and infants, and high **fertility rates** (birthrates). The decline in infant mortality affects population growth in two ways. More people live to become adults, and more women reach childbearing age. However, family planning (birth control), famine, or war may slow or stop population growth. Disease can also affect population. For example, Native American populations were **decimated** (destroyed in large numbers) by smallpox, and an influenza epidemic in 1918–1919 resulted in 15 million deaths worldwide.

FIND DETAILS

Whether you are reading a novel, a magazine, a newspaper, or other written material, it is helpful to be able to recognize details. Details are the descriptive words and the facts that support the main idea. They often answer the questions *how*, *what*, *where*, *when*, *how much*, *how many*, and *why*.

To find details in a paragraph, pay attention to words and sentences that describe a person, place, or thing. Look for words that explain when or where something happened. If you have trouble identifying details, ask yourself *how*, *when*, and *why* questions.

Read the following passage. In a notebook, list the details that you find.

> In the 1300s, Europe was struck by bubonic plague, also known as the Black Death. It is thought to have begun in China or Egypt. Rats carried the disease aboard ships sailing to Mediterranean ports. From there, the plague spread quickly throughout Europe, killing about a third of the population. Scientists today are still trying to figure out where the plague began and what path it took through Europe. Because the bubonic plague still surfaces in modern times, they hope to use this information to predict the location of future outbreaks.

One way to find the details in this paragraph is to ask questions and look for the answers. The question *Where?* is answered by the details "China," "Egypt," "Mediterranean ports," and "Europe." The question *When?* is answered by "in the 1300s." *How?* is answered with details about rats, ships, and port cities. *How many?* is answered by "a third of the population." *Why is this important?* is answered by the details in the last sentence.

WRITE TO LEARN

When you **describe** something, you give details about a person, place, thing, or event. A descriptive paragraph uses rich details to help readers visualize what the writer is describing.

After reading about diseases that have altered the world population throughout history, write a descriptive diary entry about what it would have been like to have lived through one of these periods. Use as many details as possible so the event comes alive for the reader.

THINK ABOUT SOCIAL STUDIES

Directions: Match these words with their definitions.

_____ 1. demography

_____ 2. mortality rate

_____ 3. fertility rate

_____ 4. population explosion

A. rapid growth in population

B. study of population, movement, and distribution of people

C. number of children born each year in a population

D. rate of death in a population

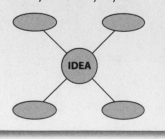

Western industrial countries no longer have a population explosion due to lower birthrates. Population has been growing more slowly in these countries. In countries with developing economies, improved living conditions have decreased mortality rates, but fertility rates have not decreased. This has created a population explosion in these countries. Therefore, even though the rate of population growth is slowing, by about 2040 there will probably be 9 billion people on Earth.

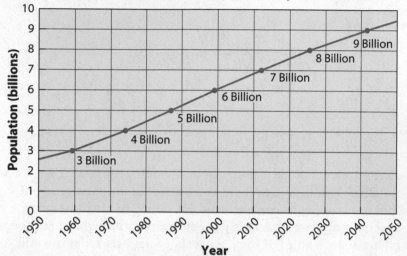

WORLD POPULATION GROWTH, 1950–2050

Source: U.S. Census Bureau, International Data Base, June 2011 Update.

Migration

Migration is the movement of people from one place to another. It has been happening since humans existed. Early people migrated to search for food or to leave harsh environmental conditions. Later people migrated to escape poor economic conditions or to find political or religious freedom.

Throughout history, most people have been free to migrate where and when they wanted. At times, however, people in certain areas have been forced to move. In the 1700s, for example, millions of Africans were forced to come to North America and South America as slaves.

Millions of people were **displaced**, or forced to move, by the changes in Europe after World War II. In recent years, political conflict has created huge numbers of refugees from countries such as Iraq, Afghanistan, Somalia, the Sudan, and Colombia. A **refugee** is a person who flees to a foreign country to escape danger. The United Nations estimates that there are more than 15 million refugees in the world today.

Whatever the cause, migration creates **cultural diffusion**, or the spread of cultural traits from one part of the world to another. The United States has absorbed people from around the world, and it has been enriched by the variety of customs these people have brought with them.

Urban Growth and Suburbs

As people migrate from place to place, demographers can often detect patterns in where people choose to live. These settlement patterns change over time. They can be greatly affected by historical events.

At one time, most people in the United States lived in rural areas. In the twentieth century, however, that changed. Cities became larger and more numerous as people came from the countryside to find better-paying jobs.

A city's location affects the city's growth and, sometimes, its decline. Access to rivers, large lakes, and oceans is very important because these waterways provide transportation routes. Access to transportation also means access to raw materials. The steel-making city of Pittsburgh, Pennsylvania, is located where the Allegheny and Monongahela rivers join to form the Ohio River, so it is on a major transportation route. It is near rich coalfields. Pittsburgh's location was ideal for the growth of manufacturing and industry.

In the 1800s, most people who worked in the city also lived in the city because it was difficult to travel long distances. Modern transportation methods—trains, trolleys, and the automobile—allowed people to work in one place and live in another. Interstate highways made it easier for people to travel from **outlying**, or surrounding, areas to the cities. With the highways came the trucking industry. Trucking allowed businesses to be located outside of cities. In the past businesses had located near railroad centers so their goods could be shipped.

> ## Research It
> Display Data
>
> The US Census Bureau conducts a census every 10 years. In the census, it collects demographic data for all areas of the country.
>
> Research your state, county, or city at the US Census Bureau website (www.census.gov). Decide which demographic information to research. For example, you might learn about ethnic groups or average family size.
>
> Then create a graph or chart displaying the data you have found. Title your graphic.

Vocabulary Review

Directions: Use these words to complete the following sentences.

demography   fertility rate   migration   mortality rates   population

1. If you wish to know the average number of children born to women in the United States, take a look at the _____.

2. The Industrial Revolution resulted in the _____ of many people from rural areas to cities.

3. When infant _____ are high, the population does not grow very quickly.

4. The _____ of an area is the people who live there.

5. The census conducted by the government every ten years is a valuable tool in the field of _____.

Directions: Read the passage below. Identify the details. Then answer the questions.

During the years following World War I, millions of African Americans moved from the South to northern cities. This mass migration continued as late as the 1960s. Over this period, 6 million African Americans relocated from the South to the North, leading historians and demographers to refer to it as "The Great Migration."

The Great Migration was caused by many factors. In the South, African Americans faced poverty and racial discrimination. At the same time, northern cities were experiencing a shortage of workers. New laws had caused a sharp drop in the number of immigrants arriving in the United States. Pushed by the unfavorable conditions in the South and pulled by the promise of better wages and living conditions in the North, African Americans swelled the populations of cities such as Chicago, Detroit, Cleveland, and New York.

Today demographers are noticing a new trend. Starting in the 1960s, African Americans began returning to the South in large numbers. Demographers call this reverse movement the "New Great Migration." Chicago, New York, and Los Angeles are losing African Americans to Atlanta, Charlotte, and Washington, DC. The new migration offers some evidence that the racial problems plaguing the South may be improving. Many African Americans talk about increased economic opportunities in the region. It appears that African American migration within the country has come full circle.

---

1. When did the mass migration of African Americans from the South to the North take place?

_____

2. How many African Americans relocated during this time?

_____

3. What name has been given to this demographic event in US history?

_____

4. What trend in African American migration began in the 1960s?

_____

Directions: Read the excerpt below. Then, in a notebook, write a paragraph in which you apply information from the article to analyze your experiences and everyday life.

For decades, city-dwellers have fled to the clean, quiet, and spacious American suburbs, where McMansions have popped up faster than you can say "Applebee's." But the suburbs are not proving to be recession-proof, as the latest census data shows—while cities are growing nationwide, suburban growth is slowing. It's good green news, considering that the average city dweller has a carbon footprint that is much smaller than a suburbanite's. . . .

There are abundant reasons why it's greener to live in the city: public transportation, walkable neighborhoods, smaller houses and lower levels of energy use, to name the big ones. . . .

Many of the people making the switch from suburbs to city this year are not motivated by environmental factors, of course—and many are not even moving out of choice. Forced to give up their homes due to foreclosure or job loss or sheer expense, these Americans are opting to move close to the city to cut their living costs and find work. The influx has its drawbacks too, though—public transit systems across the country are in peril, and . . . schools are struggling to accommodate their new students. Nevertheless, the shift could mean greener living for ex-suburbanites across the country, whether they realize it or not.

"Good News: Cities Are Growing, Suburbs Are Slowing," by Maura Judkis, *US News and World Report*, July 1, 2009

Skill Practice

Directions: Choose the one best answer to each question.

1. Which piece of data is an example of migration?

   A. the high percentage of Americans living in rural areas before 1900
   B. the population explosion in Latin America
   C. the high mortality rate in African countries
   D. the movement of people to the suburbs following World War II

2. Which describes the general migration trends in US history?

   A. North to South
   B. inland to coast
   C. rural to urban to suburban
   D. mountains to cities to farms

3. With medical advances, improved nutrition, and increased food production, which change is most likely to happen?

   A. Fertility rates will rise.
   B. Mortality rates will rise.
   C. Fertility rates will drop.
   D. Mortality rates will fall.

4. Which statement is an example of how demography is used?

   A. Soil erosion causes the coastline of California to shrink.
   B. A company's sales rise after a new marketing manager is hired.
   C. Town managers decide to build a new senior citizens' center to support population changes.
   D. The lives of people in rural Africa are improved when electricity is brought to their area.

Writing Practice

Directions: Did your family come to the United States from another country? Did they come to the region you live in from another part of the United States? In a notebook, write the story of your migration or the migration of a friend or family member. If you prefer, tell about the migration of someone famous. To do this, you may need to research that person's biography.

Nationhood and Statehood

KEY CONCEPT: Earth has been divided into nations by the forces of cooperation and conflict.

The world is a big place, but in some ways, it is getting smaller all the time. Today more people are traveling around the United States and around the world. Do you dream of traveling to another state? To another country? Most people daydream about visiting faraway places. Finding out about the places you will visit makes you a more knowledgeable traveler.

A World of Shapes, Colors, and Lines

Picture a globe. Or if there's a globe nearby, take a close look at it. What do you see? Most globes show an arrangement of shapes, colors, and lines. The shapes are countries. Colors are often used to make it easy to distinguish the countries. The lines show the outlines of countries.

Now imagine you are orbiting Earth in a spaceship. When you look down, what do you see? Not the shapes, colors, and lines of the globe. Instead, you see land undivided by borders. The real Earth looks much different than the globes that serve as models of our planet.

The difference is that globes show Earth as it has been divided by people. Every bit of land on the planet is claimed by one or more nations. Some areas are independent countries, such as the United States. However, other areas are not independent. These countries, colonies, and dependencies are controlled by other nations.

The division of Earth's surface is an important characteristic of the world we live in. Crossing a border from one country to another can be a simple action or a complex operation. The ease of traveling between countries depends on the relationship that the two countries have with each other.

In some ways, the history of the world is largely the history of shifting borders. If you look at a map made ten, twenty, or fifty years ago, some borders will be different. If you look at a very old map, you may not recognize any of the borders. Borders between countries are constantly in a state of change.

Boundaries and Borders

Boundaries are lines that separate Earth into regions. **Physical boundaries** are natural features that separate two areas. Rivers and mountain ranges are examples of physical boundaries. They are nature's way of dividing Earth's surface. **Political boundaries** are lines that separate countries and states. These boundaries are the way humans have divided the planet. Political boundaries are frequently called **borders**.

Political boundaries often **coincide** with, or follow, geographic features. Consider international borders, or borders between two nations. Many international borders follow geographic features such as rivers and mountain ranges. The border between the United States and Mexico, for example, runs along the Rio Grande. Part of the border between the United States and Canada passes through the Great Lakes. In Europe, the border between France and Spain is marked by the towering Pyrenees Mountains.

A coastline is another natural feature that forms physical boundaries. The Atlantic coastline forms the eastern border of the United States. The Pacific coastline forms the western border. The borders of many island countries are entirely coastlines. Australia's entire border, for example, is coastline.

Like international borders, many state borders are formed by natural features. Much of the border between Texas and Oklahoma runs along the Red River. The mighty Mississippi River forms part of the borders of ten states, including Arkansas, Illinois, Louisiana, and Mississippi. States along an ocean have coastlines as borders. The Appalachian Mountains in the east and the Rocky Mountains in the west form the borders of many states.

For thousands of years, these geographic features have served as natural obstacles between two areas or two groups of people. It is no wonder, then, that when humans want to divide their world, they often use natural features as division lines.

Reading Skill
Analyze Author's Purpose

When you read, you are reading for a purpose. Sometimes your purpose is to learn; sometimes it is to enjoy yourself.

Authors have a purpose for writing. An author's purpose may be to explain, to persuade, or to entertain. Knowing the author's purpose helps you get the most out of your reading.

Usually you can sum up the author's purpose in one sentence: "The author's purpose in writing this was to . . ."

To determine an author's purpose for writing, analyze the text by asking yourself these questions:

1. What am I reading? A textbook? A blog?

2. Where does the writing appear? In an encyclopedia? A sports magazine?

3. What is the title?

4. What is the main idea?

Use these questions to determine the author's purpose for writing a text you have recently read. In a notebook, name the text and state the author's purpose.

When you conduct a research project, you investigate a topic, learn information that answers your questions, and then present what you have learned.

Conduct a research project by following these steps:

1. *Choose a topic.* For this research project, your topic is the borders of your home state. Why are the borders where they are?

2. *Search for sources.* Use the Internet and library tools (and a librarian's help) to locate appropriate sources. The most reliable web sources are those that end in .gov, .edu, and .org.

3. *Get information.* Identify the sources that have the most relevant information for your project. Read these sources and take notes.

4. *Produce your project.* In a notebook, draw an outline map of your home state. Write notes along each border to tell why that border is where it is.

Geometric Borders

Long ago there were physical boundaries but no political borders. Over time, with the growth of governments and organized nations, people created borders. These borders often followed physical boundaries like rivers and mountains. Even today most international borders follow natural features.

When borders do not follow natural features, they often conform to lines of latitude or longitude. Latitude and longitude are imaginary lines used to locate places on Earth. Latitude lines run horizontally. They are known as "parallels" because they are parallel to the equator. Latitude, which is measured in degrees, tells how far north or south of the equator a place is located. The farther a place is from the equator, the larger its latitude will be. Longitude lines run from the North Pole to the South Pole. They are called "meridians." They measure how far east or west a place is from the Prime Meridian, a line that runs through Greenwich, England.

The border between the United States and Canada stretches more than 5,000 miles. It is the world's longest international border. The Great Lakes and the St. Lawrence River form part of the border. The border's longest stretch is a 2,000-mile straight line that follows the 49th parallel north.

Sometimes these straight-line borders are called **geometric borders**. A map of Africa reveals that about one-third of the continent's borders are straight lines. The reason is that nearly all of Africa was once controlled by European powers. When the Europeans divided up Africa, they drew borders that were convenient.

During the Berlin Conference of 1884–1885, the six European nations that controlled Africa divided the continent among themselves. They drew border lines on a map of Africa. Some lines followed physical boundaries, such as Lake Nyassa, which divides Malawi from Tanzania and Mozambique. Where the physical boundaries of a region were unknown, straight lines were drawn. No Africans attended the Berlin Conference. The colonizing Europeans divided Africa according to their own desires.

THINK ABOUT SOCIAL STUDIES

Directions: Write a definition of each term. Then look at a map of Central America and give one example of each term.

1. international border

   _____

2. physical boundary

   _____

3. geometric border

   _____

There are geometric borders within the United States, as well. Colorado and Wyoming are neat rectangles. Many other states—such as Pennsylvania, Oregon, and Iowa—have at least one straight-line border.

To study geometric borders and physical boundaries, look at a map of the United States. **Compare** and contrast the borders of Colorado and Arkansas. To compare the borders, determine how the northern, southern, and western borders of Arkansas are like the borders of Colorado. To contrast the borders, analyze how Arkansas's eastern border is different from Colorado's borders. What natural feature forms Arkansas's eastern border?

WRITE TO LEARN

Use the Internet to locate two maps of Europe:

before World War I
after World War I

Find information online describing the political changes that came about at the end of World War I.

In a notebook, write one paragraph explaining how conflict and cooperation played a role in changing Europe's political boundaries after World War I.

Why Borders Are Where They Are: Cooperation and Conflict

Have you wondered exactly why state and national borders are where they are? Borders are not part of nature. Even if they run along natural features, borders are human creations. The answer to the question "Why do borders exist?" is that people put them there. The question then becomes "Why did people put the borders where they are?" The answer is the "two Cs" of human history: cooperation and conflict.

Cooperation means "working together." Representatives from various countries often discuss, or negotiate, the location of borders. For example, participants in the 1884 Berlin Conference negotiated the location of borders for countries in Africa. Likewise, the border between the United States and Canada was a result of cooperation. The Jay Treaty of 1794 and the Treaty of 1818, signed by the United States and Britain, established that border. A **treaty** is a formal agreement between countries. Within the United States, the borders between most states were established through cooperation and agreement.

The opposite of cooperation is **conflict**, or fighting. Many of today's political borders have been established by war. For example, the border between the United States and Mexico is along the Rio Grande because of the American defeat of Mexico in the Mexican-American War (1846–1848). Most of the borders of Europe were redrawn after World War I and again after World War II. Even the end of the Cold War changed the map of Europe. Germany, which had been divided at the end of World War II, was reunited. In the early part of the 21st century, Yugoslavia was divided into several independent countries, including Bosnia, Croatia, and Slovenia.

As the twin forces of cooperation and conflict play out and history marches on, borders continue to change.

Vocabulary Review

Directions: Match each word with its definition.

1. _____ boundaries
2. _____ conflict
3. _____ cooperation
4. _____ geometric borders
5. _____ physical boundaries
6. _____ political boundaries
7. _____ treaty

A. working together

B. lines that separate countries or states

C. formal agreement between nations

D. fighting

E. borders

F. straight-line borders

G. natural features that separate areas

Skill Review

Directions: Follow the steps below.

Choose a topic. For this research project, your topic is identifying what forms the borders of a state you have visited or a state you would like to visit.

1. *Search for sources.* Name the state you have chosen and list the sources you found.

_____

_____

_____

_____

2. *Get information.* Identify the source you found most useful. Take notes about what you found.

_____

_____

_____

3. *Produce your project.* Write a brief paragraph describing the borders of the state that you chose.

_____

_____

_____

_____

_____

Skill Practice

Directions: Choose the <u>one best answer</u> to each question.

1. Which term describes all borders?

   A. international borders
   B. boundaries
   C. physical boundaries
   D. rivers

2. Which natural feature would be <u>least</u> likely to form an international border?

   A. a river
   B. a range of mountains
   C. a large lake
   D. a large boulder

3. Which is an example of conflict that changed international borders?

   A. World War II
   B. Jay Treaty
   C. Treaty of 1818
   D. Berlin Conference

4. Which statement about borders is most accurate?

   A. Borders rarely follow physical boundaries.
   B. All borders are straight lines.
   C. Borders tend to change over time.
   D. Most borders are created through cooperation.

Writing Practice

Directions: Choose two countries that share an international border. Go online and research how this border was determined. Then write one paragraph explaining how your example shows conflict or cooperation between people who influence the division of Earth's surface.

Sustainability

KEY CONCEPT: Earth's population growth and economic development are putting strains on the environment. These environmental problems have led many people to call for a change in policies in the use of land and resources.

Our world is changing. Population growth and changing economies mean that the world may be quite different in just a few years. As the world changes, humans must make changes too. Think about the natural resources, such as water, that you use on a daily basis. Then think about how your life would change if these resources were in short supply or were actually no longer available.

Population Growth and Economic Development

Earth currently supports a population of more than 7 billion people. That is more than *twice* the population of just 50 years ago! This population explosion is one of the most important issues of your lifetime. Why? Because all these people need the basics of life—healthful food, clean water, and safe places to live. Earth's resources are limited. Providing everyone with basic needs will prove difficult.

Moreover, most of the world's population growth is in developing countries. **Developing countries** are countries with relatively low standards of living and little industrial activity. Most of the countries in South America, Asia, and Africa are developing countries. Richer industrialized nations, like the United States and Western European countries, are considered **developed countries**.

Not only is the population growing in developing countries, but their economies are also growing. As these countries develop economically, more people are able to afford what people in developed countries already enjoy. The people of developing countries want modern homes and cars. They want nice clothes and a wide variety of goods.

The increased population and economic development have placed a huge stress on the planet. A growing demand for goods means more manufacturing. This **depletes**, or uses up, natural resources like timber and minerals. Increasing numbers of vehicles consume vast amounts of fuel and pollute the air. Growing populations strain food and water resources. Expanding cities need power plants, which often burn fossil fuels like coal. For the first time in history, people are asking a troubling question: are we using so much of Earth's resources that we are putting the future of humanity at risk?

The answer is *yes*—unless some changes are made.

Resource Depletion and Global Warming

For thousands of years, nobody worried about Earth's **carrying capacity**: the number of people that the planet can support. There seemed to be no end to the planet's forests, minerals, farmland, clean water, and other natural resources. Today population growth and increased economic activity have strained Earth in ways that were unimaginable just a few generations ago. Resource depletion is a serious concern.

Both wind and solar power are **renewable** resources, meaning there will always be a supply of these resources. But many natural resources are **nonrenewable**, meaning we cannot make more of them. The nonrenewable resources we use up today will not be available for future generations. People all around the world must learn to rely more on renewable resources.

Human activity is impacting the climate by increasing the greenhouse gases in the atmosphere. Greenhouse gases, including carbon dioxide, are a natural part of the atmosphere. They are called greenhouse gases because, somewhat like the glass windows in a greenhouse, they let in light and heat from the Sun. These gases prevent some of the heat from escaping back into space. This is called the **greenhouse effect**. Without the greenhouse effect, Earth would be extremely cold, with temperatures far below freezing.

The greenhouse effect has become a concern because population growth and economic development have led to a huge increase in the burning of oil, natural gas, and coal. These fossil fuels are used mostly to fuel vehicles, run factories, and produce electricity. As these fuels burn, they release carbon dioxide into the air, trapping more heat within the atmosphere and increasing Earth's surface temperature. A larger, wealthier world population is driving more vehicles, producing more goods in more factories, using more power, and burning more fossil fuels. The greenhouse effect is growing.

THINK ABOUT SOCIAL STUDIES

Directions: Go online to research population growth for the last 50 years in the United States and two other countries. Then answer these questions in a notebook.

1. Name the three countries you have researched and give their population (in millions) in 1950 and in 2000.

2. Which of these countries has grown the fastest in the last 50 years?

3. Using the data you have gathered, what do you predict the populations of these countries will be 50 years from now?

Recycling is one means of achieving sustainability. Individuals, businesses, and communities all have roles in recycling.

Choose a material: paper, metal, glass, or plastic. Then go online to gather information about the recycling of this material. Websites that should have the most reliable information will have addresses that end in *.gov*, *.edu*, or *.org*. One place to get started is the United States Environmental Protection Agency:

http://www.epa.gov/osw/conserve/materials/index.htm

Gather facts about the quantity of material recycled (how many tons per year). Find the percentage of recycled material used in the manufacturing of new products, if this information is available. In other words, what percentage of recycled paper goes into your daily newspaper?

In a notebook, evaluate your evidence and draw a conclusion about the effectiveness of recycling as a means to achieving sustainability.

The result is global warming, which leads to **climate change**, or a long-term alteration in weather patterns. Changing rainfall patterns lead to both floods and droughts, which negatively affect food crops. The result could be food shortages and even famines. Climate change can also lead to increased weather events like hurricanes. Warmer temperatures melt the polar ice caps, raising sea levels and flooding coastal areas. Even human health is at risk: in a warmer world, tropical diseases may become more widespread.

Sustainability

The challenges of resource depletion and global warming can best be met by a solution called sustainability, or sustainable development.

Sustainability means living within our limits when it comes to the use of Earth's resources. Sustainable activities do not deplete resources or cause long-term environmental damage. Achieving sustainability would mean that humans could maintain a healthful quality of life without exhausting the planet's resources. This would preserve resources so that future generations can meet their needs.

Sustainability is the goal of **sustainable development**. Sustainable development requires a balance between the needs of the environment and the needs of human societies. It requires people in the developed world to understand the needs of the growing populations in the developing world.

Sustainable development methods include conserving energy, recycling, and minimizing the use of fossil fuels. Often people call such practices "eco-friendly" or "green" practices. Some green practices you can adopt include taking a bus or riding a bike instead of driving and using a fan instead of turning on the air conditioning.

Going green is the best response to the problems caused by a growing population and economic development.

Vocabulary Review

Directions: Match these terms with their definitions.

1. _____ carrying capacity

2. _____ climate change

3. _____ deplete

4. _____ developed countries

5. _____ developing countries

6. _____ greenhouse effect

7. _____ sustainability

A. trapping of gases inside the atmosphere

B. living within one's means

C. nations with little industrial activity and low standard of living

D. number of people that an environment can support

E. nations with significant industrial activity and high standard of living

F. use up

G. long-term alteration in weather patterns

Directions: Number the items to show their correct order.

_____ global warming

_____ greater demand for goods

_____ increased use of fossil fuels

_____ population growth and economic development

Skill Practice

Directions: Answer the following questions. Choose the <u>one best answer</u> to <u>questions 1 through 3</u>.

1. Which continent has the largest number of developing countries?

    A. Europe
    B. North America
    C. Asia
    D. Australia

3. Which countries does climate change affect?

    A. industrial countries
    B. developing countries
    C. coastal countries
    D. all countries

2. Global warming is a *direct* result of what?

    A. climate change
    B. rising sea levels
    C. hurricanes and other violent storms
    D. increased greenhouse gases

4. Why does the burning of fossil fuels increase the greenhouse effect?

    _____

    _____

    _____

    _____

Writing Practice

Directions: Interview a business owner or an employee about green practices in a business in your community. Ask, "What eco-friendly methods does your business use?" Write one paragraph about what you learn.

Natural and Cultural Diversity

Lesson Objectives

You will be able to

- Discuss the diversity of physical geography

- Discuss the diversity of human geography

- Explain how landforms affect human settlement

Skills

- **Core Skill:** Evaluate Evidence

- **Reading Skill:** Infer

Vocabulary

climate
cultural trait
culture
diversity
landforms
multicultural
place
population density

KEY CONCEPT: Diversity is a fundamental feature of Earth and its people. Appreciating diversity is a basic part of being a world citizen.

One thing you can say about life on Earth is that there's always something going on! Billions of people around the world are engaged in all kinds of activities. Not only are people doing many different things, but they are also doing them in a wide variety of places. Someone, somewhere, is driving a tractor across open farmland. Someone else is cleaning skyscraper windows in a large desert city. Others are sunbathing on a beach. Where are you and what are you doing? Understanding the variety of our world helps you appreciate our differences.

"Earth Description"

Geography is the study of Earth. The word *geography* comes from the old Greek word *geographia*, which means "Earth description." However, geography is more than just a description of mountains, rivers, oceans, and land masses. It is also concerned with how people relate to these features. In other words, geography is the study of how people interact with the physical features of Earth.

Geographers who focus on the world's people study *human geography*. Geographers who focus on our planet study *physical geography*. In this lesson, you will read about diversity in human geography and diversity in physical geography—and then see how these two ideas intersect.

Diversity means "variety" or "differences." In physical geography, diversity is found in the different types of **landforms** on Earth. Landforms are the natural features of Earth's surface—the islands and continents, the lakes and rivers, the hills and mountains. In human geography, diversity is found in the different ways people around the world live.

The fascinating intersection of these two diversities is found everywhere people live. In geography, *place* is not simply an address. **Place** describes the physical and human characteristics of a location. Earth's many different landforms and the numerous ways people live make our world complex and fascinating.

Diversity of Places: Physical

Earth is a magnificent place. Seen from space, it is a beautiful "blue marble" floating in a sea of stars. Earth appears so blue because of its vast oceans. Seventy percent of Earth's surface is covered by water, leaving just thirty percent of our planet available for human settlement.

Geographers categorize Earth's land areas in different ways. The most natural division is by **continents**, or major land masses. The seven continents are Asia, Africa, North America, South America, Antarctica, Europe, and Australia. There are five oceans—the Pacific, Atlantic, Indian, Southern, and Arctic. Some geographers add an eighth continent, Oceania, to account for the land of the nearly 30,000 islands that dot the vast Pacific Ocean. (If you could visit one island a day, every day of the year, it would take 82 years to tour all the islands in the Pacific.)

Another way geographers categorize the land is by the type of climate a region has. **Climate** is the weather over a long period of time. The climate of a region is determined by its latitude (distance from the Equator), local landforms, nearness to the ocean, and air currents in the atmosphere. There are at least twelve types of climates on Earth, ranging from tropical wet (high temperatures and a lot of rain) to polar (bitterly cold and snowy). In addition, each type of climate has several subtypes.

Vastly differing vegetation, or types of plant life, grows in different climates. Vegetation provides geographers with yet another way to categorize land. Rain forests cover some areas, while dense pine forests or vast fields of grass flourish in other regions.

Many people categorize land by landforms. There are hundreds of types of landforms. Plains, islands, deserts, canyons, and plateaus are a few familiar examples.

Every place on Earth has physical characteristics. Because land, climate, vegetation, and landforms can all differ so dramatically, Earth easily meets the description of being diverse.

Core Skill
Evaluate Evidence

The ability to evaluate evidence is a vital skill. Today we are bombarded with advertisements, websites, sales pitches, and political campaigns, all asking us to believe what they say.

Evidence is factual support that proves a claim or an opinion. When an ad tries to convince you to buy a particular product, the ad should provide evidence to help you evaluate the claim.

Read the travel ad below. Then write down the main claim that the ad is making. Explain whether you think the evidence for this claim is believable.

Skiing   Theme Parks
Ocean Beaches

Love all three?
Then spend Winter Break at **Big Bear Lake**!

Located in southern California, Big Bear Lake is home to several of the region's premier ski resorts and just a two-hour drive from Disneyland and the beaches of the Pacific Coast.

Spend the morning skiing or snowboarding in the crystal air of Big Bear Mountain. Then enjoy the afternoon riding Space Mountain in Anaheim or strolling the warm Pacific sands in Huntington Beach.

For information on lodging and recreation, visit http://www.bigbearinfo .com/index.php

Diversity of Places: Human

Someone once said that if everyone were the same, the world would be a pretty boring place. But people are not all the same. Earth is home to thousands of different cultures.

Culture is the way of life of a society, or a human group. A society's culture includes the people's beliefs, values, language, art, customs, and behaviors. Family relationships and economic systems are also part of a group's culture.

Each aspect of a culture is called a **cultural trait**. These traits form **cultural patterns**. Traits and patterns are passed down through the generations—that is to say, culture is learned.

An important part of any culture is the language that people speak. People in a culture must speak the same language to communicate. Today about 6,000 languages are spoken in the world. Mandarin Chinese is spoken by the greatest number of people, followed by Spanish, English, Arabic, and Hindi.

Cultures are often associated with countries. For example, there is Japanese culture in Japan, where people speak Japanese, and there is French culture in France, where people speak French. Often, however, numerous cultures exist within a country. In Nigeria, more than 500 languages are spoken. This means there are many cultures within Nigeria.

Similarly, the United States is home to people of many cultures. A country with many cultures is said to be **multicultural**.

Like physical features, human features—particularly the culture of the people—help define a place. And, like physical features, the cultures of the world can certainly be described as diverse.

THINK ABOUT SOCIAL STUDIES

Directions: Go online to find answers to the following questions.

More than 300 languages are spoken in the United States. Spanish is the most commonly spoken non-English language. There are more than 34 million Spanish language speakers in the United States.

1. Which non-English languages are spoken by residents of your state? List the languages and the percentage of the population that speaks each language.

    _____

    _____

2. List at least four terms that are commonly used in English that have their roots in Spanish, French, German, or another language of your choice.

    _____

    _____

Physical and Human Diversity: Where People Settle Down

People have always lived in groups. Groups develop their own culture, or way of life. These cultures are extremely diverse.

Yet all people have the same basic needs, and every culture meets those needs. They just do so in different ways. All people need food, but Mexican food is different from Chinese food. Likewise, all people need housing. But houses around the world vary widely. Nomads construct tents because they move frequently. People living near bodies of water may build their homes on stilts to avoid flooding. City residents live in large apartment buildings because space is limited.

Population density, or the average number of people in a square mile, varies from location to location. The year 2008 was the first time in history that more people in the world lived in urban areas than rural areas. For most of history, the greatest number of people lived in villages near the fields where they farmed. With the shift to urban living, population densities have increased.

Earth's physical diversity has a lot to do with where groups of people settle. Few people settle near the North Pole or the South Pole—the climate is too cold. Few people settle in rain forests—the vegetation is too thick. Few people settle in the middle of Earth's harshest deserts—there are too few resources to support life.

Over thousands of years, many peoples have chosen to settle in river valleys. The earliest civilizations arose in river valleys, such as the valley between the Tigris and the Euphrates rivers—land that is now Iraq and Syria. River valleys provide a reliable source of water for drinking, washing, cooking, and irrigating crops. Rivers are also good transportation routes, and they provide a source of food (fish). The land along rivers is often very fertile, so crops tend to grow well there.

Other sites popular for settlements include the highest navigable point of a river—that is, the farthest place up the river that boats can travel. Geographers have noted that settlements tend to form along coastlines, especially on peninsulas and in natural harbors. Hilltops are another popular site for settlements, because the elevation makes the area easier to defend against invaders.

Wherever people have settled, the physical characteristics of a place have helped shape the culture. Local materials are used to build homes, which affects the cultural pattern of dwellings. Coastal people typically eat fish and use boats for work and recreation. Thus, diversity in the physical world is one reason for diversity in culture.

Research It
Find the Facts

Most states are broken into smaller areas called counties. Population density within your state varies from county to county.

Go online to research the population density of the county you live in or a county you know about. Also find the population density for another county you have visited. Compare the figures.

In a notebook, write one paragraph comparing the population densities of the two counties. Explain why you believe one county has a higher population density that the other.

WRITE TO LEARN

Why is your community located where it is? What landforms may have influenced settlers to move to your location?

Use the Internet to research information about your community's earliest population groups. What groups have come to your community more recently? How culturally diverse is your community? Can it be described as multicultural?

In a notebook, write two paragraphs describing the natural diversity and human diversity of your community.

Vocabulary Review

Directions: Match each word with its definition.

1. _____ climate
2. _____ cultural trait
3. _____ culture
4. _____ diversity
5. _____ landforms
6. _____ place
7. _____ population density

A. physical and human aspects of a location

B. way of life

C. variety

D. natural geographic features

E. average number of people per square mile

F. characteristic of a group of people

G. weather over a long period of time

Skill Review

Directions: Read the article. Then answer the questions.

Waterfalls determine where many cities in the eastern United States are located. The Fall Line is what geographers call the border between the flatland along the Atlantic coastline and higher ground found farther inland. Rivers flow from higher land to the sea. Waterfalls form where the river waters drop from the higher ground to the lowlands.

Many settlements grew near these waterfalls. Why? For one thing, the falls marked the highest navigable point of the river. For another, the rapidly moving water provided power for early mills and factories. Examples of eastern cities that are located near waterfalls include Philadelphia, Pennsylvania; Baltimore, Maryland; and Trenton, New Jersey.

1. What claim does the writer make?

_____

_____

2. What evidence does the writer provide?

_____

_____

_____

3. Evaluate this evidence.

_____

_____

_____

Skill Practice

Directions: Choose the <u>one best answer</u> to each question.

1. Which is the best synonym for *diversity*?
    - **A.** languages
    - **B.** assortment
    - **C.** landforms
    - **D.** cultural pattern

2. A geographer describes a region as "humid subtropical." Which characteristic is she using to define the region?
    - **A.** culture
    - **B.** climate
    - **C.** population
    - **D.** landforms

3. Which is not included in a group's culture?
    - **A.** type of food
    - **B.** traditional music
    - **C.** relationships with in-laws
    - **D.** geographic diversity

4. Which location would settlers be <u>least</u> likely to choose for their new home?
    - **A.** a swamp
    - **B.** where two rivers meet
    - **C.** a coast
    - **D.** a peninsula

Writing Practice

Directions: Is there a diversity of cultures in your community? Write a paragraph about the diversity or lack of diversity in your city or town.

Review

Directions: Choose the one best answer to each question.

Questions 1–3 refer to the following graph.

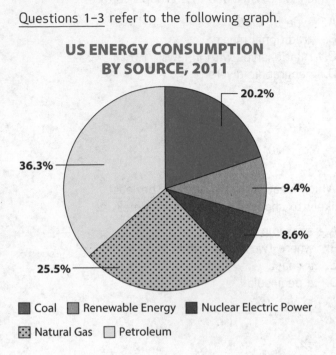

US ENERGY CONSUMPTION BY SOURCE, 2011

20.2%

9.4%

36.3%

8.6%

25.5%

- ■ Coal ■ Renewable Energy ■ Nuclear Electric Power
- ▒ Natural Gas □ Petroleum

3. Coal, natural gas, oil, and nuclear power are considered nonrenewable resources. Which statement correctly compares the percentage of nonrenewable resources used to the percentage of renewable resources used?

   A. The percentage of renewable resources used was twice the percentage of nonrenewable resources used.

   B. The percentage of nonrenewable resources used was twice the percentage of renewable resources used.

   C. Nonrenewable resources made up about 91 percent of the resources used, while renewable resources made up about 9 percent.

   D. Most of the energy used was from renewable resources.

1. Which option best summarizes the information shown in the graph?

   A. the different sources of energy used in the world in 2011

   B. the different sources of energy used in the United States in 2011

   C. the number of barrels of oil used in the United States in 2011

   D. the dependence of the United States on energy imports

4. Why would being located on a river be an advantage to a city?

   A. A river can be used to transport goods and materials to and from the city.

   B. The climate will be better suited to agriculture.

   C. People will not have to travel as far to their jobs.

   D. A river is an important source of energy for the city.

2. Which was the most used source of energy in 2011?

   A. coal
   B. natural gas
   C. nuclear power
   D. petroleum

Review

Questions 5 and 6 refer to the following graph.

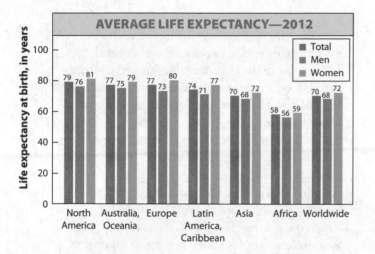

AVERAGE LIFE EXPECTANCY—2012

Legend: Total, Men, Women

North America: 79, 76, 81
Australia, Oceania: 77, 75, 79
Europe: 77, 73, 80
Latin America, Caribbean: 74, 71, 77
Asia: 70, 68, 72
Africa: 58, 56, 59
Worldwide: 70, 68, 72

5. Which geographical areas have the longest life expectancy?

   A. Asia, North America, Latin American and the Caribbean
   B. Europe, Australia/Oceania, and North America
   C. Europe, Asia, and Africa
   D. Europe, North America, and Asia

6. Which statement is best supported by the graph?

   A. All the people in the regions shown have a shorter life expectancy than people in the United States.
   B. The average person in Asia lives about five years longer than the average person in Africa.
   C. The region with a life expectancy most similar to North America's is Europe.
   D. People lived longer in 2012 than in 1912.

7. Which human activity has had the greatest impact on Earth's geography?

   A. clearing land for farms and cities
   B. sailing around the world to explore
   C. mining for metals and minerals
   D. building bridges and roads

8. Which of the following is the best example of a sustainable activity?

   A. buying a second car
   B. commuting by train
   C. burning fallen leaves
   D. heating with natural gas

9. What is the largest contributor to global warming?

   A. burning of fossil fuels
   B. depletion of resources
   C. overuse of solar power
   D. carbon dioxide occurring naturally in the atmosphere

10. How do borders between nations come to exist?

   A. They develop naturally over time.
   B. They are based on geographical features.
   C. They reflect cultural boundaries between groups of people.
   D. They result from negotiation or conflict between groups of people.

Questions 11–13 refer to the map below.

Question 14 refers to the following passage.

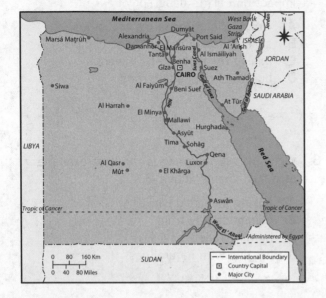

11. Which type of map is this?

    A. climate map
    B. physical map
    C. political map
    D. population map

12. Which of the following best explains why Egypt's borders are mostly straight lines?

    A. These are the historical borders of ancient Egypt.
    B. The borders follow geographic features, like rivers and mountain ranges.
    C. The Egyptians, Libyans, and Sudanese used latitude and longitude lines as borders.
    D. Europeans, who once controlled most of Africa, created geometric borders between their colonies.

13. Which best explains why most of Egypt's major cities are located along the Nile River?

    A. Throughout history, people have always chosen to live in big cities.
    B. People settled near water for drinking, washing, fishing, and irrigation.
    C. The river made it easier to defend settlements and farms against invaders.
    D. The people who lived along the river destroyed the settlements of other groups.

The official language of Egypt is Arabic, and most Egyptians speak one of several vernacular dialects of that language. . . . There are also other minor linguistic groups. The Beja of the southern section of the Eastern Desert use an Afro-Asiatic language. . . . At Siwa Oasis in the Western Desert there are groups whose language is related (but not too closely) to the Berber languages of the Afro-Asiatic family. Nubians speak Eastern Sudanic languages. . . . There are other minority linguistic groups, notably Greek, Italian, and Armenian, although they are much smaller than they once were.

At the time of the Islamic conquest, the Coptic language, a latter incarnation of the ancient Egyptian language, was the medium of both religious and everyday life for the mass of the population. By the 12th century, however, Arabic had come into common use even among Christian Copts, whose former tongue continued only as a liturgical language for the Coptic Orthodox Church.

14. According to the passage, which of these statements is true?

    A. Today Egypt's culture is mostly Arab.
    B. Today Egypt is a land of large diverse cultural groups.
    C. Egyptian culture has always been multicultural.
    D. Egyptian culture has always been predominantly Arab.

Review

Check Your Understanding

On the following chart, circle the number of any question you answered incorrectly. In the third column, you will see the pages you can review to study the content covered in the question. Pay particular attention to reviewing those lessons in which you missed half or more of the questions.

Chapter 8 Review

Lesson	Item Number	Review Pages
Physical and Cultural Landscapes	4, 7	286–291
Physical Systems	1, 2, 3	292–297
Human Systems	5, 6	298–303
Nationhood and Statehood	10, 11, 12	304–309
Sustainability	8, 9	310–313
Natural and Cultural Diversity	13, 14	314–319

ESSAY WRITING PRACTICE

Geography and People

Directions: Write an essay in response to one of the prompts below. Before planning your essay, review Lessons 8.3, 8.4, 8.5, and 8.6 to recall information about sustainability, human systems, and natural and cultural diversity.

PERSUASIVE ESSAY

Sustainability is based on the idea that people need to protect and preserve Earth for future generations. Yet many people are opposed to using sustainable practices in their homes, schools, and places of business. They may object to the costs or the inconvenience, or they may not believe their small steps can make a difference.

Write a persuasive essay to convince people that their efforts can help protect Earth. The audience for your essay should be an individual or an organization (such as a private business) that does not currently follow eco-friendly practices.

Write a five-paragraph essay. In your essay,

- Define *sustainability*. Explain the benefits of sustainability.

- Give examples of green practices.

- Anticipate objections to *going green* and respond to those objections.

INFORMATIONAL ESSAY

As you continue your education, you will study a variety of topics. For example, in this book you have learned about geography, economics, and history. These separate topics are closely related.

For example, think about the town or city where you live. Geography helped determine where it is located. Nearby natural resources helped determine what industries the economy would be built on. These events took place over time, through history.

Write a five-paragraph essay to inform your reader about the geography, economics, and history of the place where you live. You may choose to write about your whole community or just a part of it, such as a business or neighborhood. Explain how the geography, economics, and history of your community are interrelated.

Review

ESSAY WRITING PRACTICE

_____
_____
_____
_____
_____
_____
_____
_____
_____
_____
_____
_____
_____
_____
_____
_____
_____
_____
_____
_____
_____
_____
_____
_____
_____

Social Studies

This Posttest will help you evaluate whether you are ready to move up to the next level of test preparation. The Posttest consists of 50 multiple-choice questions that test your understanding of social studies concepts and your ability to read passages, maps, tables and charts, cartoons, and photographs.

Directions: Read each question carefully. Then choose the one best answer to the question.

When you have completed the Posttest, check your work with the answers and explanations on pages 343 and 344. Use the Evaluation Chart on page 345 to determine which areas you need to review.

Social Studies

1. Geographers often look at the places they study in terms of regions. A region does not have distinct boundaries or an exact population. It is simply an area with certain characteristics.

   Suppose a geographer studies precipitation patterns in the Pacific Northwest. Which of the following characteristics would best define this region?

   A. a coast-to-mountain change in altitude
   B. a high annual rate of rainfall
   C. the state boundaries of Washington and Oregon
   D. the greatest amount of cultivated farmland

Directions: Questions 3 and 4 refer to the following passage.

In 1984, Gregory Lee Johnson was protesting outside the Republican National Convention in Dallas, Texas. At one point, he burned an American flag as part of his protest. He was arrested and prosecuted for his actions, which violated a Texas law against flag desecration [disrespect]. Johnson was found guilty. He was sentenced to a year in jail and fined $2,000. He appealed, and the Supreme Court heard the case.

In a 5–4 decision, the Court ruled that Johnson's flag-burning was protected speech. The Court stated, "The Government may not prohibit the verbal or nonverbal expression of an idea merely because society finds the idea offensive or disagreeable, even where our flag is involved."

2. For several years, Ani has run a small computer repair business on the outskirts of her town. Last year a new factory opened nearby. Since then her profits have risen dramatically.

   What might explain this change?

   A. monopoly
   B. competition
   C. interdependence
   D. productivity

3. Which amendment protects Johnson's flag-burning as free speech?

   A. First Amendment
   B. Thirteenth Amendment
   C. Twenty-First Amendment
   D. Twenty-Seventh Amendment

The Supreme Court stated, "Johnson's expression of dissatisfaction with the Federal Government's policies also does not fall within the class of 'fighting words' likely to be seen as a direct personal insult or an invitation to exchange fisticuffs."

4. What could you infer from this?

   A. All speech is protected.
   B. Only political speech is protected.
   C. Political speech is not protected.
   D. There are limits to speech that is protected.

Social Studies

Directions: Questions 5 and 6 refer to the following map.

SEGREGATION IN THE UNITED STATES, 1950

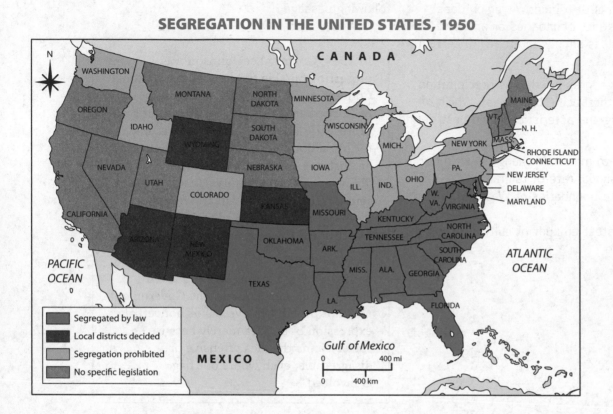

5. According to the map, which states segregated their schools by law?

- **A.** Kansas, Arizona, Wyoming
- **B.** Arkansas, Illinois, Missouri
- **C.** Texas, Georgia, Delaware
- **D.** Maine, New Hampshire, Vermont

6. Which conclusion is supported by the information shown in the map?

- **A.** The Southern states supported segregation.
- **B.** Segregation spread from east to west in 1950.
- **C.** Most Western states supported segregation.
- **D.** All Northern states prohibited segregation.

Social Studies

Directions: Questions 7 and 8 refer to the following passage.

> Many pioneers kept diaries of their incredible journeys to the American West. They wrote about their fears of hard winters, wild animals, and sickness or death. They also wrote about the loneliness of leaving behind loved ones, familiar places, and personal possessions. The pioneers described the natural beauty they saw, the friendships they formed with other travelers, and the obstacles they overcame by using all the creativity they could muster.

7. For which kind of historical project would a pioneer's personal diary be a good source?

   A. study of weather patterns in the American West
   B. report on everyday life and hardships faced by pioneers
   C. report on pioneer transportation
   D. study of the demography of pioneers

8. Which words describe what life was like for pioneers on their journey west?

   A. difficult but full of adventure
   B. exhausting and frightening
   C. surprising but easy to adjust to
   D. temporarily uncomfortable

9. Jamal mows lawns for a local landscaper. Jamal's boss asks him to work an additional four hours on Sunday afternoon. Jamal already had plans to play soccer with friends on Sunday afternoon.

If Jamal chooses to mow lawns, what is the opportunity cost of his decision?

   A. the money he earns by mowing the lawns
   B. the four hours of work mowing lawns
   C. the time playing soccer with his friends
   D. the ability to buy things in the future

10. What did political leaders do after the Civil War?

   A. Southern legislatures limited the freedom of formerly enslaved persons.
   B. Radical Republicans supported President Johnson's Reconstruction plans.
   C. Southern states built schools for formerly enslaved persons and helped them get jobs.
   D. Radical Republicans encouraged Confederate leaders to return to their former positions.

Social Studies

Directions: Questions 11–14 refer to the information shown in the map.

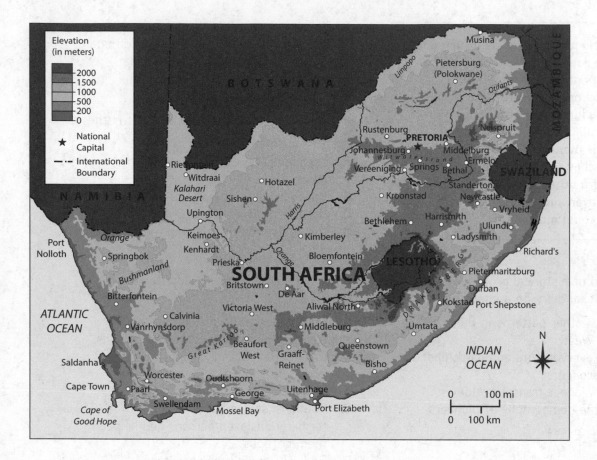

11. Which city is the capital of South Africa?

    A. Johannesburg
    B. Queenstown
    C. Pretoria
    D. Cape Town

12. Which type of map is this?

    A. physical map
    B. resource map
    C. climate map
    D. road map

13. Most of South Africa's land is at what elevation?

    A. at or above 2,000 meters
    B. at or above 1,000 meters
    C. below 500 meters
    D. at sea level

14. Which statement is supported by the map?

    A. Most of South Africa is desert.
    B. More cities are along the coast than inland.
    C. South Africa has more rivers than any of its neighboring countries.
    D. The lands at the lowest elevations are all along the coast.

Social Studies

Directions: Questions 15 and 16 refer to the following cartoon.

Directions: Question 17 refers to the following graph.

GDP PER AMERICAN FROM 1960 TO 2011

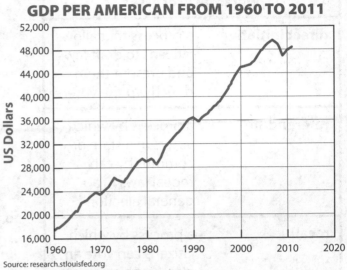

Source: research.stlouisfed.org

15. Which statement best summarizes the cartoonist's message?

A. North Korea is a dangerous enemy for the United States.

B. The United States should take better care of its ally South Korea.

C. South Korea is a dangerous enemy for the United States and China.

D. China needs to exert influence on its ally North Korea.

17. What trend does the graph show about GDP per American from 1960 to 2011?

A. no trend

B. generally increasing

C. generally decreasing

D. generally unchanged

16. What governmental role does the cartoon refer to?

A. maintaining a military defense

B. implementing fiscal policy

C. passing legislation

D. conducting diplomacy

Social Studies

Directions: Questions 18–20 refer to the following chart.

Electoral Processes	
direct initiative	a process that allows citizens to draft laws and present them directly to the voters
referendum	a process by which voters in a state or community can repeal laws in a general election
recall	a process by which citizens can vote an elected government official out of office
primary election	an election held in advance of the general election, allowing voters to select candidates for public office from one or more political parties
general election	the final election held on the same day throughout the United States

19. A person who wishes to become a political party's candidate for governor must first be selected by what process?

   A. referendum
   B. primary election
   C. direct initiative
   D. general election

20. Voters unhappy with their governor's support for denying education and health care services to illegal immigrants could have him removed from office before his term expired by what process?

   A. referendum
   B. direct initiative
   C. general election
   D. recall

18. A group of citizens writes a tax reform law. It is presented to the voters on the next ballot. This is an illustration of which electoral process?

   A. direct initiative
   B. referendum
   C. recall
   D. general election

Social Studies

Directions: Question 21 refers to the following two quotations.

> ". . . avoid the necessity of those overgrown military establishments which, under any form of government, are inauspicious [not favorable] to liberty, and which are to be regarded as particularly hostile to republican liberty."
>
> —Farewell Address, General George Washington, 1st US President, 1796
>
> "The conjunction of an immense military establishment and a large arms industry is new in the American experience. The total influence . . . is felt in every city, every state house, every office of the federal government. . . . In the councils of government, we must guard against the acquisition of unwarranted influence . . . by the military-industrial complex."
>
> — Farewell Address, General Dwight Eisenhower, 34th US President, 1961

21. What conclusion could be drawn from these statements?

A. A very large military establishment could threaten US liberty.

B. Business influence on the military has made US government more democratic.

C. Only the military-industrial complex can protect American liberties.

D. The military should be allowed more influence in US government.

22. Latin Americans made rich cultural contributions to the southwestern United States long before the twentieth century. People of Latin American background lived in the region before people migrated there from other parts of the United States. For many years, Mexico and the United States fought over the region's ownership and boundaries.

Which statement about the southwestern United States can be made on the basis of this passage?

A. Latin Americans held back the cultural development of the Southwest.

B. Mexico sold Texas to the United States to end boundary disputes.

C. There has been no Latin American influence on the cultural development of the southwestern United States.

D. Latin Americans have had a strong influence on regional culture in the southwestern United States.

Social Studies

Directions: Questions 23 and 24 refer to the following information.

> A balance sheet is a financial statement. Businesses use it to summarize their financial position at various points in time. A balance sheet has three parts:
>
> • assets (everything the business has in its possession)
>
> • liabilities (everything the business owes to someone else)
>
> • net worth (the difference between total assets and total liabilities)
>
> The balance sheet is based on this formula:
> assets − liabilities = net worth

23. How does a balance sheet describe the financial position of a business?

   A. in terms of its debts
   B. by counting its assets
   C. at certain points in time
   D. for a fiscal year

24. Jin Su's restaurant has assets totaling $75,000 and liabilities totaling $53,000. How would Jin Su find the net worth of the restaurant?

   A. Add half of the liabilities to the assets.
   B. Add the liabilities and the assets.
   C. Subtract the assets from the liabilities.
   D. Subtract the liabilities from the assets.

Directions: Questions 25 and 26 refer to the following passage.

> After the Civil War, Radical Republicans were the strongest supporters of civil rights for former slaves. One of their significant successes was the passage of three constitutional amendments guaranteeing basic civil rights. Another success was the establishment of the Freedmen's Bureau, an agency that helped former slaves make the transition from slavery to citizenship.

25. What did the Radical Republicans support?

   A. slavery
   B. civil rights for former slaves
   C. the Civil War
   D. the abolition of the Democratic Party

26. How did the Freedmen's Bureau help former enslaved persons?

   A. by teaching them to read and write
   B. by helping them find work with former slaveholders
   C. by passing Constitutional amendments on civil rights
   D. by starting the Civil War

Social Studies

Directions: Questions 27 and 28 refer to the following graph.

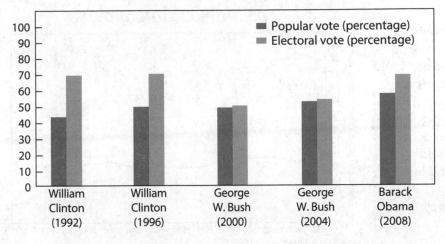

US PRESIDENTIAL ELECTION RESULTS

27. For each election, compare the percentage of popular votes to the percentage of electoral votes. Which two elections were the closest between the popular and electoral votes?

   A. 1992 and 1996
   B. 1992 and 2000
   C. 2000 and 2004
   D. 1996 and 2008

28. Which election had the greatest difference between the percentage of popular votes and the percentage of electoral votes that a president won?

   A. 1992
   B. 1996
   C. 2000
   D. 2008

Social Studies

Directions: Question 29 refers to the following passage and chart.

Jane Benson lives in a small city. She wants to open a small business in her neighborhood so she can work near her home and be her own boss. She decided to do a market survey of the area. She made up a questionnaire listing the possible products and services she could provide. Jane went from door to door asking people which business they would prefer to have in the neighborhood and how much they would spend there. The chart below shows the results of Jane's survey.

JANE'S RESULTS

Business	Number in favor		Estimated income per week
Bakery	18		$430
Drugstore	17		$500
Fabric store	9		$220
Restaurant	8		$210

29. According to the chart, which of the four businesses would be the best investment?

A. bakery
B. drugstore
C. fabric store
D. restaurant

Directions: Questions 30 and 31 refer to the following graph.

U.S. POPULATION GROWTH

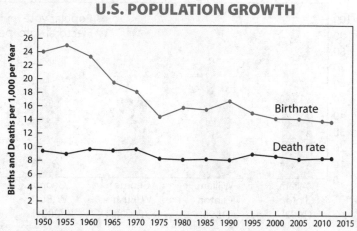

Source: CIA World Factbook, 2011

30. According to the graph, in which of the following time periods did the greatest decrease in birthrate take place?

A. from 1950–1955
B. from 1970–1975
C. from 1990–1995
D. from 2005–2010

31. What trend does the graph show about population growth rates in the United States?

A. They are exploding.
B. They have remained stable since 1950.
C. They declined during the early 1950s.
D. They have declined since 1955.

Social Studies

Directions: Questions 32 and 33 refer to the following diagram.

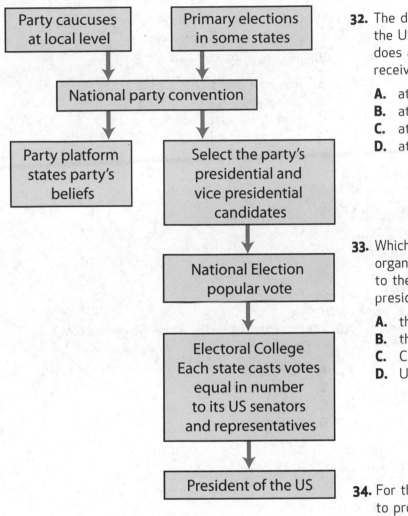

32. The diagram shows the process by which the US president is elected. At which stage does a presidential candidate officially receive the nomination of his or her party?

    A. at the electoral college vote
    B. at the national election
    C. at the national party convention
    D. at the state primary election

33. Which group seems to have the most organizational responsibility leading up to the nomination of candidates for president?

    A. the electoral college
    B. the political parties
    C. Congress
    D. US voters

34. For the most part, businesses are unwilling to produce things that the public will use free of charge. How are parks and roads produced?

    A. The government provides public goods.
    B. Businesses must give a percent of their profits to the public.
    C. The government reduces personal taxes.
    D. People know they cannot expect free goods and services.

Social Studies

Directions: Questions 35–38 refer to the following passage.

> Our first priority is making America a magnet for new jobs and manufacturing. . . .
>
> So tonight, I'm announcing the launch of three more of these manufacturing hubs, where businesses will partner with the Departments of Defense and Energy to turn regions left behind by globalization into global centers of high-tech jobs. And I ask this Congress to help create a network of fifteen of these hubs and guarantee that the next revolution in manufacturing is Made in America.
>
> —President Barack Obama, State of the Union Address, 2013

35. In these remarks, what was President Obama proposing?

   A. party platform
   B. public policy
   C. congressional reform
   D. executive appointments

36. Which statement best summarizes President Obama's proposal?

   A. Government should partner with industry to develop high-tech centers in regions experiencing decline.
   B. Congress should pass laws requiring industry to keep their manufacturing in the United States.
   C. The secretaries of the Departments of Defense and Energy should create 15 high-tech hubs.
   D. Congress should begin working on a plan to convince high-tech global industries to move to the United States.

37. President Obama's proposal reflects an important role of government.

What is that role?

   A. making a profit
   B. establishing trusts
   C. setting monetary policy
   D. creating fiscal policy

38. Which of the following is one possible goal of Obama's plan?

   A. monopoly
   B. competition
   C. inflation
   D. deflation

Social Studies

Directions: Questions 39–42 refer to the following chart.

Political Systems	
Absolute monarchy	a government where the king or queen's word is law
Constitutional monarchy	a monarchy that has elected representatives and a constitution
Direct democracy	a government where the people have a direct voice and vote in the government
Representative democracy	a democracy where people select delegates to represent them
Oligarchy	a government in which a small group of people rule
Totalitarianism	an extreme type of dictatorship in which a leader controls the political, economic, and social life of a country

39. During World War II, Benito Mussolini ruled Italy and had total control over the country. What was the political system in Italy during this period?

A. absolute monarchy

B. direct democracy

C. oligarchy

D. totalitarianism

40. Which political system does the US have?

A. constitutional monarchy

B. direct democracy

C. representative democracy

D. oligarchy

41. How are a constitutional monarchy and a representative democracy similar forms of government?

A. Both pass laws without the people knowing about the laws.

B. Both include an elected legislature.

C. Both are have a ceremonial leader with no real power.

D. Both are governments of the few.

42. Which statement or statements best summarize the difference between a representative democracy and a direct democracy?

A. In a direct democracy, the people are involved firsthand in government decisions. In a representative democracy, elected officials make decisions on behalf of the people.

B. In a direct democracy, the people elect a small group to represent them. In a representative democracy, the people elect many representatives.

C. In both a direct democracy and a representative democracy, people have no say in government decisions.

D. In both a direct democracy and a representative democracy, people elect representatives to make decisions for them.

Social Studies

Directions: Question 43 is based on the following photograph.

43. Which statement best expresses the viewpoint of the photographer?

   A. Many young women in China have good jobs today because of the world demand for inexpensive clothing.

   B. Consumers should be concerned about working conditions in factories around the world.

   C. All factory workers should join unions in order to get better pay and benefits.

   D. Raising tariffs on Chinese imports would result in fewer jobs in a country where millions of people are out of work.

44. President Franklin D. Roosevelt and British Prime Minister Winston Churchill issued the Atlantic Charter in August 1941. One of the points of this World War II document called for all nations to join together to guarantee world peace. The Atlantic Charter later evolved into the United Nations.

What can you infer from this information?

   A. The United States was finally joining the League of Nations.

   B. Congress still opposed the League of Nations.

   C. The United States still did not want to tie its foreign policy to an international organization.

   D. Wilson's idea for a League of Nations that would guarantee world peace was still alive.

Social Studies

Directions: Questions 45 and 46 refer to the following passage.

On June 12, 1987, President Ronald Reagan gave a speech at the Brandenburg Gate in West Berlin. The gate was near the Berlin Wall, and people in East Berlin could hear his speech. Below is an excerpt.

"In the West today, we see a free world that has achieved a level of prosperity [success] and well-being unprecedented [never seen before] in all human history. In the Communist world, we see failure, technological backwardness, declining standards of health, even want of the most basic kind—too little food. . . .

"There is one sign the Soviets can make that would be unmistakable, that would advance dramatically the cause of freedom and peace. General Secretary Gorbachev, if you seek peace, if you seek prosperity for the Soviet Union and Eastern Europe, if you seek liberalization: Come here to this gate! . . . Mr. Gorbachev, tear down this wall!"

—President Ronald Reagan

45. Why did President Reagan ask Gorbachev to tear down the Berlin Wall?

- **A.** He wanted Germany to be reunited.
- **B.** He thought that would end the arms race with the Soviet Union.
- **C.** He wanted the Soviet Union to show its commitment to reform.
- **D.** He believed the Soviet Union did not respect the power of the United States.

46. Why did Reagan choose the Brandenburg Gate as the site for his speech?

- **A.** He wanted people in the communist part of the city to hear the speech.
- **B.** The gate was a symbol of freedom.
- **C.** Gorbachev would be at the gate.
- **D.** He hoped it would end communism by swaying Gorbachev.

47. Among the global challenges of the twenty-first century are the issues of global warming and the overuse of nonrenewable resources. How are these issues related?

- **A.** Global warming and overuse of nonrenewable resources are both problems that can be easily solved.
- **B.** Overuse of nonrenewable resources and global warming are not real problems.
- **C.** Global warming is the cause, and overuse of nonrenewable resources is the effect.
- **D.** Overuse of nonrenewable resources is the cause, and global warming is the effect.

Social Studies

Directions: Question 48 refers to the following graph.

US UNEMPLOYMENT RATE DURING GREAT DEPRESSION

Directions: Question 50 refers to the following graph.

EQUILIBRIUM PRICE FOR COMPUTERS

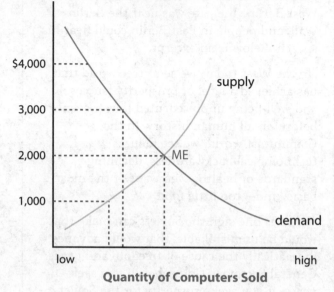

48. Look at the unemployment rate in 1929 and 1942. How would you describe the employment situation in the country in those years?

   A. high unemployment
   B. low unemployment
   C. partial employment
   D. full employment

50. The market equilibrium price of goods or services (point *ME*) takes place at the point where supply equals demand. According to the graph, what is the market equilibrium price for computers?

   A. $1,000
   B. $2,000
   C. $3,000
   D. $4,000

49. In economics, demand is the amount of a product people are willing and able to buy. According to the law of demand, what relationship exists between the price of a product and the quantity demanded of the product?

   A. When the price increases, the quantity demanded increases.
   B. When the quantity demanded decreases, the price increases.
   C. When the price decreases, the quantity demanded increases.
   D. When the quantity demanded is constant, the price increases.

Answer Key

1. **B.** *Precipitation* refers to rain or snow. The geographer would be interested in the region's annual rainfall.

2. **C.** Ani may be supplying computer services to the factory and to its employees who have moved to the area. Interdependence is the likely reason for her rising profits.

3. **A.** The First Amendment protects freedom of speech. The Supreme Court said that Johnson's flag-burning was a form of speech, which is protected under the First Amendment. The First Amendment is part of the Bill of Rights, the first ten amendments.

4. **D.** Because the Court said, Johnson's action "does not fall within the class of . . . ," you can infer that not all types of speech are protected under the First Amendment.

5. **C.** According to the map, schools in Texas, Georgia, and Delaware were all segregated by law.

6. **A.** All the states that supported segregation are located in the South.

7. **B.** A pioneer's journal would be a good source for a report describing the everyday life and struggles of a pioneer.

8. **A.** The passage states that pioneers had great difficulties but also interesting adventures.

9. **C.** Opportunity cost is the thing that was not selected when choosing between two things. The opportunity cost of Jamal's choice to mow lawns is the time he would have spent playing soccer with friends.

10. **A.** The Southern legislatures, once they were given back their power, passed laws to restrict the rights of formerly enslaved persons.

11. **C.** According to the symbols on the map and key, Pretoria is the capital of South Africa.

12. **A.** This is a physical map, since it shows the physical characteristics of South Africa. It does not show the location of natural resources, weather patterns, or highways.

13. **B.** Most of South Africa appears to be at or above an elevation of 1,000 meters.

14. **D.** The map shows that the areas of lowest elevation are all along the coast.

15. **D.** The cartoon shows Uncle Sam telling China to "do something about" its "child," North Korea.

16. **D.** One of the duties of government is to conduct diplomacy (foreign relations) by negotiating with the governments of other countries.

17. **B.** Although there are slight dips from time to time, the line on the graph shows the dollar amount rising over the years. This indicates that GDP per American has generally increased from 1960 to 2011.

18. **A.** In some states, citizens may draft laws and present them directly to voters. This is a direct initiative.

19. **B.** A political party's candidate for public office must be selected from a list of party candidates. This is done in a primary election.

20. **D.** Voters can use the recall process to remove an elected public official from office. In this case, a majority of people voting in an election would have to approve of the governor's removal.

21. **A.** Both Washington and Eisenhower warn against allowing the military to have too much influence on government. Washington says the military establishment is "hostile to republican liberty." Eisenhower says it must not be allowed to acquire too much influence.

22. **D.** Latin Americans have lived in the Southwest for a long time. Their culture—food, language, customs—is important to this region.

23. **C.** Sentence 2 says that the balance sheet is used by businesses to show their financial position "at various points in time."

24. **D.** To find net worth, subtract the liabilities from the assets.
$75,000 – $53,000 = $22,000

25. **B.** The passage states that Radical Republicans were strong supporters of civil rights for former enslaved persons.

26. **A.** The Freedmen's Bureau helped former enslaved persons make the transition from slavery to citizenship. You can infer that learning to read and write would be an important part of this process. Members of the Freemen's Bureau were not politicans, so they did not vote on Constitutional amendments.

27. **C.** The graph shows that the percentages of popular vote and electoral vote were most similar in the George W. Bush elections (2000 and 2004).

Answer Key

28. **A.** The graph shows that the difference between the percentage of popular vote won and electoral vote won was the greatest in 1992.

29. **B.** Although more people are interested in having a bakery, more money would be spent at a drugstore.

30. **B.** The graph shows that the greatest downward slope in birthrate was between 1970 and 1975.

31. **D.** The graph shows a relatively stable death rate and an overall falling birthrate. Therefore, there is a decline in population growth.

32. **C.** After voters indicate their preferences in the primary elections, the presidential candidate is officially nominated at the national party convention.

33. **B.** The political parties have the most responsibility for nominating candidates because they are responsible for local party caucuses, the national party convention, the party platform, and the selection of candidates.

34. **A.** Public goods, such as parks and roads, are provided by the government. They are paid for by taxing the public.

35. **B.** Obama was proposing public policy. This is an action that will help all citizens.

36. **A.** Obama wants businesses to work together with government to create manufacturing centers in parts of the country that have lost jobs to foreign manufacturers.

37. **D.** Through its fiscal policies, such as the one Obama proposes here, the government decides how it will spend tax money. Government spending has a great effect on the US economy.

38. **B.** Setting up high-tech industrial hubs in fifteen regions will promote competition. "Made in America" will compete with foreign-made goods.

39. **D.** Italy under Benito Mussolini was a totalitarian government. Mussolini contolled all aspects of life.

40. **C.** The United States has a representative democracy. People elect representatives to Congress, legislators, mayors, and the president to make the day-to-day decisions of government.

41. **B.** Both a representative democracy and a constitutional monarchy have a legislature that is elected by the people.

42. **A.** In a direct democracy, the people vote on government decisions. In a representative democracy, elected officials make decisions. A direct democracy would be possible only if there were a small number of citizens.

43. **B.** The photograph shows crowded factory conditions. The message to consumers is that the wages and work conditions of factory workers should be a global concern.

44. **D.** The Atlantic Charter led to the founding of the United Nations in 1945. The UN was modeled after the League of Nations, so you can infer that Wilson's goal of working for world peace was not dead.

45. **C.** Reagan said that tearing down the Berlin Wall would be an "unmistakable" sign that the Soviet Union was ready to change the way it treated its people.

46. **A.** Reagan gave his speech at the Brandenburg Gate because he knew people in communist East Berlin could hear him from there.

47. **D.** Most scientists agree that the overuse of nonrenewable resources is one of the causes of global warming.

48. **A.** In late 1929, unemployment began to rise. Throughout the Great Depression, there was high unemployment in the United States.

49. **C.** When the price of a product decreases, more people may be willing to buy that product. This is the law of demand.

50. **B.** The supply curve and the demand curve are equal at the point of intersection (*ME*). The price at this point is $2,000.

Evaluation Chart

Check Your Understanding

On the following chart, circle the number of any question you answered incorrectly. Under each lesson title, you will see the pages you can review to study the content covered in the question. Pay particular attention to reviewing those lessons in which you missed half or more of the questions.

Chapters	Item Number	Review Pages
US Government and Civics	3, 4, 18, 19, 20, 21, 22, 32, 33	18–65
US History: Revolutionary War through the Depression	7, 8, 10, 25, 26	74–101
US History: World War II through Modern Times	5, 6, 27, 28	110–143
World History and Political Systems	15, 16, 39, 40, 41, 42, 44, 45, 46, 47	152–175
Economic Foundations	2, 9, 23, 24, 29, 34, 35, 36, 37, 38, 49, 50	184–235
Economic Events in History	17, 48	244–261
Economics in the Twenty-First Century	43	270–277
Geography and People	1, 11, 12, 13, 14, 30, 31	286–319

CHAPTER 1 US Government and Civics

Lesson 1.1

Think about Social Studies, page 23
Your answer might include the following:

Declaration of Independence—Governments exist to protect people's rights.

Great Binding Law—Tribes cooperated with one another.

Magna Carta—People must be judged by their peers.

US Constitution—People cannot be deprived of life, liberty, or property without due process of law.

Virginia Declaration of Rights—All people are equally free and have certain rights.

Vocabulary Review, page 24
1. peers
2. absolute
3. democracy
4. dictatorship
5. amendments
6. confederacy
7. monarchy
8. government

Skill Review, page 24
1. **B.** A direct democracy will work only in a group that is small enough so everyone can voice an opinion and vote on every policy. A government in which leaders represent the citizens is a representative democracy, and a nation that describes government powers in a constitution is a constitutional democracy. In a nation led by an absolute ruler, the people will not be consulted.

2. **C.** In a constitutional monarchy, the king or queen has no real authority; the prime minister, who is head of the legislature, governs the country. An absolute monarchy has a king or queen, but it does not have a legislature with power to make laws and protect the rights of citizens.

3. **D.** All three documents contain statements that protect the rights of the people. They did not establish dictatorships. The Magna Carta did not create a democracy or eliminate the monarchy.

Skill Practice, page 25
Sample answers:
1. The founders knew that some rights had been abused in the past. They wanted to protect citizens in the new country.

2. The authors of the Constitution and the Bill of Rights were descended from English people, so English law would have influenced their thinking. They knew that the English Bill of Rights had protected the people from the king, and they thought all people should have those same rights.

3. The authors knew they couldn't name every right, but they wanted to protect citizens from all possible abuses by the government.

Writing Practice page 25
Your paragraph should refer to ways that the British monarchy controlled the government.

Sample Response
The colonists knew the story of how the people had forced King John to sign the Magna Carta in 1215 to prevent the king from abusing them. They also understood how King George III was taxing and abusing them. The Framers of the Constitution were determined to prevent government leaders from abusing the citizens.

Lesson 1.2

Think about Social Studies, page 27
The Constitution called for two bodies in the legislative branch. In the Senate, each state has equal representation regardless of its size.

Think about Social Studies, page 29
1. An amendment can be proposed by a two-thirds majority vote of both houses of Congress, or two-thirds of the state legislatures can ask Congress to call a convention for proposing an amendment. Amendments must be approved by either the legislatures or special conventions in three-fourths of the states.

2. Amendments extend and protect voting rights, change government function or structure, or change the powers of state and national government.

Vocabulary Review, page 30
1. guarantees
2. separation of powers
3. checks and balances
4. categories

Answer Key

Skill Review, page 30

1. **A.** Twelve amendments were passed during this time. Ten of these were in the Bill of Rights, which were agreed to before the Constitution was ratified.

2. *Sample answer:* The Twentieth Amendment was passed while Franklin D. Roosevelt was president. It changed inauguration day from March to January. This was done because of the economics problems that had increased during the months that Roosevelt waited to be inaugurated. Outgoing President Hoover had little power to solve the crisis.

Skill Practice, page 31

1. **D.** The Supreme Court tries to make decisions that prevent people from abusing freedom.

2. **B.** This case was a ruling on freedom of speech.

3. **B.** The Miranda Rights state that a suspect has the right to remain silent. This protects people from saying something that could be used against them in court.

Writing Practice, page 31

Review the list of freedoms on page 28. Then write about one of these freedoms.

Sample Response

The First Amendment guarantees the right to speak freely. Recently I felt the government had made a mistake by passing a new tax law. I wrote a letter to the editor of my local newspaper, and the letter was printed. Because I have freedom of speech, I can write what I feel, even though I am criticizing the government. Because of freedom of the press, the newspaper cannot get in trouble for printing my letter. If we did not have these freedoms, I would have had to keep silent or risk going to jail.

Lesson 1.3

Think about Social Studies, page 34

1. To become president, a person must be a natural-born US citizen and be at least 35 years old.

2. The president can refuse to sign a bill or can use a pocket veto.

Vocabulary Review, page 36

1. imbalance
2. functions
3. Judicial review
4. veto
5. delegated

Skill Review, page 36

1. **D.** The Supreme Court made very different decisions in these two cases dealing with freedom of speech. Nothing in these decisions indicates that the Supreme Court doesn't understand teenagers or doesn't like them.

2. **B.** The outcomes of the cases were different. Both cases were about events that happened in a high school and were concerned with the First Amendment, so those are not contrasts. The writer does not tell how the cases got to the Supreme Court.

Skill Practice, page 37

1. **D.** Presidential veto allows the president to refuse to sign a bill. But Congress can override the veto if two-thirds of both houses pass the bill again.

2. **C.** Two-thirds of both the Senate and the House of Representatives can overturn a veto. Then the bill would become law without the president's signature.

3. **A.** The Supreme Court must consider current events that change the way people think about the law.

4. **C.** In *Plessy v. Ferguson*, the Court ruled that segregation was legal. The passage argues that this decision was made at a time when racial discrimination was commonly accepted.

Writing Practice, page 37

When you compare and contrast, you describe similarities and differences.

Sample Response

The legislative branch consists of the Senate and the House of Representatives. The executive branch consists of the president and the cabinet. The legislative branch passes laws, and the executive branch approves and enforces these laws. The legislative branch is responsible for taxing the people, proposing amendments, and declaring war. The executive branch appoints cabinet members, agency executives, and Supreme Court justices.

Lesson 1.4

Think about Social Studies, page 39
1. federal
2. one-house
3. states

Think about Social Studies, page 41
1. The states cannot coin money, tax imports or exports, make treaties with foreign nations, or maintain an army in time of peace.
2. Local governments include counties, cities, and special districts.
3. The three kinds of city government are strong mayor/ weak city council system, weak mayor/strong city council system, and city manager/city council system.

Vocabulary Review, page 42
1. direct initiative
2. recall
3. reserved
4. referendum
5. contradict

Skill Review, page 42
1. **A.** "That year" (Sentence 4) refers to 1937, which is identified in the previous sentence.
2. **B.** The passage states that after the Nebraska legislature became unicameral, the state spent less money on its legislature and it passed more bills.
3. **C.** Sentence 4 is the first sentence to mention Nebraska.
4. **D.** Sentence 7 states that Nebraska is unique; that is, it is the only state with unicameral legislature. Sentence 3 states that before 1937, all states were bicameral. Sentences 2 and 6 do not mention how many states have bicameral legislatures.

Skill Practice, page 43
1. **C.** As commander in chief, the governor has the power to call up the state's national guard to respond to emergencies.
2. **A.** Both the states and the federal government have a written constitution, a chief executive (governor and president), and court systems.
3. **D.** A recall is an election that allows voters to vote a public official out of office before his or her term is up.

4. **C.** If voters object to a law that has been passed by the state legislature, they may vote to overturn the law. This process is called a referendum.
5. **B.** When the city council can overrule the actions of the mayor, this system is known as strong city council/weak mayor.
6. **D.** A recall gives voters power over public officials who break the law or abuse the public trust in some way.

Writing Practice, page 43
Look on the Internet or contact city officials for information about your town government

Sample Response
   My town government has a weak mayor and a strong city council. The city council is called the board of aldermen, and each alderman represents a district. The aldermen pass laws for the town, and they settle town matters like improving the snow plowing. The mayor leads parades and attends special events, but the mayor has no real power.
   The council could be more effective if it had stronger leadership. The board is very divided by party loyalties, so it is difficult to get much accomplished. A stronger mayor or a stronger chair of the board might help the aldermen get past their personal feelings and move forward to improve our community.

Lesson 1.5

Think about Social Studies, page 46
1. I
2. P
3. P
4. I

Vocabulary Review, page 46
1. platform
2. influence
3. interest group

Skill Review, page 47
1. **C.** The cartoonist shows the Republicans (elephants) and Democrats (donkeys) using all the space and all the water in the tub. The third party wants to join in, but there is clearly no room.

Answer Key

Skill Practice, page 47
1. **C.** The writer believes that poor people have little political influence because so few of them vote. When large portions of a group (such as senior citizens) vote, that group gains power.
2. **A.** If more lower-income people voted, elected officials would have to pay more attention to their interests and there might be an expansion of programs serving the poor.

Writing Practice, page 47
Newspapers have many election ads during the weeks before an election.

Sample Response
The Labor Board sponsored an ad for Representative Kelly Lawson. She usually votes in favor of bills related to worker safety and OSHA standards. Her opponent favors limiting the power of trade unions as well as reducing fines and penalties for unsafe working conditions. It makes sense that the Labor Board would sponsor an ad promoting a candidate whose policies matched the Labor Board's interests.

Lesson 1.6

Think about Social Studies, page 51
1. Women make up about half of all the people in a society. They were the largest group of people that had been denied the right to vote.
2. The South probably objected to women's suffrage. Southerners may have worried that giving voting rights to women might lead to voting rights for African Americans.

Vocabulary Review, page 52
1. suffrage
2. provision
3. civil liberty
4. seized
5. disenfranchised
6. civil rights

Skill Review, pages 52–53
1. **D.** *Best*, *spared the chaos*, and *tyranny* are words that help you understand the writer's point of view.
2. **D.** Overall, the percentage of registered voters turning out for an election is declining. If the decline continues and voter turnout is consistently less than 50%, more presidents will be elected in elections where less than half of the population has voted.

Skill Practice, page 53
1. **C.** The passage states that Radical Republicans were strong supporters of civil rights for African Americans. One of the three amendments passed at that time guaranteed African American men the right to vote. All the other choices would not have been supported by people who wanted civil rights for African Americans.
2. **A.** By providing schools for former slaves, the Freedmen's Bureau helped these people learn to read and write.

Writing Practice, page 53
Think about issues that may be important to minorities.

Sample answer
Minority groups have struggled to gain equal rights and civil liberties. To gain these rights, elected officials must believe that all people deserve the same rights. If minority groups are excluded from voting, the candidates they prefer may not be elected. Majority groups might continue to elect officials who are not concerned about equal rights for everyone.

Lesson 1.7

Think about Social Studies, page 55
1. *Sample answers:* business, education, politics, government
2. *Sample answers:* economic inequality, wars, terrorism, nuclear arms proliferation, health issues, environmental issues, human rights violations, censorship
3. the State Department

Vocabulary Review, page 58
1. fair trade
2. nonprofit organization
3. Dialogue
4. foreign aid
5. global society
6. transact

(Lesson 1.7 cont.)

Skill Review, pages 58–59

1. *Sample answer:* The cartoon deals with fair trade and organic produce. The cartoonist is implying that the cost of fair trade and organic produce is so high that people cannot earn enough money to pay for them. Cause: the high cost of fair trade and organic produce. Effect: stealing to get money.

2. A reasonable prediction is that US businesses in China will continue to make a profit. The prediction is based on the fact that most US companies that responded to a survey did well in 2007 and 2008. The survey included a large number of companies and was conducted by a reputable organization, so it is a trustworthy source of information. This strengthens the likelihood that the prediction will be correct.

Skill Practice, page 59

1. **A.** Advances in communication technologies— cell phones, satellites, and the Internet—have contributed greatly to creating a global society.

2. **C.** The fair trade movement has grown because globalization has made consumers in the United States and in other countries more aware of how goods are produced and how workers in other countries are treated.

3. **D.** US businesses have greatly benefited from opening branches overseas.

4. **B.** The World Trade Organization settles trade issues between member countries. It does not deal with nonprofit organizations that provide aid. It does not deal with the trade between states.

Writing Practice, page 59

Predictions do not always come true, but try to give logical reasons for your guess about what will happen in the future.

Sample answer
I believe that increased US business in China will cause many Chinese people to combine Chinese and western cultures. This, in turn, will increase US exports to China. In the past, the Chinese government limited what goods could come into the country. As people are exposed to new products from the United States, they will also be exposed to new ideas.

Lesson 1.8

Think about Social Studies, page 61

1. national, economic
2. state, public safety
3. local, business or economic
4. national, foreign
5. national, economic

Think about Social Studies, page 62

Sample answer: Our local elementary school has a policy about managing food allergies. It states that students with life-threatening food allergies, such as an allergy to peanut butter, must have an emergency action plan in place. The required medications must be kept in the nurse's office. However, the policy does not prevent other children from bringing peanut butter to school. The school is protecting the freedom of those children. This represents a democratic value. However, children with allergies have the right to be safe at school. The policy needs to protect the health of the students in danger.

Think about Social Studies, page 63

Sample answer: Policies must be based on facts. Policies based on opinions may not serve the general public. They will satisfy only those who agree with one point of view.

Vocabulary Review, page 63

1. D.
2. B.
3. G.
4. C.
5. F.
6. A.
7. E.

Answer Key

Skill Review, page 64

1. They are debating a local issue—whether a $1 million surplus in city funds should be spent on a playground.
2. Children currently play in the street. There is a $1 million surplus in the city budget.
3. The surplus came from taxes. Money would have to be spent to maintain and secure the park.
4. "There is nothing more important than our children." "It's only a matter of time before one of them gets hurt." "That's a lot of money!"
5. "Maybe our taxes should be refunded. We could all use more money!" "We would have to pay even more taxes in the future."
6. *Sample answer:* I agree with Maria that building a park would be a good way to protect children.

Skill Practice, page 65

1. **A.** Speed limits are public safety issues. Speed limits are set by state and federal governments for the well-being of everyone. The other choices are decisions made by a business or by individuals.
2. **D.** A declaration of war is made by the national government, not a local or state government. Because it affects our relations with another country, it is a foreign policy.
3. **D.** All three branches of government affect public policy. The legislative branch makes laws, the executive branch carries out the laws, and the judicial branch interprets the laws.
4. **C.** He is attempting to influence policy by expressing his opinion in a public space. He wants to convince others of his position. One citizen cannot make a policy.

Writing Practice, page 65

Select an issue that affects you daily. It is easiest to write about topics that are important to you.

Sample Response

I am strongly against the increase in city bus fares that has been proposed by our local transportation department. I depend on the bus to travel to classes and to my job. I realize the city may need the additional money, but a 25 percent rate hike is too much.

To get support for my position, I can research the bus-fare increases over the past few years. Then I can use that research to write to the city council and the transportation department. I can also speak to other bus riders and get them to sign a petition.

Chapter Review

Chapter 1 Review, pages 66–68

1. **C.** Before the Constitution was ratified, people insisted on changes that would guarantee their rights. The Bill of Rights, the first 10 amendments, was added two years after the Constitution was signed.
2. **A.** The Magna Carta limited the king's power. It did not lead to political elections or establish Parliament. The Magna Carta did not mention the heirs to the throne.
3. **B.** Citizens have the power to vote in a general election on a referendum. If the referendum passes, the disputed law is overturned.
4. **C.** The United States wants to promote democracy. Providing aid to developing countries helps this cause.
5. **A.** The Declaration of Sentiments and the Declaration of Independence both deal with the rights and freedom of people.
6. **C.** The writers of the Declaration of Sentiments believed they were asking for the same rights that the colonists had asked for in the Declaration of Independence. The women did not want to separate themselves from the United States. They were not trying to use a standard format or writing that they liked.
7. **B.** Establishing two houses of Congress was a compromise. All states are equally represented in the Senate. States with large populations have more representatives in the House.
8. **A.** Judicial review is the power of the Supreme Court to evaluate laws and executive actions to decide whether they are constitutional. It is part of the checks-and-balance system.
9. **D.** The US Constitution was modeled in many ways on the Virginia Declaration of Rights. The Bill of Rights was created after the Constitution. There is no evidence that the Declaration of Independence or Washington's letters influenced the Constitution.
10. **D.** Public policy is made by elected officials in all branches and at all levels of government. Citizens can influence public policy by joining political parties and interest groups, writing letters, signing petitions, demonstrating, and voting.

(Review cont.)

11. **A.** The political parties and special interest groups that hold debates, run political ads, and talk to reporters are working to educate the public on issues they care about. In a democracy it is important that the public is informed about issues.

12. **B.** In a dictatorship the person who heads the government holds power over everyone. In a democracy, the voters elect their leaders. In today's monarchies, the king or queen often has no political power.

Essay Writing Practice

Essay Writing Practice, pages 70–71
Answers will vary. Here are some points to consider.

Informative Essay

- Begin your essay with a sentence that summarizes the amendment. Examples: *Freedom of speech is important, but it can be difficult to protect. Americans today do (or do not) receive speedy trials by a fair jury.*

- Each paragraph in your essay should discuss one key idea. For example, the first paragraph might tell what the amendment says. The other paragraphs might give examples of how the government tries to protect this right or how difficult it is to protect this right.

- Edit your essay: As you proofread your essay, make sure you have capitalized proper nouns such as *Constitution* and *First Amendment*. You should also capitalize important words in the title of your essay.

Explanatory Essay

- Begin your essay by making a statement about the responsibilities of a citizen. Then state what actions you think are important.

- Each paragraph should clearly explain one action that can benefit the United States or your community. List three actions in the order of their importance. Make cause-and-effect relationships clear by using words such as such as *if . . . then*, *because*, *since*, *therefore*, and *so*.

- Edit your essay: As you proofread your essay, make sure you have capitalized proper nouns such as *Senator Schmitt* and *House of Representatives*. You should also capitalize important words in the title of your essay.

Answer Key

CHAPTER 2 US History: Revolutionary War through the Depression

Lesson 2.1

Think about Social Studies, page 76
1. **B.** One part of the English Bill of Rights gave citizens the right to a fair trial.
2. **D.** The Fundamental Orders of Connecticut was unusual because it did not mention a king.

Vocabulary Review, page 77
assembly; declaration; charter; representative government; legislature; peers

Skill Review, page 77
Sample answer: The leaders of the Iroquois League met and discussed their ideas until they all came to an agreement. Rutledge tried to use this idea in the new government for the United States.

Skill Practice, page 77
1. **C.** The Magna Carta, which was signed in 1215, was written several centuries before the other documents.
2. **B.** Delegates were likely to sign the Declaration of Independence because it contained ideas about government that were familiar to them. It was not a radical new statement.

Writing Practice, page 77
Review the documents to find ideas that became part of the government of the new nation.

Sample Response
The English Bill of Rights, Mayflower Compact, and Articles of Confederation all described duties, rights, and responsibilities. They tried to ensure that rulers and citizens followed fair rules. The Declaration of Independence described the contract that should exist between the government and its citizens. All these documents helped create societies in which people could be free.

Lesson 2.2

Think about Social Studies, page 81
1. The Constitution established a federal system of government. It divided power between the central government and the states.
2. *Sample answers:* People became more concerned about a national problem than their regional interests. It proved that the United States had strong military.

Think about Social Studies, page 82
1. **D.**
2. **C**
3. **A.**
4. **B.**

Vocabulary Review, page 83
1. Revolution; independence
2. Constitution; federal
3. expansion
4. annexed
5. sectional

Skill Review, page 83
1. Cause: the growth of the nation
   Effect: increased conflict with Native Americans; forced movement of Native Americans to Oklahoma
2. *Sample answers:* Row 1: The English government passes laws taxing the colonists. Row 2: The American Revolution begins. Row 3: The Second Continental Congress meets. Row 4: The Declaration establishes the principle that government must be based on the consent of the people. Row 5: The British surrender at Yorktown in 1781.

Skill Practice, pages 84–85
1. **C.** Most of the states that voted against annexing Texas were in the Northeast.
2. **A.** The Northern states did not want another Southern state in the Union.
3. **C.** The passage states that "unalienable rights" are given by the Creator, so these rights cannot be taken away. The other choices describe rights given by humans (colony leaders, monarch, president).
4. **A.** The founders wanted to make sure that the new government could not have complete control over the people. The people in the new nation would control the government.
5. **C.** Citizens threw tea in Boston Harbor to protest the new taxes the British government had imposed on the colonies.
6. **B.** The American Revolution encouraged other colonies to rebel against colonial control.

(Lesson 2.2 cont.)

Writing Practice, page 85
Cause-and-effect relationships explain *why* something happened.

Sample Response

A chain of events led to US independence from Britain. First, to raise money, the British government increased taxes on the American colonists. This led to the colonists protesting the new tax laws and boycotting English goods. Because of the protests, the British sent troops. The result was that the first shots of the revolution were fired. In response, US delegates met in the Second Continental Congress, where they formed an army under General George Washington. The following year, they issued the Declaration of Independence. After a five-year war, the British surrendered. Because of these events, the United States was finally free to become an independent nation.

Lesson 2.3

Think about Social Studies, page 88
Order: 3, 2, 1, 4, 5

Think about Social Studies, page 90
Sample answers:

1. The North had more people, more money, and more factories that could supply weapons for its troops. Southern military leaders could be killed and farms could be destroyed. The North had the advantage.
2. Many newly freed slaves joined the Union army, which helped the Union.

Think about Social Studies, page 91
1. C.
2. D.
3. A.
4. B.

Vocabulary Review, page 91
1. surrendered
2. secede
3. abolitionist
4. territories
5. Poll taxes
6. Reconstruction

Skill Review, page 92
Sample answers:

1. shallow men, converted, propagandist, conspiracy
    The author believes that the decision shows that slave owners have too much influence over all branches of government.
2. ridiculous, miserable, failure, deluded, pitiable, mad fanaticism, contemptible disgraceful farce
    The author thinks that abolitionists have gone too far and that their actions threaten the stability of the nation.

Skill Practice, page 92–93
1. **C.** The chart shows the largest percent of difference is iron and steel.
2. **D.** The chart shows that the North was clearly ahead in all areas of economic development.
3. **C.** Southern states believed that the North would outlaw slavery. To keep slavery, these states would have to secede from the Union and establish their own country.
4. **A.** The Emancipation Proclamation shifted the focus of the war from preserving the United States to ending slavery.
5. **A.** Few African Americans lived in the North. The industrial economy of the North did not depend on slave labor.
6. **B.** Black Codes were laws passed by Southern legislatures after the Civil War to restrict the rights of African Americans.

Writing practice, page 93
Although you may choose the side of the war you want to represent, you might consider choosing a point of view that you have not thought of before.

Sample Response

Dear Mother,

Today I signed up to fight for the Union. I don't know what awaits me, but I know I can't stay working in a cozy office while my friends and my brother march off to fight for what is right. A hundred years ago, this country was run by king and parliament. If we are going to stay a free nation, we have to stick together. The Rebels can't just decide they can strike off on their own because they don't like the president. I am not going to let that happen. I know you don't want to lose both sons to this war, but we have to think beyond the family. Please don't cry, and please be proud.

Your loving son,

Philip

Answer Key

Lesson 2.4

Think about Social Studies, page 96

1. Conditions gradually improved because social reformers pushed for new laws that would solve problems like city sanitation and unsafe factories.
2. State and local governments could not afford the reforms, and businesses were not interested in them. Help was needed from the federal government.

Think about Social Studies, page 98

1. The United States entered World War I when Germany increased submarine attacks on US ships.
2. Assembly lines meant that more goods could be produced.

Vocabulary Review, page 99

1. irony
2. social
3. progressive
4. muckrakers
5. reform

Skill Review, page 99

1. The word *nag* would probably not be used today to describe a horse. Today an artist might use a car, plane, or truck.
2. The labels say *economic recovery*, *cost of government*, *billion dollar deficit*, and *national income*—which are all economic terms.
3. The artist does not support government spending to restart the economy. He drew a very large horse that would be difficult to mount. The word *billions* is tied to the horse's leg as a little bandage.

Skill Practice, pages 100–101

1. **C.** In 1933, unemployment was at its highest point and personal income was at its lowest point. As the number of unemployed people goes up, the average income per person goes down.
2. **A.** The first graph shows that unemployment rose from 1929 to 1933. The second graph shows the gross national product declining at that time.
3. **B.** The speaker says "we have no faith in man's protection. . . . Give us the ballot, and we will protect ourselves."
4. **C.** Women often worked from their homes, particularly sewing. They worked many hours and earned very little. It was an unfair business practice.

Writing Practice, page 101

If you are unfamiliar with labor unions, talk to a friend or relative who is a member of a union.

Sample Response

From what I can tell, labor unions are just another for-profit industry. They force members to pay dues, but they do little to help the members. Over the past few years, many people have lost their jobs. Those who kept working went without raises, and some even got pay cuts. Where were the unions? Benefits were slashed. Where were the unions? It seems to me that we would all be better off if we could just keep those extra dollars in our pockets and stop paying big salaries to union bosses.

Chapter Review

Chapter 2 Review, pages 102–104

1. **C.** The United States won the Mexican War and took land that now is California, Arizona, New Mexico, Nevada, Utah, and Colorado.
2. **A.** The original 13 states are on the east coast. West was the only direction in which the country could grow.
3. **D.** The Fundamental Orders of Connecticut seems to have been the first written document that set up a government.
4. **B.** After Lincoln's election, seven Southern states decided to secede from the Union. The Civil War began as an effort to preserve the Union.
5. **B.** In every category the North had advantages over the South.
6. **A.** Social Darwinists believe that the powerful and strong members of society have the right to success and wealth. People who don't believe in Social Darwinism might think that the less powerful people need to be protected from the strong and wealthy.
7. **A.** After the Revolution, the United States was a new country without a government. Representatives from the 13 colonies met and created the Articles of Confederation.
8. **D.** Under the Articles of Confederation, the central government was weak. It had a unicameral legislature but no president or court system. The Constitution created three branches of government. It gave certain powers to the national government, such as regulating interstate commerce and printing a national currency.

(Review cont.)

9. **C.** The Missouri Compromise tried to calm the tensions between the North and the South by maintaining the balance between free and slave states.

10. **A.** All three favored the abolition of slavery. Brown was a militant who attacked the federal arsonal at Harpers Ferry, Stowe wrote the bestselling antislavery novel *Uncle Tom's Cabin*, and Douglass was a former enslaved person.

11. **B.** President Wilson, a Democrat, had proposed the League of Nations as a way to help nations settle disputes. However, Republican leaders in the Senate feared that membership could force the United States into war, so they kept the country from joining.

12. **A.** The Roaring Twenties was characterized by isolationism, which kept the United States out of world affairs. At home, business was thriving. It was a time of more jobs and higher wages.

13. **D.** Locke was writing about a social contract—an agreement between citizens and government.

14. **C.** The phrase "any number of men have so consented to make one community or government" is similar to the words "Governments are instituted among Men," which is found in the Declaration of Independence.

Essay Writing Practice

Essay Writing Practice, pages 106–107
Answers will vary. Here are some points to consider.

Summary of a Lesson

- Begin your summary by stating the main idea of the lesson. Use text features such as the lesson title and headings as a guide.
- Your paragraphs should present events in order. Use sequence words such as *first*, *second*, *then*, *next*, *later*, *soon*, and *last*.
- Edit your summary. Check that you have used commas correctly in compound sentences. In a compound sentence, two independent clauses (groups of words that could each stand alone as a complete sentence) are joined by a conjunction such as *and*, *or*, or *but*. A comma should be placed before the conjunction. Example: *George Washington led the Revolutionary Army, and later he became the first US president.*

Summary of an Event

- Begin your summary by naming the event you are describing. Provide details that tell what happened, when and where it happened, and why it happened.
- Your second paragraph should explain why the event was important and show how it affected US history.
- Edit your summary. Check that you have used commas correctly in compound sentences. In a compound sentence, two independent clauses (groups of words that could each stand alone as a complete sentence) are joined by a conjunction such as *and*, *or*, or *but*. A comma should be placed before the conjunction. Example: *George Washington led the Revolutionary Army, and later he became the first US president.*

Answer Key

CHAPTER 3 US History: World War II through Modern Times

Lesson 3.1

Think about Social Studies, page 113
1. 1
2. 4
3. 2
4. 3

Think about Social Studies, page 114
1. The United States became involved in an arms race. It wanted more weapons than the Soviet Union had in order to keep communism from spreading.
2. The Marshall Plan supplied money and material to rebuild Western Europe. The United States hoped this would keep Western European countries from turning to communism.
3. People were afraid that communists would try to take over the US government, so they were afraid of everyone who agreed with any communist ideas.

Vocabulary Review, page 115
1. rationing
2. containment
3. isolationists
4. suburbs
5. denounce

Skill Review, pages 115–116
1. Caldéron says he and other workers did any work they were asked to do.
2. The passage suggests that the *braceros* were not treated well by their employers. They had contracts (which they could not read), but the employers did not respect the contracts.
3. Caldéron says he worked seven days a week, at least 12 hours every day. Those hours would not be part of a fair work agreement.
4. The photograph shows a group of excited children standing on top of a rubble heap.
5. *Sample answer:* When people saw how excited the children were to receive the candy parachutes, they probably wanted to contribute to the project. A small gift was making many children happy.

Skill Practice, page 117
1. **D.** Stalin wanted to maintain control of all areas occupied by Soviet troops at the end of the war in order to spread communism.
2. **A.** The United States wanted places to put weapons during the arms race. It was trying to limit the spread of communism.

Writing Practice, page 117
If you want people to agree with your opinion, back up your opinion with facts.

Sample Response
I think there could be a world war today, but it would not start in Europe. I think it would be more likely to begin in the Middle East. Right now there are conflicts between the strict rulers and the people who want more control of their government in Syria, Iran, and several other Middle Eastern countries. If countries such as France and the United States support the people and countries such as China and Russia support the rulers, an international conflict could begin. Suddenly a fight in one small county could become a big war that spreads around the world.

Lesson 3.2

Think about Social Studies, page 121
1. segregation; public
2. nonviolent
3. discriminatory

Vocabulary Review, page 122
civil rights movement; discrimination; boycott; unanimously; segregation; demonstrations

Skill Review, pages 122–123
Sample answers:
1. Cause: Friedan surveys her Smith classmates.
   Effect: Friedan wrote *The Feminine Mystique*.
2. Martin Luther King Jr. was a civil rights leader in the 1960s who believed in nonviolent protests. In this picture, he was taking part in a march. The protesters have linked arms to show their unity.

(Lesson 3.2 cont.)

Skill Practice, page 123

1. **B.** When African Americans refused to ride the buses, fewer bus fares were paid. The bus company made less money.

2. **D.** Many Americans were horrified by the attacks made upon peaceful protesters. But Americans would probably also have been horrified if the protesters had used violence.

Writing Practice, page 123

Equal rights and equal opportunities affect all of us. Write about a law that affects you.

Sample Response

My grandmother, who was a widow, had to raise her children on her own. She worked hard in a factory, but she earned very little. The Equal Pay Act changed that. When my mother had to raise me on her own, she was able to get a better job and earn fair wages.

Lesson 3.3

Think about Social Studies, page 127

1. **A.** The United States hoped that the people of South Vietnam would not turn to communism if they received US aid.

Think about Social Studies, page 129

1. Nixon
2. Camp David Accords
3. market economies

Vocabulary Review, page 129

1. succeed
2. détente
3. administration
4. brinksmanship
5. repression

Skill Review, page 130

1. $112 This was about one-seventh of the world average.
2. China's GDP was increasing faster than the world average between 1980 and 1985.
3. $4,333 This was about one-half of the world average.
4. Both GDPs are continually increasing. Both had a sharp increase between 2000 and 2005.
5. China's GDP is increasing at a faster rate than the world average.
6. In a few years, China will match or beat the world average GDP.

Skill Practice, page 131

1. **D.** Miami is the only city listed that is within the 1,000-mile range from Cuba.

2. **B.** The Soviets could attack many US cities from Cuba. Cuba and the Soviet Union had not been allies for a long time. There is no evidence that the Soviets or Cubans wanted to attack South America. The United States could launch missiles at Cuba in the event of a threat.

Writing Practice, page 131

Select an issue that is important to you. Explain how you would like to see the problem solved.

Sample Response

Dear Madame President,

As you take office, I hope you will think about the needs of young people in this country. Every job seems to require a college degree. However, the price of education keeps going up, so young people can't afford to go to college. If they do, they have to borrow money for tuition, books, and living expenses. This means they may leave college with more than $50,000 of debt.

How many years do you think it will take them to pay back their debt? They will never be able to buy homes or send their own children to college. Please find a way to help Americans get the education they need without going bankrupt.

Thank you,

Eddie Kang

Lesson 3.4

Think about Social Studies, page 135

1. Government should regulate business and industry so average citizens are protected from big business. There should be strong government-funded social programs to help people who are old, disabled, or poor.

2. Advances in technology—computers, the Internet, and cell phones—made communication and the spread of information faster and easier.

3. The Internet connects computers all over the world, so businesses can communicate quickly and easily with offices or clients regardless of where they are. E-mail also helps people communicate instantly.

Vocabulary Review, page 136

conservatives and liberals (*in either order*); emissions; conserve; technologies

Answer Key

Skill Review, page 136

1. The Nashua is a river.
2. The waste was dumped into its "quiet flow." Stoddart was trying to restore it "and its tributaries." Mills were often placed beside rivers because rivers were a power source.
3. Both cartoons are about the environment. Both show that the environment is suffering. The first cartoon is about people quickly using up Earth's resources. The second cartoon is about the effect of global warming.

Skill Practice, page 137

1. **D.** Between 1990 and 2000, the national debt increased by more than $5,000 billion. This is greater than during any other 10-year period.
2. **C.** 370.1 – 284.1 = 86
3. **B.** Nixon ordered a cover-up of the break-in. Nixon himself was not a robber. He wanted to win re-election, but that was not the cause of his impeachment.
4. **B.** An increase in the population of the suburbs was one cause of increased urbanization.

Writing Practice, page 137

Every aspect of your life is affected some way by government support or regulations.

Sample Response

I receive a large number of benefits from the government. My mail is delivered by a US postal worker. I drive on roads that are paved and maintained with tax money. I went to a public school paid for with state and local money. I voted in the last election, and elections are run by the government. Every day I feel safe because police officers enforce laws. When a building in my neighborhood caught fire, firefighters put out the flames, and paramedics took the injured to the hospital.

Lesson 3.5

Think about Social Studies, page 141

1. Hillary Clinton was the first woman in one of the major political parties to run for president. Barack Obama was the first African American to be nominated by a major party and also to win the presidency.
2. *Sample answer:* I think poverty is going to be the hardest problem to solve. Some people are getting very rich, but many people continue to be poor. It will be difficult to get rich people to share more of their money with others.

Vocabulary Review, page 142

1. economic stimulus
2. surge
3. impact
4. insurgent
5. accountability

Skill Review, page 142

1. The author's opinion is that global warming is not the big problem that it is made out to be.
2. The author says that global warming is "absurd" and that there are more important "real" issues for people to be concerned about.
3. A group of people is protesting nuclear weapons by burning cardboard images of missiles.
4. The photographer supports the protest. The message of the photo is that nuclear weapons should be eliminated. The photo emphasizes that the people are protesting violence in a nonviolent way.

Skill Practice, page 143

1. **C.** The writer assumes that all three branches of government (Supreme Court, White House, and Congress) banded together to approve Obamacare against the people's wishes.
2. **B.** The writer believes Obamacare, or the Affordable Care Act, is too expensive, so it should be done away with. In the writer's opinion, people should be free to buy health insurance if they want it and can afford it.
3. **B.** The increase of troops resulted in less violence in Iraq.
4. **A.** When people have jobs, they have money to spend. When people spend money—by shopping, going out for dinner, and attending sports events—other people keep their jobs. When more people have jobs, more people pay taxes. This activity keeps the economy moving.

Writing Practice, page 143

Think about the qualities you expect of a leader.

Sample Response

Wanted: President of the United States. This position lasts four years, with a possible four-year contract extension. It includes reasonable pay, an allowance for expenses, and full benefits. The ideal candidate will have a college degree, management experience, and good people skills. He or she must be a good negotiator and problem solver. The position requires some travel. The candidate must be willing to relocate to Washington, DC. The US is an Equal Opportunity Employer.

Chapter Review

Chapter 3 Review, pages 144–146

1. **A.** US military leaders believed that Americans strongly opposed involvement in eastern Europe because people were still upset about the Vietnam War.

2. **A.** Isolationists want to focus on domestic affairs rather than foreign affairs.

3. **B.** The United States and the Soviet Union both wanted to be superior to the other. They both looked for ways to show they were the best.

4. **B.** The events of September 11, 2001, got the United States involved in a war on terrorism.

5. **A.** President Johnson's Great Society legislation dealt with the elimination of poverty.

6. **B.** When World War II began, public opinion in the United States was strongly against getting involved in the affairs of Europe and Asia.

7. **C.** In 1960 the first televised presidential debate took place. Radio had been an important medium since the early 1900s. E-mail and the Internet were not used until the late 1900s.

8. **D.** After the defeat of Nazi Germany and its allies in World War II, the United States began a policy of preventing the spread of communism. This is the reason US troops were sent to Korea and Vietnam.

9. **A.** As suburbs grew, more cars crowded the roads, so traffic increased. Gas prices rise and fall as a result of various factors, including inflation. The high price of gas has led to the development of alternative forms of energy.

10. **B.** The Freedom Riders were African Americans and white people who rode interstate buses in the 1960s to draw attention to the fact that some states would not allow integration on buses.

11. **C.** President Truman did not declare war on North Korea. Instead, he asked the UN to send troops to defend South Korea and stop the spread of communism.

12. **C.** Obama was the first African American president. When Obama took office, the United States was already involved in wars in Afghanistan and Iraq. The economic crisis was similar to the Great Depression of the 1930s. Like Presidents Roosevelt, Kennedy, Johnson, and Clinton, Obama worked to improve health care for the American people.

13. **D.** Home computers enable people to connect to the Internet and use e-mail. Electronic communication has changed the way people communicate with one another.

14. **D.** The main goal of the United Farm Workers was to improve wages and benefits for farm workers.

Essay Writing Practice

Essay Writing Practice, page 148
Answers will vary. Here are some points to consider.

Time Line

- Time line: Mark the years in which your events occurred on your time line. Add descriptions to these marks. The descriptions of the events should be short. Your descriptions can be either short phrases or complete sentences, but use the same style for each entry.

Example of short phrase:

9-11-2001, terrorists attack NYC and Washington, DC

Example of complete sentence:

Terrorists attack NYC and Washington, DC, on September 11, 2001.

- Essay: An explanatory essay is a type of informational writing. Include a lead sentence that introduces your topic. Organize the information in the paragraphs by time order, and use transition words to connect the ideas. Close with a concluding sentence that restates your main idea: the importance of this event in modern US history.

- Edit your essay: As you proofread your essay, be sure you have capitalized the names of all people, cities, states, and countries. Check that you have capitalized months of the year. If you write a date such as September 11, 2001, use a comma between the day and the year.

Answer Key

CHAPTER 4 World History and Political Systems

Lesson 4.1

Think about Social Studies, page 155
1. C.
2. D.
3. B.
4. A.

Vocabulary Review, page 156
1. administering
2. governments
3. democracy
4. institutions
5. escalate

Skill Review, pages 156–157
1. A. persuade
   B. persuade or inform
   C. inform
   D. persuade or entertain
   E. entertain

Sample answers:
2. Kim Jong-un is meeting with a group of advisors. They are all studying a large document.
3. No one in the photo is smiling. The photographer seems to be showing a negative view of Kim Jong-un.
4. Kim Jong-un is very young, but he seems to be telling all the older men what to do. He is a dictator, and he is in charge of everything, even though he may have little experience.
5. I think North Koreans might have a positive view of Kim Jong-un if they looked at this photo. They are probably happy that the leader is in charge.

Skill Practice, page 157
1. C. When only a few people control the government, the viewpoint of these people has great influence over the law. Often these people are not elected, so they have no responsibility to the citizens of the country.
2. A. All governments write laws.
3. D. Dictators control the government. A totalitarian dictator not only controls the government, he also controls all aspects of life.

Writing Practice, page 157
Presenting both sides of an argument is a good way to practice expressing your opinion.

Sample Response
(pro) Under the ten-year leadership of Wen Jiabao, China has blossomed. Today private ownership of business has led to growing prosperity of the middle classes. Many more people own cars and live in comfortable, modern homes. Because China has strengthened economic and political ties with the West, some say democracy is peeking over China's horizon.

(con) As Wen Jiabao makes his exit, he will leave behind a China characterized by poor homeless people haunting the streets of ghost cities built for an upper middle class that has never materialized. Despite his talk of a move toward democracy, his government has clamped down on free speech and has increased military spending.

Lesson 4.2

Think about Social Studies, page 160
1. C.
2. A.
3. B.

Think about Social Studies, page 161
1. Countries might feel safer knowing that another country will come to their defense if they are attacked.
2. Different leaders come into power with different goals. This affects who a country will be friendly with and who suddenly becomes an enemy.

Vocabulary Review, page 162
1. alliances
2. established
3. foreign policy
4. ratify
5. obtain
6. diplomatic

(Lesson 4.2 cont.)

Skill Review, page 162
1. Main idea: sentence 1
   Supporting details: sentences 2–6
2. Main idea: sentence 2
   Supporting details: 1 and 3–6
3. *Sample answer:* World peace is the primary goal of the United Nations. All countries should be interested in achieving that goal.

Skill Practice, page 163
1. **A.** The main idea is that the UN is an international organization. All the details emphasize this idea.
2. **B.** Economic organizations help stabilize economies. They also provide a way for countries to settle economic disputes peacefully.
3. **A.** The Security Council investigates disagreements that threaten world peace. Member nations agree to follow its decisions (though that does not always happen).
4. **B.** NATO is a military alliance formed after World War II. Its goal was to prevent aggression from the Soviet Union.

Writing Practice. page 163
Think about the effect of having two world wars within 30 years.

Sample Response
At the end of World War I, Americans felt they had helped their European allies. Then they just wanted to return to isolationist policies. However, the Great Depression proved that the economy was global. By the end of World War II, it was clear that the United States had become the leading military power in the world. Americans realized that if there was any hope of preventing future wars, the United States needed to be part of that effort.

Lesson 4.3

Think about Social Studies, page 166
1. The president cannot declare war. Only Congress has this power.
2. *Sample answer:* No, this is not a good way to choose qualified people. Ambassadors should be chosen on the basis of their diplomatic skill and their knowledge of the country they will serve. Government jobs should not go to friends.

Think about Social Studies, page 167
1. The president is the commander in chief of the armed forces, which means the president can order military action.
2. An ambassador is a diplomat sent to another country to conduct international relations.
3. The secretary of state heads the US State Department and plays a role in foreign relations.

Vocabulary Review, page 167
1. authorize; executive agreement
2. negotiate treaties
3. implementing
4. quotas

Skill Review, page 168
1.

International Affairs	Both	Domestic Affairs
involve other countries	political, economic, and social aspects	involve only the US
mainly at national level	important in any presidential administration	affect all levels of government
	the subject of laws	

2. *Sample answer:* If the government of a country is taken over by a dictator, the United States would probably not recognize the new government as a legal government. When a country is not recognized, trade agreements and other treaties are no longer in effect.

Skill Practice, page 169
1. **C.** An ambassador's job is to represent the United States in other countries.
2. **B.** Once an international treaty is signed by the president, it must be ratified by the Senate before it becomes law in the United States.
3. **D.** A treaty is more likely to affect foreign policy for many years because future presidents are required to uphold treaties. An executive agreement does not have to be upheld by future presidents.
4. **D.** The Constitution makes the president commander in chief of the armed forces. It gives Congress the power to declare war.

Answer Key

Skill Practice, page 169

You have probably heard both of these terms used on news broadcasts. Be sure you know the difference.

Sample Response

Both politicians and diplomats are involved in government. A politician is elected to public office; in contrast, a diplomat is appointed. For example, the president (who is voted into office) is a politician, while the secretary of state (who is appointed by the president) is a diplomat. Both the president and the secretary of state may discuss issues and negotiate with foreign leaders.

Lesson 4.4

Think about Social Studies, page 171

1. The European Union formed to promote free trade among the member nations. It began in 1957 as the European Common Market.

2. *Sample answer:* Using the euro makes trade between countries more efficient because the countries use the same currency. It also makes traveling in Europe simpler.

Vocabulary Review, page 174

1. fossil fuels
2. terrorism
3. global culture
4. Ethnic cleansing

Skill Review, page 174

1. **B.** Of the options, only GPS is a technology product developed in the twenty-first century.

2. A relevant source provides current information and pertains to the topic.

3. It is reasonable to predict that eliminating tariffs on goods would result in lower prices on those goods, since there is no longer a tax that will be passed on to the buyer.

4. *Since prices will go down, people will buy more goods.* Therefore, the amount of goods exported would probably increase.

Skill Practice, page 175

1. **B.** There are more cell phone subscribers per 100 people than telephones per 100 people in each country shown in the chart.

2. **D.** Germany has 4 infant deaths per 1,000 births and Italy has 3, while the United States has 6 infant deaths per 1,000 births.

3. **C.** Angola has a fertility rate of 6 children per woman. This is the highest rate of any of the countries listed.

Writing Practice, page 175

As you think about your response, consider how your use of technology has changed in recent years.

Sample Response

Some developing countries, like Angola and Bangladesh, have very few telephones (landlines). However, more than half of the people in Angola and Bangladesh now have cell phones. This is happening all over the world, and it is changing the developing world very quickly. People in these countries can quickly contact one another. They also can make contacts all around the world. When important events occur, people in the developing world know about them at once. Cell phones are also changing the way foreign aid and international business are conducted.

Chapter Review

Chapter 5 Review, pages 176–178

1. **B** A direct democracy is government in which the people vote directly about issues instead of electing representatives to make laws.

2. **D.** In a direct democracy, each individual has one vote. In a representative democracy, some representatives may represent large groups, while others represent small groups. This is true of the US Senate.

3. **A.** The author argues that new technology, such as the Internet, would make a direct democracy possible.

4. **B.** An executive agreement is an agreement between the US president and another country; it does not need Senate approval. A treaty is also an international agreement, but it does not become law without Senate approval.

5. **B.** International economic organizations help member countries increase trade and enlarge their markets for exported goods.

(Review cont.)

6. **D.** Globalization has increased communication around the world. As a result, many cultures are adopting the customs of other cultures.

7. **B.** Biofuels (coal, oil, and natural gas) are causing pollution and promoting global warming. Earth is being harmed by the use of these nonrenewable energy sources. Solar, wind, and water energy sources are better for the environment, but they are not free. Over time, however, they are less costly than biofuels.

8. **D.** Foreign aid is the help given to countries in need is. Foreign aid might include food, medicine, and technology products. It might also include expert workers who can train local staff. Trade agreements are contracts that allow for goods to be traded between two countries.

9. **B.** The League of Nations was formed after World War I. Although President Wilson had proposed it, the United States refused to join it because most Americans did not want to be involved with foreign relations. After World War II, US leaders realized that the US needed to stand behind the UN, the new international peacekeeping organization.

10. **D.** In a constitutional monarchy (like Great Britain), elected representatives make and enforce laws. The monarch's role tends to be mainly ceremonial.

11. **B.** Many of the UN agencies work to assist children in developing countries. One such agency is the UN Children's Fund. The UN does not develop common currencies, prevent communism from spreading, or determine the price of oil.

12. **A.** Both dictators and absolute monarchs have complete power over their people.

13. **C.** NATO was founded after World War II to prevent further aggression from communist Soviet Union. Member nations agree to protect one another.

14. **C.** The president chooses ambassadors, but the Senate must approve these appointments. Diplomats conduct international relations on behalf of the United States.

15. **B.** The EU was formed so trade would be easier between European countries, just as the US states trade freely among themselves. Only European countries can belong to the EU.

Essay Writing Practice

Essay Writing Practice, page 180
Answers will vary. Here are some points to consider.

Persuasive Essay

- Open your essay with a firm opinion statement. For example: *The United States has certain responsibilities toward (name of country you selected)*. In the first paragraph, mention the key ideas you will include in the essay.

- Devote one paragraph to each of your three key ideas. Support your ideas with facts and reasons. Restate your opinion in the concluding paragraph.

- Edit your essay. As you proofread your essay, check for homophones such as *role/roll*, *there/their/they're*, *four/for*, and *to/too/two*. If you are not sure which spelling to use, check a dictionary.

Explanatory Essay

- Open your essay by stating your main idea. For example: *Immigrants from (name of country you selected) bring a variety of cultural ideas when they move to the United States*. Introduce your key ideas in the first paragraph.

- Use one paragraph for each of your three key ideas. Support your ideas with facts. Restate your main idea in the concluding paragraph.

- Edit your essay. As you proofread your essay, check for homophones such as *role/roll*, *there/their/they're*, *four/for*, and *to/too/two*. If you are not sure which spelling to use, check a dictionary.

Answer Key

CHAPTER 5 Economic Foundations

Lesson 5.1

Think about Social Studies, page 186

1. Scarcity is the problem of satisfying unlimited needs and wants with limited resources.
2. In all societies, many people have wanted more than they can have.
3. Scarcity forces people to make choices because we cannot have everything we want.

Vocabulary Review, page 188

1. factors of production
2. scarcity
3. opportunity cost
4. production possibilities curve

Skill Review, pages 188–189

1. *Any three of the following:*
   A. small businesses employ fewer than 500 workers
   B. 99 percent of all US firms are small businesses
   C. small businesses create two-thirds of new jobs
   D. about half of the national output comes from small businesses
2. 450 sandwiches; Point A
3. 150 sandwiches; 300 subs
4. 50 sandwiches; at Point B, Sam would be producing 50 fewer sandwiches than he could produce.
5. 150 subs; at Point C, Sam would be producing 150 fewer subs than than he could produce.

Skill Practice, page 189

1. D. Scarcity exists because people have many wants and needs, but they have limited resources (money and time).
2. B. Production possibility curves show the number of items a supplier can produce when the supplier is making more of one item.

Writing Practice, page 189

Consider cost, time, and profit when you make your suggestion to Sam.

Sample Response

Dear Sam:

It's time to make a final decision about how much we produce each day. The deli has a long line of customers every day, and they all want a tasty lunch. I've looked at our production possibilities, and I think we should make 300 sandwiches and 200 subs every day. This is the greatest number of items we can produce, so it would allow us to satisfy the greatest number of people each day.

Sincerely,

Anna

Lesson 5.2

Think about Social Studies, page 191

1. D.
2. B.
3. A.
4. C.

Think about Social Studies, page 193

1. A demand curve generally slopes downward because the price of a product decreases as the quantity demanded increases.
2. A supply curve generally slopes upward because as the price of a product increases, the quantity a producer is willing to supply increases as well.
3. A demand curve expresses the viewpoint of a buyer because it tells the price that the consumer is willing to pay. A supply curve expresses the viewpoint of a producer (or seller) because it tells how much of an item the producer is willing to sell.

Vocabulary Review, page 194

1. market equilibrium
2. supply; demand
3. money; market

Skill Review, page 195

1. The author implies that the government is not doing enough to be sure that everyone in the United States gets an adequate education. The author argues that a lack of education is one of the causes of poverty.
2. *Sample answer:* If the government does not improve educational standards, too many people will continue to earn low incomes.
3. *Sample answer:* Poverty cannot be eliminated completely by education, but a better education will improve the lives of many people.

(Lesson 5.2 cont.)

Skill Practice, page 195
1. **B.** The market equilibrium of a product represents the point where the price and the supply of the product are balanced.
2. **C.** The law of demand states that when the price of a product decreases, the quantity demanded increases.

Writing Practice, page 195
Think about the last time you shopped at a sale.

Sample Response
I shop for sale prices by watching the websites of my favorite stores and waiting for items I like to be marked down. If I'm lucky, I can get a good deal. If I'm not lucky, the item I want will sell out before it hits the price I'm willing to pay. I think the store owners offer low prices to get rid of old merchandise and make way for new things. They may also want to get back as much money as they can at the end of a season.

Lesson 5.3

Think about Social Studies, page 198
1. Laissez-faire capitalism is a theory that says the economy will take care of itself and the government should not intervene.
2. The New Deal ended laissez-faire capitalism in the United States. During the Great Depression of the 1930s, the government adopted many programs to create jobs, assist the needy, regulate businesses, and protect workers.

Vocabulary Review, page 200
1. public goods
2. tax
3. limited government
4. Transfer payments
5. recession

Skill Review, page 201
1. *Sample answer:* The evidence describes some of the effects of the Depression. But since President Hoover took office just seven months before the crash, it is unlikely that he was the cause of the crash.
2. Government jobs will directly benefit the people who are employed. In addition, work that is needed (like building roads) will get done.
3. FDR says that it is not acceptable to simply talk about solving the economic problem. Action is needed.

Skill Practice, page 201
1. **A.** The Great Depression forced the government to help solve the economic problems of the nation.
2. **D.** The Securities and Exchange Commission is a government agency that protects investors from investment fraud.

Writing Practice, page 201
Use facts to convince readers to agree with your opinion.

Sample Response
December 18—FHA Loans
Housing in my area is expensive. I wanted to buy a house, but I couldn't make a 10% down payment. Lucky for me, I qualified for an FHA loan. With this type of loan, I only had to have a 3.5% down payment. The bank helped me figure out how much I could afford to pay every month for my mortgage and other fees. Then I knew what my price range was. Without an FHA loan, I would never have been able to buy my own place.

Lesson 5.4

Think about Social Studies, page 203
1. **D.**
2. **C.**
3. **A.**
4. **B.**

Vocabulary Review, page 206
1. credit union
2. fiat money
3. commercial bank
4. Federal Reserve System
5. savings institution
6. money supply

Skill Review, pages 206–207
1. Facts: 2, 3, 4, 5; Opinions: 1, 6, 7
2. Facts: 1, 2, 3, 4; Opinions: 5, 6, 7
3. NA
4. NA
5. A

Skill Practice, page 207
1. **B.** Store of value means that money keeps its worth over time.
2. **D.** Commercial banks lend money to businesses.
3. **A.** The FDIC insures money in savings accounts.

Answer Key

Writing Practice, page 207

You may want to read the web pages of a commerical bank and a credit union before writing your essay.

Sample Response

Banks and credit unions provide similar services to customers. A commercial bank is operated for profit; its goal is to make money for its owners and investors. A credit union is owned by its members; it is not designed to earn profits. Both institutions offer loans to individuals. Banks also offer loans to businesses.

I would like to do my banking at a credit union. The savings interest may be higher, and the loan interest lower. This is because no bank owner is making a big profit. I might be giving up some convenience because my local credit union does not have branch offices, but I would rather stick with an institution that looks out for the people it serves.

Lesson 5.5

Think about Social Studies, page 210

Monopoly	Competition
Pricing: set by the seller	Pricing: a result of supply and demand; both buyer and seller affect price
Barriers to entry: high	Barriers to entry: low
Number of suppliers: one or very few	Number of suppliers: many

Think about Social Studies, page 211

1. AT&T developed cables that went under the ocean so there could be telephone calls between Europe and the United States. It launched a communications satellite to up-date telephone service.

2. *Sample answer:* Today telephone companies have a lot of competition. They are using satellites and cables to provide service. They constantly call and e-mail customers to find out what customers want.

Vocabulary Review, page 212

1. innovation
2. demand
3. market structure
4. competition
5. monopoly
6. barrier to entry

Skill Review, pages 212–213

1. **D.** Monopoly and competition are opposites. In a monopoly, there is one seller, and prices are set by that seller. Competition involves many sellers. Prices are set by the interaction between buyer and seller. Monopolies do not have to innovate because they do not compete for customers.

2. **C.** When there is great demand for a product, sellers can raise the price and customers still buy the product. If fewer customers wanted a product, sellers might lower the price to attract customers.

3. **B.** The owner of a patent has the sole right to make a product. This prevents other companies from producing and selling that product.

4. *Sample answer:* I would like to provide a laundry service that includes pick-up and drop-off for a fee. Many people in my community have no time during the week to do their laundry. The local laundromat washes laundry, but you have to drop off the clothes and pick them up. My service would be better because I would pick up and drop off the laundry at times convenient for the customers.

Skill Practice, page 213

1. The cartoon refers to the creation of small regional phone companies after the breakup of AT&T in 1984.

2. "Competitive market" refers to a market structure based on competition. Previously AT&T had no competition within a region, so it had little reason to improve its customer service.

Writing Practice, page 213

Is there only one place to buy a particular product in your town or neighborhood? That is a monopoly.

Sample Response

The Tex-Mex Pizza Company in my neighborhood is the only pizza parlor that delivers free. I don't really like the spicy taste of their sauce, but I end up ordering their pizza anyway out of convenience. I would be happy if other pizza shops would offer free delivery, because then customers would have more choices. If there was competition, local pizza parlors might even offer coupons or specials—and that would save customers money.

Lesson 5.6

Think about Social Studies, page 216
Sample answers:

1. Recognizing workers' efforts, involving workers in developing company policies, and rewarding workers can all raise employee morale. I think the most important factor is rewarding workers, because earning money is one of the main reasons people work.

2. Morale is higher in a company that provides positive incentives for workers.

Vocabulary Review, page 216
1. C.
2. B.
3. E.
4. F.
5. D.
6. A.

Skill Review, page 217
1. high
2. high
3. high
4. low
5. low
6. high

Skill Practice, page 217
Sample answers:

1. Positive effect: reducing the cost of labor increased profits. Negative effect: workers were laid off and morale fell.

2. The new director of production can name an employee of the month. The director can ask employees to set their own job goals so they feel a sense of accomplishment. The director can also give gift certificates to workers who meet their goals.

3. The new director of marketing can create an ad demonstrating the usefulness of widgets. The ad could show how widgets help people who have trouble using their hands, such as people with arthritis.

Writing Practice, page 217
Employees often have suggestions for how to improve a business. Sometimes employees are rewarded for their suggestions.

Sample Response

I think we could improve customer service at Quick Stop if we had more training on how to bag groceries. We are wasting time and using too many plastic bags. We could improve the appearance of the shop by replacing the old mat at the front door. All of us would be happier working in a place that looked cleaner and neater. Finally, I think we could improve our profits if we found a vendor who would give us a better price for bakery goods. We are paying too much for some of the food we sell. If we pay less to vendors, we will have bigger profits.

Lesson 5.7

Think about Social Studies, page 220
Sample answer: I bought gas for my car. The gasoline came from oil that was drilled in Texas. A company refined the oil into gasoline. Another company shipped the gasoline to the gas station. The gas station was built by a construction company. The gas station bought the gas and hired employees. I paid for the gas with a credit card that was issued by a bank.

Vocabulary Review, page 221
1. G.
2. F.
3. D.
4. E.
5. A.
6. B.
7. C.

Skill Review, page 222
1. goods
2. service
3. goods
4. service
5. service
6. goods
7. service
8. goods
9. C. A service is an action performed for someone else. A shoeshine is an action. The other choices are goods, or objects.

Answer Key

10. **D.** At a laundromat, laundry is washed with laundry soap in washing machines that use electricity and water. Customers use laundry carts to carry laundry from washing machines to dryers. Therefore, all these elements are input for the laundromat.

11. *Sample answer:* An economic transaction is the process of doing business with someone. I made an economic transaction today when I paid my bus fare.

Skill Practice, page 223

1. *Sample answer:* The three owners should specialize and divide the labor. It is not efficient to have each person doing all three tasks. One person should take the orders and pass them to the second person. That person should make the sandwiches. The third person should ring up sales. All three of them will become more skilled (and faster) at their jobs when they do not keep switching tasks. If business improves, the owners may need to take on a fourth person to help make sandwiches.

2. **C.** Productivity is achieving the maximum output with the minimum input. Reaching this goal requires being efficient.

3. **D.** The manufacturer makes the object, and the buyer purchases it from the seller. The economic transaction could not take place without all these people.

Writing Practice, page 223

Even small tasks done by a team of friends can be done more efficiently when workers specialize.

Sample Response

Division of labor is the separation of tasks among various workers. Specialization occurs when individual workers do individual tasks. At a large retail store, some workers stock shelves, others help customers find items, and still others work as cashiers.

Lesson 5.8

Think about Social Studies, page 226

1. fight inflation
2. help economy grow
3. fight inflation
4. help economy grow

Vocabulary Review, page 228

1. G.
2. C.
3. B.
4. F.
5. A.
6. D.
7. E.

Skill Review, page 228

Sample answers:

1. Paul A. Volcker, chair of the board of governors of the Federal Reserve System from 1979 to 1987

2. I used these websites:
   www.ny.frb.org/aboutthefed/PVolckerbio.html
   http://www.whitehouse.gov/administration/eop
       /perab/members/volcker
   http://www.stlouisfed.org/publications/re
       /articles/?id=375.

3. Volker born 1927
   worked in US federal government for about 30 years
   two terms as chair of Fed from 1979–1987
   fought inflation that was 14 percent by 1980
   controlled money supply, making credit expensive
   brought US financial system back from near collapse

4. Paul A. Volcker, who was born in 1927, worked for the federal government for nearly 30 years. He served as chair of the board of governors of the Federal Reserve System from 1979 to 1987. Volcker fought inflation that had reached 14 percent by 1980. By making it very expensive to borrow money, Volcker helped put the US financial system back in order.

Skill Practice, page 229

1. **A.** The federal government may raise interest rates to keep the economy from growing too rapidly. The other statements are all opposite of what the federal government would do.

2. **B.** The national debt is money owed by the federal government. If less tax is collected, the federal government would need to borrow money to pay its expenses, so the national debt would be increased. If the government spent less money (federal expenditures and jobless benefits), it could pay down its debt.

3. **D.** All of these activities would increase the money that individuals and businesses have to spend. This would help the economy grow.

(Lesson 5.8 cont.)

4. **A.** The federal government collects less tax (revenue) when economic activity is decreasing. To increase economic activity, the Fed might increase the money supply. The Fed is an independent agency; the president cannot tell it what to do.

Writing Practice, page 229
Review the responsibilities of the Fed before writing your essay.

Sample Response
To help a weak economy, I would lower interest rates. This would help people who want to borrow money for big purchases, such as a car or a home. When it is easier to borrow money, people spend more money. I think this would be better than cutting taxes or increasing federal spending—which would add to the national debt.

Lesson 5.9

Think about Social Studies page 232

	Checking Accounts	Saving Accounts
Accounts located at a bank	✓	✓
Bank charges fees	✓	
Use account for paying monthly bills	✓	
Can withdraw money to pay for major purchases	✓	✓
Bank pays interest		✓
Money in account belongs to you	✓	✓

Vocabulary Review, page 234
1. D.
2. A.
3. C.
4. E.
5. B.

Skill Review, page 234
Sample answer: A credit report that gives incorrect information might mean that I would not get a loan. If an identity thief has been using my Social Security number, I might have many unpaid bills listed on my record. If my record shows unpaid bills, an employer might not hire me because I would look like an irresponsible person.

Skill Practice, page 235
1. **C.** Banks are private businesses whose goal is to make money through the fees they charge.
2. **B.** Commercial banks and credit unions both offer similar bank accounts and services. Credit unions, however, are owned by their members.
3. **A.** Checking accounts are used for paying bills and making other payments. Money in savings accounts is often used to make major purchases. Credit cards are not usually used to pay monthly bills. Your credit report is information about how well you pay bills; it is not a type of bank account.
4. **C.** Banks will charge higher interest rates to people who have not been responsible about paying bills on time.

Writing Practice, page 235
If you do not have a credit card, write about the experiences of a friend or family member.

Sample Response
My history of using credit cards has had its ups and downs. When I got my first credit card, I bought a lot of items that I didn't really need and couldn't afford. I was paying the minimum amount each month, and the interest almost made me broke. After a year, I canceled my card, but it took me a couple more years to pay off my debt. Recently I managed to qualify for another credit card. I use it very carefully. I don't want to get into financial trouble by overspending again.

Answer Key

Chapter Review

Chapter 5 Review, pages 236–239

1. **B.** The passage states that businesspeople are motivated to produce goods that will make them money; in other words, businesspeople usually act in their own interest.

2. **A.** The self-interest of the butcher, brewer, and baker refers to their interest in making a profit. There is no evidence that they are interested in increasing morale or productivity. The passage does not refer to market equilibrium.

3. **D.** The US economy began to recover when new jobs were created by Congress and the president.

4. **C.** "FDR Plans Job Creation Program to Save the Economy" would best fit the information shown in the diagram.

5. **C.** An economy is the organized way in which goods and services are produced, distributed, sold, and used.

6. **B.** *Market* means "the buying and selling of goods." A market is anywhere buyers and sellers do business.

7. **D.** When supply of a good is low, the price for the good may increase. This illustrates the law of supply.

8. **A.** The Federal Reserve can increase the money supply to help the economy grow.

9. **A.** Taxes are the way the government gets money to pay for government services.

10. **B.** Fiat money is money that has value because the government says that it has value. The United States uses fiat money.

11. **D.** In a monopoly, one seller dominates the market for a particular good or service. Often that seller uses barriers to entry, such as patents, to keep potential competitors from entering the market. Competition is the opposite—many businesses provide similar products. To attract customers, these businesses must offer lower prices, good service, and innovations.

12. **A.** One way companies can raise their profit is to lower their production costs. Often the factors of production cost less in other countries. For example, land and buildings may be less expensive. People may work for lower wages and demand fewer benefits.

13. **A.** One way companies try to increase employee morale is by providing the chance to learn new job skills. Employees with a high morale are more productive, miss fewer days of work, put extra time and effort into their work, and tend not to change jobs. This increases productivity and saves the company money.

14. **D.** Having too much money in circulation can lead to inflation, so the government will reduce the amount of money in circulation in order to fight inflation. Another factor that can increase inflation is low interest rates. Therefore, raising interest rates is also a way of fighting inflation.

15. **D.** The Federal Reserve Bank decides monetary policy and manages the US economy. This is not the job of Congress, the president, or the treasury secretary.

16. **C.** Using a credit card means you do not have to carry cash. This is because you are taking out a loan from the credit card company when you use your credit card. Using a credit card can be expensive if you do not pay your entire bill each month.

17. **B.** The credit report tells a potential lender your credit score. The credit score indicates your bill-paying habits. Having a good credit score will enable you to borrow money and pay a lower interest rate for that money.

18. **D.** When the new company moved to the town, it hired workers. These workers had money to spend in the town. Next, the local government hired workers to build new roads. Then other businesses grew, and soon more workers were hired so there was more demand for services and goods. This network of people and businesses relying on one another is an example of interdependence.

19. **B.** Business expenses are the cost of producing a product or running a store. To determine profit margin, a business subtracts its expenses from the money it receives from customers.

Essay Writing Practice

Essay Writing Practice, pages 240–241
Answers will vary. Here are some points to consider.

Pamphlet on Borrowing Money

- Your essay should open by stating its main idea. For example: *Before you borrow money, you should understand how borrowing works.*

- The paragraphs should be clearly organized. For example, the first paragraph might be about good reasons to borrow money, such as purchasing a home or financing an education. The second paragraph might be about ways in which to borrow, with information about the cost of borrowing from banks, credit unions, and loan companies. The last paragraph might remind readers that the costs of borrowing add up and that borrowing increases the final cost of an item.

- Edit your essay. As you proofread your essay, make sure you have begun every new sentence with a capital letter. Check, too, that you have indented the first line of each new paragraph.

Pamphlet on Using Credit Cards

- Your essay should open by stating its main idea. For example: *A credit card can be convenient and useful if you use it responsibly.*

- The paragraphs should be clearly organized. For example, the first paragraph could be about the importance of using credit cards responsibly and ways to keep your credit card information safe. The second paragraph might tell how to make payments, describe interest rates and minimum monthly payments, and compare debit cards and credit cards. The last paragraph might be about the final cost of items bought on credit.

- Edit your essay. As you proofread your essay, make sure you have begun every new sentence with a capital letter. Check, too, that you have indented the first line of each new paragraph.

Answer Key

CHAPTER 6 Economic Events in History

Lesson 6.1

Think about Social Studies, page 245
Canada: $1,406,300,000,000 (This is about $1.4 trillion.)
Egypt: $487,800,000,000 (This is about $500 billion.)
Japan: $4,459,000,000,000 (This is about $4.5 trillion.)

Vocabulary Review, page 247
1. I.
2. H.
3. G.
4. E.
5. C.
6. B.
7. F.
8. A.
9. D.

Skill Review, page 248
1. It was hoped that the stimulus would lead to a period of expansion. With more people working, more money would be spent and the economy would grow.
2. President Obama thought government spending would create jobs and therefore increase employment. This would help the economy.
3. When more people are working, more people pay taxes. This helps the government recover the money it spent.

Skill Practice, page 249
1. A. If all these countries have the same GDP, the GDP per capita would be highest in the country with the smallest population.
2. C. Expansion refers to growth of the GDP. Recessions and depressions are examples of relatively deep troughs in the business cycle.
3. D. People suffered greatly from the economic downturn. In response, President Roosevelt created the New Deal. The New Deal applied the ideas of Keynesian economics.
4. B. The Great Recession was a huge economic downturn, not an economic boom or expansion. The government responded to the recession by providing a stimulus, which is the opposite of laissez faire economics.

Writing Practice, page 249
Look for a program that you are familiar with. There may have been a public works program in your city.

Sample Response
The FDIC (Federal Deposit Insurance Corporation) program, which was set up during the Great Depression, was a huge help to people who had savings in a bank. Many banks failed during the Depression, and people lost all the money they had deposited. The FDIC insured accounts in banks that were members of the Federal Reserve System. Since the FDIC was established, bank customers get their money back if their bank fails. When I set up a savings account, I will make sure my bank is insured by the FDIC.

Lesson 6.2

Think about Social Studies, page 252
1. D. The Populists' goal was for government to exert greater control over monopolies. Populists did not want the government to create more monopolies. Their main goal did not involve unions or Native Americans.
2. A. Workers unionized to reduce their workday and to receive fair wages. They did not feel that they received good pay. They were not concerned with improving industrialization or credit.

Vocabulary Review, page 254
1. industrialization
2. corollary
3. imperialism
4. monopolies

Skill Review, page 254
1. sentence 1
2. sentence 1
3. C. The author states that the United States should show its power through imperialism. The author believes taking control over other countries shows strength, not weakness.
4. A. The theme of this passage is that a country increases its power by establishing colonies.

(Lesson 6.2 cont.)

Skill Practice, page 255

1. **A.** According to the maps, there were two battles in Cuba and one battle in the Philippines.

2. **D.** The arrows on the Caribbean map show that US forces landed in Cuba and then went to Puerto Rico.

Writing Practice, page 255

Think about how a lack of competition would affect you.

Sample Response

It seems like every day there are fewer gas stations here in town. One by one, the stations are closing or being bought out by Gas Guzzle. Soon there will be only one gas station in town. Gas Guzzle already has higher prices than most of the other stations. Once there is no competition, Gas Guzzle will have no reason to keep its prices down. People will have no choice but to pay whatever Gas Guzzle demands. The business will profit, but the people will suffer.

Lesson 6.3

Think about Social Studies, page 259

Scientific Revolution—theory
Industrial Revolution—steam engine
Transportation Revolution—locomotive
Digital Revolution—transistor

Vocabulary Review, page 260

1. **E.**
2. **B.**
3. **G.**
4. **H.**
5. **A.**
6. **F.**
7. **C.**
8. **D.**

Skill Review, page 260

1. (4) Digital Revolution
   (2) Industrial Revolution
   (3) Transportation Revolution
   (1) Scientific Revolution

2. **D.** Early scientists such as Galileo and Kepler used experimentation and observation to develop their theories. During the other revolutions, observation and experimentation have also been used, but these methods were first used during the Scientific Revolution.

3. Both Johannes Kepler and Nicolaus Copernicus believed that Earth and the other planets orbited the Sun. Copernicus's theory was that the planets followed circular orbits. Kepler's theory was that the orbits were oval. Kepler used Brahe's measurements to calculate the planets' paths.

Skill Practice, page 261

1. **B** The Scientific Revolution was the birth of science, which is a method of learning. Astronomy is one field of science; the Scientific Revolution did not create astronomy. Many new machines were developed to change how industry operates. These were the effects of the Scientific Revolution.

2. **D.** The Industrial Revolution moved production from homes in the country to factories in the city. Goods were now made by machines instead of by hand. Producing goods with powered machinery meant many more goods were produced.

3. **B.** More goods were available because of the factories that were built during the Industrial Revolution. Rural population decreased because people moved to towns where there were factory jobs. Factories need iron and steel, so mining activity increased.

4. **D.** The Internet relies on computers, which are digital devices. The other items were made long before the Digital Revolution.

Writing Practice, page 261

All of these revolutions affect you every day. Choose one to write about.

Sample Response

I think the Scientific Revolution was the most important because it led to the other revolutions. We would not have the inventions of the Industrial Revolution or the Transportation Revolution or the Digital Revolution without the knowledge provided by science.

Chapter Review

Chapter 6 Review, pages 262–264

1. **B.** Having a monopoly allowed business owners to charge what they wanted, limit consumer choice, and keep production costs as low as possible.

2. **D.** The union workers' signs say workers cannot live on $15 per week. Nothing in the photo mentions health benefits. The photographer seems to be supportive of the demands.

3. **A.** The Industrial Revolution began in the textile mills of Britain with the invention of spinning and weaving machines. These machines were powered first by water and later by steam.

Answer Key

4. **B.** In the 1800s, canals, steamships, and especially railroads used state-of-the-art technology and engineering to form a transcontinental transportation system. This system made it possible to move settlers and goods across the country more quickly and safely than ever before.

5. **B.** The economy grows (booms) and shrinks (busts); business does well, and then it slows down. This repetition is known as the *business cycle*.

6. **C.** Keynes believed that government spending could stimulate economic activity and that this increased activity could help end a depression or recession. Both Roosevelt (during the Great Depression) and Obama (during the Great Recession) used government policies such as unemployment benefits and job-creation programs to stimulate the economy.

7. **D.** After losing the Spanish-American War, Spain surrendered the Philippines and Cuba to the United States. Cuba later became independent, but the United States had a great deal of influence there. In the meantime, Hay's Open Door policy helped prevent any one foreign power from having too many advantages from occupying territory in China. The Spanish-American War did not involve Mexico.

8. **B.** Keynes was a British economist who believed that the government should help a struggling economy by adding money to the economy. This could be done, for example, by supporting public works projects or lowering taxes.

9. **B.** Trade unions were first organized to defend the rights of workers against business owners who wanted to keep the majority of profits for themselves. Unions often fight for better wages, benefits, and training.

10. **C.** The Populists supported the common people against large monopolies.

11. **C.** The Transportation Revolution saw the development of steamships and the railroad. Roads and canals were built. These changes improved the possibilities of worldwide shipping.

Essay Writing Practice

Essay Writing Practice, pages 266–267
Answers will vary. Here are some points to consider.

Summary of Major Events in US Economic History

- Your summary should begin by restating the main idea of Lesson 6.1 in your own words. Use key details in the lesson to support the main idea.
- Your paragraphs should describe major events in the order in which they occurred.
- Edit your summary. As you proofread your summary, refer to the lesson or look in the glossary to make sure you have correctly spelled the economics terms that you use.

Summary of the Effects of Industrialization and Scientific Innovations on the US Economy

- Your summary should begin by restating the main ideas of Lessons 6.2 and 6.3 in your own words. Use key details in the lessons to support the main ideas.
- Be sure that cause-and-effect relationships are clear in the body of your summary. Use words such as *if*, *then*, *because*, *since*, *therefore*, and *so* to show how one action caused another action.
- Edit your summary. As you proofread your summary, refer to the lessons or look in the glossary to make sure you have correctly spelled the economics terms that you use.

CHAPTER 7 Economics in the Twenty-first Century

Lesson 7.1

Think about Social Studies, page 271
Sample answers:

1. Structural unemployment: an auto assembly-line worker loses her job when robots replace workers at the plant

2. Frictional unemployment: an accountant leaves his job to look for a new job with better pay and more responsibility

3. Cyclical unemployment: a waiter at a local restaurant loses his job during an economic downturn

4. Seasonal unemployment: a home builder loses her job during the cold winter months when construction declines

Vocabulary Review, page 273

1. deflation
2. business cycle
3. full employment
4. inflation

Skill Review, page 273

1. Entrepreneurship is the skill of someone who takes the risk of starting a new business.

2. *Status quo* means keeping things the way they are. In the passage, the opposites of status quo are *innovation*, *progress*, and *positive change*.

Skill Practice, page 273

1. **B.** The long-term trend for the US economy has been one of growth.

2. **A.** Full employment is defined as the point when the unemployment rate is 5 percent.

Writing Practice, page 273
Think about a small business owner you know or a business you would like to own in the future.

Sample Response
A new business was started in my town by Moira Smalls. She opened a boutique that sells handmade candy and pastries. Before she opened her shop, many businesses on Main Street were closing. People had stopped shopping there, and they got in the habit of driving to the mall in the next town. Ms. Smalls leased an empty storefront and opened her business. With hard work and patience, the business began to grow. Her shop was featured in a national magazine. More people began visiting her shop. Other businesses on Main Street benefited from the increased foot traffic. Now Main Street is doing better, and the local economy is improving.

Lesson 7.2

Think about Social Studies, page 276
Sample answer: International organizations might be controversial because they set economic requirements for countries rather than letting the countries set their own goals. People in developing countries might question whether international organizations are just helping rich countries at the expense of poor countries.

Vocabulary Review, page 277

1. Foreign direct investment
2. Globalization
3. stabilize

Skill Review, page 277

1. **A.** The assumption is that all people, or "peoples of the world," will share the wealth gained from free trade.

Skill Practice, page 277

1. **B.** The main purpose of the World Bank is to provide grants and low-interest loans to businesses in developing countries.

2. **D.** Opponents of globalization argue that the stockholders of major international companies have the most to gain from global trade. Globalization may bring jobs to developing countries, but often they are not good jobs.

Skill Practice, page 277
Look at some of your recent purchases to see where they were made.

Sample Response
Globalization could be beneficial to everyone, but right now, everyone does not gain an equal share. The people who produce the goods or services that are shipped to developed countries usually do not see much profit from their labor. It is the investment companies and their stockholders who are gaining the most from globalization.

Answer Key

Chapter Review

Chapter 7 Review, pages 278–281

1. **D.** An expansion in the economy means the economy is getting stronger.

2. **B.** When workers are laid off, there is less demand for the product and less spending in the economy. This is a contraction.

3. **C.** Economic indicators help economists understand the state of the economy.

4. **C.** The building of businesses in foreign nations is an example of foreign direct investment.

5. **B.** Both the World Bank and the International Monetary Fund offer loans and other financial support to developing countries.

6. **D.** If prices fall, companies will cut back on their production, which will result in the layoff of workers.

7. **A.** After World War II, the world's leading economies took steps toward free trade. They wanted to increase their markets.

8. **B.** The WTO encourages trade among countries. This improves the economies of all countries.

9. **D.** Import taxes are a barrier to international trade. They cause prices to rise, which means fewer goods are sold.

10. **C.** Full employment happens when the unemployment rate is at or below 5%. This occurred in 2006 and 2007.

11. **A.** Cyclical unemployment is the result of the boom-to-bust variations in the nation's business cycle. Because the graph shows the unemployment rate rising drastically in a short time, this explanation makes the most sense.

12. **C.** Structural unemployment happens when a business changes the way it is organized. This occurs, for example, when jobs are outsourced to other countries. Choice A describes seasonal unemployment. Choice B describes cyclical unemployment. Choice D describes frictional unemployment.

13. **D.** When low-skilled jobs are moved to developing countries, there are fewer opportunities in the home country for new workers who lack skills or language proficiency.

Essay Writing Practice

Essay Writing Practice, page 282
Answers will vary. Here are some points to consider.

Analysis of the Effects of Price Stability

- Open your essay with a statement about inflation and deflation. For example: *Stable prices are an important factor in a stable US economy.*

- Your paragraphs should be clearly organized. For example, one paragraph might analyze the effects of inflation on the US economy and on American families. Another paragraph might analyze the effects of deflation on the economy and on families.

- Edit your essay. As you proofread your essay, make sure that subjects and verbs agree in number. Examples: *Price stability affects the health of the economy. Prices rise during times of inflation.*

Analysis of Global Markets

- Open your essay by making a statement that presents your main idea. For example: *Being part of the global market has both advantages and disadvantages for US car companies.*

- Your paragraphs should be clearly organized. For example, one paragraph might analyze the benefits to the US economy of sharing the global market. Another paragraph might analyze the disadvantages that US carmakers have in competing with foreign manufacturers.

- Edit your essay. As you proofread your essay, make sure that subjects and verbs agree in number. Examples: *A carmaker hires thousands of workers. US carmakers compete with foreign car manufacturers.*

CHAPTER 8 Geography and People

Lesson 8.1

Think about Social Studies, page 288

access to the sea and fresh water
flat land for farming
building materials

Think about Social Studies, page 289

Population growth made the cultivation of more farm land necessary. The invention of the steel plow made it easier to till the soil. As more land was cleared for farming and grazing, the soil on the plains was disturbed. This eventually led to the dust storms of the 1930s.

Vocabulary Review, page 290

1. drought
2. irrigation systems
3. peninsula
4. climate
5. environment
6. adapt

Skill Review, pages 290–291

1. There were 820,669 immigrants from Canada and 10,961,744 immigrants from Europe.

2. There were 150,000 more immigrants from Asia than from Latin America.

3. The number of immigrants from Europe was far greater than the total number of immigrants from all other places. The majority of the current US population is of European heritage. This is because there were so many European immigrants in the 19th century.

4. The black arrows indicate the movement of people away from Dust Bowl areas in the 1930s.

5. The Dust Bowl migrants ended up in Minnesota, Colorado, New Mexico, Arizona, and California. Some also moved to parts of North Dakota, Nebraska, Kansas, Oklahoma, and Texas that were not as affected by the drought.

6. According to the map, four states lost population during this period: South Dakota, Nebraska, Kansas, and Oklahoma.

Skill Practice, page 291

1. **D.** The Native American population living in the Southwest abandoned their villages because they needed to live where it was easier to grow food.

2. **B.** Creating land to increase the size of Boston is an example of people changing the geography of a place. All the other choices are examples of geography affecting people.

Writing Practice, page 291

You may want to do research to find photographs of the Dust Bowl and the migrants who left that area.

Sample Response

In the 1930s, farming practices and weather combined to create giant dust storms in the Great Plains. Much of the fertile topsoil in the region blew away. Where the loss of topsoil was severe, people had to leave their farms because they could no longer grow crops. Some traveled east to look for work in large cities. For example, people in the Dakotas moved to Minneapolis, and people in western Texas moved to Dallas and Houston. Others traveled west, to cities like Santa Fe and Albuquerque. Some went to California, where many of the migrants tried to find work in agriculture.

Lesson 8.2

Think about Social Studies, page 294

1. A renewable resource (like wind) is continually replaced by the environment, while a nonrenewable resource (like oil) takes millions of years to form.

2. An ecosystem is the community of organisms and natural resources in an environment.

Vocabulary Review, page 296

1. greenhouse effect
2. natural resources
3. region
4. global warming
5. ecosystem

Skill Review, pages 296–297

1. The chart shows the average monthly temperature for January, April, July, and October, average annual rainfall, and average annual snowfall for 10 US cities.

2. Fairbanks, Alaska, has the most snow, so it would be the best place to ski.

3. North America and Asia

4. Africa has the lowest carbon dioxide emissions. Africans are burning less fossil fuels. There are fewer factories and automobiles in Africa than on other continents.

Answer Key

Skill Practice, page 297
1. **C.** Cold and snowy climate is found far from the equator and at high elevations.
2. **A.** Ecosystems contain an area's natural resources. Regions may deal with people and their cultures.

Writing Practice, page 297
Use maps, tables, and reference texts to find the information you need.

Sample Response
The Pacific Northwest lies between the Pacific Ocean and the Rocky Mountains. This mountainous region includes Oregon and Washington and parts of Idaho, Montana, California, and Alaska. The Cascades, the Olympic Mountains, the Columbia Mountains, and the Coastal Range are here. These mountains include active volcanoes, like Mt. St. Helens. The majority of the rain in the Pacific Northwest falls from autumn to early spring. The Cascades keep much of the rain from reaching inland, so the inland area is drier and has greater temperature extremes. The natural resources include timber from the many forests, fish (especially salmon), and plentiful food for cattle and other grazing animals.

Lesson 8.3

Think about Social Studies, page 299
1. **B.**   3. **C.**
2. **D.**   4. **A.**

Vocabulary Review, page 301
1. fertility rate
2. migration
3. mortality rates
4. population
5. demography

Skill Review, pages 302–303
1. from the years following World War I to the 1960s
2. about 6 million
3. the Great Migration
4. the New Great Migration, which is a movement of African Americans from Northern cities to Southern cities

Sample answer: I know that many people are moving to big cities because I have seen all the new apartment buildings that are being contructed in Chicago. People want to live closer to their jobs in big cities.

Skill Practice, page 303
1. **D.** Migration is the movement of a group of people from one area to another.
2. **C.** Many early American settlers lived in rural areas. As industry developed, people moved to urban areas (big cities). Then they moved to suburbs so they would have more space.
3. **D.** Better health conditions help lower the number of deaths.
4. **C.** Demography is the study of population groups. Knowing that an area has a large number of retired people affects the kind of housing that will be built.

Writing Practice, page 303
This may be a good opportunity to learn about the origins of your family.

Sample Response
My great uncle Ralph grew up in western Texas during the 1930s. He came from a big family, and his parents had a hard time feeding all six kids during the Depression. When he was 15, Ralph enlisted in the army. He had to lie about his age to get in. The army sent him to California and trained him as a mechanic just in time to send him off to fight the Japanese in the Pacific. As a mechanic, he was lucky. He always arrived after the battle was over to take care of the jeeps, trucks, and machines. When World War II ended, Ralph decided to stay in California. Instead of trying to make a living on a dried up Texas farm, he opened a gas station in Beverly Hills, where he was surrounded by movie stars and could go to the beach every Sunday.

Lesson 8.4

Think about Social Studies, page 306
Sample answers:
1. *international border*: division between two countries between El Salvador and Honduras
2. *physical boundary*: natural features that separate areas San Juan River between Nicaragua and Costa Rica
3. *geometric border*: straight-line border some of the border lines between Mexico and Guatemala

Vocabulary Review, page 308
1. **E.**   5. **G.**
2. **D.**   6. **B.**
3. **A.**   7. **C.**
4. **F.**

(Lesson 8.4 cont.)

Skill Review, page 308
Sample answers:

1. I chose the state of Washington. I used these websites:

   http://www.mapsofworld.com/usa/states /washington/

   http://www.nationalatlas.gov/printable/reference .html#Washington

   http://www.freeworldmaps.net/united-states /washington/map.html

2. *Maps of the World* was the most useful website. western borders—Pacific Ocean and three straits geometric borders—46th and 49th parallels north borders with Canada, Idaho, and Oregon

3. **To the north**, Washington borders Canada. Most of that international border is formed by the 49th parallel north. Part of the Washington-Canada border is a natural boundary formed by three waterways: the Haro Strait and the Straits of Georgia and Juan de Fuca. **To the east**, most of the Washington-Idaho border is a straight-line geometric border, although a small portion of the border runs along the Snake River. **To the south**, the Columbia River forms most of the Washington-Oregon border. However, the eastern part of that border is formed by the 46th parallel north. **To the west**, Washington's border is the Pacific Ocean coastline.

Skill Practice, page 309

1. **B.** Boundaries are lines that separate regions. Not all borders are international borders, dividing two countries. Not all borders are determined by physical features such as rivers.

2. **D.** Physical boundaries that form international borders are large geographic features, such as rivers, mountain ranges, and large lakes. A boulder (large stone) would not be big enough to form a physical barrier between regions.

3. **A.** World War II was a conflict that led to drawing some new international boundaries. The two treaties and the Berlin Conference are examples of cooperation, which is the opposite of conflict.

4. **C.** The forces of conflict and cooperation change borders over time. Many borders follow physical features. Some borders, but not all, are straight lines. Unfortunately, many borders are the result of conflicts rather than cooperation.

Writing Practice, page 309
Learning about international borders is a lesson in world history.

Sample Response
Cooperation means "working together." Two countries, like the United States and Britain, can work together to agree on where a border should be. The United States and Britain finalized the US–Canada border by signing the Jay Treaty of 1794 and the Treaty of 1818.

Lesson 8.5

Think about Social Studies, page 311
Sample answers:

1.
	1950	2000
United States	158 million	283 million
Nigeria	30 million	114 million
India	358 million	1,009 million

2. Nigeria grew the fastest. Its population more than tripled from 1950 to 2000.

3. United States about 400 million
   Nigeria about 300 million
   India about 1,500 million

Vocabulary Review, page 312
1. D.
2. G.
3. F.
4. E.
5. C.
6. A.
7. B.

Skill Review, page 313
4 global warming

2 greater demand for goods

3 increased use of fossil fuels

1 population growth and economic development

Skill Practice, page 313

1. **C.** Many countries in Asia are considered to be developing countries. Australia and most of the countries in Europe and North America are developed countries.

2. **D.** Global warming is an effect. It is caused by increased greenhouse gases. Climate change, rising sea levels, and frequent storms are effects of global warming, not causes of it.

Answer Key

3. **D.** The atmosphere is global, so climate change affects all countries.

4. Burning fossil fuels releases the greenhouse gas carbon dioxide, which increases the greenhouse effect.

Writing Practice, page 313

As you think about eco-friendly practices, consider how Earth would be helped if everyone used green methods.

Sample Response

I decided to contact KleenHome, a cleaning service located nearby. The owner said she was happy to talk about her decision to "go green." She said that she had solar panels installed on the building's roof and that the initial costs had been offset somewhat by tax credits and rebates. Plus, she said, the panels generate more electricity than the business uses, so she gets a credit from the electricity company. In addition to using solar power, she said that all the cleaning supplies the company uses are *green* products. I asked to speak to some of the employees, and they told me that their customers all appreciate the use of the green cleaning products. Using green cleaning products has brought new customers who want only eco-friendly products used in their homes.

Lesson 8.6

Think about Social Studies, page 316
Sample answers:

1. I live in California, where the population is very multicultural. About 25 percent of Californians speak Spanish, and about 2 percent speak Chinese. Korean and Tagalog (the language of the Philippines) are each spoken by about 1 percent of the population.

2. Terms from Spanish include *coyote*, *fiesta*, *patio*, and *tortilla*. Some terms derived from French are *deluxe*, *laissez faire*, *menu*, and *souvenir*. Terms from German include *dachshund*, *glitz*, *pretzel*, and *spritz*.

Vocabulary Review, page 318
1. G.
2. F.
3. B.
4. C.
5. D.
6. A.
7. E.

Skill Review, page 318

1. Waterfalls determine where many cities in the eastern United States are located.

2. The writer provides reasons why settlements would be near waterfalls and examples of these settlements.

3. The reasons and examples are good evidence. The writer would have even stronger evidence if a geography or demography expert had been quoted.

Skill Practice, page 319

1. **B.** *Diversity* means "variety" or "assortment." Languages, landforms, and cultural patterns all contribute to the diversity of a region.

2. **B.** *Humid*, which means "damp" or "wet," hints that *humid subtropical* refers to climate.

3. **D.** Geographical diversity influences where people settle, but it is not usually part of a group's culture. Culture includes food, music, and family relationships.

4. **A.** A swamp has little usable land and often has little usable water, so settlers are unlikely to choose to live in a swamp. The other locations offer advantages for a settlement.

Writing Practice, page 319

To understand how much diversity is in your area, think about the variety of students at your school or at your child's school.

Sample Response

I enjoy living in New York. Walking around the city is like touring the countries of the United Nations. In different parts of town, there are large numbers of people from all over Central America and South America, as well as a lot of people from China, Korea, Poland, and Russia. If I want, I can go to a Mexican restaurant for tortillas and salsa at lunch and stop into a Korean restaurant for spicy barbecue at dinnertime. Many store signs are in Chinese, Korean, or Spanish. I think it's fun to try to determine what the shop is selling. Then to go inside to see if I am right.

Answer Key

Chapter Review

Chapter 8 Review, pages 320–322

1. **B.** The graph shows the various energy sources used in the United States in 2011.

2. **D.** Petroleum accounted for 36% of all the energy consumed in the United States in 2011. Petroleum is the largest section in the graph.

3. **C.** Renewable resources made up only about 9 percent of energy sources. All the other sections in the graph are nonrenewable resources. They made up about 90 percent of the resources used.

4. **A.** A river can be used for transport. For example, barges can move goods along a river to an ocean port. From there, those goods can travel by freighter to markets overseas.

5. **B.** The regions of Europe, Australia/Oceania, and North America have the longest life expectancy according to the graph.

6. **C.** The average life expectancies in North America (79) and Europe (77) are very similar. Since the United States is not the only country in North America, the graph does not provide information about US life expectancy.

7. **A.** Humans have had a huge impact on Earth's geography and climate by clearing forests and other vegetation for agriculture and settlement. As the population grows, more land is taken over for cities and large farms.

8. **B.** Commuting by train is the only sustainable activity. Buying a second car and heating with natural gas may contribute to greater use of fossil fuels. Burning leaves releases CO_2 into the atmosphere.

9. **A.** Burning fossil fuels releases extra CO_2 into the atmosphere. This increases the greenhouse effect.

10. **D.** While some borders follow geographical features, many borders are the result of cooperation or conflict between groups of people. These borders keep changing.

11. **C.** This map shows cities and national borders, so it is a political map. If it were a physical map, it would show mountains and deserts. It does not provide weather or population information.

12. **D.** The borders of Egypt are mostly straight lines, or geometric borders. When Europeans colonized Africa, their leaders drew straight lines on a map to separate the colonies.

13. **B.** Early groups often settled along rivers because the rivers provided water for drinking, washing, and irrigating crops. Fish caught in the rivers served as food and as fertilizer.

14. **A.** Since the 12th century, Egypt has been primarily an Arab culture. Although there are still other cultural and linguistic groups in Egypt, most of these groups are small.

Essay Writing Practice

Essay Writing Practice, page 324–325
Essays will vary. Here are some points to consider.

Persuasive Essay

- The first paragraph is your introduction. Open with a firm statement of your opinion. For example: *Going green is necessary so our children will have healthy lives.*

- The three bulleted points are the topics of the three middle paragraphs of your essay. The last paragraph is your conclusion.

- Review your essay. Read it from the point of view of someone you are trying to convince. Would your essay persuade this person to go green?

- Edit your essay. As you proofread your essay, check for singular and plural nouns, particularly those that have irregular plural forms, such as *company/companies.* Also check your use of singular and plural pronouns, both as subjects and as objects, such as *he, she, it/they* and *him, her, it/them.*

Informational Essay

- The first paragraph is your introduction. Open by stating your main idea. For example: *Geography, economics, and history are woven together in my community.*

- Write one paragraph about each of the three key topics: the geography of your community, the economy of your community, and the history of your community. In your last paragraph, explain how these aspects are related.

- Review your essay. Read it from the point of view of someone who does not know your community. Would the information you have presented make sense to this person?

- Edit your essay. As you proofread your essay, check for singular and plural nouns, particularly those that have irregular plural forms, such as *company/companies.* Also check your use of singular and plural pronouns, both as subjects and as objects, such as *he, she, it/they* and *him, her, it/them.*

Glossary

A

abolish (uh BOL ish) to do away with something, especially in reference to slavery

abolitionist (ab uh LISH un ist) a person who believes in ending slavery

absolute (ab soh LOOT) complete, unconditional, and unrestricted

absolute monarchy (ab suh LOOT MAHN ar kee) a form of government in which the king or queen has all the power

accountability (uh KOWNT uh BIL uh tee) responsibility

accountable (uh KOWNT uh buhl) responsible for

account balance (uh KOWNT BAL uns) the amount of money available in an account

adapt (uh DAPT) to adjust

adequate (AD uh kwit) satisfactory or sufficient

adjust (uh JUST) to change

administer (ad MIN uh stur) to manage

administration (ad MIN uh STRAY shun) in US government, the group of people in the executive branch during a president's term

alike (uh LIKE) the same, or close to being the same

alliance (uh LYE unss) a formal agreement establishing an association among nations for a particular reason

amendment (uh MEND munt) a change to a document, such as a change to a constitution

analyze (AN uh LIZE) to break information into parts

annex (AN eks) to add

anointed (uh NOYN ted) picked by divine choosing

antitrust (ANT ih TRUST) antimonopoly, or opposed to a company's having exclusive ownership of a type of product or industry

appropriations (uh PROH pree AY shunz) money set aside for a particular purpose

armistice (AR muh stus) a temporary peace agreement

arsenal (ARS uhn uhl) a place where weapons are stored

Articles of Confederation (AR tih kuhls uv kun FED uh RAY shun) the original agreement between the first 13 states, establishing a weak national government with no executive branch or court system

assemble (uh SEM buhl) to gather

assembly (uh SEM blee) a group

assumption (uh SUMP shun) an idea that is believed to be true but does not have proof

authorization (AW thuh ruh ZAY shun) approval

B

baby boom (BAY bee BOOM) a rapid growth in the birthrate

ballot (BAL ut) a paper, card, or other device that is used to record a voter's selection

barrier to entry (BAIR ee ur too EN tree) a condition that prevents competition

barter (BAR tur) the direct exchange of one product for another product

bias (BYE uss) a belief, preference, or prejudice

bicameral (BYE KAM uh ruhl) a lawmaking body with two parts, or two chambers

Black Codes (BLAK KOHDZ) a set of laws that severely restricted the rights of former slaves

blitzkrieg (BLITS KREEG) "lightning war," or fighting that has great speed and force

bloc (blok) a group of nations that join together, as in the satellite countries of the former Soviet Union

blockade (blah KAYD) an attempt to cut off all communications and supplies to an area

border (BORD ur) a political boundary or separation between two separately governed states or nations

boundary (BOWN duh ree) a border

boycott (BOY kot) the refusal to use a service or product

brinkmanship (BRINK mun SHIP) a political strategy in which two opposing sides push each other to the brink, or edge, of war

business cycle (BIZ nuss SYE kuhl) a repeating pattern of economic activity consisting of an expansion phase and a contraction phase

C

capital (KAP uh tuhl) the money and supplies needed to run a business

capitalism (KAP ut uhl IZ um) an economic system that relies heavily on the private sector (individuals and businesses) to make the majority of economic decisions

carrying capacity (KAIR ree ing kuh PASS ut ee) the number of people that Earth can support

casualties (KAZH uhl teez) deaths and injuries

category (KAT uh GOR ee) a group

cause (kawz) a reason for an action or condition

chart (chart) a visual that organizes information by horizontal rows and vertical columns

charter (CHAR tur) a written code of rules or laws

checking account (CHEK ing uh KOWNT) a bank account that lets the account holder write checks to pay for purchases

checks and balances (cheks and BAL un sez) a system that allows each branch of government to change or override acts of another branch, thus preventing any one branch from gaining too much power

circulation (SUR kyuh LAY shun) passage from one person to another, especially the interchange of money

civil liberty (SIV uhl LIB ur tee) an individual's freedom to act without interference from the government

civil right (SIV uhl RITE) a person's right to full citizenship and equality

civil rights movement (SIV uhl RITES MOOV munt) the movement for equality, especially to guarantee fair treatment of African Americans

Civil War (SIV uhl wor) American war between the North (Union) and the South (Confederacy)

clause (klawz) a section in a legal document

climate (KLYE mut) general weather conditions

climate change (KLYE mut chaynj) the long-term alteration to weather patterns

coalition (koh uh LISH un) a team made up of several groups joined together for a common purpose

Cold War (KOHLD WOR) a political conflict between the United States and the Soviet Union that did not have armed fighting

collective bargaining (kuh LEK tiv BAR gun ing) the process of workers negotiating with their employer

collectively (kuh LEK tiv lee) as a whole

commercial bank (kuh MUR shuhl BANK) a for-profit business that provides financial services to people

communism (KOM yuh NIZ um) an economic system that relies heavily on government ownership and control over businesses

compact (KOM pakt) an agreement

compare (kum PAIR) to find how two or more things are alike

competition (KOM puh TISH un) the effort to attract business by offering the best products, services, or prices; the opposite of a monopoly

conclusion (kun KLOO zhun) a judgment or an interpretation based on reasoning or logic

confederacy (kon FED er uh see) a union, or a group of people joined together for a common purpose; also, another term for the southern states during the American Civil War

conflict (KON flikt) a disagreement or a battle

Congress (KON gruss) the legislative branch of the US government, made up of the Senate and the House of Representatives

consent (kun SENT) agreement

conservative (kun SURV uh tiv) related to a political group that thinks the government should have a limited role in regulating the economy and solving social problems

conserve (kun SURV) to keep things the same or to prevent waste or overuse

constitution (KON stuh TYOO shun) a document defining the basic laws and principles of government for a state or nation

constitutional democracy (kon stuh TYOO shun uhl dih MOK ruh see) a form of government in which the citizens elect representatives whose powers and responsibilities are defined by a constitution

constitutional monarchy (kon stuh TYOO shun uhl MAHN ar kee) a form of government that has both a legislative body elected by the people and a king or queen

containment (kun TAYN munt) a foreign policy that tried to keep communism from spreading

contemporary (kun TEM puh RAIR ee) current; also, happening in the same time period

context (KON tekst) the historical situation in which an event is set; also, the text surrounding a word or phrase

continent (KON tuh nunt) one of the seven large landmasses on Earth

contraction (kun TRAK shun) a shrinking of the economy

contradict (KON truh DIKT) to oppose or conflict with

contrast (kun TRAST) to examine differences between things

convey (kun VAY) to communicate

cooperation (KOH OP uh RAY shun) working together

corollary (KOR uh LAIR ee) a conclusion, or a follow-up

cottage industry (KAH tij IN DUS tree) an industry in which people work to produce goods at home

coup d'etat (KOO day TAH) an overthrow of a government by a small group rather than by a general uprising

credit (KRED ut) the right to take ownership of something with an arrangement to pay for it later

credit score (KRED ut skor) a report of how well an individual pays debts

credit union (KRED ut YOON yun) a non-profit business that makes loans and offers other personal banking services to its members

cultural diffusion (KUHL chur uhl dif YOO zhun) the spread of cultural traits from one part of the world to another

cultural pattern (KUHL chur uhl PAT urn) a collection of cultural traits

cultural region (KUHL chur uhl REE jun) an area of land defined by the kind of people who live there

cultural trait (KUHL chur uhl TRAYT) an aspect of a culture, such as language, religion, customs, behaviors, or art

culture (KUHL chur) the way of life of a society or a human group

currency (KUR un see) money; bills and coins that are used in trade

D

data (DAY tuh) statistics or other information, often organized in a map, chart, or graph

debt (det) money owed

decimate (DESS uh MAYT) to destroy a large percentage of a population

declaration (DEK luh RAY shun) a statement

Declaration of Independence (DEK luh RAY shuhn uv IN duh PEN dunss) the US document establishing the principle that government is based on the agreement of the people who are governed

deficit (DEF uh sut) a shortage

definition (DEF uh NISH un) the exact meaning of a word

deflation (dih FLAY shun) a decrease in the overall price level for goods and services over time

delegate (DEL uh gut) a representative; also, (DEL uh GAYT) to give authority to

demand (dih MAND) the amount of a product people are willing and able to buy at a certain price at a specific time

demand curve (dih MAND KURV) a graph that plots the numbers from a demand schedule, showing how price changes affect the demand for a product

demand schedule (dih MAND SKE juhl) a table showing how price changes affect the demand for a product

demilitarized zone (DEE MIL uh tuh rized ZOHN) an area where no military force can enter

democracy (dih MOK ruh see) a type of government in which the power to rule comes from the people

demography (dih MAHG ruh fee) the study of the size, growth, movement, and distribution of people

demonstration (DEM un STRAY shun) a public protest

denounce (dee NOWNSS) to speak out against something or someone

deplete (dee PLEET) to use up

deposit (dee PAH zit) to put money into an account

depression (dee PRESH un) a severe low point in the economy that lasts a long time

describe (dih SKRIBE) to provide details about a person, place, thing, or event

détente (day TAHNT) an ease in tensions between nations

developed countries (dih VEHL upt KUN trees) nations that are relatively rich and industrialized

developing countries (dih VEHL up ing KUN trees) countries with a relatively low standard of living and little industrial activity

dialogue (DYE uh lawg) a discussion, or a conversation

dictator (DIK TAYT ur) a ruler who has absolute power

dictatorship (dik TAYT ur SHIP) a form of government in which one ruler has complete control over a country

different (DIF urnt) unlike or not similar

Digital Revolution (DIJ it uhl rev uh LOO shun) the period beginning about 1980 when digital computer technology has been growing very quickly, changing the way businesses and the economy are run

diplomacy (duh PLOH muh see) the act of conducting negotiations between nations

diplomatic (DIP luh MAT ik) involved with managing relations between countries

diplomatic recognition (DIP luh MAT ik rek ug NISH un) the formal acceptance of the legal existence of a country

direct democracy (duh REKT de MOK ruh see) a form of government in which citizens vote on policies and laws

direct initiative (duh REKT in ISH ut iv) the right of citizens to draft proposed laws

discrimination (dis KRIM uh NAY shun) unfair treatment

disenfranchise (DIS un FRAN chize) to deprive someone of the right to vote

displace (dis PLAYSS) to move by force

distribute (dis TRIB yut) to spread out

diversity (duh VUR sut ee) variety or differences

diverted (duh VURT ed) directed away from something

divine right (duh VINE RITE) the belief that a monarch's right to rule comes from God

division of labor (duh VIZH un uv LAY bor) the way work is divided among workers

domestic (duh MES tik) within a country

double jeopardy (DUB uhl JEP urd ee) the procedure of putting someone on trial twice for the same offense

downsize (DOWN SIZE) to cut back

draft (draft) the requirement that young men serve in the armed services involuntarily

drought (drowt) a long period without rain

E

economic growth (EK uh NAHM ik GROHTH) an increase in the gross domestic product (GDP) over a significant period of time

economic stimulus (EK uh NAHM ik STIM yoo luss) government spending intended to boost the economy or encourage it to grow

economists (ih KON uh musts) people who study the economy

economy (ih KON uh mee) the production, distribution, and consumption of goods and services

ecosystem (EE koh SISS tum) a community of living things and their environment

effect (uh FEKT) something caused by an action or a condition

efficiently (ih FISH unt lee) done with the least cost and effort

Emancipation Proclamation (IH mant suh PAY shun PROK luh MAY shun) the official declaration by President Abraham Lincoln that freed enslaved persons living in Confederate states

emissions (ee MISH unz) pollution released into the air

environment (in VYE run munt) the surroundings in a particular area

era (AIR uh) a period of time

escalate (ESS kuh layt) to increase

establish (ess TAB lish) to set up

ethnic cleansing (ETH nik KLENZ ing) the killing of groups of people based on their nationality, religion, language, or cultural background

European Union (YUR uh PEE un YOON yun) a group of European nations joined together to reduce trade barriers, promote economic growth, and encourage environmental and human rights awareness

executive agreement (ig ZEK yuh tiv uh GREE munt) a formal agreement between two or more nations, arranged by the president but not requiring the US Senate's approval

executive branch (ig ZEK yuh tiv BRANCH) the branch of US government that oversees the day-to-day activities of the government

expand (ik SPAND) to increase

expansion (ik SPAN shun) the process of making something larger

expenditure (ik SPEN dih chur) money that is paid out

exports (EK SPORTS) goods and services sold to other countries

F

fact (fakt) a statement that can be verified or proven

factor of production (FAK tur uv pruh DUK shun) a key resource used to produce goods and services

fair trade (FAIR TRAYD) trade that meets certain standards, such as workers being paid a living wage and having safe working conditions

faulty logic (FAWL tee LOJ ik) an error in reasoning that often leads to an inaccurate or incomplete conclusion

federal (FED uh ruhl) national government; or governmental power that is divided between a central government and the states

Federal Reserve System (FED uh ruhl ree ZURV SISS tum) the central bank of the United States, which provides services to strengthen the nation's financial system and sets monetary policy to stabilize the economy

fertility rate (FER TIL ut ee RAYT) birthrate

fiat money (FEE ut MUN ee) money that has value because of government order

financial planning (fuh NAN chuhl PLAN ing) organized steps that guide the spending, saving, and investing of money

fiscal policy (FISS kuhl PAH luh see) the taxing and spending policies of a government

fluctuations (FLUK chuh WAY shunz) changes, such as an increase or decrease in supply or demand

foreign aid (FOR un AYD) the help that a wealthy country offers to developing countries

foreign direct investment (FOR un duh REKT in VEST munt) an investment that a company makes in a foreign country

foreign policy (FOR uhn PAH luh see) the plan a country has for interacting with other countries

forum (FOR um) a public meeting to discuss an issue

fossil fuels (FOSS uhl FYOOLZ) natural resources such as oil, coal, and natural gas that are used for fuel

free trade (FREE TRAYD) trade between countries without trade barriers

full employment (FUUL em PLOY ment) the economic condition in which only about 5 percent of the labor force is without work

function (FUNK shun) the role or purpose of something

fundamental (FUN duh MEN tuhl) basic, essential

fundamentalist (FUN duh MEN tuhl ist) a person who believes in strict traditional interpretation of religious beliefs or principles

G

geography (jee OG ruh fee) the study of Earth and the places on it

geometric borders (JEE uh MEH trik BORD ers) straight-line borders between states or nations, not related to a physical feature of Earth

global culture (GLOH buhl KUL chur) the acceptance of common aspects of life—such as music, food, and fashion—throughout the world

globalization (GLOH buh luh ZAY shun) the process of creating an economy that connects countries on a worldwide scale

global society (GLOH buhl suh SYE uh tee) a way of life in which people of the world are interconnected through technology

global warming (GLOH buhl WORM ing) an increase in the average temperatures on Earth

goods (guudz) products

government (GUV urn munt) the institution that makes and manages society's laws

governor (GUV urn ur) the chief executive of a state

gravity (GRA vuh tee) the physical force drawing two heavenly bodies (such as Earth and the Moon) together

Great Depression (GRAYT dee PRESH un) the very severe trough in the business cycle that occurred in the 1930s

greenhouse effect (GREEN howss ih FEKT) the trapping of energy from the Sun by carbon dioxide and other gases in Earth's atmosphere, leading to increased temperatures

gross domestic product (GROHSS duh MES tik PRAH dukt) GDP; the total market value of goods and services produced by a country in a single year

guarantee (gair un TEE) a promise or an assurance

guerilla (guh RIL uh) a member of an independent armed force

H

HIV/ AIDS (H-I-V ADZ) global disease known as Human Immunodeficiency Virus (HIV) that causes acquired immunodeficiency syndrome

hemisphere (HEM uh SFIR) a half of Earth, as divided by the equator or by a meridian

home rule laws (HOHM ROOL LAWZ) state laws that give local governments a great deal of freedom to set up their own systems of government

House of Representatives (HOWS uv REP ri ZENT ut ivz) one of the two bodies in the legislative branch of US government; representation is determined by the size of each state's population

I

identify (eye DEN tuh fye) to figure out or to name

imbalance (im BAL unss) the state of being out of proportion or unequal

impact (IM pakt) an effect

imperialism (im PIR ee uh LIZ um) the policy of a nation's ruling over a foreign land

implement (IM pluh munt) to carry out

imply (im PLI) to read into

implication (im pluh KAY shun) something suggested rather than stated directly

implied main idea (im PLIDE MAYN eye DEE uh) an idea suggested by information or evidence but not directly stated

imports (IM ports) goods and services brought from other countries

inadmissible (IN ad MISS uh buhl) not allowed

incentive (in SENT iv) motivation

independence (in duh PEN dunss) freedom from outside control

independent (in duh PEN dunt) a person who is not part of one of the major political parties

industrialization (in DUS tree uh luh ZAY shun) the changing of a country's economy so it is based on industry

Industrial Revolution (in DUS tree uhl REV uh LOO shun) the period from the late 1700s through the early 1800s when technology for producing goods grew rapidly, resulting in the establishment of factories

inference (IN fur unss) a form of "educated guess" based on facts

inflation (in FLAY shun) an increase in the overall price level for goods and services over time

inflation rate (in FLAY shun RAYT) the percentage of increase in the price for goods and services

influence (IN FLOO unss) to have an effect on

innovation (IN uh VAY shun) the development of new products, technologies, or services or creative changes to existing ones

input (IN puut) everything that goes into making a product

institution (IN stuh TYOO shun) an organization

insurgent (in SUR jent) an armed rebel

interdependence (IN ter dih PEN dunss) the state of relying on one another

interest group (IN trist GROOP) a group that tries to influence political decisions

interest rate (IN trist RAYT) the money that a lender charges a borrower, usually stated as a percentage

international trade (INT ur NASH uh nuhl TRAYD) the buying and selling of goods and services across national borders

internment (in TURN munt) the state of being confined or locked up

interpret (in TUR pret) to explain or make sense of

intrastate (IN truh STAYT) within the state

irony (EYE run ee) the use of words to describe the opposite of reality

irrigation system (ir uh GAY shun SISS tum) a system of ditches or canals that brings water to dry areas

isolationism (EYE suh LAY shuh niz um) the policy of not participating in international relations

isolationist (EYE suh LAY shuh nust) someone who wants his or her country to remain neutral or to stay out of world affairs

issue (ISH OO) a topic that concerns the public

isthmus (ISS muss) a narrow strip of land connecting two larger land areas

J

judge (juhj) to evaluate

judicial (joo DISH uhl) having to do with a judge or a court system that interprets the law

judicial branch (joo DISH uhl BRANCH) the branch of US government that interprets laws

judicial review (joo DISH uhl ree VYOO) the power of the judicial branch to rule on the constitutionality of laws passed by the legislative branch or on actions taken by the executive branch

K

key (kee) the part of a map explaining the symbols used on the map

L

laissez-faire capitalism (leh say FAIR KAP ut uhl IZ um) the idea that a government should not interfer with the economy

landform (LAND FORM) a natural feature, such as a mountain or river, on Earth's surface

latitude (LAT uh tyood) a line running parallel to the equator, measured in degrees north and south of the equator

law of demand (LAW uv di MAND) a principle stating that as the price of a product increases, the number of products consumers are willing to buy decreases

League of Nations (LEEG uv NAY shunz) an international organization that helped nations settle disputes from 1919 to 1945

legislative branch (LEJ uh SLAYT iv BRANCH) the branch of a government that writes laws

legislature (LEJ uh SLAY chur) a lawmaking body

liberal (LIB ur uhl) related to a political group that thinks the government should regulate industries and be involved in social issues to protect citizens

limited government (LIM uh tud GUV urn munt) a government that restricts its role in the economy

lobbyist (LOB ee ust) a person who works to influence legislation

longitude (LON juh tyood) lines that run from the North Pole to the South Pole, measured in degrees east and west of the prime meridian

M

Magna Carta (MAG nuh KAR tuh) the document King John of England was forced to sign in 1215, limiting the power of the monarch and ensuring the rights and privileges of the people

main idea (MAYN eye DEE uh) the most important information in a paragraph or text

Manifest Destiny (MAN uh FEST DESS tuh nee) the belief that the United States should occupy all the land to the Pacific Ocean

market (MAR kut) any situation in which a buyer and a seller freely exchange one thing for another

market equilibrium (MAR kut EE kwuh LIB ree um) the economic situation in which there is a balance between supply and demand

market structure (MAR kut STRUK chur) the way a market is organized, for example as a monopoly or with competition

meaning (MEE ning) the message that a word or phrase expresses

mechanization (MEK uh nuh ZAY shun) the use of machinery

migration (mye GRAY shun) the movement of people from one country or place to another

monarchy (MON urk ee) the form of government in which a king or queen is the head of state

monetary policy (MAHN uh TAIR ee PAH luh see) the government's control of the money supply and interest rates

money (MUN ee) anything people will accept as a method of payment

money supply (MUN ee suh PLYE) the amount of money available for use at any one time

monopoly (muh NOP uh lee) a control over a service or product by one business

morale (mor AL) the confidence and enthusiasm of a group

mortality rate (mor TAL uh tee RAYT) death rate

muckraker (MUK RAYK ur) a radical journalist who exposes corruption in business or politics

multicultural (MUHL tee KUHL chur uhl) a country, region, or group that includes many cultures

multiple-meaning word (MUL tuh puhl MEEN ing WURD) a word with more than one definition; for example, *scale* (tool used for weighing objects; thin plate covering a fish)

N

national debt (NASH uh null DET) money the federal government owes to lenders

naturalized (NACH uh ruh LIZED) made a citizen

natural resources (NACH ur uhl REE sorss uz) the land, water, and raw materials that occur naturally in the environment

negotiate (nih GOH shee AYT) to come to an agreement

negotiation (nih GOH shee AY shun) a discussion to end a dispute

New Deal (NYOO DEE uhl) President Franklin Delano Roosevelt's programs and federal actions designed to counter the hardships of the Great Depression

nonpartisan (NON PART uh zun) politically independent

nonprofit (NON PRAHF ut) not for the purpose of making money

nonprofit organization (NON PRAHF ut ORG uh nuh ZAY shun) a private group that puts the money it makes toward reaching its overall goals

O

obtain (ob TAYN) to get or secure

oligarchy (OHL uh GAR kee) a type of government in which only a few people rule

opportunity cost (op ur TYOO nut ee KAWST) the cost of giving up one option to choose another

outcome (OWT kum) the result of something

outlying (OWT lye ing) surrounding, distant

output (OWT puut) the product or service provided by a business

P

paraphrase (PAIR uh FRAYZ) to use one's own words to restate an idea

pardoned (PARD und) forgiven

Parliament (PAR luh munt) the highest law-making branch of the government in England, Canada, France, and some other countries

parliamentary democracy (PAR luh MENT uh ree dih MOK ruh see) a form of government where citizens elect representatives to their legislature and the executive branch of the government is accountable to the legislature

peak (peek) a high point

peer (pir) someone who is of equal standing to another

peninsula (puh NIN suh luh) a body of land surrounded by water on three sides

per capita (PUR KAP ut uh) for each person

personal budget (PER sun uhl BUJ ut) an outline showing how much money a person will be spent on various expenses

persuade (pur SWAYD) to convince

petition (puh TISH un) a statement saying that a person wants to run for office

physical boundaries (FIZ i kuhl BOWN duh reez) natural features of Earth, such as rivers, that separate two areas

place (playss) the physical and human characteristics of a location

plain (playn) a large area of level land

plank (plangk) an issue in the policy statement of a political party

plateau (pla TOH) a flat area of land raised above nearby land

platform (PLAT form) a statement of beliefs and issues that a political party supports

point of view (POYNT uv VYOO) a way of looking at issues; an opinion or attitude

political boundaries (puh LIT i kuhl BOWN duh reez) lines that separates states and countries

political cartoon (puh LIT i kuhl kar TYOON) a drawing that expresses the artist's opinion by showing the subject in a humorous or ironic way

political science (puh LIT i kuhl SYE enss) the study of governments and how they work

poll tax (POHL TAKS) a fee that must be paid before a person can vote

popular vote (POP yuh lur VOHT) the votes cast in an election

population (POP yuh LAY shun) the inhabitants of an area

population density (POP yuh LAY shun DEN sut ee) the average number of people per square mile

population explosion (POP yuh LAY shun ik SPLOH shun) rapid population growth

precipitation (pri SIP uh TAY shun) rain, hail, snow, or other forms of falling water in the atmosphere

prediction (pri DIK shun) a guess about something that will happen or come next

preview (PREE vyoo) to quickly review something before reading it to get an idea about the subject or content

price ceiling (PRISE SEE ling) a maximum price for a good, service, or resource

price controls (PRISE kuhn TROHLZ) price-setting for goods or services by the government

price floor (PRISE FLOR) a minimum price for a good, service, or resource

price instability (PRISE IN stuh BIL ut ee) drastic changes in the prices of goods and services

price stability (PRISE stuh BIL uh tee) the absence of large upswings or downswings in the price of goods and services

prime meridian (PRIME muh RID ee un) the 0° line of longitude that circles the globe, passing through the North Pole and the South Pole and running through Greenwich, England

prime minister (PRIME MIN uh stur) the head of the legislature

proclamation (PROK luh MAY shun) a formal public statement

production possibilities curve (pruh DUK shun POS uh BIL ut eez KURV) a graph showing all possible combinations of the number of products a supplier might produce

productivity (PROH duk TIV ut ee) the pace at which work is completed

profit (PRAHF ut) income left after subtracting expenses

profit margin (PRAHF ut MAR jun) the measurement of how much money a business keeps out of every dollar of its sales

progressive (pruh GRESS iv) interested in new ideas

provision (pruh VIZH un) a legal condition or requirement

public goods (PUB lik GUUDZ) goods that the government provides for all people to use; for example, parks

public policy (PUB lik PAH luh see) actions or decisions that affect everyone

purpose (PUR puss) a reason

Q

quota (KWOH tuh) a fixed amount

R

ratify (RAT uh fye) to approve

rationing (RA shun ing) limiting the availability of products, sometimes including food

real GDP (REEL JEE DEE PEE) the size of the economy, as adjusted for price changes and inflation (real gross domestic product)

realm (relm) an area or kingdom

real wages (REEL WAYJ ez) wages adjusted for inflation

recall (RE KAWL) a special election that permits citizens to vote an official out of office before his or her term is over

recession (ri SESH un) an economic downturn in which business activity slows, unemployment rises, and investment decreases

Reconstruction (REE kun STRUK shun) the period of rebuilding the nation after the Civil War ended in 1865

recruit (ree KROOT) to enlist, to encourage to sign up

referendum (REF uh REN dum) the right of voters to overturn legislation that has already been passed by voting against it in a general election

reform (ri FORM) a change to improve society and remove abuses

refugee (REF yuu JEE) a person who flees a country to escape danger

region (REE jun) an area of land that has a number of common elements

regulation (REG yuh LAY shun) a rule

relevant information (REL uh vunt in fur MAY shun) knowledge that is related or connected to a topic

repeal (ri PEEL) to end or take back

representation (REP ri zen TAY shun) the act of having someone speak or act on behalf of another person; also, a visual that shows information

representative democracy (REP ri ZENT ut iv dih MOK ruh see) a form of government in which the people elect representatives to run the government and make decisions on their behalf

representative government (REP ri ZENT ut iv GUV urn munt) a form of government in which the people elect others to represent them in government

repression (ri PRESH un) control by force

reserve (ri ZURV) to set aside

revenue (REV uh NYOO) income from a certain source, such as from taxes

revolution (REV uh LOO shun) the removal of one government or ruler and replacement with another

S

savings account (SAY vingz uh KOWNT) a bank account where money is stored

savings institution (SAY vingz IN stuh TYOO shun) a business that makes loans to individuals rather than to businesses

scarcity (SKAIR sut ee) a shortage of resources required to meet the unlimited wants and needs of the people

science (SYE unts) a method of learning about the natural world

Scientific Revolution (SYE un TIF ik REV uh LOO shun) the period from the late 1500s to the early 1600s during which scientific knowledge grew rapidly

secede (si SEED) to withdraw or break off from

sectional (SEK shun uhl) regional

segregation (SEG rih GAY shun) the practice of separating people or groups on the basis of race or another factor

seize (seez) to arrest someone or take possession of something

Senate (SEN ut) one of the two bodies in the legislative branch of US government; each state has two senators

separation of powers (SEP uh RAY shun uv POW urz) the division of government into branches; each branch has its own duties and responsibilities

sequence (SEE kwuns) a series; also, the order of events

services (SUR vus es) work done by a person to benefit another person

shah (shah) Persian word for "king"

social (SOH shuhl) relating to human society

social contract (SOH shuhl KAHN trakt) the idea that government is a contract between leaders and the people

Social Darwinism (SOH shuhl DAR wuh NIZ um) the belief that society follows the biological principle of the survival of the fittest, where wealth and power go to those who are best suited or more fit

specialization (SPESH uh luh ZAY shun) the training, skill, and focus of working on one task

spheres of influence (SFIRZ uv IN FLOO unss) areas or regions controlled by a government or organization

stabilize (STAY buh LIZE) to support and make steady

stipulate (STIP yuh LAYT) to demand certain conditions

subpoena (suh PEE nuh) to issue a formal command requiring a person to testify in court

suburbs (SUB urbz) small communities outside urban areas

succeed (suk SEED) to follow or come after

suffrage (SUH frij) the right to vote

summarize (SUM uh RIZE) to restate the most important information from a text

supply (suh PLYE) the amount of a product businesses are willing and able to produce at a certain price at a specific time

supply curve (suh PLYE KURV) a graph that plots the numbers from a supply schedule, showing the impact of price changes on the quantity of a product supplied

supply schedule (suh PLYE SKEJ uhl) a table showing the impact of price changes on the quantity of a product supplied

supporting details (suh PORT ing DEE taylz) information that expands upon a main idea or makes it clearer

surge (surj) a rapid rise

surrender (suh REN dur) to stop fighting by giving in to the opposing power

sustainability (suh STAY nuh BIL ut ee) living in a way that does not deplete resources or damage the environment

sustainable development (suh STAYN uh buhl dee VEL up munt) the process of meeting human needs while conserving resources so those resources will be available to future generations

synthesize (SIN thuh SIZE) to combine information from various sources

T

table (TAY buhl) a visual that organizes information by horizontal rows and vertical columns

tariffs (TAIR ufs) taxes on an imported product

tax (taks) a required payment by people to the government

technology (tek NOL uh jee) the machines and equipment developed from advances in scientific knowledge

term (turm) a period of time

territory (TAIR uh TOR ee) a government-controlled area that is not officially a state

terrorism (TAIR ur IZ um) the use of violence and fear to advance a cause

terrorist (TAIR ur ust) a person who uses fear and violence to advance a cause

text structure (TEKST STRUK chur) the organization of ideas in a text

theory (THIR ee) a general statement that explains facts observed by scientists

third party (THURD PAR tee) a political party other than the two major parties

totalitarianism (toh TAL uh TAIR ee uh NIZ um) a type of government in which people are completely subject to one ruler who has all the power

trade agreement (TRAYD uh GREE munt) a legal contract relating to trade between countries

transact (tranz AKT) to carry out or perform

transfer payment (TRANS fur PAY munt) money given to help people in need, funded by tax revenues

Transportation Revolution (TRANS pur TAY shuhn REV uh LOO shun) the period during the 1800s and early 1900s when steam engines were developed and new trade routes were established, enabling large quantities of goods to be moved around the world

treaty (TREE tee) a formal agreement between two or more nations that requires the US Senate's approval

trend (trend) the general direction of change

trough (trawf) the low point of the economy

U

unanimous (yoo NAN uh muss) without dissent or disagreement

unicameral (yoo ni KAM uh ruhl) a lawmaking body with only one part, or one chamber

urbanization (UR buh nuh ZAY shun) the development and growth of cities as populations move away from rural areas

V

variety (vuh RYE uh tee) a type; or diversity

Venn diagram (VENN DYE uh gram) a graphic organizer with two or more overlapping circles, used to compare and contrast information

veto (VEE toh) an action taken by a government leader, such as the president, to prevent a bill from becoming a law

W

weapons of mass destruction (WEP unz uv mass dee STRUK shun) chemical, biological, and nuclear weapons designed to harm many people

withdraw (with DRAW) to take money out of an account

Y

yellow journalism (YELL oh JURN uhl IZ um) reporting that is exaggerated and shows only one point of view

Index